BOOKS FOR YOU

A Booklist for Senior High Students

SCHOLASTIC BOOK SERVICES
New York Toronto London Auckland Sydney Tokyo

BOOKS FOR YOU

A Booklist for Senior High Students

New Edition

Prepared by

Kenneth L. Donelson, Editorial Chairman,
and the Committee on the Senior High School Booklist
of the National Council of Teachers of English

National Council of Teachers of English
1111 Kenyon Road, Urbana, Illinois 61801

Sixth Edition
NCTE Stock Number 03626
ISBN 0-8141-0362-6

Library of Congress Cataloging in Publication Data
National Council of Teachers of English.
  Books for you.
  Includes indexes.
  1. Bibliography—Best books. 2. Children's literature—Bibliograhy. I. Donelson, Kenneth L. II. Title.
Z1037.N266 1976   028.52   76-41688
ISBN 0-8141-0362-6

ACKNOWLEDGMENTS

As chairman of the Committee on the Senior High School Booklist, my appreciation must first go to the members of the committee. Given the maturity of high school students, we were faced with the task of sorting and selecting from a universe of books written for the public at large, mindful particularly, however, of what would most appeal to high school readers. The basis for organization upon which the committee finally agreed was related to the elective courses common to high school English departments today. The first broad categories for this booklist came from a study of curriculum guides from all over the nation. Beyond that survey, the collective professional experience of committee members furnished numerous other categories. After that, it was mostly a matter of reading and vainly trying to keep up to date with the books arriving from publishers. If in the final stages committee members wearied, they nonetheless were always a pleasure to work with.

Credit and thanks must also go to the publishers who provided review copies of books; to friends and fellow teachers who jogged our minds, challenged our ideas, and gave specific suggestions; to members of the Secondary Section and the Executive Committee of the National Council of Teachers of English for their honest and frequent help; and to Paul O'Dea, director of NCTE Publications, who pestered and persisted and helped me to pester and persist with the booklist committee.

Several individuals deserve special mention. My wife Annette helped in all ways at all times, but along with Betty Whetton, she helped particularly with the Science Fiction section. Linda Hope, Kathy McCool, and Liz Celis—coworkers all—helped in so many ways to make the job a little easier and a lot more fun. Thanks also to Norma Willson, West High School, Torrance, California; Nancy Wells, San Pedro (California) High School; and

Joanne Wilkinson, graduate student at the University of Illinois, for valuable last-minute contributions to the I Am Woman section.

Joy Scott assisted with correspondence, catalogued the many books as they came in, edited many annotations, and did all sorts of odd jobs that were sometimes difficult but still necessary, almost always happily and always efficiently. Joy may have started her job as my secretary, but by the time we were halfway through, she had become coeditor in almost every way save the title. I herewith award her the title and say that I am most grateful for everything she has done.

Finally, I would like to thank the editorial staff of the NCTE Publications Department: William Ellet, project editor, ably assisted by Carol Schanche, Kathy Stevens, Elaine Dawley, Diane Dieterich, Patricia Leedecke, and especially Lois Haig, who has persevered in this project from the beginning.

Kenneth L. Donelson

CONTENTS

BOOKS FOR YOU

A Booklist for Senior High Students

INTRODUCTION TO THE STUDENT

Reading very often has an immediate purpose: checking the time a movie begins, making sure a comma is in the right place, learning a skill. But much reading is simply for pleasure—from the uncomplicated enjoyment found in a mystery or adventure book to the intellectual fun of puzzling out an idea or theory found in a philosophical or scientific work. The problem is where to begin. Publishers produce thousands of titles each year and even with the recommendations of parents, teachers, librarians, and friends, locating books that fit specific interests is sometimes frustrating.

Books for You is intended to make the search easier by providing suggestions for all kinds of readers with all sorts of interests. Teachers and librarians may use this book to recommend this or that title, but its primary purpose, from section headings to annotations, is to be of use to you, the student. No book is included just because of its literary reputation as a classic or because it is considered a necessary part of everyone's reading experience. The sole standard of selection for this booklist is pleasurable reading.

What sort of reading will this booklist lead you to? That depends upon what you want a book to do for you. If it's relaxation and imaginative escape, see the sections Mystery, Adventure, Science Fiction, Beyond Belief, Sports, All the World's a Stage, Short Stories, and Humor and Satire.

Do you wonder about yourself and whether your problems and experience are shared by others? Beyond the concerns of the moment, what are the possibilities for your future? Books about such personal concerns are in the sections Coming of Age, Love, Problems and Young People, and Careers.

Each of us occasionally encounters ideas that have been argued for centuries and even now make us wonder, question, and doubt. Sometimes these encounters reward us with something more than the pleasure of thinking things through: a better understanding of humanity.

The sections Problems of Modern Humanity, Reflections, Our Languages, Our Religions, Utopias and Communes, Fine Arts, and Poetry ` pose such universal concerns.

Almost inescapable today is an awareness of social injustice in our country and others. If you worry about this issue or are simply looking for more information on it, see I Am Woman; the five Ethnic Experiences sections; Urban Life, Urban Concerns; Politics, the Law, and Humanity; and the two Third World sections.

The people and event of the past—and the perspective they can provide on the present—are the subjects of Western Frontier; Lives, Then and Now; the three sections on the United States; War; Myth and Folklore; and Digging into Our Past.

Contemporary culture and leisure activities—television, movies, music, comic books, backpacking, auto racing—are covered in Mass Media, Popular Culture, and On the Move.

Our physical environment is the object of many investigations and the setting for much adventure. Accounts of these and of questions they frequently raise, such as what people and the sciences have done to help the earth or befoul it, are included in Science, Today and Tomorrow; Nature; Ecology; Skies and Mountains; and Oceans.

Before turning to these sections, you should be aware of a few problems faced in putting this booklist together, since some of these problems are really warnings to you, the reader. We would also like to explain a few features of the booklist's organization.

Books are like readers: they seldom allow simple descriptions and quick categorizations. Thus, be sure to glance through several sections and the indexes before assuming that a certain book isn't listed. Of course, some books are easy to place. For example, Zander Hollander and Hal Bock's *The Complete Encyclopedia of Ice Hockey* clearly belongs in the Sports section. But others are difficult to categorize and could be placed in several sections. For example, Malcolm X and Alex Haley's *The Autobiography of Malcolm X* is in the Black Experiences section, but it could just as easily have been put in Lives, Then and Now; Problems of Modern Humanity; or the United States Since the Civil War. The book is in Black Experiences because it seemed that if you were searching for that book, you would expect to find it there; if you didn't know the work but were interested in the section, it seemed likely that you would enjoy the autobiography of a famous black leader.

Although the committee that put together *Books for You* tried to be comprehensive in its selection of titles, you may find a book you like has been left out. If this is so, the reason could be the inevitable differences in people's reading tastes. However, book selection was limited both by space considerations and the committee's desire to include as many recent works as possible.

We have indicated in the annotations of some books that they have explicit sexual scenes or language which may be offensive to some readers; but modern literature is frank and realistic, so you should be warned that we may not have spelled out all the problems you or your friends may see in a book. A few teachers and librarians suggested that we note certain controversial books with statements like "This book is antifeminist" or "Some readers may object to the racism implied." Yet almost every book could be objected to by someone for some reason (believe it or not, that applies to books as different as the Bible, *Silas Marner, Treasure Island, Moby Dick, Slaughterhouse-Five,* and *Go Ask Alice*). To leave out a book simply because of a hypothetical objection to it was not a convincing argument to us. You are therefore warned that some books included here may offend, irritate, or anger you. But books that please and books that disturb may serve equally valid purposes by making you think or by challenging your beliefs. A book, almost by definition, is subversive: it can alter what you believe to be true by testing ideas or theories you have too easily accepted.

The organization of the booklist requires a brief explanation. The books in each section are arranged alphabetically by author or editor; books by the same author or editor in a section are arranged alphabetically by title. If you are looking for a particular book or books by a particular author, see the title or author index. We have indicated "fiction" or "nonfiction' for many books. However, these designations have been omitted in sections containing only fiction or nonfiction (for example, Short Stories and Mass Media). Some books are also described as "mature," which means they are difficult, quite long and complex, or sophisticated in tone or style.

A typical entry for an annotated book reads this way:

Aiken, Joan. **Night Fall** (© 1969). HR&W 1971.

The first date, enclosed in parentheses, is the copyright date; the second is the publication date for the edition used in annotating the book. When the two dates are the same, only the one date, of course, is given. In the few cases where we could not determine a publication date, "n.d." appears. An abbreviated form of the publisher's name precedes the publication date. The Directory of Publishers at the end of the book lists these abbreviations with the publishers' full names and ordering addresses.

At the end of many annotations, you will find in parentheses "see also" suggestions for further reading. These books are not annotated anywhere in the booklist but are mentioned as worthwhile reading on the same topics as the annotated books. When the author is the same for both the annotated book and the "see also" title, the author's name is omitted in the "see also" entry.

With this information, you should be able to use *Books for You* as a convenient starting point for your ventures into reading and the pleasures it offers.

MYSTERY

Aiken, Joan. **Night Fall** (© 1969). HR&W 1971.

Nineteen-year-old Meg Frazer sets out for the rugged coast of Cornwall to escape from a nightmare which has haunted her for fourteen years, only to find herself at the center of an unsolved murder she witnessed as a five year old. Fiction.

Allan, Mabel Ester. **A Chill in the Lane.** Nelson 1974.

Lyd, a sixteen-year-old orphan, visits the wild and lonely Trelonyan Cove in Cromwell with her foster parents and experiences visions of an earlier time when murders were sanctioned by superstitions. Through her visions, she begins to discover her true identity. Fiction.

Armstrong, Charlotte. **The Balloon Man** (© 1968). Fawcett World 1974.

Sherry is the victim of her father-in-law's terror tactics designed to destroy her sanity so that he can win the custody of his grandson and punish Sherry, who he believes ruined his son. Fiction.

Asimov, Isaac. **Asimov's Mysteries** (© 1968). Dell 1969.

An anthology of mystery stories taking place in the future by science fiction writer Isaac Asimov. Included are stories about the first murder on the moon, the case of the stranded spaceman, and the wrong-way time-traveler. Fiction.

Ball, John. **In the Heat of the Night.** Har-Row 1965.

Virgil Tibbs, a black homicide detective from California, becomes involved in solving a murder in the rural South. The story emphasizes investigative procedure and the conflicts of racial prejudice. Fiction.

Bleeck, Oliver. **The Highbinders.** Morrow 1974.

Ross Thomas, writing under the pseudonym of Oliver Bleeck, adds another chapter to the adventures of the introspective and witty Philip St. Ives, who here attempts to recover a stolen antique sword from con men and murderers. Mature fiction.

Buchan, John. **The 39 Steps** (© 1915). Popular Lib 1970.

Hannay, a fugitive wanted for murder, sets out to save himself and his country by solving the riddle of the thirty-nine steps, which he found on a scrap of paper clutched in a dead man's hand. Fiction.

Carr, John Dickson. **The Three Coffins** (© 1935). Award Hse 1974.

This is a mystery of the "locked room" school of detective fiction in which an apparently impossible murder is committed by a seemingly invisible murderer. Fiction.

Chandler, Raymond. **The Long Goodbye** (© 1953). Ballantine 1971.

Phillip Marlowe, one of America's most famous fictional private investigators, helps a troubled man, then finds himself harrassed by unethical cops and involved in the mysterious death of a beautiful heiress. Mature fiction.

Chesterton, G. K. **The Man Who Was Thursday** (© 1908). Cap Putnam 1960.

Chesterton's sophisticated writing and intellect make this much more than an account of the brilliant policemen who discover the identity of Sunday, a traitor working at the highest levels of the British government. Mature fiction.

Christie, Agatha. **And Then There Were None** (© 1940). PB 1975.

The author's most famous tale in which a group of strangers find themselves on a desert island where, one by one, they are killed. (See also *The Murder of Roger Ackroyd,* PB; *The ABC Murders,* PB; and *A Murder Is Announced,* PB.) Fiction.

Christie, Agatha. **Death on the Nile** (© 1938). Bantam 1974.

Hercule Poirot, Christie's famous detective, eventually solves the murder of a wealthy and lovely woman, but even he cannot fit the clues together in time to keep the killer from striking again. Fiction.

Christie, Agatha. **Murder on Board.** Dodd 1974.

Three mystery novels—*The Mystery of the Blue Train, Death in the Air,* and *What Mrs. McGillicuddy Saw*—featuring detectives Hercule Poirot and Miss Marple. Fiction.

Collins, Michael. **The Silent Scream.** Dodd 1973.

A routine investigation takes Dan Fortune, a one-armed private investigator, into the violent world run by the Syndicate and populated with lonely, defeated people. Mature fiction.

Collins, Wilkie. **The Moonstone** (© 1868). Penguin 1966.

Often called the first mystery novel, this Victorian tale centers on a fabulously costly jewel stolen from the forehead of a statue in India. Fiction.

Crowe, John. **Bloodwater.** Dodd 1974.

A wealthy businessman is found murdered in a sleazy motel and before the killer is found, three generations of international greed and guilt are exposed. Fiction.

Dickens, Charles. **Bleak House** (© 1853). NAL 1964.

The lawsuit *Jarndyce* v. *Jarndyce* has dragged on for years. Whole families are caught up in the suit, their futures hinging on how the case will be settled. (See also *Our Mutual Friend,* Penguin; and *Dombey and Son,* NAL.) Fiction.

Doyle, Sir Arthur Conan. **The Hound of the Baskervilles** (© 1902). Dell 1959.

Sherlock Holmes and Dr. Watson solve the mystery of the fiendish hound which has terrorized the Baskerville family for four generations. Fiction.

Doyle, Sir Arthur Conan. **The Adventures of Sherlock Holmes** (© 1892). Har-Row 1930.

A fine collection of the adventures of Sherlock Holmes, whose deductive powers allow him to solve many baffling cases. Fiction.

Ellis, Mel. **No Man for Murder.** HR&W 1973.

Seventeen-year-old Danny Stuart finds himself standing trial for a murder he did not commit. Trying to

establish his innocence, he only makes the case against
him stronger. Fiction.

Eyerly, Jeannette. **Good-Bye to Budapest.** Lippincott
1974.

Megan acquires a strange and crudely drawn map.
Before she can find out who sent it and what it means,
she is kidnapped and on her way to a real mystery.
Fiction.

Fenner, Phyllis R., compiler. **Consider the Evidence.**
Morrow 1973.

Ten stories of mystery and suspense dealing with the
capture of criminals through the use of many types
of evidence. Fiction.

Francis, Dick. **Slayride** (© 1973). Har-Row 1974.

David Cleveland, an investigator for the English
Jockey Club, travels to Norway to investigate the disappearance of a British steeplechase jockey. Instead,
he becomes a hunted man. Fiction.

Francis, Dorothy Brenner. **Golden Girl.** Schol Bk Serv
1974.

Lisa, a level-headed and talented girl, is terrified: she
is a finalist in the Golden Girl Scholastic Pageant, but
someone is trying to force her out of the contest even
if it is necessary to murder her. Fiction.

Garfield, Brian. **The Threepersons Hunt.** M Evans 1974.

Arizona state trooper Sam Watchman, a Navajo Indian, is on the trail of escaped murderer Joe Threepersons on the White River Apache Reservation. The
chase ultimately involves a militant Indian group, white
ranchers, and Joe's sister. Fiction.

Gloag, Julian. **Our Mother's House** (© 1963). PB 1971.

Seven children decide not to report the death of their
mother. They bury her in the garden and pretend
to the outside world that she is only ill. Then a
stranger appears claiming he is their father. Fiction.

Greene, Graham. **Brighton Rock** (© 1938). Viking Pr
1956.

Greene takes the reader on a probing journey into the
tortured mind of a sadistic murderer. Mature fiction.

Hamilton, Virginia. **The House of Dies Drear.** Macmillan 1968.

Thirteen-year-old Thomas explores the secrets of a house which was a station on the underground railroad traveled by slaves escaping from the South before the Civil War. Fiction.

Hammett, Dashiell. **The Maltese Falcon** (© 1929). VinRandom 1972.

The valuable statue called the Maltese Falcon is missing in San Francisco; Sam Spade must track it down while avoiding the treachery of a beautiful woman and underworld figures who are also looking for the statue. (See also *The Thin Man,* VinRandom; and *The Glass Key,* VinRandom.) Fiction.

Hillerman, Tony. **The Blessing Way.** Har-Row 1970.

An Indian lawman and an anthropologist set out to track down the identity of a "Wolf," a Navajo witch who is spreading death on the reservation. An unusual combination of mystery, Navajo beliefs, and witchcraft. (See also *Dance Hall of the Dead,* Har-Row.) Fiction.

Kemelman, Harry. **Tuesday the Rabbi Saw Red** (© 1973). Fawcett World 1975.

A bomb explodes in a dean's office and a body is found in the English office. Everybody on campus is a suspect until Rabbi Small unravels the clues and finds the murderer. Fiction.

Le Carré, John. **Tinker, Tailor, Soldier, Spy.** Knopf 1974.

The author of the popular spy thriller, *The Spy Who Came in from the Cold,* writes of George Smiley, a British agent assigned to find the double agent who has worked himself into the upper ranks of British Intelligence. Fiction.

L'Engle, Madeleine. **The Arm of the Starfish.** FS&G 1965.

Adam Eddington is to spend the summer working for a brilliant scientist who is studying the starfish's ability to regenerate its limbs. Adam becomes tangled in international intrigue involving the scientist's work and has to decide which of the opposing forces really stands for what he believes. Fiction.

Liebman, Arthur, editor. **Thirteen Classic Detective Stories.** Rosen Pr 1974.

Beginning with selections from the Bible and the works of Voltaire, Liebman presents British and American stories tracing the form of the detective tale from its early complexity and ingenuity to its present simplicity and directness. Fiction.

Macdonald, Ross, editor. **Ross Macdonald Selects Great Stories of Suspense.** Knopf 1974.

The creator of the Lew Archer detective series edited this anthology of novels by Dick Francis, Agatha Christie, Kenneth Fearing, and Macdonald; and short stories by such authors as Graham Greene, Flannery O'Connor, and James M. Cain. Fiction.

Macdonald, Ross. **Sleeping Beauty.** Knopf 1973.

The story begins with an oil spill and a murder on the California coast. As Lew Archer pursues the case, he exposes the corruption, greed, and infidelity of three generations of the wealthy Lennox family. Fiction.

Manley, Seon, and Gogo Lewis, editors. **Grande Dames of Detection.** Lothrop 1973.

Many of the better short stories of detection written by women over the past two centuries are collected here. Included are stories by Baroness Orczy, Agatha Christie, Dorothy L. Sayers, and Ngaio Marsh. Fiction.

Marsh, Ngaio. **A Man Lay Dead** (© 1934). Little 1972.

Chief Detective-Inspector Roderick Alleyn must solve the murder which was the unexpected ending to a party game; in solving the crime, Alleyn must deal with greed, jealousy, and hints of the supernatural. Fiction.

McQueen, Ian. **Sherlock Holmes Detected.** Drake Pubs 1974.

An examination of the life and career of Sherlock Holmes as it is given in four novels and fifty-six short stories. Nonfiction.

Meyer, Nicholas. **The Seven Percent Solution.** Dutton 1974.

A contemporary addition to Sherlock Holmes's adven-

tures in which the detective travels to Vienna on the
trail of archvillain Professor Moriarty. Fiction.

Platnick, Kenneth B. **Great Mysteries of History** (©
1971). Har-Row 1973.

This book details sixteen famous, unsolved cases of
murder, royal intrigue, missing persons, and some
mysteries of the ancient world, including the search
for lost continents. Nonfiction.

Platt, Kin. **Sinbad and Me** (© 1966). Dell 1974.

While attending summer school, Steve and his bulldog
become involved in solving a 100-year-old mystery, escape from underworld characters, and discover a fortune in treasure. Fiction.

Rendell, Ruth. **Some Lie and Some Die** (© 1973). Bantam 1975.

At a rock festival a young woman is murdered. To
find her murderer, a British homicide detective must
explore the twisted personalities of all concerned and
finds important clues in the lyrics of a contemporary
love ballad. Mature fiction.

Sayers, Dorothy L. **Murder Must Advertise.** Har-Row
1959.

Incognito, Lord Peter Wimsey joins an advertising
agency to solve the murder of a copywriter, managing to crack the case and break up a London-based
drug smuggling ring. Fiction.

Sjöwall, Maj, and Per Wahlöö. **The Abominable Man**
(© 1972). Bantam 1974.

Martin Beck, a Swedish homicide detective, tracks
down the brutal murderer of a hospitalized police
officer. The setting is Sweden and the language is
realistic. Mature fiction.

Sleator, William. **Blackbriar** (© 1972). Avon 1975.

A British schoolboy and his guardian suddenly move
from London into a country house named Blackbriar
where the boy becomes caught up in the evil history
and secret passages of the house. Fiction.

Steinbrunner, Chris, and Otto Penzler. **Encyclopedia of
Mystery and Detection.** McGraw 1976.

Biographical information on writers and descriptions

of fictional characters and of genres provided here will answer practically any question readers might have about mystery literature. Nonfiction.

Stout, Rex. **The Doorbell Rang** (© 1965). Viking Pr 1968.

Nero Wolfe, an overweight, orchid-collecting private detective, must cope with bugging devices and police surveillance while exposing a murderer. Fiction.

Sullivan, Mary W. **The Indestructible Old Time String Band.** Nelson 1975.

Some boys form their own bluegrass musical group; when a mystery causes problems in their lives, the group is tied together both by their love of music and the desire to solve the mystery. Fiction.

Whitney, Phyllis A. **Mystery of the Angry Idol** (© 1965). NAL 1974.

Jan Pendleton visits an old, reconstructed village in Connecticut and becomes involved in discovering the secret of a stolen Chinese idol. Fiction.

Wilhelm, Kate. **City of Cain.** Little 1974.

An apparently innocent proposal is made to the U.S. Senate to develop a secret underground complex in Washington, D.C., for use in case of nuclear war. Peter Roos, the brother of a senator involved in the proposal, discovers sinister implications in the project. Fiction.

ADVENTURE

Ambler, Eric. **The Levanter** (© 1972). Bantam 1973.

Businessman Michael Howell suddenly finds himself battling for survival against an Arab terrorist group determined to use him in their attempt to destroy Israel. Fiction.

Bennett, Jay. **The Long Black Coat** (© 1973). Dell 1974.

Phil Brant's brother is dead, and Phil is being hunted by two of his brother's army buddies. Phil doesn't know why they are after him, but his terror is not as bad as his pain when he finds out why. (See also *Shadows Offstage,* Nelson.) Fiction.

Bosworth, J. Allan. **White Water, Still Water.** PB 1966.
Chris and his homemade raft are swept miles down
river into the Canadian wilderness. Without shoes and
armed only with a pocketknife, Chris must fight his
way back to civilization before winter. Fiction.

Branscum, Robbie. **Me and Jim Luke** (© 1971). Avon
1975.
While hunting possums, two boys find a murdered
man. They set out to discover the killer and learn
that the dread Ku Klux Klan may be involved in the
murder. Fiction.

Butterworth, W. E. **Road Racer.** Tempo G&D 1969.
Steve Haas, a high school dropout with an interest in
cars, not only returns to school but wins a scholarship
for a year of study abroad. His knowledge of German
and engineering talent serve him well when he comes
into contact with a millionaire racing ace working
on an experimental racing car. Fiction.

Clark, Mavis Thorpe. **Wildfire.** Macmillan 1974.
A story of five young characters united in a desperate
struggle to survive a raging wildfire in the parched
forests of Victoria, Australia. Fiction.

Condon, Richard. **The Manchurian Candidate** (© 1959).
NAL 1962.
Raymond Shaw, a war hero, has been programmed by
enemy agents to assassinate the vice-president-desig-
nate in this story of spies, greed, and political corruption. Mature fiction.

Creasey, John. **The Masters of Bow Street.** S&S 1974.
Creasey's story of Scotland Yard does not idealize
human nature or the past but captures the squalor,
bawdiness, and rawness of eighteenth-century London,
and depicts the search for social justice. Mature
fiction.

Crichton, Michael. **The Great Train Robbery.** Knopf
1975.
Every possible precaution, from armed guards to special locks, has been taken to safeguard a shipment of
gold on a train leaving London. However, master thief
Edward Pierce still believes he can pull off the perfect
robbery. Based on an actual 1855 case. Fiction.

Deighton, Len. **Spy Story.** HarBraceJ 1974.

Many of the characters made famous in *Funeral in Berlin* reappear in this novel of cold war politics in which Anglo-American war games, underwater spying expeditions, and double agents are the basic elements. Mature fiction.

Dulles, Allen, editor. **Great Spy Stories from Fiction.** Har-Row 1969.

Dulles, a former director of the C.I.A., gathers together spy stories ranging from the Trojan War to World War II. Fiction.

Du Maurier, Daphne. **Jamaica Inn** (© 1935). Doubleday 1970.

Trapped in the Jamaica Inn, a haven for smugglers and murderers, Mary Yellan learns of the horrors planned by her fiendish uncle and struggles to escape his evil hold on her. Fiction.

Eckert, Allan. **Incident at Hawk's Hill** (© 1971). Dell 1972.

In 1870 a shy six-year-old boy is lost in the Canadian wilds and survives the summer only because he is protected and cared for by a female badger. Fiction.

Edmonds, Walter D. **Wolf Hunt.** Little 1970.

Danny Gallagher and his uncle set out in the winter of 1784 to track down the "stump-toed wolf." After spending many days in the wilderness, both their lives change once the wolf has been killed. Fiction.

Evarts, Hal G. **Bigfoot.** Scribner 1973.

Dingo, a high school student, finds himself leading a hunting party into the wilds when his grandfather, a professional guide, breaks his shoulder. But the hunt is not like any Dingo has ever heard of: they are hunting for "Bigfoot," a huge, gorilla-like creature said to be the American cousin of the Abominable Snowman. Fiction.

Fisher, Vardis. **The Mothers** (© 1971). Swallow 1973.

What begins as an optimistic journey across the Sierras in 1846 results in treachery, deceit, and murder. The primitive instincts of the wives and mothers of the Donner party take over as they struggle to save their children from the blizzard which has trapped them in the mountains. Mature fiction.

Forester, C. S. **Hornblower and the Hotspur** (© 1937). Bantam 1973.

Hornblower commands the *Hotspur,* a sloop of war, in efforts to thwart Bonaparte's invasion of Ireland. Fiction.

Garve, Andrew. **Boomerang: An Australian Escapade.** Har-Row 1970.

Peter Talbot, a successful businessman and gambler, plans a stock market swindle which carries him into the Australian bush country and will bring him either incredible wealth or utter ruin. Fiction.

Gipson, Fred. **Savage Sam** (© 1962). PB n.d.

The Texas frontier is the setting of this story about a dog's attempt to rescue his young master from Apache raiders. Fiction.

Greene, Graham. **Travels with My Aunt** (© 1969). Bantam 1971.

Timid Henry Pulling meets his Aunt Augusta at his mother's funeral. Upon learning that the deceased woman isn't his mother, he embarks with his flamboyant and eccentric aunt on a series of adventures that involve his mother's funeral urn, Interpol, the C.I.A., and war criminals. Fiction.

Hall, Adam. **The Tango Briefing** (© 1973). Dell 1974.

Quiller, a master British spy, is sent on a suicide mission into the Sahara to find and destroy a mysteriously downed aircraft. Fiction.

Hallstead, William F. **Ghost Plane of Blackwater.** Har-BraceJ 1974.

Nineteen-year-old Greg Stewart arrives in Blackwater, South Carolina, to take his first job as a crop duster, but soon finds himself in a search for a B-24 bomber which mysteriously crashed in the area's snake-infested swamp in 1944. Fiction.

Hemingway, Ernest. **For Whom the Bell Tolls** (© 1940). Scribner 1968.

Robert Jordan, an American, goes to Spain to fight in

the Spanish civil war. He experiences terror in battle and pleasure in love, only to meet death with his guerrilla comrades. Mature fiction.

Hemingway, Joan, and Paul Bonnecarrére. **Rosebud.** Morrow 1974.

Five young girls are kidnapped by Arabs in a plot to turn the world against Israel. A French agent is hired to try to save the girls—and world peace. Fiction.

Holt, Victoria. **The House of a Thousand Lanterns.** Doubleday 1974.

Jane Lindsay attempts to escape the sadness of a shattered romance and a "marriage of convenience" by traveling to Hong Kong and the strange House of a Thousand Lanterns. Soon she finds her life in danger. Fiction.

Hope, Anthony. **Ruritania Complete: The Prisoner of Zenda and Rupert of Hentzau** (© 1894). Dover 1961.

Rudolph Rassendyll travels to Ruritania to see the coronation ceremonies. To his surprise he finds that he and the new king could easily be mistaken for twins. Because of a plot against the king by Black Michael, Rudolph agrees to take the king's place temporarily. Fiction.

Huff, Tom. **Nine Bucks Row.** Hawthorn 1973.

A Gothic romance set in Victorian England in which Susannah, an eighteen-year-old orphan, becomes frighteningly involved in the capture of Jack the Ripper. Fiction.

Huffaker, Clair. **The Cowboy and the Cossack** (© 1973). PB 1974.

Fifteen American cowboys and fifteen Russian Cossacks work together on a 4,000-mile cattle drive through Siberia. Fiction.

Jacks, Oliver. **Man on a Short Leash.** Stein & Day 1974.

Todd, a British intelligence agent, spots and tails an enemy agent, only to find himself sentenced to thirty years for treason. Todd must discover those who set him up, but first he has to escape from a maximum security prison. Fiction.

Jennings, William Dale. **The Cowboys** (1971). Bantam n.d.

In 1877 a group of schoolboys are hired to herd Wil Andersen's cattle to market. During the 400-mile trip, the boys become accomplished cowhands and learn the realities of human hate. Fiction.

Leasor, James. **Green Beach.** Morrow 1975.

A true account of how the British learned the secrets of a Nazi radar installation by sending an electronics specialist into occupied France. Eleven Canadian rangers went with him to insure that he would not be taken alive. Mature nonfiction.

Leslie, Robert Franklin. **In the Shadow of a Rainbow.** Norton 1974.

An Indian youth and a wolf develop a remarkable friendship in the wilderness of British Columbia, and the Indian attempts to protect the wolf from trappers and bounty hunters. Nonfiction.

Levitin, Sonia. **Roanoke: A Novel of the Lost Colony.** Atheneum 1973.

Sixteen-year-old William Wythers tells of the adventures, mysteries, and hardships he encountered as a member of the ill-fated "Lost Colony" during England's early attempts to colonize America. Fiction.

Littell, Robert. **The Defection of A. J. Lewinter** (© 1973). Popular Lib 1974.

A. J. Lewinter, an M.I.T. defense scientist, defects to Russia. The U.S. wants to know what secrets Lewinter carried, while Russia wants to know if the secrets are real. So begins a spy-chess game of bizarre gambits and double crosses. Fiction.

Ludlum, Robert. **The Rhinemann Exchange.** Dial 1974.

A treasonous exchange of war materials necessary for the continuation of World War II takes place between the industrial communities of the U.S. and Nazi Germany. Mature fiction.

Lytle, Andrew. **The Long Night** (© 1936). Avon 1973.

During the Civil War, a young boy becomes obsessed with avenging his father's murder, and the obsession dramatically affects all those around him. Fiction.

MacDonald, John D. **The Dreadful Lemon Sky.** Lippincott 1975.

Travis McGee meets an old friend who leaves $104,200 with him. When the friend dies, Travis investigates and finds himself battling a drug smuggling ring run by a lawyer who has a promising political career if he can control his criminal activities and sex habits. Mature fiction.

MacInnes, Helen. **The Snare of the Hunter.** HarBraceJ 1974.

A band of civilians tries to smuggle a young woman out of Czechoslovakia into Switzerland, an act which leads to romance, adventure, and intrigue. Fiction.

Maclean, Alistair. **The Guns of Navarone** (© 1957). Fawcett World 1974.

When an all-out naval bombardment fails to silence the German artillery on the cliffs at Navarone, five men, each a specialist in violence, death, and destruction, are sent on a commando raid to destroy the guns. Mature fiction.

Maybury, Anne. **Walk in the Paradise Garden.** Random 1972.

Spending a holiday on a beautiful Greek island with her amorous suitor, Justin becomes intrigued by the puzzling death of a wealthy woman and by the woman's mute daughter, who holds the key to solving the mystery. Fiction.

Mazer, Harry. **Snow Bound** (© 1973). Dell 1975.

Tony Laporte runs away from home to teach his parents a lesson. A car accident leaves Tony and Cindy, the hitchhiker he has picked up, stranded in the wilderness on the U.S. side of the Canadian border, where they must survive a raging blizzard. Fiction.

Melville, Herman. **Typee** (© 1846). Penguin 1972.

Melville jumped ship at Typee in the Sandwich Islands of the South Pacific. In this book he presents a semi-autobiographical account of his stay on the island, including his capture by cannibals. Nonfiction.

Neufeld, John. **Sleep Two, Three, Four!** (© 1971). Avon 1972.

It is 1983. Six idealistic young people join the underground to fight a dictatorship that has taken over the United States. Fiction.

Nicole, Christopher. **Operation Neptune** (© 1972). Dell 1973.

Jonathan Anders struggles with overzealous Irish rebels, an ex-Nazi, and determined Russian agents to discover a secret device designed to aid in the exploration and control of the sea. Fiction.

Nordhoff, Charles, and James Norman Hall. **The Bounty Trilogy.** Little 1946.

The trilogy contains *Mutiny on the Bounty,* the crew's seizure of a British sailing ship because of what they consider the inhumanity of Captain Bligh; *Men Against the Sea,* Captain Bligh's heroic struggle to sail an open boat across 3,600 miles of the Pacific after the mutiny; and *Pitcairn's Island,* the mutineers' attempt to build a new home for themselves on a remote tropical island. Fiction.

North, Sterling. **The Wolfling** (© 1969). Bantam n.d.

A fast-paced story about a young man and a wolf growing up in the wilderness of Wisconsin in the years following the Civil War. Fiction.

Orczy, Baroness Emmuska. **The Scarlet Pimpernel** (© 1909). NAL 1974.

After the French Revolution, a group of men try to seize control of France, but even their terror tactics cannot succeed until they stop the mysterious man who fights for human rights and leaves as his calling card the flower called the Scarlet Pimpernel. Fiction.

Peck, Richard. **Through a Brief Darkness** (© 1973). Avon 1974.

Karen, the daughter of a Syndicate chief, finds herself pulled out of school, hurried off to England, and plunged into terror as she battles to escape captors who are using her to control her father. Fiction.

Polk, Dora. **The Linnet Estate.** McKay 1973.

A young English girl visits the ranch of an eccentric California widow interested in the occult and becomes the object of what appears to be a supernatural campaign to drive her away. Fiction.

Preussler, Otfried (translator Anthea Bell). **The Satanic Mill.** Macmillan 1973.

A young boy in seventeenth-century Germany attempts to escape from a master of necromancy, a conjurer of spirits from the dead. Fiction.

Pyle, Howard. **Men of Iron.** Har-Row 1891.

In the days of chivalry, young Myles Falworth fights his way to knighthood and battles his father's mortal enemy in order to remove the stigma of traitor from the family name. Fiction.

Ray, Mary. **The Ides of April.** FS&G 1974.

After Roman senator Caius Pomponius is found murdered in A.D. 62, his slaves are to be immediately executed according to Roman law. Seventeen-year-old Hylas manages to hide and is determined to find the killer. Fiction.

Roth, Arthur. **The Iceberg Hermit.** Four Winds 1974.

Seventeen-year-old Allan Gordon is shipwrecked in the Arctic where he is stranded for seven years, much of the time alone. Based on a historical incident. Fiction.

Ryder, Jonathan. **The Cry of the Halidon.** Delacorte 1974.

International economic and political conspiracy explodes in Jamaica, and an innocent individual is caught in the middle. Mature fiction.

Scott, Sir Walter. **Ivanhoe** (© 1819). WSP 1963.

Ivanhoe returns to England from the Crusades and falls in love with Rowena, but runs afoul of Bois-Guilbert and the Knights Templar who serve the grasping Prince John. Fighting to free himself and others from John's tyranny, Ivanhoe also seeks to restore the throne to its rightful holder. Fiction.

Stevenson, Robert Louis. **Kidnapped** (© 1886). NAL 1959.

In the early eighteenth century, David Balfour is kidnapped by his uncle and put aboard a ship to the British colonies, but David escapes to a fugitive's life in the Scottish Highlands. Fiction.

Stevenson, William (with Uri Dan). **90 Minutes at Entebbe.** Bantam 1976.

An inside account of the July 1976 commando raid into East Africa to rescue over 100 hostages held by a group of terrorists who were being aided by the Ugandan government. Nonfiction.

Taylor, Theodore. **The Cay** (© 1969). Avon 1970.

During World War II Phillip, a young boy prejudiced against blacks, finds himself temporarily blinded and shipwrecked on a barren island where he must rely upon an old black man to help him survive. Fiction.

Thiele, Colin. **Fire in the Stone.** Har-Row 1974.

Australian Ernie Ryan discovers an opal mine while on a school vacation, but his dreams of wealth turn into a nightmare when the opals are stolen. Ernie and his aborigine friend track the thief through the rugged Australian Outback. Fiction.

Titler, Dale M. **Unnatural Resources: True Stories of American Treasures.** P-H 1973.

True stories of lost American treasure grouped in sections on buried, underwater, and pirate treasure, and lost mines. Includes a picture glossary. Nonfiction.

White, Robb. **Deathwatch** (© 1972). Dell 1973.

Hired as a guide for a bighorn sheep hunting expedition, Ben, by witnessing a killing and refusing to be a party to a cover-up, finds himself fair game. (See also *The Frogmen,* Dell.) Fiction.

Woods, George A. **Catch a Killer** (© 1972). Dell 1973.

A young man slowly turns into a psychotic killer and kidnaps a young boy. A determined detective then sets out to find and capture the disturbed man. Fiction.

Wyss, Johann. **The Swiss Family Robinson** (© 1812). Dell 1967.

Through ingenuity and cooperation, a family survives, and even prospers, on a deserted island after their sailing ship sinks. Fiction.

WESTERN FRONTIER

Abbey, Edward. The Brave Cowboy (© 1956). Ballantine n.d.

John W. Burns, a self-sufficient cowboy who hates fences and all they represent, deliberately gets arrested to help a friend. When Burns breaks out of jail, the police go after him. Made into the movie *Lonely Are the Brave*. Fiction.

Adams, Andy. The Log of a Cowboy (© 1903). U of Nebr Pr 1964.

From his own experiences as a trailhand and cowboy, Adams creates an authentic picture of the unromantic cowboy—the dust, the boredom, the cattle, and the horses that made up his world. Fiction.

Baker, Betty. The Spirit Is Willing. Macmillan 1974.

The problems mount up when Carrie, bored with summer and with not being able to do anything "interesting," decides she *has* to see the Indian mummy on display in the local saloon. Fiction.

Benedict, Rex. Goodbye to the Purple Sage. Pantheon 1973.

Sagebrush Sheridan I, sheriff of Medicine Creek, gathers around him a strange posse of Apache kids, Comanche chiefs, and singing outlaws as he gallops off after the Pecos Gang. Fiction.

Bourne, Eulalia. Woman in Levi's. U of Ariz Pr 1967.

The author writes of her experiences as a teacher, a homesteader, and a woman engaged in ranching, a world traditionally controlled by and limited to men. Nonfiction.

Burke, John. The Legend of Baby Doe. Putnam 1974.

Baby Doe Tabor survived a scandalous divorce, the snubs of Denver society, and the unwise generosity of her husband, only to die virtually forgotten, protecting the silver mine which her husband said would some day make her rich again. Nonfiction.

Camp, Walter (editor Kenneth Hammer). Custer in '76. Brigham 1976.

A study of the Little Bighorn Battle based on the unpublished notes of Camp, who, between 1876 and 1920, interviewed both army and Indian participants in the battle. Nonfiction.

Capps, Benjamin. **A Woman of the People** (© 1966). Fawcett World 1971.

Nine-year-old Helen Morrison is captured by Comanches. At first she pretends to accept her fate while awaiting a chance to escape, but slowly she becomes willing to accept Indian ways. (See also *The White Man's Road,* Ace Bks.) Fiction.

Cary, Diana Serra. **The Hollywood Posse.** HM 1975.

During the early years of this century, some genuine cowboys left their ranches and became extras in movie westerns. The author's cowboy-father, his friends, and their descendants are the heroes of this book. Nonfiction.

Cather, Willa. **My Antonia** (© 1918). HM 1961.

When her bohemian father commits suicide, Antonia assumes the burden of working her family's poor Nebraska farm. She finds her greatest satisfaction there in a struggle with the land which demands both energy and optimism. (See also *O Pioneers,* HM; *The Professor's House,* VinRandom; and *Death Comes for the Archbishop,* VinRandom.) Fiction.

Collinson, Frank (editor Mary Whatley Clarke). **Life in the Saddle** (© 1963). U of Okla Pr 1972.

The author, an Englishman who went to Texas in 1872, tells of his life in the Old West, including buffalo hunting, trail drives, and confrontations with the Plains Indians. Nonfiction.

Cook, D. J. **Hands Up; or, Twenty Years of Detective Life in the Mountains and on the Plains** (© 1958). U of Okla Pr 1971.

Cook, once superintendent of the Rocky Mountain Detective Association, first published this story of his life as a detective and tracker of criminals in 1882. The language may seem old-fashioned but these stories of crime, hangings, and shootings are true. Nonfiction.

Cornelius, Temple H., and John B. Marshall. **Golden Treasures of the San Juans** (© 1961). Swallow 1973.

Much mining activity took place in the San Juan

Mountains of southwestern Colorado before 1900. The locations of many mines worked by only one man were lost over the years, and rumors of these lost mines persist even today. Nonfiction.

Crawford, Thomas Edgar (editor Jeff C. Dykes). **The West of the Texas Kid, 1881–1910.** U of Okla Pr 1962.

These are the recollections of the Texas Kid, an outlaw, a rancher, and a gold miner. Included are some of the activities of Hole in the Wall outlaws. Nonfiction.

Custer, Elizabeth B. **"Boots and Saddles," or Life in Dakota with General Custer** (© 1885). U of Okla Pr 1968.

The wife of General George Custer tells of her experiences living in Dakota while her husband was stationed there. She presents a personal portrait of her husband unlike that found in many other sources. Nonfiction.

Decker, William. **To Be a Man.** Fawcett World 1967.

A realistic tale of the rough, dirty, back-breaking life of the old-time cowboy. Fiction.

Durham, Marilyn. **Dutch Uncle.** HarBraceJ 1973.

In March 1880, former gunfighter and current gambler Jake Hollander comes to New Mexico with two Mexican orphans in his custody. At first anxious to dump the kids, Hollander changes his mind and instead becomes a town marshal. Fiction.

Durham, Marilyn. **The Man Who Loved Cat Dancing.** HarBraceJ 1972.

Catherine Crocker runs away from her husband, only to get mixed up with a train-robbing gang and its leader—the man who loved Cat Dancing. Mature fiction.

Durham, Philip, and Everett L. Jones. **The Adventures of the Negro Cowboys** (© 1966). Bantam 1969.

More than 5,000 blacks—cowboys, rustlers, homesteaders, and miners—were a significant factor in the development of the American West after the Civil War. Nonfiction.

Eunson, Dale. **Up on the Rim.** FS&G 1970.

The year is 1910, and the Eunsons are setting out for the last American frontier—Montana—with adventure and hardship ahead of them. Nonfiction.

Evarts, Hal G. **The Man from Yuma** (© 1958). PB 1972.

Disguised as a murderer, John Hazard sets out to capture a group of army deserters terrorizing the settlers along the Colorado River. Fiction.

Fisher, Vardis. **Mountain Man** (© 1965). PB 1972.

When the mountain man returns from a round of his traplines to find his pregnant wife dead, he becomes a person whose only thought is revenge against those who took her life. Fiction.

Flynn, Robert. **North to Yesterday.** Knopf 1967.

A group of misfits decides to drive a trail herd north more than ten years after all the cattle trails have dried up. Fiction.

Gard, Wayne. **The Chisholm Trail** (© 1954). U of Okla Pr 1969.

Beginning in 1865, the Chisholm Trail was the main route followed by Texas cowboys taking cattle to railroads in Kansas. The trail drives were hard on men, horses, and cattle, but at the end, they promised wealth, saloons, and gambling. Nonfiction.

Grey, Zane. **To the Last Man** (© 1922). PB n.d.

Ellen Jorth and Jean Isbel are in love, but their families hate each other. The feud erupts into the bloody Pleasant Valley War in Arizona. Based on fact. (See also *Robbers' Roost,* PB; and *Riders of the Purple Sage,* PB.) Fiction.

Gulick, Bill. **Liveliest Town in the West.** Doubleday 1969.

Dustville is the sleepiest, dullest town in the Old West until the editor of the *Dustville Clarion* concocts some legends and a hero to go with them. The Eastern press picks up the stories, and tourists begin heading west for thrilling Dustville. Fiction.

Guthrie, A. B., Jr. **The Big Sky** (© 1949). Bantam 1972.

Boone Caudill, a rugged Kentucky boy, makes his way

to the mouth of the Missouri, falls in with tough frontiersmen, and follows the life of a rough-and-tumble trapper, always keeping ahead of the crush of settlers moving westward. Fiction.

Guthrie, A. B., Jr. **The Way West** (© 1952). Bantam 1972.

The trail to Oregon is taken by several kinds of persons—the old mountain man, the power-hungry leader, the quiet but forceful true leader—and by Brownie, who grows up as the caravan wends its way west from Independence, Missouri. Fiction.

Henry, Will. **The Bear Paw Horses.** Lippincott 1973.

Before his death, Crazy Horse commands Crowfoot, his seventy-year-old medicine man, to steal horses from the whites and take them to Chief Joseph, who is leading his Nez Percé tribe away from their home in Oregon to safety in Canada. Fiction.

Henry, Will. **From Where the Sun Now Stands** (© 1960). Bantam 1972.

Based on the 113-day war between the Nez Percé Indians, led by Chief Joseph, and the white man, the story portrays the chief as heroic and dignified. (See also *One More River to Cross,* Bantam; and *The Fourth Horseman,* Bantam.) Fiction.

Horgan, Paul. **Lamy of Santa Fe: His Life and Times.** FS&G 1975.

Juan Bautista Lamy was only thirty-seven in 1851 when he was sent to New Mexico as a Catholic bishop. Though he had enemies and faced one attempt on his life, his frontier drive and strength of character won him friends and increased the power of the Catholic Church in the Southwest. Winner of the 1976 Pulitzer Prize for history. Nonfiction.

Hosford, Jessie. **You Bet Your Boots I Can.** Nelson 1972.

Though teenager Judy Hoffman enjoys her high school days in a remote town and her year as teacher in a rural school, she values most her life with her parents on the Nebraska frontier at the turn of the century. Fiction.

Jackson, W. H. (with Ethel Dassow). **Handloggers.** Alaska Northwest 1974.

The author tells of his life as a handlogger in Alaska from the early years of the twentieth century to the present. Nonfiction.

Jennings, Gary. **The Terrible Teague Bunch.** Norton 1975.

In 1905, four inexperienced desperadoes plan to stop and rob a payroll train by running a herd of cattle onto the tracks. Fiction.

Johnson, Annabel, and Edgar Johnson. **A Golden Touch.** Har-Row 1963.

When Andy goes off to a gold-mining town to live with his father, he finds problems for which his earlier life with his grandparents has not prepared him. Why does the sheriff keep coming around and who is stealing gold from the mine? Fiction.

Johnson, Dorothy M. **The Bloody Bozeman: The Perilous Trail to Montana's Gold.** McGraw 1971.

The Bozeman Trail led to the goldfields of Montana, but along the way Indians and road agents lay in wait. (In the same American Trails series, see also Wallace Stegner, *The Gathering of Zion: The Story of the Mormon Trail*, McGraw; and Ferol Egan, *The El Dorado Trail: The Story of the Gold Rush Routes Across Mexico*, McGraw.) Nonfiction.

Jordan, Grace. **Home below Hell's Canyon.** U of Nebr Pr 1962.

Jordan relates her family's experiences after they move to a sheep ranch in Idaho and find themselves living on the Snake River just below Hell's Canyon, virtually isolated from the rest of the world. Nonfiction.

L'Amour, Louis. **Down the Long Hills.** Bantam 1968.

An Indian attack that kills all their friends and relatives forces seven-year-old Hardy and three-year-old Betty Sue to set out for safety with only a horse and a knife to help them. (See also *Under the Sweetwater Rim*, Bantam; and *The Ferguson Rifle*, Bantam.) Fiction.

L'Amour, Louis. **The Quick and the Dead.** Bantam 1973.

The McKaskels, inexperienced in the ways of the West, are joined by Con Vallian, who knows both the good and the bad of frontier life. Together, they find a new home for the family, fighting off an outlaw gang and a band of Indians along the way. Fiction.

Laune, Seigniora Russell. **Sand in My Eyes** (© 1956). Northland 1974.

Laune describes, through anecdotes from her own life, the pioneer life in a small town in western Oklahoma, starting with its raw early days following the land run and continuing through the time when the town has paved streets and a library. Nonfiction.

Le May, Alan. **The Searchers.** Har-Row 1954.

A six-year-old white girl is taken by Comanches in a raid, and Amos and Martie set off to rescue her. (See also *The Unforgiven*, Har-Row.) Fiction.

Locke, Charles O. **The Hell Bent Kid.** Norton 1957.

When young Tot Lohman shoots another cowboy in a dance brawl, the dead cowboy's family swears revenge. Lohman is forced to become a fugitive—and a man. Fiction.

Lott, Milton. **Dance Back the Buffalo** (© 1959). PB 1968.

When the glories of the Sioux Indians seemed dead, a great Indian messiah came to them preaching that they must do a ceremonial dance which would bring back the buffalo and make them safe from white men's bullets. (See also *The Last Hunt*, HM.) Fiction.

MacConnell, C. E. **Xit Buck.** U of Ariz Pr 1968.

The author relates his experiences as a young boy who goes west and grows up living the life of a cowboy on the largest fenced ranch in the world. Nonfiction.

Manfred, Frederick. **Lord Grizzly** (© 1954). NAL 1971.

Mauled by a bear, Hugh Glass is deserted by his companions. His will to live and to revenge himself on his former friends leads him to crawl for weeks to safety. (See also *Conquering Horse*, NAL; and *Scarlet Plume*, NAL.) Fiction.

Manfred, Frederick. **Riders of Judgment** (© 1957). NAL 1973.

The three Hammett brothers love the same girl, but her marrying one of them does not separate them. When the range wars between the cattle barons and the small ranchers begin, they are caught in the middle. Cain, the oldest brother, finally has to seek revenge for the entire family. Fiction.

McNichols, Charles L. **Crazy Weather** (© 1944). U of Nebr Pr 1967.

Two boys, one an Indian and the other white, go off together during a four-day storm and find themselves to be quite different people when they return home. Fiction.

McNitt, Frank. **Richard Wetherill, Anasazi** (© 1966). U of NM Pr 1974.

Wetherill discovered the Indian ruins of Mesa Verde, Colorado, when he was a young cowboy. Later, he ran a trading post in New Mexico where he was murdered. Nonfiction.

Michener, James A. **Centennial.** Random 1974.

Michener weaves together the stories of the land, various people—including Indians, trappers, farmers, cattlemen, and laborers—and events to present a fictionalized history of an area along the South Platte River in Colorado. Fiction.

Moody, Ralph. **Riders of the Pony Express** (© 1958). Dell 1967.

In spite of weather, lack of rest, and personal danger, eighty riders rode 400 fast horses to relay the mail almost 2,000 miles from St. Joseph, Missouri, to San Francisco in ten days and nights. This is an account of the Pony Express in the years 1860–61. Nonfiction.

Neihardt, John G. **The River and I** (© 1910). U of Nebr Pr 1968.

In a highly readable style, the author relates his experiences along the Missouri River. Nonfiction.

Portis, Charles. **True Grit.** NAL 1968.

Fourteen-year-old Mattie Ross gains the assistance of Marshal Rooster Cogburn in tracking down her father's murderer. Mattie never loses her nerve in the uproarious adventures which follow. Fiction.

Rhodes, Eugene Manlove. **Pasó Por Aquí** (© 1925). U of Okla Pr 1973.

Ross McEwen robs a bank and flees, pursued by Sheriff Pat Garrett. In his attempt to get away, McEwen runs across a family dying of diphtheria. (See also *The Proud Sheriff*, U of Okla Pr; and *Copper Streak Trail*, U of Okla Pr.) Fiction.

Rhodes, Eugene Manlove. **The Trusty Knaves** (© 1934). U of Okla Pr 1972.

The hero of this story is based on Bill Doolin, an Oklahoma Territory outlaw who was befriended by the author. A plot to rob a bank provides the action. Fiction.

Rickey, Don, Jr. **Forty Miles a Day on Beans and Hay: The Enlisted Soldiers Fighting the Indian Wars** (© 1963). U of Okla Pr 1972.

A picture of the life of the regular army soldier during the 1866–1891 Indian Wars: the dusty drudgery of frontier life, the recreation of privates and noncoms, and the Indian battles. Nonfiction.

Rosa, Joseph G. **The Gunfighter: Man or Myth?** (© 1969). U of Okla Pr 1973.

The Western gunfighter has been regarded as a hero by some, a villain by others. The author tries to separate fact from myth to get at the truth. Nonfiction.

Russell, Andy. **The High West.** Viking Pr 1974.

The text and photographs give a glimpse of the high West, its inhabitants, its beauties, and its hazards. Nonfiction.

Sandoz, Mari. **Cheyenne Autumn** (© 1953). Avon 1969.

Kept on the reservation by whites, a band of Cheyenne Indians breaks out to return to their ancient home. Based on fact. Fiction.

Savage, William W., Jr., editor. **Cowboy Life: Reconstructing an American Myth.** U of Okla Pr 1974.

A collection of observations, memoirs, and reminiscences, this book shows what the cowboy's life was really like. Mature nonfiction.

Schaefer, Jack. **Shane** (© 1949). Bantam 1969.

Shane, a mysterious gunfighter, drifts into the middle of a range war and sides with the homesteaders. Fiction.

Schoenberger, Dale T. **The Gunfighters.** Caxton 1971.

Wyatt Earp, Doc Holliday, Bat Masterson, Clay Allison, Ben Thompson, Luke Short, and Wild Bill Hickok are the subjects of the author's attempt to show gunfighters as they really were. They turn out to be much less romantic than they usually appear on television or in films and novels. Nonfiction.

Seelye, John. **The Kid.** Viking Pr 1972.

A slender blond youth and a towering black man ride into a Wyoming town which is spoiling for a fight. When it is learned that the pair has gold and plans to buy sheep, the local cowboys become even more upset. The outcome of this novel, which contains some harsh language, is quite unexpected. Fiction.

Stewart, George R. **Ordeal by Hunger: The Story of the Donner Party** (© 1960). PB 1971.

The story of the Donner Party, including the hardships that led to some members surviving only through cannibalism, told in part through letters and diaries of some of the members of the party. Nonfiction.

Swarthout, Glendon. **The Shootist.** Doubleday 1975.

John Bernard Books, last of the shootists or gunfighters, rides into El Paso in 1901. The doctor he seeks confirms an earlier doctor's prognosis that Books is dying of cancer. Bothered by those wanting something from him, Books decides just how and when he will die. Frank language of the times. Fiction.

Vestal, Stanley. **Jim Bridger, Mountain Man.** U of Nebr Pr 1970.

Jim Bridger was a great mountain man, an explorer, trapper, Indian fighter, and trailblazer. This biography covers, among other things, his discovery of the Great Salt Lake and his work trapping for the Rocky Mountain Fur Company. Nonfiction.

Vestal, Stanley. **The Missouri** (© 1945). U of Nebr Pr 1964.

The author recounts the events in American history

in which the Missouri River has been involved. Non-fiction.

Wagoner, David. **The Road to Many a Wonder.** FS&G 1974.
Twenty-year-old Ike Bender and his young bride-to-be Millie set out on a 500-mile journey to Denver during the Pikes Peak Gold Rush of 1859. Fiction.

Wilson, Elinor. **Jim Beckwourth.** U of Okla Pr 1972.
Born a slave around 1800, Jim Beckwourth became in turn a fur trapper, an army scout, a trader to the Indians, and a war chief of the Crow Indians. In short, he was one of the great mountain men of his time, living and finally dying among the Indians. Nonfiction.

Wister, Owen (editor Robert L. Hough). **The West of Owen Wister: Selected Short Stories.** U of Nebr Pr 1972.
Wister's stories in this collection of his Western literature take place in settings ranging from a mining camp in the Rockies to a territorial capitol in the Northwest. Fiction.

Young, Otis E., Jr. **The Mining Men.** Lowell Pr 1974.
This is the story of a gold mine, the Molly Pitcher, and the many persons who are involved with her in one way or another. Starting in 1871 and ending in 1932, the author portrays the events that might have taken place around a single mine. Fiction.

SCIENCE FICTION

Anderson, Poul. **Orbit Unlimited** (© 1961). Pyramid Pubns 1973.
Colonists disenchanted with earth are on their way to another planet when they receive word that they can go back to a new government. They must decide if they will return or continue toward their original destination.

Anthony, Piers. **Var the Stick.** Bantam 1973.
Var, who is animal-like in many ways, fights a duel to settle a dispute between two warring factions. The

duel's unexpected results lead him to flee into exile—
with the opponent he was supposed to defeat.

Asimov, Isaac. **Foundation** (© 1951). Avon 1970.

The Foundation is created by Hari Seldon to protect
civilization against the expanding Galactic Empire,
which uses psychology and history to control the behavior of the masses. Following the Seldon Plan, the
Foundation achieves supremacy at the edges of the
galaxy and the battle begins for control of the entire
galaxy. (See also *Foundation and Empire,* Avon; and
Second Foundation, Avon.)

Asimov, Isaac. **Pebble in the Sky** (© 1950). Fawcett
World 1973.

Joseph Schwartz is transported into the future, where
he becomes involved in earth's vicious attempt to
control the galaxy. He decides to use his newly developed special powers to save the planet.

Asimov, Isaac, editor. **The Hugo Winners,** 2 vols. Doubleday 1970.

The only complete collection of best science fiction
stories selected yearly at the World Science Fiction
Convention.

Bellamy, Francis Rufus. **Atta** (© 1953). PB 1974.

When Brokell wakes from whatever has caused him
to lose consciousness, he is insect-sized and apparently
stands little chance of survival in the terrifying world
that was once his orchard.

Bioy Casares, Adolfo. **Diary of the War of the Pig.** Mc-
Graw 1972.

The theme of aging is explored in this story about a
war of extermination of the elderly. The novel is set
in Buenos Aires during the final political struggles of
the Peron regime.

Blish, James. **Cities in Flight** (© 1955). Avon 1970.

The four novels of Blish's epic of the future are
brought together here. *They Shall Have Stars* begins
the cycle on Jupiter, anticipating the time when Earth
will be too worn out to support life. *A Life for the
Stars* takes the cities, wrenched from their positions
in space by the spin-dizzy, on galactic wanderings in
search of means of support. In *Earthman, Come Home*

this planet's original inhabitants return to destroy their ancient home. *The Triumph of Time* continues the journey through inter-galactic space to the birthplace of continuing creation.

Blish, James. **The Quincunx of Time.** Dell 1973.

Earth's empire has become so far-flung that even the fastest spaceships take months to deliver messages. A solution is found in the Dirac transmitter, but the problems become even more complex when someone starts tapping Dirac's secret transmissions.

Boulle, Pierre. **Planet of the Apes.** Vanguard 1963.

Two men from earth land on a planet governed by intelligent but cruel apes, who have taken over as humans have become weaker. One of the men, Ulysse Merou, is captured and fights for his freedom.

Bova, Ben. **As on a Darkling Plain.** Dell 1974.

The answer to the machines on Saturn's star must be found, since it is believed they intend to destroy Earth. Dr. Lee sets out to find the secret and finds his arch-rival thwarting his plans.

Brackett, Leigh. **The Long Tomorrow** (© 1955). Ballantine 1974.

Len's grandmother remembers the time of supermarkets, TVs, and movies, all swept away by the Destruction. Only those who could adapt to the old Mennonite ways have survived in a United States bereft of machines, with all towns bigger than 1,000 people prohibited by the Thirtieth Amendment. (See also *The Ginger Star,* Ballantine.)

Bradbury, Ray. **The Illustrated Man** (© 1951). Bantam 1969.

A man completely covered with colorful illustrations which move and tell stories tries to find peace and some way of ridding himself of the illustrations. Nineteen stories, which make up the book, are illustrated on the man's body.

Bradbury, Ray. **The Martian Chronicles** (© 1950). Bantam 1974.

The chronicles trace man's exploration and colonization of Mars, ending, finally, when the Martians are the only humans left in the solar system.

Bradbury, Ray. **S Is for Space** (© 1966). Bantam 1970.

A collection of science fiction short stories by one of the better-known writers in the field.

Clarke, Arthur C. **Against the Fall of Night** (© 1953). Pyramid Pubns 1960.

Alvin is the only child to have been born in his city during the last 7,000 years. When his quest for truth and knowledge leads him to the discovery that another city still exists, his people face a very difficult choice.

Clarke, Arthur C. **Childhood's End** (© 1953). Ballantine 1972.

Earth is suddenly invaded by starships whose masters never appear on earth but still control its inhabitants. Karellen, the only Overlord to have any contact with humans, is never seen. As years pass, the populace grows used to the spaceships' presence, but one day the ships descend and Karellen disembarks. (See also *Rendezvous with Rama,* Ballantine; and *The Sands of Mars,* HarBraceJ.)

Clarke, Arthur C. **2001: A Space Odyssey** (© 1968). NAL 1972.

A strange monolith, apparently left by an alien being, is the object of a space voyage which includes a computer that goes crazy and the survival of only one of the original five space voyagers.

Cogswell, Theodore R. **The Wall around the World** (© 1962). Pyramid Pubns 1973.

The author uses fiction to explore some possible worlds of the future—or are they possible?

Crichton, Michael. **The Andromeda Strain** (© 1969). Dell 1971.

A secret satellite, intended to analyze the upper atmosphere and then return to earth, lands in a tiny Arizona town, and all but two of its inhabitants die. The effort to discover the cause of the deaths turns into a race to prevent atomic self-destruction.

Crichton, Michael. **The Terminal Man** (© 1972). Bantam 1974.

The author explores the consequences of mind and

behavior control by computer. Criminal Harry Benson is brought to University Hospital for an experiment but escapes, and the doctors discover they have unleashed a human time bomb on the public. (For other medical mysteries see Robert Silverberg, *To Live Again,* Doubleday, *Recalled to Life,* Doubleday, and *Born with the Dead,* Random; Isaac Asimov, *Fantastic Voyage,* HM; and Clifford Simak, *Why Call Them Back from Heaven,* Ace Bks.)

De Camp, L. Sprague. **Lest Darkness Fall** (© 1939). Ballantine 1974.

When Martin Padway is hurtled back to sixth-century Rome, he quickly adapts himself and sets about to prevent the coming of the Dark Ages by using his knowledge of historical events and by introducing "new" inventions.

Del Rey, Lester. **The Eleventh Commandment.** Regency 1962.

"Be fruitful and multiply" is the eleventh commandment, and taken literally and enforced by the Church, earth becomes an overpopulated hell. Bitter, logical, and frightening, even more today than when first published.

Dick, Philip K. **The Man in the High Castle** (© 1962). Berkley Pub 1974.

A story about an alternate universe pertinent to our own time. Germany and Japan win World War II and divide the United States between them.

Dickson, Gordon R. **Sleepwalker's World.** DAW Bks 1972.

Rafe Arnaul Harald investigates the force using earth's buried energy to paralyze society and prevent a voyage to the stars. A special wolf and a crippled girl become his allies against the world which is exploiting their planet.

Dickson, Gordon R. **The Star Road** (© 1968). DAW Bks 1973.

A collection of Dickson's short stories first published in science fiction magazines. (See also *The Book of Gordon Dickson,* originally published as *Danger—Human,* DAW Bks.)

Dunstan, Mary J., and Patricia W. Garlan. **Worlds in the Making: Probes for Students of the Future.** P-H 1970.

This collection of materials about various topics related to the future can be used by anyone trying to cope with a changing world. Nonfiction.

Elwood, Roger, editor. **Chronicles of a Comer and Other Religious Science Fiction Stories.** John Knox 1974.

Religion as it pertains to the imagined worlds of tomorrow is explored in this collection of short stories. (See also *The Learning Maze,* Messner; and *Showcase,* Har-Row.)

Engdahl, Sylvia Louise. **Beyond the Tomorrow Mountains.** Atheneum 1973.

Noren has become a Scholar, one of his society's elite, though he once scorned the teachings of his order. Now, however, he finds himself in despair because there seems no chance for the survival of his planet.

Engdahl, Sylvia Louise. **Enchantress from the Stars.** Atheneum 1970.

Elana is a stowaway on a mission sponsored by a highly advanced civilization. The mission is to save a primitive planet from destruction by a technological society attempting to colonize it.

Farmer, Philip Jose. **To Your Scattered Bodies Go** (© 1971). Berkley Pub 1973.

In the Riverworld, millions of resurrected humans retain their hatreds and prejudices, but they cannot die.

Fast, Howard. **A Touch of Infinity.** Morrow 1973.

Thirteen offbeat short stories, most of them set in the present, about humanity and its attempts to understand puzzling aspects of nature.

Frank, Pat. **Alas, Babylon.** Lippincott 1959.

When an accident triggers World War III, the inhabitants of a small survival area in Florida search for leadership that will help them build a new life.

Franke, Herbert W. (translator Christine Priest). **The Orchid Cage** (© 1961). DAW Bks 1973.

Though the city attempts to repel them, two teams

of competing explorers are able to enter it. But they find that solving the mysteries of the city's inhabitants is not so easy.

Freedman, Nancy. **Joshua Son of None** (© 1973). Dell 1974.

In November 1963, a dying president is rushed to a hospital where a surgeon takes some cells from the president's neck and through a process of cloning reproduces an apparent identical twin of the president.

Gerrold, David. **When Harlie Was One** (© 1970). Ballantine 1975.

Harlie is a computer who thinks he's human, and his psychologist believes that Harlie indeed has an id, an ego, and a superego. But which of these may control Harlie at any one moment is the problem, for Harlie has the emotional characteristics of a child. (See also *The Man Who Folded Himself,* Popular Lib.)

Gilman, Robert C. **The Rebel of Rhada.** Ace Bks 1968.

Kier, the warleader of the planet Rhada, lives far in the future when society has reverted to feudalism and science has become suspect.

Goulart, Ron, editor. **What's Become of Screwloose? And Other Inquires** (© 1970). DAW Bks 1973.

These are stories of mechanical devices gone wild and people's ability or inability to cope with the cyborgs we find around us now, berserk washing machines and neurotic automobiles included.

Gutteridge, Lindsay. **Cold War in a Country Garden** (© 1971). PB 1973.

Matthew Dilke is the first man to experiment with a process which reduces him to the size of a small insect. When the experiment succeeds, he and the companions who have joined him are assigned to a secret mission behind the Iron Curtain.

Haldeman, Joe W., editor. **Cosmic Laughter.** HR&W 1974.

The lighter side of science fiction is featured in this collection of short stories subtitled "science fiction for the fun of it."

Harrison, Harry. **The Deathworld Trilogy.** Doubleday 1960.

Jason din Alt, a successful gambler, chances his life on three deadly planets with separate challenges. On *Deathworld 1,* he is reconditioned to survive the horrifying assaults of both plants and animals. Kidnapped and removed to *Deathworld 2,* a world where man either kills or lives as a slave; on *Deathworld 3,* man is bred to attack and kill. Jason finds the mental powers he has developed in his life as a gambler his most important weapon.

Harrison, Harry, and Carol Pugner, editors. **A Science Fiction Reader.** Scribner 1973.

An overview of science fiction writing with stories by authors like Arthur Clarke and Isaac Asimov.

Heinlein, Robert A. **Stranger in a Strange Land** (© 1961). Berkley Pub 1968.

To a young man newly arrived on Earth after being raised by natives on Mars, human civilization is indeed very strange, and he, with his nonhuman reasoning and talents, is very much the stranger.

Herbert, Frank. **Dune** (© 1965). Ace Bks 1974.

The desert planet Arrakis (Dune) is the background for the development of a young alien and his ultimate confirmation as religious leader of the planet's nomadic natives.

Hoyle, Fred. **The Black Cloud** (© 1957). NAL 1973.

Earth is threatened by a black cloud which has somehow entered the solar system. When all other theories prove unsatisfactory, one of the scientists studying the cloud decides that it contains an alien intelligence and that he must communicate with it.

Hoyle, Fred, and Geoffrey Hoyle. **Seven Steps to the Sun.** Fawcett World 1973.

Mike Jerome is exploring the possibility of writing a science fiction novel when he suddenly finds himself living in the future.

Jones, Raymond F. **Man of Two Worlds** (© 1944). Pyramid Pubns 1971.

Ketan does not like much of what he knows about his

native world, but his attempts to change it lead him to other worlds which have their own problems.

Keyes, Daniel. **Flowers for Algernon** (© 1959). Bantam 1970.

As a result of extraordinary surgery, Charlie Gordon progresses from mental dullness to brilliance. His journal reflects his intellectual and social growth—and his fear of unpredictable dangers which may lie ahead.

Klein, Gerard (translator John Brunner). **The Overlords of War** (© 1971). DAW Bks 1974.

After an accident transports George Corson 6,000 years into the future, he continues to move across space and time as he becomes part of a master plan to end war.

Knight, Damon, editor. **Toward Infinity.** S&S 1968.

The subjects handled in this volume include monsters from outer space and superior intelligences caused by mutation.

Laumer, Keith. **The Glory Game** (© 1973). Popular Lib 1974.

Tan Dalton, of Terran's Space Navy, is approached by both the Softliners and the Hardliners as they seek to gain support for their political positions. When he actually confronts his planet's enemies, he has to decide which faction he will support.

Le Guin, Ursula K. **The Dispossessed.** Har-Row 1974.

Facing many problems on his isolationist planet, Shevek travels to the mother planet, hoping to share his discoveries and to break down some of the barriers between peoples, nations, and planets. Mature.

Le Guin, Ursula K. **A Wizard of Earthsea** (© 1968). Ace Bks 1973.

On the planet Earthsea, a world governed by laws of magic as exact and inevitable as those of science, the boy Sparrowhawk begins a journey in the company of wizards, dragons, shadows, and some ordinary people. (See also *The Tombs of Atuan,* Atheneum; and *The Left Hand of Darkness,* Ace Bks.)

L'Engle, Madeleine. **A Wrinkle in Time.** Schol Bk Serv 1962.

When a father fails to return to his children, they are taken on a chilling journey through a wrinkle in time into terrors beyond four-dimensional space.

Levin, Ira. **This Perfect Day** (© 1970). Fawcett World 1974.

Uni controls everything, including the selection of names, the administering of the proper amount of depressants to keep people content, and the decision about who may and may not have children. Chip tries to rebel against the control.

Lightner, A. M. **The Day of the Drones** (© 1969). Bantam 1970.

Many years after the nuclear war which destroyed most of the world, "black" people who think they are the only survivors decide there may be other life on the planet, and they set out to find it.

Lightner, A. M. **Gods or Demons?** Four Winds 1973.

A time machine takes two boys and a girl thousands of years into the past where they must cope with a landscape and people quite different from what they are used to.

Lundwall, Sam. **Bernhard the Conqueror.** DAW Bks 1973.

Ex-private Bernhard, sentenced to hard labor on a prison planet, escapes to the biggest spaceship in the galaxy where all the machinery has been accidentally programmed to adore him, while its inhabitants would gladly cut his throat.

McCaffrey, Anne. **Dragonflight** (© 1968). Ballantine 1973.

Abandoned by Earth and faced with destruction by the dread silver threads, the men of Pern develop a life form of their planet into winged, tailed, and fire-breathing dragons. (See also *Dragonquest,* Ballantine; and *Decision at Doona,* Ballantine.)

McCaffrey, Anne. **The Ship Who Sang** (© 1961). Ballantine 1970.

The perfect brain in a tiny, useless body is rescued

by technology and placed in a new body. No one fore-
sees what will happen to the personality developing
along with the brain.

Meredith, Richard C. **We All Died at Breakaway Station.** Ballantine 1969.

Breakaway Station, a vital communications link between the rim worlds and earth, is endangered, and
its only defenders are injured officers restored to a
temporary, artificial life by medical and mechanical
means. Headed by Captain Absalom Bracer, these
part machine, part humans are the galaxy's only hope
for survival. (See also *At the Narrow Passage,* Berkley Pub.)

Miller, Walter M., Jr. **A Canticle for Leibowitz** (© 1959).
Bantam 1972.

A nuclear holocaust renders earth a barren world
inhabited by people who have forgotten how to use
the machines and knowledge left behind and who return to a feudal society with all its fears and superstitions.

Niven, Larry. **Ringworld** (© 1970). Ballantine 1972.

Four unlikely travelers explore an artificial world so
enormous it encircles the sun.

Niven, Larry, and Jerry Pournelle. **The Mote in God's
Eye.** S&S 1974.

Humans have explored and colonized the galaxy to
its farthest reaches but are challenged by an equal
power. The first contact with that world ends in the
accidental death of the alien emissaries, forcing earth
to send representatives on a dash through space to
explain the incident and avert war.

Norton, Andre. **Moon of Three Rings** (© 1966). Ace
Bks 1972.

Krip Vorland discovers that although Yiktor is a neu-
tral planet, with the power of the three-ringed Moon,
the Old Ones can exchange spirits among other beings
as they will. (See also *The Crystal Gryphon,* DAW
Bks; and *Iron Cage,* Viking Pr.)

Nourse, Alan E. **The Bladerunner.** McKay 1974.

Billy Gimp is a "bladerunner," one who obtains medical supplies for doctors who practice illicit medicine

outside the rules of Health Control. The elaborate system of medicine which Health Control has established works until an epidemic strikes, and then both Billy and his doctor become involved in correcting the problems in the system.

O'Brien, Robert C. **Z for Zachariah.** Atheneum 1975.

Sixteen-year-old Ann Burden thinks she may be the only person in the world to have survived the nuclear holocaust until she sees smoke from a campfire.

Offutt, Andrew J. **The Galactic Rejects** (© 1973). Dell 1974.

Bernie, Cory, and Rinegar are stranded on an unknown planet after the ship taking them from the war area is destroyed. They find themselves still involved in the war, however, but also find that their special talents are helpful in resisting the enemy.

Pesek, Ludek (translator Anthea Bell). **The Earth Is Near** (© 1973). Bradbury Pr 1974.

A psychiatrist relates the experiences of men who make the first manned flight to Mars and find that the mental challenges of the journey may be more troublesome than the physical ones.

Pohl, Frederik, editor. **The Expert Dreamers** (© 1961). Avon n.d.

Sixteen stories of science fiction by scientists such as Isaac Asimov, Arthur C. Clarke, and Fred Hoyle. (See also Carol and Frederik Pohl, editors, *Science Fiction: The Great Years,* Ace Bks.)

Pohl, Frederik. **The Gold at the Starbow's End.** Ballantine 1972.

Science fiction short stories, including one about space travelers who search for a planet which does not exist and then create their own planet. Mature.

Pohl, Frederik, and C. M. Kornbluth. **The Space Merchants.** Ballantine 1974.

Mitchell Courtenay has been assigned the task of selling people on emigrating to Venus. He encounters all kinds of problems, even though advertising has taken over the world.

Serling, Rod. **Night Gallery 2.** Bantam 1972.

These stories from the television series contain a mix of science fiction and horror in many forms.

Silverberg, Robert, editor. **Chains of the Sea** (© 1973). Dell 1974.

Three short science fiction novels, each dealing with a different theme, including one which explores the deaths of all members of certain animal species.

Silverberg, Robert, editor. **Deep Space** (© 1968). Dell 1974.

Eight stories of ventures into uncharted deep space.

Silverberg, Robert. **Dying Inside** (© 1972). Ballantine 1973.

All his life, David Selig has known what others think and feel. At first fascinated, he wants finally to control his "gift." Then he finds his power disappearing. (See also *Hawksbill Station,* Avon; *The World Inside,* Avon; *Downward to the Earth,* Doubleday; and *The Book of Skulls,* Scribner.)

Silverberg, Robert, editor. **The Mirror of Infinity** (© 1967). Canfield Pr 1973.

This anthology represents the critics' choice of science fiction and illustrates the evolution of the field. Each of the thirteen stories is accompanied by a commentary by other science fiction writers and critics. Includes a bibliography of science fiction criticism.

Stapledon, Olaf. **Odd John** (© 1935). Dover 1972.

Half-humorous, half-serious, *Odd John* is the study of a mutated superman who must accept the fact that he is different and decide what he will do with his gifts. (See also *Sirius,* Dover.)

Stewart, George R. **Earth Abides** (© 1949). Fawcett World 1974.

A catastrophe has wiped out almost the entire population of the United States. Ish sets out to build a new life for himself and for the few other persons he finds alive.

Sturgeon, Theodore. **The Synthetic Man** (© 1950). Pyramid Pubns 1974.

"Kiddo" runs away and joins a carnival, never wondering why he remains child-sized even as he grows older. When his benefactor tells him he must run away again, the secret of his origins begins to unfold.

Verne, Jules. **20,000 Leagues under the Sea** (© 1869). Bantam 1964.

Years before the submarine was invented, Verne wrote about life under the sea in this classic of science fiction.

Walker, David. **The Lord's Pink Ocean** (© 1972). DAW Bks 1973.

Two families living in the last fertile valley of North America are involved in a feud. The land around them is gray and the ocean is pink with death and destruction.

Walters, Hugh. **First Contact?** Nelson 1973.

Mysterious radio signals from the planet Uranus lead to a trip through space for two highly trained crews. The real reason behind the radio signals turns out to be even more amazing than any of them had dared to guess.

Warrick, Patricia, and Martin Harry Greenberg, editors. **The New Awareness: Religion through Science Fiction.** Delacorte 1975.

Science fiction short stories and excerpts from science fiction novels are used to explore questions about God.

Weinbaum, Stanley G. **The Best of Stanley G. Weinbaum.** Ballantine 1974.

A collection of stories by Stanley G. Weinbaum, one of the best science fiction writers of his time.

White, James. **The Dream Millennium.** Ballantine 1974.

Since earth is a dying planet, a large group of people have set out to find a new home.

White, Ted. **Trouble on Project Ceres.** Westminster 1971.

The "enemies" of Project Ceres, an experiment in growing food on desert land, could be any of a number of people. Larry McCombs, whose father heads the project, becomes involved, along with two friends, in trying to find the enemy and prevent disaster.

Wilhelm, Kate, editor. **Nebula Award Stories Nine.**
Har-Row 1974.

The winners of the 1973 Nebula Awards, presented
by the Science Fiction Writers of America, are included in this collection of stories along with two
essays about science fiction.

Williams, Jay. **The People of the Ax.** Walck 1974.

Arne has grown up believing that the crom are an
inferior, dangerous people. When an encounter with
one of them leads to his being sent to a mysterious
woman with strange powers, he begins to wonder if
his people may be wrong about the crom.

Yep, Laurence. **Sweetwater.** Har-Row 1973.

Tyree is taught music by Amadeus, the great Argan
songmaster of the planet Harmony. But when Amadeus gives a special gift to Tyree's blind sister, Tyree's
people become frightened.

Yolen, Jane, editor. **Zoo 2000, Twelve Stories of Science
Fiction and Fantasy Beasts.** Seabury 1973.

How will men and animals relate to each other in the
future? These tales of science fiction and fantasy, all
centering on animals, give some imaginative answers
to the question.

Zamyatin, Yevgeny (translator Mirra Ginsberg). **We.**
Bantam 1972.

D-503, living in a world of Reason, discovers he has
a soul. This Russian novel is summed up in the
heroine's comment, "I do not want anyone to want for
me—I want to want for myself." Written in 1920–21,
the book has not yet been published in Russia.

Zelazny, Roger. **Nine Princes in Amber** (© 1970). Avon
1972.

All worlds are a reflection of Amber, and Corwin,
long exiled to the Shadow Earth, must try to return
to Amber before Eric crowns himself king. (See also
The Guns of Avalon, Avon.)

BEYOND BELIEF

Adams, Richard. **Watership Down** (© 1972). Macmillan
1974.

Hazel is the leader of a maverick band of wild rabbits who search for a new home after one of their number prophesies death for those who stay behind. To establish their new warren, they must outwit men and animal predators and battle their own kind. Fiction.

Allen, Sybil, and Roma Tomelty. **Lissamor's Child.** Nelson 1975.

Kate has always both loved and feared her ancestral home, but when she returns to it, she becomes more aware that another girl lives there and that a fearful secret needs to be unravelled. Fiction.

Anderson, Margaret J. **To Nowhere and Back.** Knopf 1975.

A young American girl in England with her family travels through a time-warp into the life and daily problems of a peasant girl 100 years ago. Fiction.

Andreae, Christine. **Seances and Spiritualists.** Lippincott 1974.

A brief history of spiritualism, starting with experiments in hypnosis in the eighteenth century, covering famous mediums like the Fox sisters, Douglas Home, Edgar Cayce, and Arthur Ford, and ending with the author's own experiences with a medium. Nonfiction.

Bartell, Jan Bryant. **Spindrift: Spray from a Psychic Sea.** Hawthorn 1974.

Jan Bartell moves from one place to another, but mysterious happenings occur in every place she lives. This book seems like fiction, but it is a true story of incredible events. Nonfiction.

Beagle, Peter. **The Last Unicorn** (© 1968). Ballantine 1973.

A lovely but lonely unicorn is captured by carnival people, and she travels with them until a magician turns her into a young princess. Although the plot may seem to be a fairy tale, this novel is not a child's book. Fiction.

Benedict, Stewart H., editor. **Tales of Terror and Suspense.** Dell 1963.

Such master mystery writers as Edgar Allan Poe and Sir Arthur Conan Doyle lead the willing reader to the brink of the unknown. Fiction.

Berlitz, Charles. **The Bermuda Triangle.** Doubleday 1974.

A mysterious "force field," UFO activity, magnetic pull from the sunken continent of Atlantis, a time-warp—all are possible explanations for the disappearances of ships and planes in the sinister Bermuda Triangle off the Florida coast. Nonfiction.

Blatty, William Peter. **The Exorcist** (© 1971). Bantam 1972.

Two priests struggle to free twelve-year-old Regan from the powerful demon that possesses her. Fiction.

Bleiler, E. F., editor. **Three Gothic Novels.** Dover 1966.

This work contains the unabridged reprints of these Gothic novels: Walpole's *The Castle of Otranto,* Beckford's *Vathek,* and Polidori's *The Vampyre.* Mature fiction.

Borges, Jorge Luis. **Doctor Brodie's Report** (© 1970). Bantam 1973.

"The queen of the Yahoos expresses the royal good by pricking her favorite subjects with pins. . . ." Such events are highlighted in these tales of the occult and bizarre by this Argentine author. Fiction.

Bradbury, Ray. **The Halloween Tree** (© 1972). Bantam 1974.

On Halloween eight boys are escorted through the land of the dead, from ancient times to the present, to discover what Halloween has meant through the ages. Their guide, Mr. Carapace Clavicle Moundshroud, helps them to retrieve their good friend Pipkin from an untimely end. Fiction.

Brown, Rosemary. **Unfinished Symphonies** (© 1971). Bantam 1972.

Brown has had little formal musical training, yet she composes excellent classical music. Her compositions are dictated, she says, by the spirits of such composers as Beethoven and Bach. Nonfiction.

Burford, Lolah. **The Vision of Stephen: An Elegy.** Macmillan 1972.

Stephen, the son of a warrior-king in seventh-century England, is suspected of treason and tortured. His spirit escapes his pain-wracked body and travels through time to Victorian England, where he meets two children who live at the site of his former home. Fiction.

Canning, John, editor. **50 Great Horror Stories.** Bantam 1973.

Stories about graves, ghouls, and goblins weird enough to frighten any reader. Fiction.

Cerf, Bennett, editor. **Famous Ghost Stories** (© 1944). VinRandom 1956.

The editor collects some of the most famous and scary ghost stories in English, among them W. F. Harvey's "August Heat" and W. W. Jacobs's "The Monkey's Paw." Fiction.

Christopher, Milbourne. **Mediums, Mystics, and the Occult.** T Y Crowell 1975.

The author covers many occult mysteries including ESP and the powers of Uri Geller, the Israeli mentalist. Nonfiction.

Clapp, Patricia. **Jane-Emily** (© 1969). Dell 1973.

Louisa, an aunt at eighteen, takes her niece to spend the summer at the Canfield mansion. While there, the spirit of a dead child tries to take possession of the niece and ruin Louisa's romance. Fiction.

Cohen, Daniel. **Curses, Hexes, & Spells.** Lippincott 1974.

A collection of grisly and ghostly tales of curses, beginning with the ancient Greeks and including some shivery ones of recent origin, such as those associated with the Bermuda Triangle. Nonfiction.

Cohen, Daniel. **ESP: The Search beyond the Senses.** HarBraceJ 1973.

Scientific investigation of parapsychology—supranormal occurrences such as telepathy, clairvoyance, and spirit communication—began in the nineteenth century and continues up to the present day, when the predictions and accomplishments of psychics such as Croiset, Peter Hurkos, and Jeanne Dixon are the subject of research by scientists. Nonfiction.

Cohen, Daniel. **The Mysteries of Reincarnation.** Dodd 1975.

Reincarnation, living a series of lives one after the

other, appeals to many people and religions. The author examines those religious beliefs which seem to suggest the reality of reincarnation and concludes with a discussion of the scientific evidence underlying and attacking it. Nonfiction.

Dickinson, Peter. **The Gift** (© 1973). Little 1974.

Davy was born with the gift to see the thoughts of other people in his own mind. Unfortunately, his gift leads him into the planning of a bank robbery and a confrontation with a man he knows only as "Wolf." Fiction.

Dinsdale, Tim. **Monster Hunt.** Acropolis 1972.

The author gave up his job to become photographic director of the Loch Ness Investigation Bureau. The Loch Ness monster, a beast reputedly living in a Scottish lake, and its legends are investigated along with alleged monsters in other countries. Nonfiction.

Ebon, Martin, editor. **Reincarnation in the Twentieth Century** (© 1960). NAL 1970.

Fifteen true stories of people who claim to remember living other lives. Nonfiction.

Ehrlich, Max. **The Reincarnation of Peter Proud.** Bobbs 1974.

Peter Proud is a handsome, young college professor with everything going for him. He only has one problem: he keeps having weird dreams. Then Peter finds that the dreams are really manifestations of a previous life. Mature fiction.

Florescu, Radu, and Raymond T. McNally. **Dracula: A Biography of Vlad the Impaler, 1431–1476.** Hawthorn 1973.

Dracula, born Vlad Tepes in 1431, was a Rumanian prince whose cruelties have become legendary. In his short lifetime, Dracula allegedly killed between 40,000 and 100,000 people by driving a stake through his victims. Nonfiction.

Ford, Arthur. **Unknown but Known** (© 1968). NAL 1969.

One of the world's most famous mediums, Arthur Ford, discusses his unique talent, describes some of the more famous readings he has given, and gives some theories about the nature of psychic phenomena. (See also *Nothing So Strange,* Paperback Lib.) Nonfiction.

Geller, Uri. **Uri Geller: My Story.** Praeger 1975.

The Israeli psychic-performer-clairvoyant learned about his mental powers when he was very young. His performances and mental tricks are currently being investigated by scientists. Nonfiction.

Goodavage, Joseph F. **Write Your Own Horoscope** (© 1968). NAL 1971.

A do-it-yourself guide to self-knowledge through astrology, with charts showing the positions of the planets during the last century and sections describing their influence. Nonfiction.

Gregor, Arthur S. **Witchcraft and Magic: The Supernatural World of Primitive Man.** Scribner 1972.

Do witches really exist? Can magic do what it says it can? Can black magic kill? Answers are based on long traditions of witchcraft and magic in primitive and advanced societies. Nonfiction.

Harris, Marilyn. **The Conjurers.** Random 1974.

In an isolated English town, a woman whose husband disappeared years before opens her house to some strange young people. One of them begins a series of frightening mental experiments, and sinister events finally lead to a series of murders. Fiction.

Heaps, Willard A. **Superstition!** Nelson 1972.

Superstition! is a resource book about the origins, persistence, and bases for superstitions in all areas of life. The book includes a bibliography for further reading. Nonfiction.

Holt, Victoria. **The Curse of the Kings** (© 1973). Fawcett World 1974.

Judith Osmond knows that two archaeologists have died, supposedly because of the curse of Egyptian kings. She is not personally touched until a young archaeologist who will carry on the investigations into the kings' tombs asks her to marry him. Fiction.

Horwitz, Elinor Lander. **The Soothsayer's Handbook— A Guide to Bad Signs & Good Vibrations.** Lippincott 1972.

Readers interested in ESP, astrology, palmistry, numerology, and the like will find this informal exploration of psychic feats informative. Nonfiction.

Jackson, Shirley. **We Have Always Lived in the Castle.**
Viking Pr 1962.

Two sisters and their senile uncle live in comfortable isolation, avoided by the townspeople who think one of the sisters poisoned four other members of the family. The arrival of "cousin" Charles and a fire contribute to the tension before the murderer is identified. Fiction.

Kahn, Joan, editor. **Some Things Dark and Dangerous.**
Har-Row 1970.

This volume contains sixteen suspense stories that will keep readers delightfully scared and entertained. Fiction.

Key, Alexander. **Escape to Witch Mountain** (© 1968).
PB 1973.

Two orphan children from another planet try to find their way back to their own people. Tony and Tia are pursued by a villain who wants to capture them and use their extraordinary powers for evil. Fiction.

Konvitz, Jeffrey. **The Sentinel.** S&S 1974.

After her father's death, Allison Parker wants only the peace and quiet she seems to have found in an old brownstone apartment. Then the headaches begin and her neighbors look less and less normal and more and more frightening. Fiction.

Kusche, Lawrence D. **The Bermuda Triangle Mystery—Solved.** Har-Row 1975.

The Bermuda Triangle area of the Caribbean Sea has been the subject of much mystery and investigation since ships and airplanes have been lost in it. The author analyzes the evidence and comes up with his own original theory. Nonfiction.

Lawrence, Louise. **The Wyndcliffe.** Har-Row 1975.

When Ruth and Anna Hennessy move to an old cottage near Wyndcliffe, England, Ruth starts a busy social life, but Anna is lonely until she meets the spirit of John Hollis who lived in Wyndcliffe 150 years ago. Fiction.

Le Guin, Ursula K. **The Farthest Shore.** Atheneum 1972.

Young Arren and Ged, Earthsea's chief enchanter, travel beyond the world's end to the land of the dead to stop the disappearance of magic from Earthsea. Fiction.

Manley, Seon, and Gogo Lewis, editors. **Bewitched Beings: Phantoms, Familiars and the Possessed in Stories from Two Centuries.** Lothrop 1974.

These eleven stories about the supernatural include ones about a boy who turns his teacher into a rabbit and a young man who is afraid of mirrors. Fiction.

Manley, Seon, and Gogo Lewis, editors. **Ladies of Horror: Two Centuries of Supernatural Stories by the Gentle Sex.** Lothrop 1971.

Fourteen authors, from Mary Shelley to Shirley Jackson, tell stories about ghosts and goblins and things that go bump in the night. Fiction.

Marasco, Robert. **Burnt Offerings.** Delacorte 1973.

"Unique Summer Home, restful, secluded. Perfect for large family." Marian and David Rolfe look into this summer retreat and find unbelievable evil and horror. Mature fiction.

Mayne, William, editor. **Ghosts.** Nelson 1971.

Ghosts is a collection of tales by famous authors from all over the world. Some are "true" and others are purely fiction. Fiction.

Montgomery, Ruth. **A Search for the Truth** (© 1967). Bantam 1969.

The author relates true stories of psychic experiences, including her own communications with spirits through automatic writing. (See also *Here and Hereafter,* Fawcett World; *A Gift of Prophecy,* Bantam; and *A World Beyond,* Coward.) Nonfiction.

Moss, Thelma. **The Probability of the Impossible: Scientific Discoveries and Explorations in the Psychic World.** J P Tarcher 1974.

A parapsychologist who works in a laboratory at the University of California, Los Angeles, reports on research in Kirlian photography, telepathy, and the reaches of the mind. Nonfiction.

Pike, James A. (with Diane Kennedy). **The Other Side: An Account of My Experiences with Psychic Phenomena** (© 1968). Dell 1969.

After Bishop Pike's son Jim committed suicide, strange things began to happen in his father's house. As a result of this "haunting" and a televised sitting with medium Arthur Ford, the bishop came to believe that Jim's soul was alive and existed in another dimension. Nonfiction.

Roberts, Jane. **Seth Speaks: The Eternal Validity of the Soul** (© 1972). Bantam 1974.

The spirit of Seth speaks through the body of the author on such subjects as reincarnation, life after death, the nature of the soul and of reality. Mature nonfiction.

Roueché, Berton. **Feral.** Har-Row 1974.

Amy and Jack Bishop move to Long Island, New York, so Jack will be able to write and edit. The peace and quiet they seek turns into a nightmare when a few stray cats near their farm multiply and start attacking humans. Fiction.

Sefton, Catherine. **The Haunting of Ellen.** Har-Row 1975.

Ellen discovers that the ghost of a young woman who died tragically many years before is inhabiting her body in order to uncover an old mystery. Fiction.

St. Clair, David. **The Psychic World of California** (© 1972). Bantam 1973.

Interviews with Californians interested in and involved with the occult, voodoo, Tarot, witches and warlocks, mediums, UFOs, astrology and Satanism. Nonfiction.

Seton, Anya. **Green Darkness** (© 1972). Fawcett World 1974.

The lives of newlyweds Richard and Celia are threatened by memories of a tragic love affair in another lifetime when he was a priest and she was his mistress in sixteenth-century England. Fiction.

Shelley, Mary. **Frankenstein (or, the Modern Prometheus)** (© 1818). Dell 1965.

Victor Frankenstein, student of science and venturer into the unknown, successfully creates life in the form of a monster. Mistreated and misunderstood by society, the monster gains a measure of revenge. Fiction.

Sherburne, Zoa. **Why Have the Birds Stopped Singing?** Morrow 1974.

On a school bus trip, epileptic Katie visits an antique shop and sees a portrait of a woman long dead who looks exactly like Katie. Frightened and yet fascinated, she has a seizure and crosses the boundary of time into the past. (See also *The Girl Who Knew Tomorrow,* Morrow.)   Fiction.

Skurzynski, Gloria. **The Poltergeist of Jason Morey.** Dodd 1975.

After young Jason Morey has been present in the Kessler home for a time, the Kesslers find that a poltergeist, a noisy and mischievous ghost, has also taken up residence with them. The family then tries to rid themselves of their unwanted visitor. Fiction.

Sleator, William. **House of Stairs.** Dutton 1974.

Five sixteen-year-old orphans are taken daily to the "house of stairs" where they are guinea pigs in a psychological experiment. Although they do not know it, they are being prepared for a future society where they will be robots for a master class. Fiction.

Stearn, Jess. **Edgar Cayce: The Sleeping Prophet** (© 1967). Bantam 1969.

The story of the mystic Edgar Cayce, who could diagnose other people's physical and mental ailments in his sleep. (See also *Yoga, Youth, and Reincarnation,* Bantam; *The Miracle Workers,* Bantam; and *The Search for a Soul: Taylor Caldwell's Psychic Lives,* Fawcett World.)   Nonfiction.

Steele, Mary Q. **Journey Outside.** Viking Pr 1969.

Floating down an underground river on a raft with his grandfather, Dilar jumps onto a rock and from there into a completely new, frightening, and beautiful world. Fiction.

Stevenson, Robert Louis. **Dr. Jekyll and Mr. Hyde** (© 1886). Bantam n.d.

Dr. Jekyll is respected and admired, but his experiments lead to discovering a formula which drastically changes his appearance and personality. Fiction.

Stoker, Bram. **Dracula** (© 1897). Dell n.d.

The famous horror story set in the forests of Transylvania about the century-old vampire Dracula and his lust and need for human blood. Fiction.

Stolz, Mary. **Cat in the Mirror.** Har-Row 1975.

Erin lives in New York City today, and Irun lives in ancient Egypt, but both girls have much in common. Erin is fascinated by the past, Irun thinks constantly of the future, and a cat named Ta-she is prominent in both their lives. Fiction.

Tolkien, J. R. R. **The Lord of the Rings** (© 1965). Ballantine 1974.

In this trilogy *(The Fellowship of the Ring, The Two Towers,* and *The Return of the King)* the mythical world of Middle Earth is inhabited by many fantastic creatures, including the peaceful and fun-loving Hobbits. Frodo, a Hobbit and the hero of the cycle, is entrusted with a magic ring which he must protect on his long, eventful journey to Mount Doom, the center of all evil in Middle Earth. Mature fiction.

Valiente, Doreen. **An ABC of Witchcraft Past and Present** (© 1973). St Martin 1974.

An encyclopedia of people, places, and things associated with the history and practice of witchcraft. Nonfiction.

Von Daniken, Erich. **Chariots of the Gods?** (© 1969). Bantam 1971.

Prehistoric visits to earth by beings from other planets are one man's explanation for some of the archaeological mysteries of our world. Nonfiction.

Wharton, Edith. **The Ghost Stories of Edith Wharton.** Scribner 1973.

These stories have creepy settings: bleak corners of New England, haunted houses in old England, the misty coast of the English Channel, American country mansions with long passageways leading to distant servants' quarters. Mature fiction.

Wilde, Oscar. **The Picture of Dorian Gray** (© 1891). NAL 1962.

When his portrait is completed, Dorian Gray regrets

that the portrait will forever remain youthful while he ages. He says that he would sell his soul to keep his youth. Before long, friends begin to notice changes in the picture. Fiction.

Wilson, Colin. **The Occult** (© 1971). VinRandom 1973.
A comprehensive history of magic, mysticism, and manifestations of latent psychic abilities that everyone possesses but which few develop. Includes a section on spiritualism and reincarnation. Mature nonfiction.

Windsor, Patricia. **Home Is Where Your Feet Are Standing.** Har-Row 1975.
American Sara Watt and her three children live in Rosegrove Cottage in England, along with several poltergeists, amid many erratic and unexplainable happenings. (See also *Something's Waiting for You, Baker D.*, Har-Row.) Fiction.

Wyndham, John. **The Midwich Cuckoos** (© 1959). Ballantine 1972.
After the village of Midwich is mysteriously sedated for a short time, all of the women in the village become pregnant. The babies who are born become the focal point of concern among high government officials. Fiction.

Zindel, Paul. **Let Me Hear You Whisper: A Play** (© 1970). Har-Row 1974.
Scientists try to teach a dolphin to speak. The dolphin, however, knows they are up to no good and will talk only to the kindly old cleaning lady. Fiction.

LOVE

Agee, James. **A Death in the Family** (© 1957). Bantam 1971.
In this novel about love's power to hold a family together in the face of tragedy, a man dies in an auto accident, leaving behind his wife and his family. Mature fiction.

Asinof, Eliot. **Craig and Joan: Two Lives for Peace.** Dell 1971.
On October 15, 1969, two seventeen year olds killed

themselves so that people would begin to think about
love and peace. Asinof, a magazine writer, was assigned to interview families and friends about why
Joan and Craig, both popular and bright, would commit suicide. Nonfiction.

Austen, Jane. **Sanditon.** HM 1975.

When author Jane Austen died in 1817, she left an
unfinished fragment of a novel, *Sandition,* behind.
"Another Lady," using Austen's style and tone, completed the story of Charlotte Heywood who is invited
to stay at a seaside resort where she meets fortune
hunters and finds love. Fiction.

Avery, Curtis E., and Theodore B. Johannis, Jr. **Love
and Marriage: A Guide for Young People.** HarBraceJ
1971.

Focuses on questions dealing with finances, use of leisure time, sex and family planning, and relationships
with inlaws and friends. Relevant to young people
whether marriage is an immediate reality or a distant
possibility. Nonfiction.

Baldwin, James. **If Beale Street Could Talk.** Dial 1974.

In frank street talk, Tish tells her love story. She is
nineteen, black, pregnant by and in love with Fonny,
a sculptor who planned to marry her before he was
put in jail on a false charge. Mature fiction.

Banks, Lynne Reid. **The L-shaped Room** (© 1961). PB
1972.

An unwed pregnant girl goes to a roominghouse to
await the birth of her baby. Her few months there
change her life and the lives of the other boarders.
Fiction.

Bergman, Ingmar. **Scenes from a Marriage.** Bantam
1974.

Johann and Marianne, a quiet, conventional married
couple, believe their marriage is nearly perfect.
Slowly, Marianne recognizes that something is wrong,
and then Johann reveals he is in love with someone
else. Much later they meet again. Mature fiction.

Blume, Judy. **Forever . . . .** Bradbury Pr 1975.

Katherine and Michael both believe that their love

and passion will last forever, and the excitement of
first love and first sex seems overwhelming, but. . . .
Some language and situations will offend some readers. Fiction.

Bronte, Emily. **Wuthering Heights** (© 1847). Dell 1966.
Heathcliff, an orphan, falls in love with Catherine
Earnshaw. Although class differences prevent their
marriage, their love continues long after her death.
Fiction.

Chute, Marchette. **The Innocent Wayfaring** (© 1943).
Dutton 1955.
A historical romance set in fourteenth-century England. Anne Richmond, a rebellious sixteen year old,
refuses to stay at her aunt's convent to learn womanly
skills and instead runs away to London with the hope
of becoming an entertainer. Fiction.

Davis, Gwen. **Kingdom Come.** Putnam 1973.
A young couple, much in love, are killed in a motor-
cycle accident and struggle to be reunited in heaven.
A novel about people and religion and love. Fiction.

Dwyer-Joyce, Alice. **The Rainbow Glass.** St Martin
1973.
After the sudden death of her husband, Lalage goes
to Coolna-Grena, a lovely but decaying house on the
Irish coast. She rebuilds the house and her life with
the help of the handsome and mysterious Gregory.
Fiction.

Fitzgerald, F. Scott. **The Great Gatsby** (© 1925). Bantam 1974.
Nick, a young Midwesterner, lives in a cottage near
Jay Gatsby's fabulous East Coast estate. He learns
that the great Gatsby is the self-created myth of a
young man from the wrong side of the tracks who
happened to fall in love with socialite Daisy. Fiction.

Flaubert, Gustave (translator Lowell Bair). **Madame
Bovary** (© 1856). Bantam 1959.
The love story of Emma Bovary, married to a dull
but faithful husband whom she leaves in search of
her great love and finds nothing but tragedy. Mature
fiction.

Gardam, Jane.. **A Long Way from Verona** (© 1971).
Macmillan 1972.

Thirteen-year-old Jessica Vye wants to be a writer.
This ambition causes conflicts with her straight teachers, giggly schoolmates, and socially conscious mother,
but it also leads her to romance. Fiction.

Greene, Graham. **The Heart of the Matter** (© 1948).
Viking Pr 1974.

Scobie, an assistant police commissioner in West Africa and a devout Roman Catholic, is torn between
his love for his wife and his passion for a young girl.
Mature fiction.

Hamilton, Virginia. **M. C. Higgins the Great.** Macmillan 1974.

M. C. Higgins daydreams on a forty-foot flagpole
towering over his home on Sarah's Mountain. His
encounter with a young wanderer helps him to realize
that fleeing the hills is not the answer for him. Fiction.

Harris, Rosemary. **The Seal Singing.** Macmillan 1971.

The summer that three cousins—Cat, Toby, and
Miranda—spend in their ancestral home, a castle on
a Scottish island, not only opens the door on the past
but foreshadows problems for Cat. Fiction.

Hartley, L. P. **The Go-Between** (© 1953). Avon 1968.

During one summer, a beautiful and wealthy lady becomes the lover of a farmer. A very young boy who
becomes their go-between is more changed by the experience than the two lovers. Fiction.

Hudson, W. H. **Green Mansions** (© 1904). Bantam
1965.

Living in the South American jungle, Abel finds that
Indians will not go near one area they think is
haunted. The ghost turns out to be a mysterious girl
named Rimi with whom Abel falls in love. Fiction.

Huffaker, Clair. **One Time, I Saw Morning Come Home.**
S&S 1974.

The author writes about a Utah mining town, unem-
ployment in the 1920s and 1930s, his mother and
father, and a deep love they felt for each other despite adversity. Nonfiction.

Kawabata, Yasunari. **Thousand Cranes** (© 1958). Berkley Pub 1965.

Kikuji's father may be dead, but the father's love life and his women haunt his son who seeks out elements of his father's past to appease his own feelings of guilt. (See also *The Sound of the Mountain,* Berkley Pub.) Fiction.

Knowles, John. **Spreading Fires.** Random 1974.

Neville, the mad cook who comes with the house Brenan Lucas rents for a summer in the south of France, disrupts the love among Brenan, his mother, sister, and a friend who is also the sister's fiance. Mature fiction.

Lurie, Alison. **The War between the Tates.** Random 1974.

The Tates declare war in a four-way conflict involving Brian, Erica, and their adolescent son and daughter, with some minor battles with the environment, academia, friends, and the counter culture. Mature fiction.

May, Rollo. **Love and Will** (© 1969). Dell 1974.

Psychotherapist Rollo May has treated many patients who are guilt-ridden or deeply disturbed by the sexual and moral revolution. In this frank book, May shows how sex and love are interrelated and not separable. Mature nonfiction.

McKay, Robert. **Dave's Song** (© 1969). Bantam 1970.

Kate Adams, pursued by the town's most eligible fellow, is strangely attracted to Dave Burdick, a ruggedly individualistic classmate who is more interested in raising chickens than in belonging to the "in" crowd. Fiction.

Miller, Albert G. **Mark Twain in Love.** HarBraceJ 1973.

Mark Twain fell in love with Livy Langdon when he first saw her in a small photograph. His campaign to win her over the objections of her family is covered in this somewhat fictionalized account of a true story. Fiction.

Nichols, John. **The Sterile Cuckoo** (© 1965). Avon 1972.

On his way to his freshman year in college, Jerry Payne meets Pookie Adams. Their love affair runs into problems because of Pookie's personality. Fiction.

Paterson, Katherine. **Of Nightingales that Weep.** T Y
Crowell 1974.

A beautiful young Japanese girl finds love and adventure with a young samurai warrior during a civil
war in feudal Japan. Fiction.

Renvoize, Jean. **A Wild Thing** (© 1971). Bantam 1972.

Feared by townspeople, Morag is a wild child of the
woods who wants only love and companionship. An
airplane crash provides Morag with a temporary companion, a kind of love, and some reason for living.
Fiction.

Robinson, Jill. **Bed/Time/Story.** Random 1974.

Born of Hollywood film parents, the author was the
divorced mother of two and a speed addict when she
fell in love with a gentle, brilliant mathematician. In
frank language she relates how their mutual love
brought them from the depths of an emotional hell
into a genuine and abiding relationship. Mature nonfiction.

Roth, Philip. **Goodbye Columbus** (© 1959). Bantam
1970.

The love story of Neil Klugman, librarian, and Brenda
Patimkin, beautiful daughter of a nouveau-riche
plumber, that satirizes the romance and the contrast
between the two lifestyles. Fiction.

Rowe, Terry. **To You with Love** (© 1971). NAL 1975.

Brief poems about nature and the many faces of love.

Rushing, Jane Gilmore. **Mary Dove.** Doubleday 1974.

After she shoots him and then nurses him back to
health, Mary Dove, orphaned daughter of a sheep
farmer, and Red, a cowboy, fall in love. Then Red
comes to realize that the innocent Mary Dove is
different. Fiction.

Sarton, May. **Mrs. Stevens Hears the Mermaids Singing.** Knopf 1975.

Mrs. Stevens attempts to help Mar, a poetically talented college dropout, deal with a powerful homosexual experience involving one of his professors; this
action brings her to consider her own situation: what

does it mean to be a woman and a writer? Mature fiction.

Stanford, Gene, and Barbara Stanford, editors. **Love Has Many Faces.** WSP 1973.

Short stories, poems, essays, and interviews with teenagers which explore romance, differences in male and female views of love, cultural views of love, and qualities of mature and lasting love.

Stolz, Mary. **A Love, or a Season.** Har-Row 1964.

Nan and Harry have been friends since childhood, but in her sixteenth summer, Nan discovers that their relationship is changing toward a physical love she both wants and fears. Fiction.

Thackeray, William Makepiece. **Vanity Fair** (© 1847). Penguin 1969.

Becky Sharp and Amelia Sedley become friends at Miss Pinkerton's school for girls. Apparently doomed to rise no higher in life than a governess, Becky's beauty, cleverness, and heartlessness cause her fortunes to improve. Fiction.

Tolstoy, Leo (translator Rosemary Edmonds). **Anna Karenina.** Penguin 1960.

Although she loves her young son, Anna finds her husband cold and distant. She falls in love with Count Vronsky, and they run off together despite the condemnation of society. First published in 1875. Mature fiction.

Tyler, Ann. **The Clock Winder.** Knopf 1972.

At twenty, easygoing Elizabeth Abbott is the kind of girl who takes a job as a handyman, finds rides from the nearest bulletin board, and says "I don't" when she gets to the altar. Fiction.

Wakefield, Dan. **Starting Over.** Dell 1974.

Told with compassionate humor, this is the story of Phil Potter, recently divorced and starting over. First as lovers and finally as friends, Phil and Marilyn, also recently divorced, help each other through frustrations, temptations, promiscuous sex, alcohol, women's lib, and group therapy. Mature fiction.

Walsh, Jill Paton. **Goldengrove** (© 1972). Avon 1973.

Separated most of the time by the hatred of their parents, Madge and Paul spend summers at their grandmother's seaside home and learn something about themselves. (See also *Fireweed*, Avon.) Fiction.

Westheimer, David. **My Sweet Charlie** (© 1965). NAL n.d.

A black intellectual man and a not too bright Southern girl are both fugitives. Forced to share shelter and food, their relationship gradually changes from hate to fear to love. Fiction.

Willis, Jack, and Mary Willis. **". . . But There Are Always Miracles."** Viking Pr 1974.

Paralyzed from the waist down in a surfing accident, Jack Willis struggles through months of treatment and therapy. His fiancee struggles just as hard. Nonfiction.

COMING OF AGE

Bach, Alice. **Mollie Make-Believe.** Har-Row 1974.

Mollie's strict and conventional family has always controlled her and what she thinks she wants. Her grandmother's illness and an accidental meeting with a boy make her question her too easy acceptance of other people's values. (See also *They'll Never Make a Movie Starring Me,* Dell.) Fiction.

Barnouw, Victor. **Dream of the Blue Heron.** Delacorte 1966.

Wabus is raised by his Chippewa grandparents in the old ways of the tribe and then is suddenly thrust into a white school by his father who lives and works in the modern white world. Fiction.

Benchley, Nathaniel. **Only Earth and Sky Last Forever** (© 1972). Schol Bk Serv 1973.

Dark Elk, an inexperienced brave, seeks desperately to prove himself in battle against the white soldiers in order to gain the hand of the beautiful Lashuka. His efforts eventually take him with Crazy Horse to the Little Big Horn. Fiction.

Blume, Judy. **Then Again, Maybe I Won't** (© 1971). Dell 1973.

When Tony Miglione's father suddenly becomes prosperous, he finds affluence can create problems. They move to a swank suburban neighborhood where Tony finds the preteen years difficult to adjust to. Fiction.

Bonham, Frank. **Durango Street** (© 1965). Dell 1972.

Rufus Henry, on probation for auto theft, struggles to escape from the violent world of street gangs. Fiction.

Borland, Hal. **When the Legends Die** (© 1963). Bantam 1972.

Young Thomas Black Bull knows the songs and ways of his Ute ancestors. Following his parents' deaths, he is dragged into the white people's world where he gains fame as a rodeo star. Fiction.

Borland, Kathryn, and Helen Speicher. **Goodbye to Stony Crick.** McGraw 1975.

Young Jeremy hates to leave Stony Crick in the Appalachians, but he hates even more his family's move to Chicago. The big city proves even more ominous than he had feared. Fiction.

Bradbury, Ray. **Dandelion Wine** (© 1957). Bantam 1969.

The summer of 1928 was the last summer Doug was a kid. Miracles then were everyday occurrences to this extraordinary boy who wants to squeeze every last drop out of summer. Fiction.

Bradford, Richard. **Red Sky at Morning** (© 1968). PB 1971.

A southern boy, Josh Arnold, is sent with his mother to a little New Mexico town to wait out World War II. Coping with the Mexican-American language and customs, Josh learns about another culture and about himself. Mature fiction.

Campbell, Hope. **No More Trains to Tottenville** (© 1971). Dell 1972.

Jane's mother runs off to India, her father takes off again, and Jane goes off to Tottenville to find herself. (See also *Meanwhile, Back at the Castle,* Dell; and *Why Not Join the Giraffes?,* Dell.) Fiction.

Carlson, Dale. **Baby Needs Shoes.** Atheneum 1974.

Little Janet Walsh earns a living for her ding-a-ling sister by calling the numbers in Fat Charlie's floating crap game, while evading the neighbors, her social worker, and the law. Fiction.

Cleaver, Vera, and Bill Cleaver. **The Mimosa Tree.** Lippincott 1970.

Crop failure strikes a North Carolina family, and they set off for Chicago, the city of promise. (See also *Grover,* Lippincott.) Fiction.

Clements, Bruce. **The Face of Abraham Candle.** FS&G 1969.

Fatherless Abraham Candle leaves his Colorado home to seek Indian artifacts at the Mesa Verde ruins. While he is digging for his fortune, he remembers the parables his father had once told him. (See also *I Tell a Lie Every So Often,* FS&G.) Fiction.

Colman, Hila. **Friends and Strangers on Location.** Morrow 1974.

An eighteen-year-old girl sees the realities of the movie world when she becomes a script supervisor for a film being shot in Mexico. Fiction.

Corcoran, Barbara. **The Lifestyle of Robie Tuckerman.** Nelson 1971.

When Robie's father, a Hollywood writer, decides to take the family off to Mexico to find himself, she decides to go along. Fiction.

Craig, John. **Zach.** Coward 1972.

Young Zach Kenebec, the last living member of the Agawa tribe, sets out on a cross-country odyssey to find some clues to his tribal identity. Fiction.

Crane, Stephen. **The Red Badge of Courage** (© 1895). Bantam 1964.

This realistic story of a young soldier during the Civil War is a powerful account of the horror of war and how it changes a boy into a man. Mature fiction.

Crawford, Charles P. **Bad Fall** (© 1972). Bantam 1973.

The influence of an ill-chosen friend introduces conflict and tragedy into the life of a ninth grade boy. This book contains language which may be objectionable to some. Fiction.

Crawford, Charles P. **Three-legged Race.** Har-Row 1974.

Brent falls through a trap door in the barn and breaks his back. His stay in the hospital is made tolerable through his friendship with his roommate, Kirk, and a girl named Amy. Fiction.

Daly, Maureen. **Seventeenth Summer** (© 1942). PB n.d.

Angie Morrow at seventeen finds herself propelled into the "in" group, largely because of her dates with Jack Duluth, basketball star. Fiction.

Donovan, John. **I'll Get There. It Better Be Worth the Trip** (© 1969). Dell n.d.

Davy moves to New York City to live with his mother and is lonely until he makes friends with a bright but moody classmate. Fiction.

Donovan, John. **Wild in the World** (© 1971). Avon 1974.

A large farm family dies one by one leaving only John to run the farm on a desolate, rattlesnake-ridden mountain. Then a stray animal becomes an important part of John's life. Fiction.

Engebrecht, P. A. **Under the Haystack** (© 1973). Dell 1975.

Three girls, abandoned by their mother, attempt to keep neighbors from finding out about their situation. Fiction.

Erno, Richard. **Billy Lightfoot.** Crown 1969.

When Billy leaves his reservation and comes to an Indian school in Phoenix, he has trouble adjusting to his new classmates. Fiction.

Fair, Ronald L. **Hog Butcher** (© 1966). Bantam 1973.

A ten-year-old black boy sees policemen kill a young black basketball star. The policemen claim the victim was involved in a robbery, and the community brings pressure on the boy to go along with the policemen's story. Fiction.

Fitzhugh, Louise. **Nobody's Family Is Going to Change.** FS&G 1974.

The black Sheridan family has two problems: a fat, eleven-year-old daughter who wants to be a lawyer and a skinny seven-year-old son who wants to tap-dance his way to stardom. Fiction.

Fox, Paula. **The Slave Dancer** (© 1973). Dell 1975.

Jessie Bollier, thirteen, is kidnapped and taken aboard a slave ship bound for Africa. On the trip back to America he is ordered to play his fife so that the slaves will dance and thus stay in decent physical condition for sale in the United States. For Jessie the voyage home is a bitter experience of oppression, human suffering, and compassion for the victims transformed into hate. The book was awarded the 1974 John Newbery Medal but has been criticized for an inaccurate presentation of the slave trade and an insensitive treatment of black characters. Fiction.

Frank, Anne. **The Diary of a Young Girl** (© 1952). WSP 1972.

In a diary, Anne, a young Dutch Jewish girl, details the events from June 1942 when she and her family hide from the Gestapo until August 1944 when the family is captured. Nonfiction.

Frederikson, Edna. **Three Parts Earth** (© 1972). Popular Lib 1974.

Delphie Doud's growing-up years are spent moving from place to place as her impoverished father tries to make a living for his family. Fiction.

George, Jean Craighead. **Julie of the Wolves.** Har-Row 1972.

Alone and without food among a pack of Arctic wolves, a thirteen-year-old Eskimo girl discovers love as she struggles to survive on the vast tundra. Fiction.

Gordon, Ethel Edison. **Where Does the Summer Go?** (© 1967). PB 1971.

Fifteen-year-old Freddy has looked forward all year to returning with her family to their vacation home so she can renew her summer relationship with long-time friend Dave. But college has changed him. Fiction.

Greenberg, Joanne. **Rites of Passage.** HR&W 1972.
Stories that speak about the experiences of adolescence.
Fiction.

Green, Constance C. **A Girl Called Al.** Viking Pr 1969.
Al (short for Alexandra) and her best friend deal with
the twin problems of divorce and growing up by trying
hard to be nonconformists. Fiction.

Hale, Janet Campbell. **The Owl's Song.** Doubleday 1974.
When Billy White Hawk's mother dies and his best
friend commits suicide, Billy knows he must leave his
Idaho reservation. But his move to San Francisco
only makes things worse. Fiction.

Harker, Herbert. **Goldenrod.** Random 1972.
Jesse Gilford, a broken-down rodeo rider, and his sons
try to face life without the wife and mother who has
deserted them. Mature fiction.

Harris, Marilyn. **The Runaway's Diary** (© 1971). PB
1974.
Sixteen-year-old Cat (short for Catherine Anne) runs
away from a father and mother who fight and ends up
in Canada in a highway accident. Fiction.

Head, Ann. **Mr. & Mrs. BoJo Jones** (© 1967). NAL
1973.
Two young people who "have to get married" find
that the love they shared as high school students isn't
enough to hold a marriage together. Fiction.

Hentoff, Nat. **I'm Really Dragged but Nothing Gets Me
Down** (© 1968). Dell 1969.
Nearing his eighteenth birthday, Jeremy must decide
whether he will protest the Vietnam War and stay
at home or flee to Canada. Fiction.

Hentoff, Nat. **In the Country of Ourselves** (© 1971).
Dell 1972.
A rabble-rousing teacher and several young revolu-
tionary students disrupt an entire high school. Fiction.

Hinton, S. E. **That Was Then, This Is Now** (© 1971).
Dell 1972.
Byron confronts the problems of drugs, alcohol, and
betrayal when he faces losing his best friend. Fiction.

Holland, Isabelle. **Of Life and Death and Other Journeys.** Lippincott 1975.

Peg lives in Italy with her unconventional mother and stepfather. Curious about her real father, Peg keeps questioning her mother only to discover that he is coming to visit and her mother is dying. Mature fiction.

Hull, Eleanor. **The Second Heart.** Atheneum 1973.

This is the story of what happens when four young people meet and change each other because of the Second Heart, the ancient Indian metaphor for courage. Fiction.

Hunt, Irene. **Across Five Aprils.** Follett 1964.

Young Jethro Creighton is left home to work the Illinois farm while the men in his family go off to fight the Civil War. Fiction.

Hunt, Irene. **Up a Road Slowly** (© 1966). Tempo G&D 1968.

Julie Trelling's growing-up years are made difficult by the death of her mother, the marriage of her beloved sister, and the close supervision of her strict Aunt Cordelia. Fiction.

Joyce, James. **Portrait of the Artist as a Young Man** (© 1916). Viking Pr 1968.

Stephen Daedalus, a sensitive and artistic Irish-Catholic growing up in Dublin, rebels against his family, school, and traditional religion. Mature fiction.

Kerr, M. E. **If I Love You, Am I Trapped Forever?** (© 1973). Dell 1974.

Handsome and popular sixteen-year-old Alan Bennett has his entire world toppled when plain and balding Duncan Stein begins a school paper and becomes the most popular boy in the school. Fiction.

Kerr, M. E. **The Son of Someone Famous** (© 1974). Ballantine 1975.

Adam hides from the fame his father gained as a presidential advisor who dates starlets, and Brenda fights her mother's concept of what a woman should be. Fiction.

Knowles, John. **A Separate Peace** (© 1960). Bantam 1969.

Gene, the narrator, both admires and envies Finny, his athletic and handsome friend. One summer during the early years of World War II, Finny is injured diving from a tree into a river near their English boarding school, and Gene has to face himself and his involvement in the accident. Fiction.

Koenig, Laird. **The Little Girl Who Lives Down the Lane.** Coward 1974.

Is Rynn a lonely, innocent young girl trying to build a life for herself in a hostile world—or is she a clever murderer? Fiction.

LaPointe, Frank. **The Sioux Today.** CCPr Macmillan 1972.

High school-age Sioux Indians in twelve short stories about ranching, poverty, sports, a beauty pageant, protest, education, and suicide. All experience the conflict between tribal culture and the ways of the dominant white society. Fiction.

Lee, Mildred. **Fog** (© 1972). Dell 1974.

Luke Sawyer, whose life has been centered on his boyhood gang and their clubhouse in a Southern river town, meets Milo and learns what it is to have a broken heart. Fiction.

Lee, Mildred. **The Rock and the Willow** (© 1963). PB 1970.

Enie longs to escape from Tired Creek, Alabama, and a widowed father she has grown to dislike, but college and a teaching career seem unlikely destinations for her. Fiction.

Llewellyn, Richard. **How Green Was My Valley.** Macmillan 1941.

As he examines his life, Huw Morgan recognizes the coal mines as a dominant force in his Welsh community and in his own youth. Fiction.

Lockett, Sharon. **No Moccasins Today.** Nelson 1970.

Offered a basketball scholarship, Jay hopes that attending college will allow him to leave his home on the Chuala Indian Reservation forever. Fiction.

Lofts, Norah. **The Maude Reed Tale** (© 1971). Dell 1974.

Maude Reed, a fifteenth-century British girl, seems destined for a role as a royal lady, but she wants to be a wool merchant.

Lorenzo, Carol Lee. **Heart-of-Snowbird.** Har-Row 1975.

Laurel is anxious to leave her small mountain town in the South, but her plans change when a young Indian boy moves to her neighborhood. Fiction.

Lyle, Katie Letcher. **I Will Go Barefoot All Summer for You** (© 1973). Dell 1974.

Lonely Jessie lives with a cousin and dreams of becoming important and famous. When Toby comes for a visit, Jessie falls in love and decides to travel by cab to see him. Fiction.

Mann, Peggy. **My Dad Lives in a Downtown Hotel.** Doubleday 1973.

When Joey's parents get a divorce he thinks it must be his fault. He can't see why his dad won't come home if Joey promises to change. Fiction.

McCullers, Carson. **The Member of the Wedding.** HM 1946.

Frankie Addams, twelve years old, is a loner but feels she finally has someone to belong to when her brother returns home from the army. Her feelings are crushed, however, when he marries and doesn't take her on his honeymoon, yet slowly she recovers from her imagined rejection. Mature fiction.

McMurtry, Larry. **The Last Picture Show** (© 1966). Dell 1974.

Three young people, Sonny, Jacy, and Duane, grow up in dusty and desolate Thalia, Texas, where the most exciting event is going to the movies. Some sexually explicit scenes. (See also *Hud,* original title *Horseman, Pass By,* Har-Row.) Fiction.

Momaday, N. Scott. **House Made of Dawn** (© 1968). NAL 1969.

Written by a Kiowa Indian, this Pulitzer Prize novel tells the story of Abel, a World War II veteran who returns to his reservation after the war but finds the old beliefs and traditions are now meaningless to him. After committing a murder and serving out a prison sentence, he takes a job in Los Angeles and becomes involved with an Indian mission. Eventually he returns to the reservation at the moment of his grandfather's death. Mature fiction.

Murphy, Patrick J., and Shirley Rousseau Murphy. **Carlos Charles.** Viking Pr 1971.

Set in Panama City, this story is about a boy paroled to a Spanish boat builder and how he learns to play a role in shaping his own life. Fiction.

Murray, Michele. **The Crystal Nights.** Seabury 1973.

Elly, a high school junior, has always wanted to know her beautiful German cousin, Margot. But she finds that Margot and her mother are not what she expected when they flee Hitler's Germany during World War II and move in with Elly's family. Fiction.

Ney, John. **Ox, the Story of a Kid at the Top** (© 1970). Bantam 1971.

Ox is a fat twelve year old who has spent two years in fourth grade. His wealthy parents are drunks and nobody care much about him. Assigned to write a paper on cows, he takes a week-long trip with his father. Fiction.

O'Dell, Scott. **Island of the Blue Dolphins** (© 1960). Dell 1971.

The story of a young Indian girl left to fend for herself on an island off the California coast for nearly twenty years. Fiction.

Paterson, Katherine. **The Sign of the Chrysanthemum.** T Y Crowell 1973.

A young Japanese boy searching for his father, a samurai warrior, finds himself caught up in the violence of feudal Japan. Fiction.

Peck, Robert Newton. **A Day No Pigs Would Die** (© 1973). Dell 1974.

A thirteen year old narrates the story of his growing up as a farmboy in Vermont in the 1920s. Maturity comes early for young Rob when hard times bring the loss of the creatures he holds dear. (See also *Soup,* Knopf.) Fiction.

Platt, Kin. **The Boy Who Could Make Himself Disappear** (© 1968). Dell 1971.

Roger's mother is too concerned with herself to pay any attention to him, and his father is wrapped up in his career in California. Handicapped by this and his severe speech impediment, Roger withdraws into schizophrenia. Fiction.

Potok, Chaim. **The Chosen.** S&S 1967.

Two Jewish boys grow up in Brooklyn, one Hasidic, one Orthodox. Danny and Reuven are good friends but live in entirely different worlds. Fiction.

Rabe, Bernice. **Naomi.** Nelson 1975.

Naomi is only eleven but she is worried about what she will grow up to be and about her life and the lives of her five brothers and one sister. Fiction.

Raucher, Herman. **Summer of '42.** Dell 1971.

Three young adolescent boys live their last moments of innocence during the early years of World War II. Mature fiction.

Rawlings, Marjorie Kinnan. **The Yearling** (© 1938). Scribner 1962.

Jody Baxter learns that life isn't always good in this classic animal story involving a fawn, dogs, bears, and all the other creatures that inhabit the Florida backwoods. Fiction.

Rawls, Wilson. **Where the Red Fern Grows** (© 1961). Bantam 1974.

Young Billy Coleman is convinced his Old Dan and Little Ann are the finest coon hounds anywhere. They get a chance to prove themselves in a championship hunt. Fiction.

Rhodes, Evan H. **The Prince of Central Park.** Coward 1975.

Eleven-year-old Jay-Jay runs away and becomes a modern Robinson Crusoe with Central Park in New York as his desert island. Fiction.

Richard, Adrienne. **Pistol** (© 1965). Dell 1970.

Billy Catlett loves his summer work as a horse wrangler; for him, it's a perfect life. Then the Depression comes, and Billy faces one problem after another; but in losing his perfect life, he gains maturity. Fiction.

Richler, Mordecai. **The Apprenticeship of Duddy Kravitz.** Little 1959.

Duddy Kravitz, an ambitious Jewish boy from the streets of Montreal, schemes and hustles his way to his heart's desire. His adventures are full of zest and humor, but they could offend some readers. Fiction.

Rikhoff, Jean. **One of the Raymonds.** Dial 1974.

The adventures of Raymond Buttes and his teacher show Raymond growing up in the nineteenth-century world of the Adirondacks. Fiction.

Robbins, Harold. **A Stone for Danny Fisher** (© 1952). PB 1972.

To Danny Fisher, growing up in Flatbush with his depression-scarred and stern father and the frustrations of poverty, the prizefighting ring promises a way out. Mature fiction.

Rockowitz, Murray, editor. **Insight and Outlook.** Globe 1970.

Chosen to help young people gain insight into themselves, the stories concern growing up and outlooks for the future. Fiction.

Roy, Carl. **The Painter of Miracles.** FS&G 1974.

Sixteen-year-old Maclovio finds that, as a result of the 1914 Revolution, he can no longer paint miracles but becomes a man who lives and sees them. Fiction.

Russ, Lavinia. **The April Age.** Atheneum 1975.

In 1925, Peakie is almost eighteen and full of dreams and fantasies about life but especially about men and love. Then on a trip to Europe she meets a handsome British lord. Fiction.

Ryan, Betsy. **The Sexes: Male/Female Roles and Relationships.** Schol Bk Serv 1975.

A collection of cartoons, pictures, poems, ads, and articles about love and about being male or female today.

Salinger, J. D. **The Catcher in the Rye** (© 1951). Bantam 1970.

Holden Caulfield is dismissed from Pencey Prep and, without telling his parents, returns home to New York City. Sometimes haltingly and sometimes humorously, he tells his story of inescapable encounters with hypocrisy and the "phonies" among his classmates and in the adult world. Fiction.

Sugarman, Daniel A., and Rolaine Hochstein. **The Seventeen Guide to You and Other People** (© 1972). WSP 1974.

Aimed at teenage girls, this book explores the development of values in several areas: jobs, marriage, religious beliefs, family relationships, drugs, and sex. Jointly written by a clinical psychologist and a professional writer. Nonfiction.

Swarthout, Glendon, and Kathryn Swarthout. **Whichaway.** Random 1966.

An awkward, self-conscious young man, "Whichaway" is ignored by almost everyone and expected only to keep the windmills running. His enduring three days in great pain trapped on a windmill begins to turn his life around. Fiction.

Townsend, John Rowe. **Goodbye to the Jungle.** Lippincott 1967.

Two English youngsters go to live with their shiftless uncle after the death of their parents. Fiction.

Townsend, John Rowe. **Good Night Prof, Dear.** Lippincott 1971.

Almost seventeen, Graham Hollis is left alone for the first time when his parents go on a week vacation. He takes a part-time restaurant job and meets a waitress who has been around. Fiction.

Van Leeuwen, Jean. **I Was a Ninety-eight Pound Duckling.** Dial 1972.

Thirteen-year-old Kathy (the ninety-eight-pound duckling) begins her slow transformation into a swan in this novel about the awkward age. Fiction.

Walker, Mildred. **Winter Wheat** (© 1944). HarBraceJ 1966.

Ellen blames her parents when her fiance visits their

Montana wheat farm and, finding her family and their life dull and different from his own, breaks their engagement. Fiction.

Webb, Charles. **The Graduate** (© 1963). NAL 1971.

Benjamin Braddock graduates from college and returns to his home town. His parents and his friends are all interested in helping him into business but are not willing to listen to his doubts about himself and his future. An affair and then real love clear up some of his confusion. At times, a very funny book, but some situations may offend some readers. Mature fiction.

Wells, Rosemary. **None of the Above.** Dial 1974.

When Marcia's widowed father marries a perfectionist with kids who are near geniuses, Marcia begins to conform to their high standards and finds that she is losing her own personality. Mature fiction.

West, Jessamyn. **Cress Delahanty.** HarBraceJ 1954.

In this delightful and sensitive novel set on a ranch in California, Cress Delahanty changes from a twelve-year-old girl to a sixteen-year-old woman. Fiction.

Wojciechowska, Maia. **Shadow of a Bull.** Atheneum 1964.

His friends and community expect Manolo Olivar to follow in the footsteps of his father, a great Spanish bullfighter. Confused, frightened, but wanting to prove himself, Manolo learns to recognize his limitations and overcome his fears. Winner of the 1965 John Newbery Medal. Fiction.

Wojciechowska, Maia. **A Single Light** (© 1968). Bantam 1971.

A young deaf girl is drawn into the world of humanity by a baby and a marble statue of the Christ Child. Fiction.

Wood, Phyllis Anderson. **Your Bird Is Here, Tom Thompson.** Westminster 1972.

Tom Thompson just can't seem to put his life together and is given one more chance when an injured seagull becomes mascot at Last Chance High. Fiction.

Woods, George A. **Vibrations** (© 1970). Dell 1971.

A seventeen-year-old boy struggles to deal with the truths about himself—his fear of failure, his con man father, his friends who have died. Fiction.

PROBLEMS AND YOUNG PEOPLE

Aitmatov, Chingiz (translator Mirra Ginsburg). **The White Ship.** Crown 1972.

An unwanted Russian orphan boy tries to survive in a world made up of adults who do not want him. Fiction.

Aldridge, James. **A Sporting Proposition** (© 1973). Dell 1975.

Both a poor thirteen-year-old boy and the crippled daughter of a wealthy rancher claim ownership of a wild Welsh pony, a dispute that eventually involves an entire community. Fiction.

Balducci, Carolyn. **Is There Life After Graduation, Henry Birnbaum?** (© 1971). Dell 1973.

Unusual things happen when David Schoen begins college at M.I.T. and Henry Birnbaum, his closest friend, goes to Oberlin. (See also *Earwax,* HM.) Fiction.

Beckman, Gunnel. **Admission to the Feast.** HR&W 1972.

A sixteen-year-old Swedish girl, learning that she is going to die of leukemia, leaves her mother and fiance and goes off to a summer cottage to write a long searching letter to a friend. Fiction.

Birmingham, John. **Our Time Is Now: Notes from the High School Underground** (© 1970). Bantam n.d.

The author explains the need for underground publications in high schools and describes the development of the one he edited. Some frank language. Nonfiction.

Blume, Judy. **It's Not the End of the World.** Bradbury Pr 1972.

The three Newman children, ranging in age from six to fifteen, all experience repercussions when their mother and father separate and plan a divorce. Fiction.

Braber, Eleanor, and Lou Jacobs, Jr., editors. **Teen-Agers Inside Out.** WSP 1974.

Mini-essays written by teenagers on subjects such as friendship, the drug scene, suicide, and love. Accompanying photographs taken by teenagers. Nonfiction.

Butler, Beverly. **Gift of Gold** (© 1972). PB 1973.

Cathy Wheeler, blind since she was fourteen, is stunned when her college's speech department chairman suggests that she abandon her plans to become a speech therapist. (See also *Light a Single Candle,* PB.) Fiction.

Byars, Betsy. **The Summer of the Swans.** Viking Pr 1970.

It's not until fourteen-year-old Sara's mentally retarded brother, Charlie, is lost that she takes her mind off her own troubles. Fiction.

Cleaver, Bill, and Vera Cleaver. **Where the Lilies Bloom** (© 1969). NAL 1974.

Fourteen-year-old Mary Call keeps her orphaned brothers and sisters together and provides strength and help for them. (See also *The Whys and Wherefores of Littabelle Lee,* Atheneum; *Grover,* Lippincott; *Lady Ellen Grae,* Lippincott; and *I Would Rather Be a Turnip,* Lippincott.) Fiction.

Collier, James Lincoln. **The Hard Life of the Teenager.** Four Winds 1972.

Feelings of anxiety, desire for popularity, the war between parents and their children, sexual changes, sexual feelings and their consequences are teenage problems dealt with frankly here. Nonfiction.

Cormier, Robert. **The Chocolate War** (© 1974). Dell 1975.

Jerry Renault, freshman in a Catholic boys' school, discovers the devastating consequences of refusing to join the school's annual fund raising drive. Frank language and situations. Fiction.

Davies, Peter. **Fly Away Paul.** Crown 1974.

The treatment Paul receives from a sadistic headmaster and his growing friendship with a German boy make him want to run away from a Montreal boys' home. Candid language. Fiction.

Divoky, Diane, editor. **How Old Will You Be in 1984?** (© 1969). Avon 1971.

A collection of articles and editorials and cartoons from recent high school underground newspapers, including recommendations by students for improving one school system. Nonfiction.

Donovan, John. **Remove Protective Coating a Little at a Time** (© 1973). Dell 1975.

Harry, fourteen and a cynic with an unstable home life, meets Amelia, a seventy-two-year-old rebel who cusses like a sailor and begs for a living. Fiction.

Elfman, Blossom. **The Girls of Huntington House** (© 1972). Bantam 1973.

A young English teacher, bored with regular public schools, takes a job teaching in a home for young unwed mothers and learns that understanding the problems of her girls is more important than any subject matter. Fiction.

Ellson, Hal. **Tomboy** (© 1950). Bantam 1969.

Tomboy, a fifteen-year-old deb in the Harps street gang is tougher than most of the guys and plans their cruel capers. Fiction.

Eyerly, Jeannette. **Bonnie Jo, Go Home** (© 1972). Bantam 1973.

Her parents do not want Bonnie Jo to have an abortion, but she gets enough money together to travel to New York City and to a doctor who will operate. (See also *The Phaedra Complex,* Berkley Pub; *The Girl Inside,* Berkley Pub; *Escape from Nowhere,* Berkley Pub; and *A Girl like Me,* Berkley Pub.) Fiction.

Farber, Jerry. **The Student as Nigger** (© 1969). PB 1970.

Biased but perceptive comments about the treatment of young people in schools, grades, and suggestions for changing the system. Some strong language and many ideas that will offend adults. Mature nonfiction.

Fox, Paula. **Blowfish Live in the Sea.** Bradbury Pr 1970.
Twelve-year-old Carrie and her half brother Ben go
to Boston to search for a stranger with a habit of vanishing. Fiction.

Go Ask Alice (1971). Avon 1972.
"Alice" is the pseudonym of a normal, fifteen-year-old
girl from a good home who turned on to drugs and
found they really make the world a better place—for
a while. Realistic language and sometimes shocking
episodes. Mature fiction.

Gold, Robert S., editor. **Point of Departure—Nineteen
Stories of Youth and Discovery** (© 1967). Dell 1969.
William Melvin Kelley, John Updike, and Carson Mc-
Cullers are some of the authors whose works appear in
this collection which focuses upon the frequent anguish
of adolescence. Fiction.

Green, Hannah. **I Never Promised You a Rose Garden**
(© 1964). NAL 1973.
A schizophrenic at sixteen, Deborah Blau is committed to a mental institution where she begins the slow
process of abandoning the self-destructive forces of
her inner world. Fiction.

Guy, Rosa. **The Friends** (© 1973). Bantam 1974.
Phyllisia Cathy, a bright West Indian girl, is rejected
by everyone in her school except Edith when she moves
to Harlem. Fiction.

Haggard, Elizabeth. **Nobody Waved Goodbye.** Bantam
1971.
With just a few weeks to go until graduation, Peter
Marks gets arrested for speeding in a "borrowed" car.
Out on probation, Peter finds those remaining weeks
the rockiest of his life. Fiction.

Hall, Lynn. **Sticks and Stones.** Dell 1972.
Tom Naylor and his mother move to a small Iowa
town after his mother's divorce. Because Tom plays
the piano and is sensitive, people begin to suspect he
is a homosexual. Fiction.

Hamilton, Virginia. **The Planet of Junior Brown.** Macmillan 1971.
Junior Brown, a 300-pound musical prodigy with a

neurotic, overprotective mother, and Buddy Clark, a loner known to dozens of homeless waifs like himself as Tomorrow Billy, spend most of their time in a secret cellar in the school where Mr. Pool, the janitor, has made a model of the solar system. Fiction.

Hinton, S. E. **The Outsiders** (© 1967). Dell 1968.

Ponyboy Curtis, a tough but sensitive member of a street gang, learns the meaning of tragedy as his friends and enemies are hurt or killed in a senseless series of rumbles. Fiction.

Holland, Isabelle. **The Man without a Face** (© 1972). Bantam 1973.

After flunking his entrance exams for prep school, Chuck leaves home and his mean sister to be tutored by a horribly scarred former teacher. Their relationship grows slowly and almost becomes homosexual. (See also *Heads You Win, Tails I Lose,* Lippincott.) Fiction.

Johnson, A. E. **A Blues I Can Whistle.** Schol Bk Serv 1969.

After an unsuccessful try at suicide, Cody is hospitalized and tries to figure out who and what and why he is. Fiction.

Johnson, Eric W. **V.D.** (© 1973). Bantam 1974.

Information about the nature and causes and problems of veneral diseases, particularly syphilis and gonorrhea. Many illustrations and specific help for young people in trouble. Nonfiction.

Kellogg, Marjorie. **Like the Lion's Tooth.** FS&G 1972.

All of the "problem children" in the school have been damaged by warped love. Julie's father figure deserted her; fifteen-year-old Madeline was raped by her father; and Ben hides in the school from a father who abused him. Fiction.

Kerr, M. E. **Dinky Hocker Shoots Smack.** Har-Row 1972.

Dinky has a terrific fat problem. Natalia, her cousin, has to go to a school for the mentally disturbed. But Dinky's mother has no sympathy for them until one night when Dinky gets her attention in a shocking way. Fiction.

Kerr, M. E. **Is That You, Miss Blue?** Har-Row 1975.
After her mother runs off with a younger man, Flanders Brown is sent to an Episcopal boarding school by her father. There, Flanders begins to work out her mixed feelings about herself and her unusual parents. Fiction.

Kingman, Lee. **The Peter Pan Bag** (© 1970). Dell 1971.
When runaway Wendy Allardyce finds herself friendless and broke, she accepts shelter in a crash pad in Boston. There she meets a new way of life and a crowd deep in the drug culture. Fiction.

Kirkwood, James. **Good Times/Bad Times** (© 1968). Fawcett World 1973.
Peter Kilburn's account of how he is involved in the death of the headmaster of a small private school shows a young boy's rude awakening to the harsh realities of the adult world. Fiction.

Klein, Norma. **Mom, the Wolfman and Me** (© 1972). Avon 1974.
Brett doesn't mind having a mother who has never married, wears jeans, and keeps irregular hours. Then the Wolfman comes into their lives. Fiction.

Lee, Mildred. **The Skating Rink** (© 1969). Dell 1970.
Branded as a dummy because he stutters, Tuck Faraday spends most of his spare time watching the construction of a new skating rink. The owner of the rink befriends Tuck and helps him to understand himself and others. (See also *Sycamore Year,* Lothrop.) Fiction.

Mazer, Harry. **The Dollar Man.** Delacorte 1974.
Marcus's fiercely independent mother, Sally, chooses to raise him without assistance from his father, whom she never married. At fourteen Marcus, a Walter Mitty type dreamer, decides to find his father. Fiction.

Mazer, Norma Fox. **A Figure of Speech.** Delacorte 1973.
When grandpa is moved out his basement apartment to make room for her brother and his new bride,

thirteen-year-old Jenny and eighty-three-year-old grandpa attempt to make it on their own. Fiction.

McCord, Jean. **Deep Where the Octopi Lie.** Atheneum 1968.

McCord's short stories are recollections of her own adolescent years. Fiction.

Neufeld, John. **Lisa, Bright and Dark** (© 1969). NAL 1970.

Sixteen-year-old Lisa Shilling knows she is slowly going insane. Her parents will not believe her, though her friends do. Lisa becomes more and more withdrawn and self-destructive before her parents take notice. (See also *Edgar Allan,* NAL; and *Twink,* published in hardback as *Touching,* NAL.) Fiction.

Peck, Richard. **Don't Look and It Won't Hurt** (© 1972). Avon 1973.

The three Patterson sisters live with their mom in Claypitts, Illinois, until seventeen-year-old unwed Ellen has to leave home to have a baby. Then Carol, fifteen, goes to Chicago to try to help her. Fiction.

Peck, Richard. **Representing Super Doll.** Viking Pr 1974.

When Verna's friend Darlene is named Central United States Super Doll in a beauty contest, the girls see firsthand the sexism practiced by many people. Fiction.

Peck, Robert Newton. **Millie's Boy.** Knopf 1973.

Tit Smith, son of the local prostitute, sets off into an 1898 Adirondack wilderness to find his mother's killer and also to find his father. Fiction.

Raab, Robert A. **The Teenager and the New Morality.** Rosen Pr 1970.

The response of teenagers to the new morality. What are the new standards and norms of conduct? Is there such a thing as morality and immorality? These are some of the questions explored. Nonfiction.

Reynolds, Pamela. **Will the Real Monday Please Stand Up.** Lothrop 1975.

Poor Monday! Her brother has been expelled from school for smoking marijuana and at nearly the same time she has her first date with a soccer star five years older than she. Fiction.

Rivera, Geraldo. **A Special Kind of Courage.** S&S 1976.
Rivera, host of a youth-oriented TV talk show, tells the stories of contemporary people, many of them teen-agers, who have faced and withstood severe tests of courage and character. Nonfiction.

Samuels, Gertrude. **Run, Shelley, Run.** T Y Crowell 1974.
Her mother an alcoholic and her father an unknown, Shelley Clark escapes from a center for girls in New York and is put in solitary confinement until a sympathetic judge begins to understand her. Fiction.

Schulman, M. L., editor. **The Loners: Short Stories about the Young and Alienated.** Macmillan 1970.
Ten short stories about lonely young people often frightened by the world around them. Fiction.

Scoppettone, Sandra. **Trying Hard to Hear You.** Har-Row 1974.
Camilla discovers that Phil, the man she loves, and Jeff, her close friend for years, are lovers. Fiction.

Segal, Lore. **Other People's Houses.** HarBraceJ 1964.
The story begins in Vienna in 1937. The narrator, ten years old and Jewish, records honestly her experiences growing up a rootless exile. Fiction.

Sgroi, Suzanne M. **VD: A Doctor's Answers.** HarBraceJ 1974.
Facts about VD, how venereal diseases are spread, what and where treatments are available. Ways to avoid VD are discussed by Dr. Sgroi. Nonfiction.

Sillitoe, Alan. **The Loneliness of the Long Distance Runner** (©1959). NAL 1971.
The title story in this collection is about a reform school boy who is pressured by the authorities to represent his school as a long distance runner. For a time he almost knuckles under to them. Fiction.

Southall, Ivan. **Josh.** Macmillan 1972.
Josh tells his own story about a visit to his eccentric Aunt Clara. Poet and dreamer, Josh finds romance

and agony when he reluctantly enters into the activities of the town's young people. Fiction.

Stolz, Mary. **By the Highway Home.** Har-Row 1971.

Thirteen-year-old Catty is bewildered by the impact of her brother's death in Vietnam on the rest of her family. Then she learns her father has lost his job and an even greater change is coming to the family. (See also *The Edge of Next Year,* Har-Row.) Fiction.

Stolz, Mary. **Leap before You Look** (© 1972). Dell 1973.

Fourteen-year-old Jimmie's attempt to understand her parents' divorce explores the relationships of the whole family—Gram, Grandmother Prior, her little brother Goya, as well as her easygoing father and intellectual but unhappy mother. Fiction.

Summers, James. **Don't Come Back a Stranger.** Westminster 1970.

His college freshman year overwhelms Dan and turns him into a person neither his girlfriend nor his parents know. (See also *Senior Dropout,* Westminster.) Fiction.

Summers, James. **The Iron Doors Between.** Westminster 1968.

Two foster parents sincerely try to help Vic Shan find a place in the world outside of the prison life Vic has known. Fiction.

Swarthout, Glendon. **Bless the Beasts and the Children** (© 1970). PB 1973.

Six misfits at an Arizona summer camp for rich but unwanted boys try to stop the annual buffalo hunt. Fiction.

Taggard, Ernestine, editor. **Twenty Grand Short Stories** (© 1947). Bantam 1969.

Chosen by high school students as their most favorite, the twenty stories represent a cross section of themes which concern young adults. Ring Lardner, Maureen Daly, and John Steinbeck are some of the writers represented. Fiction.

Thompson, Jean. **The House of Tomorrow** (© 1967). NAL 1968.

Jean Thompson is a twenty-year-old college girl who

is pregnant by a married man. Unwilling to involve her parents, Jean moves to a home for unwed mothers and keeps a journal of her feelings and ideas during this difficult time. Fiction.

Thompson, Thomas. **Richie** (© 1973). Bantam 1974.

George Diener is extremely proud of his son Richie, but the changes in his son, often caused by drugs, lead to a confrontation. Fiction.

Thrasher, Crystal. **The Dark Didn't Catch Me.** Atheneum 1975.

Seely, a courageous eleven-year-old, tells her own story about the difficult years during the 1930s when she moves into a new neighborhood and has a falling out with her parents. Fiction.

Wagner, Robin S. **Sarah T.—Portrait of a Teen-Age Alcoholic.** Ballantine 1975.

Sarah, at thirteen, got her first taste of alcohol at her mother's second wedding. The drink marked the beginning of a habit that lasted for two years—when this story begins. Fiction.

Weesner, Theodore. **The Car Thief** (© 1972). Dell 1973.

Alex Housman, sixteen years old, steals automobiles to find respect and manhood and love in the only way he knows possible. Fiction.

Wersba, Barbara. **The Dream Watcher.** Atheneum 1968.

Albert Scully is a misfit. He's failing in school, driving his status-conscious mother crazy and his salesman father to drink. Fiction.

Wersba, Barbara. **Run Softly, Go Fast** (© 1970). Bantam 1972.

Dave Marks and his father have a love-hate relationship. The death of the father provokes Dave into examining his own life, his values, and his beliefs. Fiction.

Windsor, Patricia. **The Summer Before** (© 1973). Dell 1974.

Alexandra is hurt physically and emotionally in the car crash that kills Bradley, her best friend and the first person she has ever really loved. Fiction.

Wohl, Burton. **That Certain Summer.** Bantam 1973.

Nick's parents are divorced, but he doesn't know why. When he goes to visit his father, he discovers the reason: his father is a homosexual. Fiction.

Woolley, Bryan. **Some Sweet Day.** Random 1973.

Gate Turnbolt looks back without bitterness to the last two poverty-stricken years he spent with a father filled with rage, violence, and love. Fiction.

Zindel, Paul. **The Pigman.** Dell 1970.

John and Lorraine, outsiders in their families and school, find each other and then Mr. Pignati, a lonely old man living on dreams and daily visits to the zoo. The unlikely trio do zany things, like roller skating in Mr. Pignati's house, as if they were trying to escape into the irresponsibility of childhood. Fiction.

Zolotow, Charlotte, editor. **An Overpraised Season: Ten Stories of Youth.** Har-Row 1973.

The communication gap between members of different generations sets the theme for this collection of stories. Fiction.

PROBLEMS OF MODERN HUMANITY

Anselment, Carol, and Donald B. Gibson, editors. **Black & White: Stories of American Life.** WSP 1971.

Selections by Baldwin, Wright, Faulkner, Welty, and Ellison demonstrate the universality of the human condition. Subheadings such as "Loneliness and Isolation," "Humor and Fantasy," and "Victory" indicate the book's range of concerns. Fiction.

Böll, Heinrich (translator Leila Vennewitz). **The Lost Honor of Katharina Blum.** McGraw 1975.

Katharina Blum attends a party, dances with a young radical wanted by the police, and stays all night with him. The police question her, but newspaper reporters hound her mercilessly until she takes drastic action. Fiction.

Brown, Christy. **Shadow on Summer.** Stein & Day 1974.

Irish author Riley McCombe, a cripple, comes to America. His stay and the people he stays with lead him

slowly to a recognition of his own emotional cowardice.
Mature fiction.

Burgess, Anthony. **Enderby** (© 1963). Ballantine 1969.
Enderby is a middle-aged poet who suffers through
many indignities. The one thing no one can take from
him is his ability to create. Mature fiction.

Caldwell, Taylor. **Wicked Angel** (© 1965). Fawcett
World 1973.
The chilling story of Angelo, a young psychopath. The
author weaves various psychological theories into her
story. Fiction.

Camus, Albert. **The Stranger** (© 1942). VinRandom
1954.
Having committed a pointless murder, Meursault is
convicted in part because he has demonstrated a cold
indifference toward the death of his mother. While
awaiting execution, he weighs the value of life and
the certainty of death. Mature fiction.

Capek, Karel, and Josef Capek. **R. U. R.** (© 1921). WSP
1969.
Rossum's Universal Robots manufactures robot-work-
ers in human form. When a new and brighter kind of
robot is manufactured, the robots revolt and destroy
all except one human being. Fiction.

Clark, Walter Van Tilburg. **The Track of the Cat** (©
1949). NAL 1961.
Two brothers set out to track down a panther that has
been killing their cattle while a third brother is left
to tend the ranch. Mature fiction.

Coover, Robert. **The Universal Baseball Association,
Inc., J. Henry Waugh, Prop.** Random 1968.
This is not a baseball book. It is the story of a man,
baffled by fate, who escapes into an illusionary world.
Fiction.

Cronin, A. J. **The Citadel** (© 1937). Bantam 1971.
A young doctor, Andrew Manson, compromises his
ambition to serve humanity as his desire for recognition and wealth increases. Fiction.

Davies, Peter. **The Truth about Kent State: A Challenge to the American Conscience.** FS&G 1973.

On May 4, 1970, four Kent State University students were shot by the Ohio National Guard. Seventy-four photographs indicate what led to the shootings, and the author chronicles the incidents before and after the tragedy. Nonfiction.

Dreiser, Theodore. **An American Tragedy** (© 1900). NAL 1973.

Clyde Griffiths, a sensitive and unhappy young man, murders the woman who threatens his opportunity to rise socially. Fiction.

Earle, William. **Public Sorrows and Private Pleasures.** Ind U Pr 1976.

In this collection of essays on modern America, Earle invites philosophy to step once again into public affairs as a counterweight to the "public sorrows" of ideology and radical reformers and to reconnect politics with the broader concerns of the human spirit such as religion and art. Mature nonfiction.

Faulkner, William. **The Sound and the Fury** (© 1929). VinRandom 1966.

The Compson family had once been one of Mississippi's proudest families, but the remaining members have little faith in the Compson name and even less liking for each other. A complex tale of family relationships, suicide, and greed. (See also *Light in August,* VinRandom; *Absalom, Absalom!,* VinRandom; and *Sanctuary,* VinRandom.) Mature fiction.

Fitzgerald, Zelda. **Save Me the Waltz** (© 1932). NAL 1974.

This autobiographical novel by the wife of F. Scott Fitzgerald is the love story of Alabama Beggs and David Knight, both extremely sensitive and creative. Fiction.

Froman, Robert. **Racism** (© 1972). Dell 1973.

Racism from the beginnings when Europeans first made contact with Indians and blacks until today with emphasis on the ways humanity might overcome racism. Nonfiction.

Fuller, R. Buckminster. **Operating Manual for Spaceship Earth** (© 1969). PB 1970.

Fuller suggests that humanity is in deep trouble unless we face up to what we are doing to our planet. He suggests that we act as if our planet were a spaceship and devise systems which would allow the spaceship to survive in its long trip ahead. Mature nonfiction.

Fuller, R. Buckminster. **Utopia or Oblivion: The Prospects for Humanity.** Bantam 1969.

Fuller argues that humanity has the willingness and technical knowledge to solve the problems of the future if we can avoid a nuclear holocaust in the next few years. Mature nonfiction.

Golding, William. **Lord of the Flies.** Cap Putnam 1959.

Golding explores human nature in this account of a group of English schoolboys stranded on a tropical island. A struggle for power evolves between Ralph, who strives for order and government, and Jack, who represents anarchy. Fiction.

Hamner, Earl, Jr. **Spencer's Mountain** (© 1961). Dell 1973.

The story of Clay-Boy Spencer's becoming a man was the basis of the popular television series, "The Waltons." The author pays attention to the details of daily life among a close-knit family. Fiction.

Harrison, William. **Roller Ball Murder.** Morrow 1974.

The title story in this collection is set in the future when the most popular spectator sport is Roller Ball. During the average contest, deaths and injuries are acceptable and even welcomed by the crowds. Fiction.

Hatch, Alden. **Buckminster Fuller at Home in the Universe.** Crown 1974.

Fuller has been called both genius and crackpot. He is a poet, a scientist, the inventor of the Geodesic Dome, a man worried about the future and where we are heading—or drifting.

Heller, Joseph. **Something Happened.** Knopf 1974.

In words that may offend some readers, the narrator Robert Slocum tells about his middle-age existence with a wife he pities but cares little about, and with his children, especially his imbecile son, whom he tries not to think about. Mature fiction.

Hemingway, Ernest. **A Farewell to Arms** (© 1929). Scribner 1967.

Frederic Henry experiences love and war in the tragic story of an American lieutenant in the Italian ambulance corps during World War I. Mature fiction.

Hemingway, Ernest. **The Old Man and the Sea** (© 1952). Scribner 1961.

Hemingway probes the mind of Santiago, an old Cuban fisherman, and reveals the story by exploring relationships of the old man with a young boy, with the sea, with the fish, and with himself. Fiction.

Herlihy, James Leo. **Midnight Cowboy** (© 1965). Dell 1969.

Cowboy Joe Buck comes to New York sure that he is the answer to the problem of all lovely rich women. But all he finds are loneliness, pettiness, and Ratso Rizzo, a dying derelict. Some use of four-letter words; some people will object to the sexual situations. Mature fiction.

Hesse, Hermann (translator Michael Roloff). **Beneath the Wheel** (© 1906). Bantam 1970.

Hans Giebenrath is a disciplined student, but when he goes away to school he meets Hermann, a free spirit whose unwillingness to yield to society's demands creates a terrible dilemma for Hans. Mature fiction.

Hesse, Hermann (translator Ursule Molinaro). **Narcissus and Goldmund** (© 1930). Bantam 1971.

Set in the Middle Ages, this novel depicts in its dual protagonists the struggle between spirit and nature and the synthesis they achieve. Fiction.

Himes, Chester. **Cast the First Stone** (© 1952). NAL 1972.

For five years James Monroe is in prison. This novel attempts to give a total picture of prison life and all aspects of a closed society where money, good looks, and intelligence still play an important part. Mature fiction.

Kafka, Franz (editor and translator Stanley Corngold). **The Metamorphosis** (© 1916). Bantam 1972.

George Samsa awakes one morning to find himself transformed into a man-sized cockroach. Life is seen through his eyes in this new state until he meets with tragedy. Mature fiction.

Karl, Frederick, and Leo Hamalian, editors. **The Naked I: Fictions for the Seventies.** Fawcett World 1971.

Ken Kesey, LeRoi Jones, and Franz Kafka are included in this collection of contemporary fiction. From Jones's "Answers in Progress" to Kafka's "A Country Doctor," the writers communicate their own personal visions of the world. Fiction.

Kerouac, Jack. **On the Road** (© 1957). NAL 1960.

One of the early statements of the Beat Generation, this novel focuses on the adventures of Sal Paradise as he embarks on a search for self. Ultimately he must choose between a stable existence and the wandering life of his friend, Dean Moriarity. Fiction.

Kesey, Ken. **One Flew Over the Cuckoo's Nest** (© 1962). NAL 1975.

A fun-loving rebel who feigns insanity to escape from a work farm leads a group of inmates in a mental hospital in their struggle against the dehumanizing influence of their ward nurse. Some language may be objectionable. Mature fiction.

Klein, Norma. **Sunshine.** Avon 1974.

At sixteen Kate marries David to escape her unhappy home. At eighteen, the day she learns she is pregnant, she leaves him. When she meets Sam, a guitar player on a motorcycle, it is love at first sight. Fiction.

Kostelanetz, Richard, editor. **Twelve from the Sixties.** Dell 1967.

Madness and the absurdity of society are the two themes in this volume. Alienation and rejection are examined by such talented writers as Saul Bellow, Bernard Malamud, and Tillie Olsen. Fiction.

Larson, Charles R., editor. **Prejudice: Twenty Tales of Oppression and Liberation.** NAL 1971.

The author terms prejudice "one of the vilest diseases

of all mankind." His collection includes stories from many cultures and religions. Fiction.

Lee, Harper. **To Kill a Mockingbird** (© 1960). Popular Lib 1974.

Scout Finch recalls the summer when her father, Atticus, an Alabama lawyer, defended a black man unjustly accused of a crime. Fiction.

Lewis, Sinclair. **Arrowsmith** (© 1924). HarBraceJ 1949.

Martin Arrowsmith makes his way through a maze of commercialism and quackery as he establishes his medical career, first as a general practitioner and finally as a brilliant researcher. Fiction.

Lewis, Sinclair. **Babbitt** (© 1922). NAL 1961.

Conservative George F. Babbitt is a successful small-town businessman, but also, as he begins to recognize, empty of soul or real purpose. Fiction.

Malamud, Bernard. **The Assistant** (© 1957). Dell 1971.

Down and out, Frank Alpine helps to rob a grocer. Guilt-ridden because the grocer has been injured, Alpine devotes his life to atoning for his guilt and trying to find his own redemption. Mature fiction.

Malamud, Bernard. **The Fixer** (© 1966). Dell 1968.

During a period of violent anti-Semitism in czarist Russia, a Jewish handyman is wrongly imprisoned for murdering a Gentile boy. Mature fiction.

Malamud, Bernard. **The Magic Barrel** (© 1958). PB 1972.

Thirteen short stories about people today, their fears and amusements and loves but most of all about their essential humanness. (See also *Rembrandt's Hat*, PB.) Fiction.

Maugham, W. Somerset. **Of Human Bondage** (© 1915). PB 1971.

Though Philip Carey's deformity affects his view of life, he, like most intellectual youths, struggles with religious beliefs, tragic love affairs, and the necessity of selecting a vocation. Mature fiction.

McCord, Jean. **Bitter Is the Hawk's Path.** Atheneum 1971.

Each of the ten persons who appear in these stories is isolated from others either by social status, language or physical characteristics, or just because they feel different; nevertheless, all of them learn to cope with their differences. Fiction.

McCullers, Carson. **The Heart Is a Lonely Hunter** (© 1940). Bantam 1970.

Story of five misfits and outcasts of a Southern town who have one thing in common—an aching loneliness and the need to communicate with other human beings: Mick Kelly, an awkward teenage girl; a bitter black doctor; a drunken radical; the owner of an all-night bar; and a deaf mute from whom they seek understanding. Fiction.

Miller, Arthur. **Death of a Salesman.** Viking Pr 1949.

Having mistaken platitudes for personal values, salesman Willy Loman is tragically shaken when his sons turn against him and, at sixty-three, he loses his job. A classic of modern drama.

Morris, Desmond. **The Human Zoo** (© 1969). Dell 1970.

The author is concerned with the ways in which the modern city is making people much like animals in a zoo, bound in with bars and space and emotional restrictions. (See also *The Naked Ape,* Dell.) Mature nonfiction.

Nathanson, E. M. **The Latecomers** (© 1965). PB 1973.

Early one morning in the plastic world of a Los Angeles amusement park, Cocert finds the body of the man who has been hired to play Christ in a Passion play hanging from the cross. Fiction.

Paley, Grace. **Enormous Changes at the Last Minute.** FS&G 1974.

Paley's stories contain wit and humor and are filled with the affairs of ordinary human beings as they move through life. Fiction.

Pines, Maya. **The Brain Changers: Scientists and the New Mind Control.** HarBraceJ 1973.

Scientists have been working for years to uncover the

mysterious workings of the human brain. The author summarizes their work in this field and reports on the implications and dangers of brain research for our lives today and tomorrow. Nonfiction.

Potok, Chaim. **My Name Is Asher Lev** (© 1972). Fawcett World 1973.

A young artist-genius disappoints his father, who views art as undignified foolishness, and creates a scandalous monument to his mother which threatens to cut him off from his family. Fiction.

Pynchon, Thomas. **The Crying of Lot 49** (© 1966). Bantam 1967.

The adventures and discoveries of the unusual heroine, Oedipa Maas, provide a social satire on America in the 1960s. Sexually explicit, the book is frank in its exploration of contemporary life. Mature fiction.

Rikhoff, Jean. **Buttes Landing.** Dial 1973.

The Adirondack Mountain region of New York is the setting for this novel about three generations of mountain farmers. Fiction.

Schulberg, Budd. **What Makes Sammy Run?** (© 1941). Fawcett World 1970.

Sammy Glick fights his way from the lower East Side of New York City to great financial success in Hollywood. His success is won at the expense of former friends and associates he runs roughshod over. Mature fiction.

Shute, Nevil. **On the Beach** (© 1957). Ballantine 1974.

An American and his Australian friends, the last of the human race, attempt to fulfill their dreams as they await inevitable death from radiation following an atomic war. Fiction.

Singer, Isaac Bashevis. **Enemies, a Love Story** (© 1972). Fawcett World 1973.

Herman Broder finds himself in the unusual predicament of having three wives. His struggle to resolve this complicated situation takes several interesting turns. Mature fiction.

Spark, Muriel. **The Prime of Miss Jean Brodie** (© 1961).
Dell 1966.

Muriel Spark explores the relationship between Jean
Brodie, an unusual and remarkable teacher, and six
of her favorite students in a private English girls'
school and how she influences their lives. Fiction.

Stallworth, Anne Nall. **This Time Next Year.** Vanguard
1971.

The title of this work echoes the sentiments of the
Birdsong family as each member longs for a better life
on or away from their tenant farm in Alabama. Fiction.

Stein, Sol. **The Magician** (© 1971). Dell 1972.

Ed Japhet, a popular and gifted sixteen-year-old magician, is attacked by a psychopathic classmate after
a successful magic show at a high school prom. Though
there is no question of guilt, a clever defense attorney
proves that law and justice may be perverted. Fiction.

Steinbeck, John. **The Grapes of Wrath** (© 1939). Bantam 1970.

Victims of the Dust Bowl of the Thirties, the Joad family join thousands of farmers in the great migration to
California, the promised land, where they hope to find
a new life. Mature fiction.

Steinbeck, John. **Of Mice and Men** (© 1937). Bantam
1970.

Ranchhands George and his retarded friend Lennie
long for a place of their own, a place where they can
find peace and quiet. (See also *Tortilla Flat,* Bantam.)
Fiction.

Tryon, Thomas. **The Other** (© 1971). Fawcett World
1972.

All male members of the Perry family have met with
untimely and violent deaths. Exactly how the twelve-
year-old twins, Niles and Holland, are involved in
these and other strange events creates a most unusual
plot. Fiction.

Toffler, Alvin. **Future Shock** (© 1970). Bantam 1971.

Toffler contends that humanity is the victim of "future
shock," a disorientation caused by the too-sudden tech-

nological changes taking place all around us. Mature nonfiction.

Updike, John. **Rabbit, Run** (© 1960). Fawcett World 1974.

Harry (Rabbit) Angstrom, finding married life frustrating after his glorious high school years as a basketball star, deserts his wife and sets out for the freedom he longs for. This leads him to adventures that may seem sordid and offensive to some readers. Mature fiction.

Vonnegut, Kurt, Jr. **Slaughterhouse-Five** (© 1969). Dell 1974.

A satirical condemnation of violence and war and those who create them. Billy Pilgrim lives three lives: an American soldier in World War II in the Dresden firebombing; a happily married postwar optometrist; and an exhibit transported to a Tralfamadorian zoo to meet with a young moviestar. Mature, sometimes shocking reading. Fiction.

Warren, Robert Penn. **All the King's Men** (© 1946). Bantam 1973.

Poorly educated Willie Stark fights the political corruption in his state, but after winning the governorship, he becomes as tyrannical and power-obsessed as the system he had originally fought. Fiction.

West, Nathanael. **Miss Lonelyhearts** (© 1933). FS&G 1957.

A newspaper reporter who writes a lovelorn column is horrified by his editor's heartlessness and his own inability to find answers to the letters. Mature fiction.

Wharton, Edith. **Ethan Frome.** Scribner 1911.

Ethan Frome, a New England farmer, marries an older woman out of loneliness. Their lives are complicated when her young female cousin comes to live with them. Fiction.

Williams, John. **Stoner** (© 1965). PB 1972.

A professor of English who is a dull person to most of his fellow teachers comes alive when he finds a young love outside of his conventional and dull marriage. Fiction.

Young, Leontine. **The Fractured Family** (© 1973). Mc-
Graw 1974.

The family as an institution has been both attacked
and defended by modern society. The author analyzes
the causes of family breakup and parental problems
and the attitudes of young people toward the family
unit. Nonfiction.

REFLECTIONS

Abbey, Edward. **Fire on the Mountain** (© 1962). Ballantine n.d.

An old man and his twelve-year-old grandson defy the
U.S. Air Force when the government decides to con-
dem a ranch to extend the White Sand Missile Range.
(See also *Black Sun,* PB.)   Fiction.

Arvio, Raymond Paavo. **The Cost of Dying and What
You Can Do About It.** Har-Row 1974.

What can people do about the multibillion-dollar, un-
regulated funeral industry which Arvio feels is secre-
tive and hides under the cloak of the American flag
and conventional religion? The author advocates consumer control—"memorial societies" and completely
consumer-owned and controlled facilities. Mature nonfiction.

Bach, Richard. **Jonathan Livingston Seagull** (© 1970).
Avon 1974.

A brief poetic story about seagulls. Jonathan decides
that there is much more to life than eating and becomes an outcast when he dares to probe the unknow-
able. Fiction.

Baker, Daisy. **Travels in a Donkey Trap.** St Martin
1974.

At seventy-six, Daisy Baker acquires a donkey and a
cart. While traveling to the woods or the beach, Daisy
finds joy in her recollection of the past and her continuing link with life beyond her lane. Nonfiction.

Baldwin, James. **Go Tell It on the Mountain** (© 1954).
NAL 1963.

An evangelist and his family are spiritually locked in
the ghetto of Harlem. The fanatic father battles against

his own nature to find God, and his son John fights
to escape to find himself. Mature fiction.

Barry, Anne. **Bellevue Is a State of Mind.** HarBraceJ
1971.

Anne Barry feigned mental illness in order to be committed to the psychiatric ward at New York's Bellevue
Hospital. This investigative report includes impressions of her week-long stay in one of nation's most controversial hospitals. Nonfiction.

Berry, Wendell. **The Memory of Old Jack.** HarBraceJ
1974.

Old Jack, a retired farmer, spends one day reliving his
life and trying to find some meaning and purpose in
it. Fiction.

Billing, Graham. **Forbush and the Penguins** (© 1966).
Fawcett World n.d.

A young man on a solitary mission in Antarctica tries
to study a penguin rookery and skuas which prey on
penguin chicks and finds he develops a messianic drive
to protect the penguins against all enemies, bird or
man. Fiction.

Bloomfield, Harold H., Michael Peter Cain, and Dennis
T. Jaffe. **TM: Discovering Inner Energy and Over-
coming Stress.** Delacorte 1975.

Transcendental Meditation (TM) is a technique for
making humanity master of its own emotions and
nerves and stresses. This book suggests ways of using
TM for mental and physical problems. Nonfiction.

Buck, Pearl S. **To My Daughters with Love.** John Day
1967.

Thoughts on youth, love, marriage, and eternal truths
which are not invalidated by new views of morality.
Nonfiction.

Castañeda, Carlos. **The Teachings of Don Juan: A Yaqui
Way of Knowledge** (© 1968). S&S 1973.

Castañeda is introduced to the wisdom of the peyote
cult by Don Juan, a Yaqui Indian medicineman/
sorcerer. The experience leads Castañeda into strange
and fascinating worlds of thought and perception in
his quest to become "a man of knowledge." (See also

A Separate Reality: Further Conversations with Don Juan, S&S; *Journey to Ixtlan: The Lessons of Don Juan,* S&S; and *Tales of Power,* S&S.)   Mature nonfiction.

Conrad, Joseph. **Lord Jim** (© 1900). Penguin 1971.

An officer on a ship, Jim escapes with other officers while the ship slowly sinks with all passengers still on board. Though the passengers are rescued, Jim's sense of guilt forces him to begin a life as a wanderer seeking redemption.   Mature fiction.

Conrad, Joseph. **The Secret Sharer** (© 1917). NAL 1971.

Having taken aboard an escaped confessed murderer, a young captain hesitates to return the man to his captors because he feels somehow that, under similar circumstances, he too might have committed the murderer's act.   Fiction.

Dillard, Annie. **Pilgrim at Tinker Creek** (© 1974). Bantam 1975.

The author lives by Tinker Creek in Virginia's Blue Ridge Mountains and writes of simple mysteries and wonders like stars and hawks and winter and time and stalking animals and insects and death. (See also her collection of poetry, *Tickets for a Prayer Wheel,* Bantam.)   Mature nonfiction.

Dostoyevsky, Fyodor (translator David Magarshack). **Crime and Punishment.** Penguin 1970.

Raskolnikov, a poor student, believes that he is not bound by normal moral codes. He kills an old woman, but through the love of the prostitute Sonia he recognizes his common bond with others. First published in 1866.   Mature fiction.

Dostoyevsky, Fyodor. **The Idiot.** Dell 1959.

Prince Myshkin lives a saintly life, trying constantly to help others as much as he can. First published in 1868–1869, this is a novel of compassion and love and torture and frustration.   Mature fiction.

Dostoyevsky, Fyodor (translator Mirra Ginsburg). **Notes from Underground.** Bantam 1974.

In this 1864 novel, a nameless narrator, one of literature's first antiheroes, launches into a tirade about

humanity and the endless questions for which there
are no easy answers. Mature fiction.

Douglas, William O. **Points of Rebellion.** Random 1970.
In this little book a justice of the Supreme Court tells
why he values the rebellion so characteristic of the
young: "This period of dissent based on belief in man
will indeed be our great renaissance." Mature nonfiction.

Falk, Irving A., editor. **Prophecy for the Year 2000.**
Messner 1970.
Over 100 sketches by noted people, including Ralph
Nader and Jackie Robinson, about life in A.D. 2000:
multi-level cities, a new role for religion, test tube
babies, and new roles for the sexes. Nonfiction.

Gibran, Kahlil. **The Prophet.** Knopf 1923.
Poetic prose statements concerning some of humanity's
deepest concerns: friendship, beauty, love, teaching.
Nonfiction.

Golden, Jeffrey. **Watermelon Summer.** Lippincott 1971.
Diary of an idealistic young Northern white man during a summer spent as a laborer on a black cooperative
farm in Georgia. Nonfiction.

Harris, Sydney J. **For the Time Being.** HM 1972.
Harris selects some of his "Strictly Personal" newspaper columns for this book. The columns include
comments on truth, God, the second rate, pro sports,
TV violence, obscenity, and education. Nonfiction.

Haskins, Jim. **Diary of a Harlem Schoolteacher.** Grove
1969.
A frank account of the frustrations which make Haskins's job of teaching elementary school almost impossible. Nonfiction.

Hendin, David. **Death as a Fact of Life.** Norton 1973.
Advances in medical technology have led to new questions about death. When is a person legally dead?
Should a person have the right to determine the time
and means of death? What kind of therapy is most
helpful to the dying? Can freezing the newly dead
really lead to possible revival at a later time? Nonfiction.

Hesse, Hermann (translator Hilda Rosner). **Siddhartha** (© 1951). Bantam n.d.

Encouraged by the Buddha to find the ultimate good on his own, Siddhartha abandons his friends, rejects the teachings of his elders, and travels to the city. (See also *Steppenwolf,* Bantam; *Demian,* Bantam; and *The Journey to the East,* Bantam.) Fiction.

Hesse, Hermann (editor Theodore Ziolkowski and translator Ralph Manheim). **Stories of Five Decades.** FS&G 1973.

This selection of stories offers a spectrum of Hesse's writings from 1899–1948 concerning his own secret dreams and his own anguish. Fiction.

Hesse, Hermann (translator Denver Lindley). **Strange News from Another Star & Other Tales.** FS&G 1972.

Hesse's collection contains stories concerned with dream worlds, the subconscious, and magical thinking. Mature fiction.

Howland, Bette. **W-3.** Viking Pr 1974.

Sent to the psychiatric ward of a large university hospital when she had a nervous breakdown, Howland had time to consider what it means to be "crazy" and to observe others in the W-3 community. Some frank language. Nonfiction.

Issawi, Charles. **Issawi's Laws of Social Motion.** Hawthorn 1973.

An economics professor enunciates laws and aphorisms, some funny, some ironic, many profound, about history, politics, economics, revolution, and America. Nonfiction.

Kafka, Franz. **Selected Short Stories.** Random 1952.

Stories dealing with themes of human isolation and frustration and paradoxical human quests for freedom and responsibility. Mature fiction.

Langone, John. **Death Is a Noun: A View of the End of Life.** Little 1972.

A provocative study of death written for young adults. Examines new definitions of death, euthanasia, why people murder, capital punishment, suicide, abortion, the scientific quest for longer life, and some conjectures about the hereafter. Nonfiction.

Langone, John. **Vital Signs: The Way We Die in America.** Little 1974.

Honest, open discussion of death is taboo for many people. The author argues that we need to understand death, and he offers medical and legal definitions of death along with interviews of those who are dying and those who take care of the dying. Mature nonfiction.

Lifton, Robert Jay, and Eric Olson. **Living and Dying.** Praeger 1974.

Sex and death are human realities, but they have often been sources of embarrassment or ignorance. The authors present some facts about creation and death. Nonfiction.

Lindbergh, Anne Morrow. **Gift from the Sea.** Pantheon 1955.

Walking along the shore, the author reflects upon the joys of the simple life and the intricacies of the patterns which together form the complex fabric of modern life. Nonfiction.

Lindbergh, Anne Morrow. **Hour of Gold, Hour of Lead.** HarBraceJ 1973.

When sheltered, introspective Anne Morrow married famous pilot Charles Lindbergh in 1929, he took her into his world of action. These diary entries and letters tell of her learning to fly and take aerial photographs, to live in the glare of fame and publicity—and to live with the loss of their kidnapped son. Nonfiction.

Manchester, William. **Controversy and Other Essays in Journalism, 1950–1975.** Little 1976.

Manchester records his dispute with the Kennedy family over his book on the assassination of President Kennedy and profiles individuals and institutions prominent in America over the last twenty-five years. Nonfiction.

Mannes, Marya. **Last Rights: The Case for the Good Death.** Morrow 1974.

The author believes that anyone should have the right to choose the manner of death with dignity rather than be kept alive with tubes and medicine. Nonfiction.

Mitford, Jessica. **The American Way of Death** (© 1963). Fawcett World 1973.

The author attacks businesses and people that make money out of the sadness of death. Nonfiction.

Pasternak, Boris (translator Frederick Manfred). **Doctor Zhivago** (© 1958). NAL 1973.

Yuri Zhivago—doctor, poet, philosopher—struggles to preserve his integrity and his spiritual independence during the Russian Revolution. Mature fiction.

Pirsig, Robert M. **Zen and the Art of Motorcycle Maintenance** (© 1974). Bantam 1975.

A father and son travel around the West on a motorcycle finding out who and what and why they are. Mature fiction.

Robbins, Jhan, and David Fisher. **Tranquility without Pills: All about Transcendental Meditation** (© 1972). Bantam 1973.

Two skeptical writers discover people whose lives have improved because they set aside two twenty-minute periods each day for meditation. Nonfiction.

Saint Exupèry, Antoine de (translator Lewis Galantiere). **Wind, Sand and Stars** (© 1939). HarBraceJ 1967.

Artistic reminiscences of a pilot who flew during the exciting first days of airplane flight. Nonfiction.

Sarton, May. **As We Are Now.** Norton 1973.

At seventy-six, Caroline Spencer, intelligent, witty, and dignified, is taken to Twin Elms Nursing Home, where she writes her journal to ward off senility and her fear of death. Fiction.

Solzhenitsyn, Alexander (translators Max Hayward and Ronald Hingley). **One Day in the Life of Ivan Denisovich.** Bantam 1963.

A novel about a single day in the life of an inmate of one of Stalin's forced labor camps in Siberia. The narrator's account of his feelings, thoughts, and conversations in the barracks, filled with the raw and vulgar language of the peasant, serves as a significant and authentic political document. Fiction.

Steinbeck, John. **The Pearl** (© 1947). Bantam 1971.

When Kino finds a very large pearl of great value, he is confident that it will purchase health and happiness for his family. Instead, it calls forth the dark spirits in Kino and those who covet the pearl. Fiction.

Thoreau, Henry David. **Walden** (© 1854). NAL 1973.

Fearing the consequences of the emerging machine age, Thoreau lived a solitary life near Walden Pond for two years. This daily journal is a record of his observations about man and nature. Mature nonfiction.

Watts, Alan. **The Book** (© 1966). VinRandom 1972.

The Hindu philosophy of Vedanta explores the self and the fear of knowing the self. (See also *Beyond Theology,* VinRandom; *Nature, Man and Woman,* VinRandom; and *In My Own Way: An Autobiography,* VinRandom.) Mature nonfiction.

West, Jessamyn. **Hide and Seek: A Continuing Journey.** HarBraceJ 1973.

Living by herself for three months in a travel trailer on a remote bank of the Colorado River, the author shares her experiences, observations, and thoughts on solitude. Mature nonfiction.

White, E. B. **The Points of My Compass.** Har-Row 1962.

Essays written in various sections of the country, describing a hurricane on the Maine coast, a gale in the north Pacific, and a circus in its winter quarters. Nonfiction.

Wibberley, Leonard. **The Last Stand of Father Felix.** Morrow 1974.

When civil war hits a small East African country, eighty-year-old Father Felix is told to flee the opposing armies, but he decides to take a stand at his mission. Fiction.

Wilder, Thornton. **The Bridge of San Luis Rey** (© 1927). PB 1972.

Brother Juniper, the only witness of the collapse of a bridge over a deep chasm in Peru, decides to inquire into the secret lives of the five victims. Fiction.

Wyatt, John. **The Shining Levels: The Story of a Man Who Went Back to Nature.** Lippincott 1974.

Like a modern Thoreau, John Wyatt took to the woods in order to rediscover himself and achieve a harmony with his environment unattainable in urban life. Nonfiction.

Young, I. S. **Uncle Herschel, Dr. Padilsky, and the Evil Eye.** HarBraceJ 1973.

A very young boy remembers the life and problems of his uncle, a Russian herb dealer, during the early 1900s. Fiction.

LIVES, THEN AND NOW

Aaron, Jan. **Gerald R. Ford: President of Destiny.** Fleet 1975.

The thirty-eighth president of the United States, from boyhood to the first 100 days in office.

Agee, James. **Letters of James Agee to Father Flye.** HM 1971.

Agee's life as a writer and as a human being unfolds through a series of letters written to his dearest friend, an Episcopalian priest.

Ambrose, Stephen E. **Ike: Abilene to Berlin.** Har-Row 1973.

From childhood on the Kansas prairies to a mediocre career at West Point, Dwight D. Eisenhower became the leading Allied general in World War II.

Angelou, Maya. **Gather Together in My Name.** Random 1974.

Continuing the story of her life and the obstacles she overcame to find security for herself and her son Guy, Angelou relates how she narrowly escaped drug addiction. (See also *I Know Why the Caged Bird Sings*, Bantam.) Mature.

Apsler, Alfred. **The Sun King: Louis XIV of France.** Messner 1965.

From 1643 (when he was five years old) until his death in 1715, Louis XIV was king of France. Under his reign, France became the center of the Western world in power and the arts.

Arnold, Adele R. **Red Son Rising.** Dillon 1974.

An Apache Indian, captured by Pima Indians and sold to a white photographer, becomes well-known physician Carlos Montezuma.

Barrett, S. M., and Frederick W. Turner III, editors. **Geronimo: His Own Story** (© 1970). Ballantine 1974.

Geronimo's personal account of his life, from his early Apache family life to his capture and life as a prisoner.

Block, Alex Ben. **The Legend of Bruce Lee.** Dell 1974.

An intimate portrait of one of the "most exciting legends of our time," Bruce Lee. Views his childhood and training in the martial arts, his career in moviemaking, his marriage, his friends, his overall philosophy of life, and the mystery surrounding his untimely death.

Born, Franz (translator Juliana Biro). **Jules Verne: The Man Who Invented the Future** (© 1960). P-H 1964.

The story of the life of Jules Verne, the nineteenth-century science fiction writer whose novels often accurately predicted the future.

Brant, Charles S., editor. **Jim Whitewolf: The Life of a Kiowa Apache Indian.** Dover 1969.

Whitewolf's life was buffeted by the radical changes brought by reservations, education, Christian missionaries, and alcohol in the first half of the twentieth century.

Burnett, Avis. **Gertrude Stein.** Atheneum 1972.

Gertrude Stein was a born rebel, a lover of art and fine cooking, a friend to writers and musicians in Paris during the 1920s and 1930s, and a writer of unusual poetry.

Caine, Lynn. **Widow** (© 1974). Bantam 1975.

A woman shares and suffers with her cancer-stricken husband for months and then begins the period of adjustment to being alone again.

Carter, Rubin "Hurricane." **The Sixteenth Round: From Number One Contender to #45472.** Viking Pr 1974.

Before May 26, 1967, "Hurricane" Carter was the top

contender for a bout with the world middleweight boxing champion, but on that date Carter and another
man were found guilty of the murder of three white
people in a Paterson, New Jersey, bar. In prison he
maintained his innocence and fought for his freedom.

Chamberlain, Wilt (with David Shaw). **Wilt: Just Like
Any Other Seven-Foot Black Millionaire Who Lives
Next Door.** Macmillan 1973.

Chamberlain, a controversial figure both on and off the
basketball court, tells about his career in basketball,
his travels, his friends, his political activities, his views
about and his experiences with women, and his relations with other players and coaches.

Cochise, Ciyé "Niño" (with A. Kinney Griffith). **The
First Hundred Years of Niño Cochise.** Pyramid Pubns
1971.

Born in 1874, the grandson of Cochise tells of his colorful life, from Apache customs and the exploits of his
uncle Geronimo to watching the astronauts on TV
walking on the moon.

Cooper, Paulette, editor. **Growing Up Puerto Rican.**
NAL 1972.

Tape-recorded stories by seventeen young Puerto Ricans who frankly describe what life is like growing up
and coping with two distinct cultures.

Crowder, David L. **Tendoy, Chief of the Lemhis.** Caxton
1969.

Unlike most Indian leaders, Tendoy befriended the
white settlers, protected them against other Indians,
and was in turn honored by many whites when he
died in 1907. The life of the Indians in the Lemhi
Valley of Idaho and of their distinguished chief is described by Crowder's use of many original documents
and news articles.

Curtis, Richard. **The Berrigan Brothers: The Story of
Daniel and Philip Berrigan.** Hawthorn 1974.

Philip and Daniel Berrigan are radical Catholic priests
deeply involved in legal battles over protesting the
Vietnam War and draft conscription.

D'Ambrosio, Richard. **No Language but a Cry.** Dell 1970.

An abused child, Laura, is nursed back to life by a courageous doctor and concerned Sisters.

Davidson, Donald (with Jesse Outlar). **Caught Short.** Bantam 1972.

Only four feet tall, Donald Davidson was hired by the Boston Red Sox as a mascot and part-time batboy in 1938. By 1970 he had become assistant to the president of the Atlanta Braves and the team's traveling secretary.

Dempsey, Hugh A. **Crowfoot: Chief of the Blackfeet.** U of Okla Pr 1972.

Crowfoot was a strong and devoted leader who saw the futility of fighting superior white armies in both the U.S. and Canada and so guided his people through the humiliating transition from freedom to reservation farming.

Dickson, Lovat. **Wilderness Man: The Curious Life of Archie Belaney Called Grey Owl.** Atheneum 1973.

At eighteen, Archie Belaney left England and moved to Canada. Adopting the Indian name of Grey Owl and Indian ways, he married an Iroquois girl and wrote. His earlier identity as a non-Indian was not discovered by the public until after his death.

Douglas, William O. **Go East, Young Man: The Early Years.** Random 1974.

The life and thoughts of the Supreme Court justice from his boyhood in Yakima, Washington, until his appointment to the Supreme Court in 1939. His love of nature and hiking in the mountains is obvious.

Drimmer, Frederick. **Very Special People.** Bantam 1976.

Drimmer writes compassionately about the problems and triumphs of people too often called circus freaks— Siamese twins, armless and legless wonders, hairy people, short and tall people, and others.

Eastman, Charles A. **Indian Boyhood** (© 1902). Dover 1970.

A Santee Sioux who grew up in the white world and became a physician describes his youth among his people between 1858 and 1873, before his life was changed forever by white institutions.

Eckert, Allan W. **Blue Jacket: War Chief of the Shawnees.** Little 1969.

The true story of a white boy who always wanted to be an Indian and one day finds himself captured by Shawnees.

Eiseley, Loren. **All the Strange Hours: The Excavation of a Life.** Scribner 1975.

The great popularizer of science begins his life story with his Nebraska boyhood and school in Pennsylvania and then details his career as an anthropologist and writer.

Fecher, Constance. **The Last Elizabethan: A Portrait of Sir Walter Raleigh.** FS&G 1972.

The multifaceted life of one of the most extraordinary men who lived during the Elizabethan age.

Fiore, Carlo. **Bud: The Brando I Knew—The Untold Story of Brando's Private Life.** Delacorte 1974.

An intimate view of the private life of Marlon Brando, one of America's most celebrated contemporary actors, as told by one of Brando's closest friends.

Giovanni, Nikki. **Gemini: An Extended Autobiographical Statement on My First Twenty-five Years of Being a Black Poet** (© 1971). Viking Pr 1973.

Metaphorical portrait of one of America's most enterprising black female poets.

Greene, Graham. **A Sort of Life.** S&S 1971.

The English writer describes through personal recollections, memoirs, observations, and experiences his childhood and his early years as a writer. Mature.

Gridley, Marion E., editor. **American Indian Women.** Hawthorn 1974.

An anthology of biographies of some native American women who have made significant contributions to their people as well as to their country: Sacajawea, Winema, Susan La Flesche, Picotte (the first woman physician), Maria Montoya Martinez (master artisan), Elaine Abraham Ramos (college vice president), and others.

Gridley, Marion E. **Contemporary American Indian Leaders.** Dodd 1972.

Concise biographies of twenty-six contemporary Indians in a variety of fields, from education and art to politics and social action.

Haskins, James. **Adam Clayton Powell: Portrait of a Marching Black.** Dial 1974.

Blacks in Harlem saw Adam Clayton Powell as a savior, a protector of their interests; whites, many of them in the U.S. Congress, tried to force him out of Congress.

Hayman, LeRoy. **O Captain! The Death of Abraham Lincoln.** Four Winds 1968.

Fast-moving biography captures and recreates a momentous event in American history.

Hellman, Lillian. **An Unfinished Woman.** Little 1969.

An American dramatist covers her painful childhood through the days of her writing career.

Herriot, James. **All Creatures Great and Small.** St Martin 1972.

A young Scottish veterinarian comes to a northern English town to practice and learns to handle animals and people, birth and death. (See also *All Things Bright and Beautiful,* St Martin.)

Higham, Charles. **Katie: The Life of Katherine Hepburn.** Norton 1975.

Katherine Hepburn's friendships with Humphrey Bogart, Cary Grant, and especially Spencer Tracy make her life story almost a history of Hollywood from 1930 to the present.

Hook, Donald D. **Madmen of History.** Jonathan David 1976.

Eighteen short biographies of often terrifying characters whose "madness" (variously defined here) had an impact on the history of their times.

Hough, John T., Jr. **A Peck of Salt: A Year in the Ghetto.** Little 1970.

A VISTA volunteer candidly recounts his experiences in an inner-city junior high school and community.

Howard, Helen Addison, and Dan L. McGrath. **War Chief Joseph** (© 1941). U of Nebr Pr 1964.

Claiming to be the most complete story of Chief Joseph's life, this biography tells the story of the early history of the Nez Percé Indians, the various treaties of the mid-1800s, the unparalleled military campaign of 1877, and the events following Joseph's surrender.

Howat, Gerald, editor. **Who Did What.** Crown 1974.

A series of brief biographies, alphabetically arranged, of more than 5,000 famous men and women.

Hurwitz, Howard L. **Donald: The Man Who Remains a Boy.** PB 1973.

At birth, Donald Hurwitz weighed less than two pounds. Today, at twenty-eight, he is 5′ 8″ tall and weighs 150—but he is mentally retarded. His parents have resisted placing Donald in an institution and have struggled to prepare him to live in a normal environment.

Hyde, George E. **Spotted Tail's Folk: A History of the Brulé Sioux** (© 1961). U of Okla Pr 1974.

Unlike his Sioux contemporaries Red Cloud and Sitting Bull, Spotted Tail felt it was wise not to fight the white armies. (See also *Red Cloud's Folk: A History of the Oglala Sioux,* U of Okla Pr; *The Pawnee Indians,* U of Okla Pr; and *Indians of the Woodlands: From Prehistoric Times to 1725,* U of Okla Pr.)

Ishigo, Estelle. **Lone Heart Mountain** (© 1972). Ritchie 1973.

The author tells of her experiences in a Japanese war relocation center during World War II.

Kaufman, Louis, Barbara Fitzgerald, and Tom Sewell. **Moe Berg, Athlete, Scholar, Spy.** Little 1974.

A catcher with the Boston Red Sox, Moe Berg was fluent in at least twelve languages, was a brilliant student in many fields, and was also a spy for the United States before and during World War II.

Kelen, Emery. **Mr. Nonsense: A Life of Edward Lear.** Nelson 1973.

This short biography of Edward Lear reveals the loneliness, wanderlust, ill health, and frustrated hopes that saddened the life of a thoroughly charming and loving man who wrote so many limericks.

Kennedy, John F. **Profiles in Courage.** Har-Row 1956.
Sketches of eight men who demonstrated great moral courage in the face of overwhelming opposition. By defending his principles, each man helped to maintain American democracy. Mature.

Ketchum, Richard M. **Will Rogers: The Man and His Times** (© 1973). S&S 1975.
Part Cherokee Indian and raised on the Oklahoma frontier, Rogers's lassoing ability took him to vaudeville and Broadway plays and from there on to Hollywood. He became one of the most popular political commentators and humorists of his time.

Killilea, Marie. **Karen.** Dell 1952.
The Killileas and their friends knew little about cerebral palsy until it struck little Karen.

Komroff, Manuel. **Napoleon.** Messner 1954.
Traces his career from artillery officer to emperor: his enormous influence both within France and throughout Europe, his many successful battle campaigns, and his restructuring of social, political, and legal conditions in France.

Krents, Harold. **To Race the Wind.** Bantam 1972.
Blind since birth, Harold Krents was the inspiration for the young blind hero of the Broadway and film hits, *Butterflies Are Free.* Determined to live in the world of the sighted, Harold played football, graduated from Harvard College and Law School, and is now a New York lawyer.

Kroeber, Theodora. **Ishi, Last of His Tribe.** Bantam 1961.
Biography of a gentle man who was the last surviving member of the Yahi tribe. When the whites had encroached on the Indians' territory and killed most of them, only Ishi eventually remained to tell his story and live his remaining years in a California museum.

Kubiak, Daniel James, editor. **Ten Tall Texans.** Naylor 1970.
Ten biographical sketches of Texans who helped shape

that state include Jose Antonio Navarro (signer of the Texas Declaration of Independence), Sam Houston, David Crockett, and Jim Bowie.

Kugelmass, J. Alvin. **Ralph J. Bunche: Fighter for Peace.** Messner 1972.

Orphaned at twelve, Ralph Bunche was reared by his grandmother, who guided him toward a higher education. Out of poverty and discrimination, he became an outstanding anthropologist and undersecretary for the United Nations.

Lacy, Leslie Alexander. **The Life of W. E. B. DuBois: Cheer the Lonesome Traveler** (© 1970). Dell 1972.

A portrait of W. E. B. DuBois: the writer, teacher, and statesman, and his role in the struggle of today's black Americans.

Lame Deer and Richard Erdoes. **Lame Deer, Seeker of Visions.** S&S 1972.

With earthy humor, Lame Deer tells of his life as a boy, a sheepherder, a policeman, a rodeo performer, and, most importantly, a medicine man—a *wicasa wakan,* a Sioux holy man, experienced with visions, healings, and sacred things.

Lash, Joseph P. **Eleanor: The Years Alone.** Norton 1972.

Eleanor Roosevelt is portrayed during her later years in the roles of teacher, writer, lecturer, worldwide traveler, and ally of the United Nations and Israel. Mature.

L'Engle, Madeleine. **The Summer of the Great-Grandmother.** FS&G 1974.

A memoir of a much loved parent; a story of the aged and the dying and of sensitive living and life.

Lincoln, C. Eric, editor. **Martin Luther King, Jr.: A Profile.** Hill & Wang 1970.

Commentary and analysis of a culture and of a man it produced, by thirteen close associates and acquaintances of King.

Linderman, Frank B. **Plenty-Coups, Chief of the Crows** (© 1930). U of Nebr Pr 1962.

Reminisences about the old days, before the passing of

the buffalo, especially fighting with General Crook against the Crow enemies: the Sioux, Cheyennes, and Arapahoes.

Linderman, Frank B. **Pretty-Shield: Medicine Woman of the Crows** (© 1932). U of Nebr Pr 1974.

The experiences and insights of Pretty-Shield, a Crow medicine woman, who describes her youth and early life.

Loeper, John J. **Men of Ideas.** Atheneum 1970.

Lives and ideas of such philosophers as Socrates, Lao-tzu, Confucius, St. Augustine, René Descartes, Voltaire, Soren Kierkegaard, and Friedrich Nietzsche.

Lund, Doris. **Eric.** Lippincott 1974.

At seventeen, the author's son found he had leukemia. Given from six months to two years by doctors, Eric went to college, played varsity soccer, and proved that a person can crowd a lot of living into a very few years.

Marriott, Alice. **Maria: The Potter of San Ildefonso** (© 1948). U of Okla Pr 1973.

Although Maria Martinez's productivity continued long after this 1948 publication, the biography covers her life with her husband Julian and their world famous pottery designs and process, especially their legendary black-on-black ware. Illustrated.

Martin, Ralph G. **Jennie: The Life of Lady Randolph Churchill, the Romantic Years 1854–1895.** P-H 1969.

Aside from being the mother of Winston Churchill, this girl from Brooklyn became a forceful figure in the British monarchy and society.

Maser, Werner (translator Arnold Pomerans). **Hitler's Letters and Notes.** Har-Row 1973.

Hitler's public and private memorabilia encompass a wide range of subjects and the full chronology of his life. Mature.

Massie, Robert, and Suzanne Massie. **Journey.** Knopf 1975.

The Massies discover that their son, Robert, has hemophilia, and the family faces many problems learning to live with the blood defect.

Neihardt, John G. **Black Elk Speaks: Being the Life Story of a Holy Man of the Oglala Sioux** (© 1932). PB 1972.

Black Elk describes his life among the Oglala Sioux, his visions and religious experiences as a holy man, his boyhood experiences at the Custer battle and years later at Wounded Knee. (See also, *When the Tree Flowered: An Authentic Tale of the Old Sioux World*, PB.)

Nelson, Mary Carroll. **Maria Martinez.** Dillon 1972.

A short biography of Maria Martinez, one of the finest makers of Indian pottery in the world, describes how Maria and her husband Julian developed their world-famous pottery-making techniques that brought fame and relative wealth to the San Ildefonso Pueblo, New Mexico.

Newcomb, Franc Johnson. **Hosteen Klah: Navaho Medicine Man and Sand Painter** (© 1964). U of Okla Pr 1971.

Biography of Hosteen Klah, Navajo medicine man, sand painter, and weaver is told in part by the author's personal reminiscence.

North, Sterling. **Thoreau of Walden Pond.** HM 1959.

Devoted to the outdoor life, Henry David Thoreau lived by himself for more than two years at Walden Pond on a budget of twenty-seven cents a week.

O'Connor, Richard. **Heywood Broun: A Biography.** Putnam 1975.

Heywood Broun (1888–1939) was a fighting liberal newsman and columnist, a friend of President Franklin Delano Roosevelt and other powerful people, and a man unhappy in his marriage and afraid of death.

O'Donnell, Kenneth P., and David F. Powers (with Joe McCarthy). **"Johnny, We Hardly Knew Ye": Memories of John Fitzgerald Kennedy.** Little 1972.

A detailed biography which reveals the personal and political life of the late president.

Ojigbo, A. Okion, editor. **Young and Black in Africa.** VinRandom 1971.

Eight Africans from Ghana, Guinea, Kenya, Malawi, Nigeria, and South Africa reveal their experiences in the rapidly changing African world.

Olsen, Viggo (with Jeanette Lockerbie). **Daktar, Diplomat in Bangladesh.** Moody 1973.

A dedicated surgeon relates his adventures as doctor and diplomat during the tumultous days in war-ravaged Bangladesh.

Orrmont, Arthur. **James Eades: The Man Who Mastered the Mississippi.** P-H 1969.

One of the greatest self-taught engineers in history, Eades invented the diving bell, removed snags and wrecks from the Mississippi, and designed the "impossible" Eades Bridge, which spans the river at St. Louis.

Panger, Daniel. **Ol' Prophet Nat.** Blair 1967.

The life story of Nat Turner, leader of a slave uprising almost thirty years before the Civil War.

Pappas, Martha R., editor. **Heroes of the American West.** Scribner 1969.

A collection of twenty-nine biographical sketches, tales, letters, and ballads of the men and women in nineteenth-century Western America who helped build a nation from the stuff of dreams.

Pilat, Oliver. **Drew Pearson: An Unauthorized Biography.** PB 1973.

A candid profile of one of America's most controversial journalists. Mature.

Radin, Paul, editor. **The Autobiography of a Winnebago Indian.** Dover 1920.

S. B. tells of his youth, education, marriage, hunting, jail, drinking, peyote, and visions.

Red Fox, Chief William (editor Cash Asher). **The Memoirs of Chief Red Fox.** Fawcett World 1970.

Parts of this book were plagiarized, but it is nevertheless an insightful autobiography of Crazy Horses's nephew who survived the Battle of the Little Big Horn.

Sanderlin, Owenita. **Johnny.** Pyramid Pubns 1968.

A mother tells about her son, a chess and tennis player, good student and amateur journalist, who contracts leukemia when he is only sixteen.

Sandoz, Mari. **Crazy Horse: The Strange Man of the Oglalas** (© 1942). U of Nebr Pr 1961.

The legendary Sioux chief from his boyhood in the 1840s through his battles with other Indian tribes and then against white soldiers, culminating at the Rosebud and then the Little Big Horn.

Saroyan, William. **Places Where I've Done Time** (© 1972). Dell 1973.

Autobiography of the Armenian-American author traces some of his most humorous and most serious experiences.

Scott, Lalla. **Karnee: A Paiute Narrative** (© 1966). Fawcett World 1973.

Annie Lowry, a half-blood, rejected her white heritage and chose to live with her Paiute people near Lovelock, Nevada. She tells of her mother's hard life as well as hers, trying to live above the cruelties of two cultures.

Sherman, Diane. **The Boy from Abilene: The Story of Dwight D. Eisenhower.** Westminster 1968.

This book traces the life of Dwight David "Ike" Eisenhower from his boyhood days in Abilene, Kansas.

Stalvey, Lois Mark. **The Education of a WASP** (© 1970). Bantam 1971.

The author believes America is basically a racist country, and in her autobiography she candidly relates her experiences as a WASP who comes face to face with this dilemma. Mature.

Standing Bear, Luther (editor E. A. Brininstool). **My People the Sioux** (© 1928). U of Nebr Pr 1975.

Luther Standing Bear tells of his Sioux boyhood, how he entered the white world, became a teacher and a rancher, toured Europe with Buffalo Bill, but never lost his identification with his Lakota heritage.

Steiner, Nancy Hunter. **A Closer Look at Ariel.** Popular Lib 1973.

A personal account of crucial years in the life of Sylvia

Plath, the tragic young poetess and author of *The Bell Jar,* as told by her former college roommate.

Sullivan, Tom (with Derek Gill). **If You Could See What I Hear.** Har-Row 1975.

Blind since birth, Tom Sullivan has become an athlete, composer, TV personality, husband, and father.

Thrapp, Dan L. **Victorio and the Mimbres Apaches.** U of Okla Pr 1974.

The guerrilla fighter Victorio is less well known than Geronimo and Cochise, but he was an important Apache warrior.

Vecsey, George. **One Sunset a Week.** Sat Rev Pr 1974.

A *New York Times* reporter recounts seven consecutive days in the life of coal miner Dan Sizemore and the economic system which chains him and his family to the Appalachia mines.

Wechsler, James A. (with Nancy F. Wechsler and Holly W. Karpf). **In a Darkness.** Norton 1972.

Despite a loving family and a secure home, the author's son killed himself when he was twenty-six. He had suffered for ten years from schizophrenia.

Wicker, Tom. **Kennedy without Tears: The Man Beneath the Myth.** Morrow 1964.

John F. Kennedy "as he really was" by a former White House reporter.

Wilson, Dorothy Clarke. **Bright Eyes: The Story of Susette la Flesche, An Omaha Indian.** McGraw 1974.

The daughter of an Omaha chief in the mid-1800s, educated in Eastern white schools and without political skills or experience, sought justice for the Omahas and Poncas in public meetings and before the U.S. Senate.

Wilson, Ellen. **They Named Me Gertrude Stein.** FS&G 1973.

Gertrude Stein from her childhood through her career as a writer and philosopher. Includes accounts of people who directly influenced her—Ernest Hemingway, her two brothers, Matisse and Picasso, Juan Gris, and Alice B. Toklas.

CAREERS

Arnold, Arnold. **Career Choices for the '70s.** CCPr Macmillan 1971.

Arnold bases practical advice on the premise that it is wiser for one to make a vocational commitment and to pursue answers to questions about that vocation. Contains chapters directed to minorities and girls and numerous lists of free or inexpensive sources of information.

Barth, George Francis. **Your Aptitudes—You Do Best What You Are Best Fitted to Do.** Lothrop 1974.

Do you like paperwork? Can you think in three dimensions? Do you enjoy solving puzzles? Such aptitudes may help to determine a career in which you can find satisfaction.

Berger, Gilda. **Jobs That Help the Consumer and Homemaker.** Lothrop 1974.

Careers in social work, fashion design, home health care, product design, and home economics.

Berger, Melvin. **Jobs in Fine Arts and Humanities.** Lothrop 1974.

Careers in acting, painting, writing, dance, and music, including behind-the-scenes jobs in those fields.

Biegeleisen, Jacob I. **Careers and Opportunities in Teaching.** Dutton 1969.

An experienced teacher offers detailed information and advice on teaching positions of all types, from kindergartens through colleges and universities.

Brown, Judy, and Donald Grossfield. **I Wish I'd Known That Before I Went to College.** S&S 1966.

Things students wish they had been told before they made the big switch to college—college choices, study skills, academic and social life, finances—are assembled here to benefit younger brothers and sisters.

Burt, Jesse, and Robert Ferguson. **So You Want to Be in Music!** Abingdon 1970.

Information vital to a professional in popular song-writing and recording: what it takes to be a pro; how songs are selected for recording; copyright procedures; roles of sidemen, producers, and engineers; royalties and other profits.

Colby, Jean Poindexter. **Building Wrecking.** Hastings 1972.

Tells why and how buildings are reduced to rubble by wrecking balls or bulldozers, and describes the variety of careers in the industry.

Coleman, Ken. **So You Want to Be a Sportscaster: The Life, Times and Lessons of a Sports Announcer.** Hawthorn 1973.

A twenty-five year veteran of radio and TV sports announcing, Coleman suggests how young people might enter the field and sprinkles his advice with anecdotes recalling his associations with sports heroes.

Corwen, Leonard. **Your Future in Publishing.** Arco 1973.

Describes careers in several aspects of the publication of magazines, books, newspapers, and house organs, including editorial, art, production, advertising, and circulation careers.

Coyne, John, and Tom Hebert. **This Way Out.** Dutton 1972.

An informal guide to alternatives to traditional college education—independent study, experimental colleges, and foreign study programs.

Criner, Beatrice, and Calvin Criner. **Jobs in Personal Services.** Lothrop 1974.

Reviews personal services careers open to young people with a high school or technical school education and on-the-job training—interior designer, plumber, florist, caterer, travel agent, and others.

Criner, Beatrice, and Calvin Criner. **Jobs in Public Service.** Lothrop 1974.

Short sketches on careers whose workers are paid by government taxes: teachers, police officers, foresters, child welfare workers, and customs officials.

Darby, Patricia, and Ray Darby. **Your Career in Physical Therapy.** Messner 1969.

Heat, cold, ultraviolet light—three of the physical

therapist's most important tools. Learning how to use such tools with skill and compassion is the subject of this collection of personal experiences and factual information.

de Mille, Agnes. **To a Young Dancer.** Little 1962.

One of America's greatest dancers guides the movement of prospective dancers from their first ballet lessons to their performance as professionals.

Dobrin, Arnold. **Jobs in Recreation.** Lothrop 1974.

Emphasizes jobs in park and recreation departments and in our national parks, and hospitality careers in restaurants and hotels.

Dodd, Ed. **Careers for the '70s: Conservation.** CCPr Macmillan 1971.

The creator of the conservation comic strip "Mark Trail" outlines careers in forestry, wildlife, national parks, fish, and soil conservation. Includes sources of summer employment and a directory of colleges offering courses in conservation. (See also Virginia McCall and Joseph R. McCall, editors, *Your Career in Parks and Recreation,* Messner.)

Dowdell, Dorothy, and Joseph Dowdell. **Your Career in the World of Travel.** Messner 1971.

Information on career fields that have direct contact with the touring public: travel agencies, car rental, sightseeing, airline stewardess, airline sales, tour operation, and hotel/motel management.

Duckat, Walter. **A Guide to Professional Careers.** Messner 1970.

Detailed information on seventy-seven professional careers: duties, income, and training; and lists of jobs with the federal government based on various college majors.

Englebardt, Stanley N. **Jobs in Health Care.** Lothrop 1973.

Lab technicians, nurses, nurses' aides, medical secretaries, and administrative personnel describe their duties. Also includes information about medical health associates, jobs in dentistry, physical therapy, pharmacy, and optometry.

Evers, Dora R., and S. Norman Feingold. **Your Future in Exotic Occupations.** Rosen Pr 1972.

Auctioneer, diamond cutter, treasure hunter, dance therapist, tunnel worker—some of the thirty occupations described here.

Gammage, Allen Z. **Your Future in Law Enforcement.** Rosen Pr 1974.

Detailed descriptions of the jobs of patrol officer and other aspects of law enforcement, including general investigation work, criminalistics, vice control, and work with juveniles. Includes a self-evaluation test.

Gay, Kathlyn. **Careers in Social Service.** Messner 1969.

Educational requirements, special skills, and desirable personality traits and attitudes are necessary for serving others through social services administered by government agencies, church institutions, and private foundations.

Goldstein, Kenneth K. **New Frontiers of Medicine.** Little 1974.

Computerized medical histories, plastic and metal body part replacements, genetic manipulation, drug-induced brain activity—all are aspects of the new frontiers of medicine which demand thoughtful consideration and responsible action. Somewhat technical, but of special interest to prospective doctors. Mature.

Gray, Genevieve. **Jobs in Transportation.** Lothrop 1973.

Transportation offers a wide variety of careers: tugboat hands, flight engineers, mechanics, bus drivers, and train dispatchers. Many illustrations. (See also Robert A. Liston, *Your Career in Transportation,* Messner.)

Grumich, Charles A., editor. **Reporting—Writing from Front Row Seats.** S&S 1971.

Twenty-five Associated Press writers describe their jobs and reporting specialties, including religion, wars, Hollywood, and sports.

Gummere, Richard M., Jr. **How to Survive Education: Before, During and After College.** HarBraceJ 1971.

Answers common questions about admissions routines, dormitory rules, and curricula, and also deals with more important concerns such as college life today, the grading systems, the agonies of career search, and the chances for survival.

Haskins, James. **Jobs in Business and Office.** Lothrop 1974.

Accounts of six people and their jobs: an office machine operator, a secretary, a computer programmer, a personnel manager, an owner of a day care center, and an owner of a record store. (See also I. J. Seligsohn, *Your Career in Computer Programming,* Messner.)

Henle, Fay. **Careers for the '70s: Securities.** CCPr Macmillan 1972.

A private company or branch of the government seeking new money requires the skills of increasing numbers of people in sales, research, trading, and operations. Glossary describes nearly fifty securities-related careers.

Houlehen, Robert J. **Jobs in Agribusiness.** Lothrop 1974.

One out of every five jobs is in the food industry. Jobs described here include raising crops, running a tree nursery, caring for sick animals, and selling seed or tractors. (See also J. J. McCoy, *To Feed a Nation: Farming in America,* Nelson.)

Jackson, Gregory. **Getting into Broadcast Journalism: A Guide to Careers in Radio and TV.** Hawthorn 1974.

A veteran news correspondent for ABC-TV addresses young people, especially women and minority group members, who think they might like a career in radio and television news but don't know how to get started. (See also John R. Rider, *Your Future in Broadcasting,* Arco.)

Jackson, Jacqueline. **Turn Not Pale, Beloved Snail.** Little 1974.

Advice to young writers from the author of ten books for young people.

Jessup, Claudia, and Genie Chipps. **Supergirls.** Har-Row 1972.

Personal services business begun by two young women with $900 capital started with walking dogs and stuffing mailboxes. Now they plan promotional campaigns and develop marketing ideas.

Johnson, George. **Your Career in Advertising.** Messner 1966.

Johnson describes a typical advertising agency and the jobs of those who make it tick: copy writer, artist, sales person, and market researcher.

Joseph, James. **Careers Outdoors.** Nelson 1969.

Over 100 usual and unusual outdoor jobs which pay well, some of them very well.

Kesselman, Judi R. **Stopping Out: A Guide to Leaving College and Getting Back In.** M Evans 1976.

The matters to be considered in the frequently difficult decision to leave college are spelled out by the author, as are the work and study alternatives once the decision is made.

Kolodny, Rosalie. **Fashion Design for Moderns.** Fairchild 1968.

The work of a fashion designer and the building of a designer's collection from its inspiration to its formal showing.

Lee, Essie E. **Careers in the Health Field.** Messner 1974.

Of every hundred health workers, only nine are physicians. This is a narrative survey of the kinds of work which the other 93 percent perform, some of which require relatively short training periods.

Lembeck, Ruth. **Teenage Jobs.** Dell 1971.

Hundreds of job suggestions for ages twelve to twenty, based on real experiences of young workers: animals, writing, science, and so on.

Liebers, Arthur. **Jobs in Construction.** Lothrop 1973.

Describes some careers in construction which can begin right after high school, others which require college training: steel worker, bricklayer, carpenter, engineer, architect, purchasing agent, draftsperson.

Liston, Robert A. **On the Job Training and Where to Get It.** Messner 1973.

Aimed at the high school graduate who cannot go to

college, this book emphasizes the skills in greatest demand in a technological society.

Liston, Robert A. **Your Career in Law Enforcement.** Messner 1973.

Because a serious crime occurs in the United States every five seconds, law enforcement officers are in great demand. Relevant to those interested in careers as F.B.I. and treasury agents, state patrol, county, and local officers.

Liston, Robert A. **Your Career in Selling.** Messner 1967.

Offers advice concerning sales careers in such diverse fields as real estate, securities, automobiles, industrial and business equipment, insurance, and retail sales.

MacCloskey, Monro. **Your Future in the Military Services.** Rosen Pr 1974.

Careers in the all-volunteer services suit a wide range of interests and skills and offer attractive benefits, including excellent pay and educational opportunities.

McCoy, J. J. **The World of the Veterinarian.** Lothrop 1964.

The evolution of veterinary medicine and planning a career in the field.

McDonnell, Virginia B. **Careers in Hotel Management.** Messner 1971.

Hotels and motels are miniature cities which demand imaginative control and thus offer a growing number of career opportunities in management. College list.

McGonagle, Robert, and Marquita McGonagle. **Prepare for a Career in Radio and Television Announcing.** Lothrop 1974.

Two experienced broadcasters share their practical knowledge with prospective announcers. Includes practice scripts and college list.

McLeod, Sterling, and Science Book Associates Editors. **Careers in Consumer Protection.** Messner 1974.

After demonstrating the need for increased consumer protection, McLeod describes careers in consumer education, inspection, and law enforcement; and science, engineering, and noncollege careers in consumer protection.

Millard, Reed, and Science Book Associates Editors. **Careers in Environmental Protection.** Messner 1974.

The Environmental Protection Agency predicts that the need for environmental professionals will triple by 1980. There will be challenging jobs in ecology, the physical and environmental sciences, and in agricultural, chemical, and civil engineering.

Myers, Arthur. **Careers for the '70s: Journalism.** CCPr Macmillan 1971.

Journalist Myers describes the varieties of education available to would-be journalists and tells how students can get valuable experience in high school.

Norton, Joseph L. **On the Job.** Doubleday 1971.

Sixty-five people tell what their jobs are like. A wide range of careers is included, among them legal secretary, dress shop owner, airline ticket salesman, plumber, and architect.

Oakes, Vanya. **Challenging Careers in the Library World.** Messner 1970.

A librarian describes career opportunities in public and school libraries. List of library schools accredited by the American Library Association.

Richter, Edward. **The Making of a Pilot.** Westminster 1966.

What it feels like to fly a plane, what it takes to be a private, commercial, or military pilot. (See also Dick O'Kane, *Making of an Aircraft Mechanic,* Westminster; and Ross R. Olney, *Air Traffic Control,* Nelson.)

Ross, Frank, Jr. **Jobs in Marine Science.** Lothrop 1974.

Many kinds of oceanographers band together to explore, study, and understand the mysteries of the marine world. Some are specialists in physics, biology, or chemistry, while others are marine engineers or technicians.

Rusk, Howard A. **A World to Care For.** Readers Digest Pr 1972.

The success of his rehabilitation program for war-damaged men led Dr. Howard Rusk to establish the Institute of Rehabilitation Medicine (New York University Medical Center), which serves physically disabled patients from all over the world.

Sandman, Peter M., and Dan Goldenson. **The Unabashed Career Guide.** Macmillan 1969.

What it's really like to be an ad person, a banker, a lawyer, or a teacher. Takes you through typical days, explodes illusions, and issues warnings.

Sarnoff, Paul. **Careers in the Legal Profession.** Messner 1970.

Descriptions of specializations within the legal profession, information on qualifications for the various fields, lists of law schools, and advice on state bar exams and the young lawyer's first professional steps.

Searight, Mary. **Your Career in Nursing.** Messner 1970.

Describes the scope of modern nursing, explains the training and personal qualities required, and lists scholarship sources. Also, what the future holds for nurses in an age of outer space and ocean exploration.

Seide, Diane. **Careers in Medical Science.** Nelson 1973.

Describes more than fifty careers in the medical field, including nursing, psychiatric social worker, speech therapist, dental hygienist, optometrist, and medical doctor. Includes health career self-evaluation test.

Spencer, Lila. **Exciting Careers for Home Economists.** Messner 1967.

Trained home economists may work in many specialized fields: textiles, food, fashion, writing, art, chemistry, teaching, and radio-TV. The author emphasizes practical experience in addition to formal training. Bibliography and college lists.

Splaver, Sarah. **Nontraditional Careers for Women.** Messner 1973.

Brief descriptions of more than 500 nontraditional occupations now open to women in law, medicine, the helping professions, science and math, engineering,

the creative arts, business, manual trades, and government services.

Splaver, Sarah. **Paraprofessions.** Messner 1972.

Paraprofessionals assist full-fledged professionals in
numerous fields: law, architecture, education, medicine, library science, engineering, and science. Their
education is not as lengthy and demanding as that of
the professional, but they share the same sense of
service and satisfaction.

Splaver, Sarah. **Your Career if You're Not Going to
College.** Messner 1971.

Assists high school graduates in assessing their interests and capabilities, in matching their qualifications
with those required for hundreds of jobs described in
the book, and in choosing jobs in which they can find
success and gain advancement. Bibliographies.

Stein, M. L. **Blacks in Communications.** Messner 1972.

Opportunities for blacks in journalism are increasing
and should continue to grow during the next few years.
In addition to historical information, Stein offers short
sketches on dozens of black Americans currently active
in all aspects of journalism.

Terry, Walter. **Careers for the '70s: Dance.** CCPr Macmillan 1971.

A dancer and critic offers advice to young men and
women who want onstage or behind-the-scenes careers
in dance. Includes a chapter on special problems and
opportunities of the male dancer.

Turner, S. E. **So Who's Afraid of a Polygraph Test?**
Naylor 1974.

What happens when a prospective employer wants to
give you a polygraph (lie detector) test before hiring
you? It is a growing practice—and many people panic
because they do not understand the machine or the
test.

Wakin, Edward. **Jobs in Communications.** Lothrop 1974.

Brief descriptions of the wide range of careers in television, radio, public relations, advertising, magazine
and newspaper publishing, and movies.

I AM WOMAN

Alexander, Shana. **A State-by-State Guide to Women's Legal Rights.** Wollstonecraft 1975.

Reports across the United States about the legal rights of women in marriage, in having or adopting children, in divorce, in employment, and other areas. Nonfiction.

Babcox, Deborah, and Madeline Belkin, editors. **Liberation Now!** Dell 1971.

An anthology of articles about the women's liberation movement and what led to it, discrimination against women in jobs, the role of modern woman and the family, and the cultural identity of women. Mature nonfiction.

Bacon, Margaret Hope. **I Speak for My Slave Sister: The Life of Abbey Kelley Foster.** T Y Crowell 1974.

One of the first to see parallels between the role of women and that of slaves in nineteenth-century America, Abbey Kelley Foster fought the conservative and the overcautious in helping to clear the path for the abolition of slavery and universal suffrage. Nonfiction.

Baez, Joan. **Daybreak.** Dial 1968.

Joan Baez takes the reader into the days of her childhood, her antiwar protest, and her music. She writes with feeling about her parents, her friends, and her dreams. Nonfiction.

Barker, Mildred. **Women.** Eakins 1972.

A collection of stories by nine authors about women, young and old, affluent and poor, who are often trapped by the harsh circumstances of their lives, but sometimes see their way through them. Includes a photo essay. Fiction.

Bird, Caroline. **Born Female** (© 1970). PB 1974.

Discussing the subject of prejudice against women, the author supplies information about the occupational advancement possibilities, changing roles, and new feminism in the women's movement. Nonfiction.

Bolton, Carole. **Never Jam Today.** Aladdin 1971.

A high school girl becomes a Suffragist and makes her own decisions. Fiction.

Brownmiller, Susan. **Against Our Will: Men, Women and Rape.** S&S 1975.

A study of rape as a method used historically by men to keep women in a perpetual state of fear and subjugation. The author argues that rape is intertwined with racism and war and the cult of violence. Mature nonfiction.

Burt, Olive W. **First Woman Editor: Sarah J. Hale.** Messner 1960.

The biography of a woman who fought for women's rights at a time when women were considered good for nothing but bearing children, sewing, knitting, and housecleaning. Sarah J. Hale overcame many obstacles, including the death of her husband and having to raise their five children alone. Nonfiction.

Cade, Toni, editor. **The Black Women: An Anthology** (© 1970). NAL 1974.

Black women's voices in poetry and essays, talking about life as they see it, sometimes with love, sometimes with anger. The language is colorful and expressive. Mature.

Cahill, Susan, editor. **Women and Fiction.** NAL 1975.

Twenty-six stories about women growing up, playing roles men seem to expect women to play, and being what they want to be, by writers Carson McCullers, Joyce Carol Oates, Doris Lessing, and others. Fiction.

Canning, Victor. **The Finger of Saturn.** Morrow 1974.

Robert Rolt's wife, Sarah, suddenly disappears from a seemingly comfortable marriage. Two years later she is found, unable to recall why she left home or any of the events of her previous life. Fiction.

Carlson, Dale. **Girls Are Equal Too.** Atheneum 1973.

An explanation of the whys and hows of the women's liberation movement. The introduction concludes, "Tired of being inferior? Read on." The text illuminates the problems that women encounter and offers suggestions on how to solve them. Nonfiction.

Carson, Josephine. **Silent Voices: The Southern Negro Woman Today.** Delacorte 1969.

The author believes that black women have been

forced into silence both because they are black and because they are women. The book is a result of many interviews with women from all walks of life: a woman in charge of adult literacy, a housewife, and a chairperson of a college English department. Nonfiction.

Chamberlin, Hope. **A Minority of Members: Women in the U.S. Congress.** Praeger 1973.

Brief biographies of eighty-five women representatives and senators from 1917, when Montana voters elected Jeannette Rankin to the House of Representatives, to the contemporary scene. Nonfiction.

Chesler, Phyllis. **Women and Madness.** Doubleday 1972.

Chesler shows how psychiatry forces women to behave in certain "acceptable" ways. Those who break the norms by independent behavior are often viewed as mentally ill. She discusses the treatment women receive in mental asylums and cites the case histories of Sylvia Plath and Zelda Fitzgerald, among others. Nonfiction.

Chester, Laura, and Sharon Barba, editors. **Rising Tides: Twentieth-Century American Women Poets.** WSP 1973.

Selections from seventy women poets, ranging across the years from Gertrude Stein to Erica Jong.

Chopin, Kate. **The Awakening.** Cap Putnam 1964.

Living in New Orleans around 1900, a mother of two becomes painfully aware that her artistic and sexual needs are not being filled. She tries to forget her problems on a family vacation, but the sea surrounding them only reminds her of how all-enclosing Victorian society is. Fiction.

Clarke, Mary Stetson. **Bloomers and Ballots: Elizabeth Cady Stanton and Women's Rights.** Viking Pr 1972.

Best known for her work with Susan B. Anthony and the women's suffrage movement, Elizabeth Stanton had actually broken ground much earlier when she urged passage, in 1848, of a bill allowing married women the right to own property. Nonfiction.

Cooke, Joanne, Charlotte Bunch-Weeks, and Robin Morgan, editors. **The New Women** (© 1970). Fawcett World 1973.

This anthology of women's liberation writings discusses

the role of women in today's society and what can be predicted as their roles in the future. It contains selections from the writings of Diane Di Prima, Jean Tepperman, Marlene Dixon, and others. Nonfiction.

Dizenzo, Patricia. **An American Girl.** HR&W 1971.

The fictional diary of a Hackensack high school girl in the 1950s. Problems at home—an alcoholic mother, a bad-tempered father—are set against the backdrop of cheerleading tryouts and homework. Fiction.

Dobrin, Arnold. **A Life for Israel: The Story of Golda Meir.** Dial 1974.

After a lifetime of service to Israel, Ambassador Meir retired in 1966. Soon she was recruited to head the Israeli Labor Party and three years later became her country's first female prime minister. Nonfiction.

Epstein, Cynthia Fuchs. **Woman's Place.** U of Cal Pr 1970.

A study of the sociology, psychology, and economics of women at work. Mature nonfiction.

Forfreedom, Ann, editor. **Women Out of History: A Herstory Anthology.** Ann Forfreedom 1975.

"Her"-storical perspective from the Amazons to the Redstockings (a 1960s radical women's group). Some sections for mature readers only. Nonfiction.

Gerson, Noel B. **Because I Loved Him: The Life and Loves of Lillie Langtry.** Morrow 1971.

Born in 1853, Lillie Langtry became the toast of London society and the darling of the American stage. Nonfiction.

Gilman, Charlotte Perkins. **The Yellow Wallpaper.** Feminist Pr 1973.

A semi-autobiographical short story from the late 1800s that accurately depicts the psychological breakdown of a proper Victorian woman. Fiction.

Giovanni, Nikki. **ego-tripping.** Lawrence Hill 1973.

Poems from this immediate, fresh poet selected especially for junior high and high school students.

Greer, Germaine. **The Female Eunuch** (© 1971). Bantam 1972.

With acid wit and personal experience, Greer analyzes the conflict between what society expects women to be and what women need to be fulfilled. Nonfiction.

Griffin, Susan. **The Sink.** Shameless Hussy Pr 1974.

Six short stories, including the title story about a housewife whose life has come to a mad night vigil under her kitchen sink and another which presents a portrait of lesbian love. Mature fiction.

Grimstad, Kirsten, and Susan Rennie, editors. **The New Woman's Survival Catalog.** Berkley Pub 1973.

Like the *Whole Earth Catalog,* this woman's reference book is printed on newsprint and consists of ads and resources focused on the needs of modern women. The products and services offered are all by women. Nonfiction.

Gurko, Miriam. **The Ladies of Seneca Falls.** Macmillan 1974.

The first group of feminists joined together in 1848 to work for women's rights. The book describes those early contributors, among them Susan B. Anthony, the Grimke sisters, and Amelia Bloomer. Nonfiction.

Hahn, Emily. **Once upon a Pedestal.** T Y Crowell 1974.

The struggle of American women to leave the pedestal men had placed them on and to gain freedom and self-respect is chronicled by the author. She covers almost everything from the pioneer woman to the women's liberation movement. Nonfiction.

Hall, Nancy Lee. **A True Story of a Drunken Mother.** Daughters 1974.

A book for high school students with some frank language and some real incidents. Nonfiction.

Haney, Lynn. **The Lady Is a Jock.** Dodd 1973.

The author traveled the country interviewing women jockeys. She found out how they started horseracing, what they like and dislike about their lives, and where they see their careers heading. Nonfiction.

Hardwick, Elizabeth. **Seduction and Betrayal.** Random 1974.

This study of women in literature includes Ibsen heroines, the Brontes, Sylvia Plath, and Zelda Fitzgerald. Nonfiction.

Heyman, Abigail. **Growing Up Female.** HR&W 1974.

A very personal essay about the author and what it means to grow up as a woman but not quite as a human being. Photographs and diary entries document the state of being a woman today. Some photographs may offend some people. Mature nonfiction.

Hogrefe, Pearl. **Tudor Women: Commoners and Queens.** Iowa St U Pr 1976.

The Tudor women whose lives Hogrefe traces circumvented English legal and social restrictions of their times (1485–1600) to lead full lives in commercial, political, or intellectual pursuits. Nonfiction.

Holland, Cecelia. **Great Maria.** Knopf 1974.

A tapestry from the eleventh century comes to life in the story of Maria. Maria's marriage to the brother of the man she loves is a convenience for her lover but brings her little happiness. Fiction.

James, Edward T., Janet Wilson James, and Paul S. Boyer, editors. **Notable American Women: A Biographical Dictionary,** 3 vols. Harvard U Pr 1971.

Short biographies of hundreds of American women from 1607 to 1950. Except for the wives of presidents, women cited are all well known in their own right. Nonfiction.

Janeway, Elizabeth. **Between Myth and Morning: Women Awakening.** Morrow 1974.

The history and background of the women's movement serves as an introduction to a discussion of the practical problems and potential of women today and the careers and services women now have open to them. Mature nonfiction.

Josephson, Hannah. **Jeannette Rankin: First Lady in Congress.** Bobbs 1974.

Jeannette Rankin was the first woman elected to the United States Congress. A leading feminist at all times, she was likely even better known as the only member of Congress to vote against America's entry into either World War. Nonfiction.

Kane, Paula, and Christopher Chandler. **Sex Objects in the Sky.** Follett 1974.

The life and training of the stewardess and an attack on the profession pointing up the subservient and demeaning nature of the job. Eighty percent of the training is devoted to beauty and only twenty percent to the safety procedures necessary in an aircraft. Nonfiction.

Katz, Naomi, and Nancy Milton, editors. **Fragment from a Lost Diary and Other Stories: Women of Asia, Africa, and Latin America.** Pantheon 1973.

A collection of short stories by women from Asia, Africa, and Latin America, each story illustrating a woman trying to find herself and a valid role in her society. Mature fiction.

Key, Mary Ritchie. **Male/Female Language.** Scarecrow 1975.

A source book of sociolinguistics: the study of how language shapes society, and vice-versa. Excellent bibliography and index. Nonfiction.

King, Billie Jean (with Kim Chapin). **Billie Jean.** PB 1974.

Billie Jean King, champion tennis player, tells about her struggle to become a champion athlete and her wish to become involved in the women's rights movement. Nonfiction.

Klägsbuen, Francine, editor. **The First Ms. Reader.** Paperback Lib 1973.

A collection of articles from *Ms.* magazine. Explains the meaning behind the rhetoric of the women's liberation movement: sexism, feminism, consciousness-raising sessions, and other topics. Nonfiction.

Knudson, R. R. **Zanballer** (© 1972). Dell 1974.

Suzanne Hagen (she prefers the name Zanballer) loves sports. Even worse for her principal, she believes girls have a right to play team sports. She becomes a thorn in her school's side until girls are given

a time and place to play football before an audience.
Fiction.

Lader, Lawrence, and Milton Meltzer. **Margaret Sanger:
Pioneer of Birth Control** (© 1969). Dell 1974.

As a young woman, Sanger discovered how horrifying life was for the poor who were unable to find
ways to control the size of their families. She devoted her life to educating the world about the necessity of family planning. Nonfiction.

Levin, Ira. **The Stepford Wives.** Random 1972.

Women become domestic drones after moving to a quiet
suburban community known as Stepford. Fiction.

Lichtenstein, Grace. **A Long Way Baby: Behind the
Scenes in Women's Pro Tennis.** Morrow 1974.

Until recently, women pro tennis players were not as
well paid as men players and their matches were not
as well attended. With the coming of women players
like Billie Jean King, Francoise Durr, Margaret Court,
Chris Evert, and Evonne Goolagong, changes took place
slowly so that most spectators now agree that women's
tennis is as exciting as men's play. Nonfiction.

Lutzker, Edythe. **Women Gain a Place in Medicine.**
McGraw 1969.

The story of five young women who fought against the
medical practice of the Victorian age to become doctors.
Nonfiction.

Mackenzie, Midge. **Shoulder to Shoulder.** Knopf 1975.

A documentary about British Suffragettes from 1903 to
1918 centering on Emmeline Pankhurst and her two
daughters and using speeches, newspaper articles, photographs, and letters to illustrate the struggle and pain
and final victory. Nonfiction.

Mackey, Mary. **Split Ends.** Ariel 1974.

Poems by a rising young feminist who speaks of both
youthful and adult female experience.

Manley, Seon, and Susan Belcher. **O, Those Extraordinary Women! or The Joys of Literary Lib.** Chilton
1972.

The lives and writings of women authors from Mary

Wollstonecraft and her *Vindication of the Rights of Women* to modern writers like Virginia Woolf and Dorothy Parker. Nonfiction.

Medea, Andra, and Kathleen Thompson. **Against Rape.** FS&G 1974.

The authors discuss the frequency and causes of rape, how to avoid entrapment, and how to cope with rape physically and emotionally. Nonfiction.

Meigs, Cornelia. **Jane Addams: Pioneer for Social Justice.** Little 1970.

In 1889 Jane Addams established a settlement house in one of Chicago's teeming immigrant districts "to respond to the immediate primitive needs of the community." She became an important force in fighting for improved social conditions in an era prior to labor laws. Nonfiction.

Milford, Nancy. **Zelda: A Biography.** Har-Row 1970.

The life story of Zelda Fitzgerald details her marriage to F. Scott, their reckless life style, and her later breakdown and confinement in a sanitarium. Fond of outrageous stunts and discouraged from pursuing her artistic ambitions, she was unable to assert her own identity apart from her husband. Nonfiction.

Moffat, Mary Jane, and Charlotte Painter, editors. **Revelations: Diaries of Women.** Random 1974.

Thirty-three women share their thoughts and feelings through excerpts from their diaries. Divided into three sections, "Love," "Work," and "Power," the book includes the words of women like Anais Nin, Anna Dostoevsky, Anne Frank, Louisa May Alcott, Sylvia Ashton-Warner, George Eliot, and others. Nonfiction.

Montagu, Ashley. **The Natural Superiority of Women.** Macmillan 1968.

An anthropologist asserts that women are superior to men physically, psychologically, and socially. He argues that this knowledge has been available for years, but a male-dominated culture and a female submissiveness to the male ego have maintained the myth of male superiority. Mature nonfiction.

Morgan, Robin, editor. **Sisterhood Is Powerful.** Vin-Random 1970.

An anthology of writings from the women's liberation movement: articles, poems, and photographs about birth control, television, high school, college, careers, law, and medicine. Mature.

Mortimer, Penelope. **The Pumpkin Eater** (© 1962). Daughters 1975.

Adrift in her fourth marriage, surrounded by her numerous children, the heroine is still trying to figure out how all her adolescent dreams got away from her. Mature fiction.

Myers, Elizabeth P. **Madam Secretary: Frances Perkins.** Messner 1972.

Secretary of labor under Franklin Roosevelt in the 1930s and 1940s, Frances Perkins is a model for the current women's movement because of her ability and willingness to act when the times demanded it. Nonfiction.

Orloff, Katherine. **Rock 'n Roll Woman.** Nash 1974.

A collection of interviews with twelve women who make their living in rock and roll. A range of performers from vocalist Grace Slick to electric guitarist Alice Stuart answer questions about the women's movement and the music industry. Nonfiction.

Perl, Lila. **That Crazy April.** Seabury 1974.

Cress Richardson, age eleven, is forced to examine questions such as the importance of a college degree versus marriage, or about girls engaging in "masculine" activities. Fiction.

Plath, Sylvia. **The Bell Jar.** Har-Row 1971.

Twenty-year-old Esther Greenwood goes to New York to serve on a fashion magazine's editorial board. The hectic and hollow tone of her stay there captures for women the adolescent experience that Holden Caulfield, in *Catcher in the Rye,* captures so well for men. Fiction.

Price, Reynolds. **A Long and Happy Life** (© 1961). Avon 1973.

Rosacoke, a young woman, works at a tedious job in

North Carolina while waiting for Wesley to decide to settle down, but he is more interested in fast motorcycles and women. Mature fiction.

Ross, Pat. **Young and Female.** VinRandom 1972.

Eight women describe the turning point in their lives, the time each decided upon a career to pursue. The list includes Shirley MacLaine, Shirley Chisholm, Emily Hahn, Margaret Sanger, Althea Gibson, Edna Ferber, Dorothy Day, and Margaret Bourke-White. Nonfiction.

Rossi, Alice S., editor. **The Feminist Papers** (© 1973). Bantam 1974.

Ideas by and about women concerning education, freedom, sex, equality, politics, and the law, among other things. Mature nonfiction.

Sanders, Marion K. **Dorothy Thompson: A Legend in Her Time.** HM 1973.

Dorothy Thompson was called "The First Lady of American Journalism." She traveled widely in Europe during the 1920s, knew almost anybody of political importance, and was a highly influential reporter before and after World War II. Mature nonfiction.

Sayre, Anne. **Rosalind Franklin and DNA.** Norton 1975.

One of four scientists to work on the molecular structure of DNA (the key to heredity), she was never given credit for her work. Her contributions were downgraded by male scientists apparently unable to accept a woman as an equal. Nonfiction.

Schneir, Miriam, editor. **Feminism.** VinRandom 1971.

A historical collection of writings by and about women, their rights, their self-images, their responsibilities, their freedoms, and their social roles from the eighteenth century until today. Mature nonfiction.

Schulman, L. M., editor. **A Woman's Place.** Macmillan 1974.

A collection of stories written by women, each struggling to be master of herself and her destiny. Katherine Mansfield, Jessamyn West, and eight other authors. Fiction.

Seed, Suzanne. **Saturday's Child** (© 1973). Bantam 1974.

Thirty-six women talk about their jobs—vocations as different as painter, sportswriter, musical conductor, biophysicist, pilot, brigadier general, policewoman, bank vice-president, veterinarian, and filmmaker. Nonfiction.

Shulman, Alix Kate. **Memoirs of an Ex-Prom Queen** (© 1972). Bantam 1973.

The adventures of beautiful Sasha Davis, product of the white middle class, as she grows from little girl to twice-married housewife. One woman's search for self and a reflection of the sexist values of society. Fiction.

Smedley, Agnes. **Daughter of Earth.** Feminist Pr 1973.

An autobiography with unique political perspective from an American woman involved in the struggle for India's independence until 1928. Nonfiction.

Spinner, Stephanie, editor. **Feminine Plural.** Macmillan 1972.

A collection of ten gifted writers, including Carson McCullers, Doris Lessing, and Colette, who explore growing up and find it is not always a painless and carefree experience. Fiction.

Stanford, Barbara, editor. **On Being Female.** WSP 1974.

The essays and short stories underscore the inequality of opportunity for women, from nursery school to training for astronauts, from the typist to the prize fighter.

Tanner, Leslie B., editor. **Voices from Women's Liberation.** NAL 1970.

A collection of excerpts from many women crying out for freedom to govern their own destinies, beginning with Abigail Adams in 1776 and ending with Shulamith Firestone in 1970. Nonfiction.

Terrell, John Upton, and Donna M. Terrell. **Indian Women of the Western Morning: Their Life in Early America.** Dial 1974.

The role of Indian women in early American history. Dispelling many myths, the authors examine living conditions, clothing, family life, adornments, sexual rituals and activities, labor, health, and status. Mature nonfiction.

Tharp, Louise Hall. **The Peabody Sisters of Salem** (© 1950). Pyramid Pubns 1968.

Sophia, Mary, and Elizabeth were bright and energetic young women of the nineteenth century. Each was specially talented and each left her own mark on those with whom she came into contact. Nonfiction.

Tolchin, Susan, and Martin Tolchin. **Clout—Womanpower and Politics.** Coward 1974.

Women are getting into politics, often with great success. The authors report on how and why women get into the political arena and some get elected to political office. Nonfiction.

Walker, Greta. **Women Today: Ten Profiles.** Hawthorn 1975.

Ten biographies of women who have fashioned worthwhile careers for themselves in fields as different as medicine and TV and police work. Nonfiction.

Wasserman, Barbara Alson, editor. **The Bold New Women** (© 1966). Fawcett World 1970.

A collection of contemporary writing by twenty-three women journalists, poets, playwrights, and novelists. Writers like Doris Lessing turn inward to the emotional life of love and breakup while journalists like Joan Didion look at women's roles in society.

Weldon, Fay. **Down among the Women** (© 1972). Warner Bks 1974.

Recreating the 1950s with black humor, Weldon tells the story of Wacky Wanda, her daughter, and her friends. Their lives center on troubled relationships with men. Fiction.

Westcott, Jan. **Set Her on a Throne.** Little 1972.

Married to the man who will become Richard III of England, Anne Neville becomes queen when Richard usurps the throne. Fiction.

AMERICAN INDIAN EXPERIENCES

Allen, Terry D., editor. **Arrows Four: Prose and Poetry by Young American Indians.** WSP 1974.

American Indian students from many schools and tribes wrote for this collection of poetry and prose. Some of the students celebrate nature, and many allow the reader to get some understanding of what it means to be an Indian.

Anderson, Susanne (editor David Brower). **Song of the Earth Spirit** (© 1973). Ballantine 1974.

Living with some Navajo families, Susanne Anderson captures on film a lifestyle, customs, and beliefs that are foreign to her. Nonfiction.

Armstrong, Virginia Irving, editor. **I Have Spoken: American History through the Voices of the Indians.** Swallow 1971.

Armstrong's collection of Indian speeches reflects the historical development of this country from the seventeenth century to the 1970s. Indians speak about the heritage of the land, broken treaties, and their hopes for peace and for the future. Nonfiction.

Astrov, Margot, editor. **American Indian Prose and Poetry** (© 1946). Cap Putnam 1962.

A collection of songs, prayers, poems, and stories from many tribes revealing deep belief and feelings about Indians and their relationship with each other, to the earth, and to their maker.

Beal, Merrill D. **"I Will Fight No More Forever": Chief Joseph and the Nez Percé War** (© 1963). Ballantine 1973.

The Nez Percé tribe in Oregon did not fight whites until tribal land was taken. Then Chief Joseph, one of the greatest Indian war chiefs and military generals in history, and his tribe tried to fight their way from Oregon to Canada. Nonfiction.

Belous, Russell E., and Robert A. Weinstein. **Will Soule: Indian Photographer at Fort Sill, Oklahoma, 1869–74.** Ritchie 1968.

A fascinating collection of 100-year-old glass-plate photographs of American Indians of the southern Plains who were then in almost constant battles with the U.S. Army. Interspersed with brief histories of the Kiowa, Comanches, Apaches, and others are short biographies of selected individual Indians. Nonfiction.

Berger, Thomas. **Little Big Man** (© 1964). Fawcett World 1974.

An adopted Indian, the only white survivor of the Battle of the Little Big Horn, tells the story of his life both as a white frontiersman and as a Cheyenne Indian. Fiction.

Bonham, Frank. **Chief** (© 1971). Dell 1973.

With the aid of his wine-guzzling uncle and a kind but crazy lawer, Henry Crowfoot seeks to confirm the authority of an old treaty proving that his impoverished band owns half of downtown Harbor City. Fiction.

Boyd, Doug. **Rolling Thunder.** Random 1974.

Rolling Thunder is a medicine man of the Cherokee and Shoshone Indians. He reveals to the author secrets that have been passed down for centuries and demonstrates that they are not fairy tales but real powers Indians accept. Nonfiction.

Brandon, William. **The American Heritage Book of Indians.** Dell 1961.

A general overview of the history of American Indians—including Eskimos, Mayans, and Aztecs—from prehistory to the beginning of the twentieth century. Mature nonfiction.

Brill, Charles. **Indian and Free: A Contemporary Portrait of Life on a Chippewa Reservation.** U of Minn Pr 1971.

A combination of 160 photographs and brief textual comments presents an unusual portrait of both early and modern life among the Red Lake Band of the Chippewa Indians who live in northern Minnesota. Nonfiction.

Brown, Dee. **Bury My Heart at Wounded Knee: An Indian History of the American West** (© 1971). Bantam 1972.

Dee Brown presents the Indians' side of the "Winning

of the West" during the second half of the nineteenth century, using the words of famous Indians themselves wherever possible. (Some readers might prefer the simplified version of Brown's book adapted by Amy Ehrlich, *Wounded Knee: An Indian History of the American West,* HR&W.) Nonfiction.

Brown, Dee (with Martin F. Schmitt). **Fighting Indians of the West.** Ballantine 1974.

A pictorial description of the battles between white men and Indians like Red Cloud and Sitting Bull of the Sioux, and Black Kettle of the Cheyenne. Nonfiction.

Burt, Jesse, and Robert B. Ferguson. **Indians of the Southeast: Then and Now.** Abingdon 1973.

Less visible and less publicized than the Indians of the Southwest are the tribes of the Southeast—the Cherokees, Choctaws, Seminoles, and other smaller tribes. This book describes—along with numerous photographs and drawings—the histories, lifestyles, games, foods, music, crafts, and beliefs of those peoples. Nonfiction.

Burton, Jimalee. **Indian Heritage, Indian Pride.** U of Okla Pr 1974.

A Cherokee Indian artist writes about her childhood and the legends, prayers, and stories she heard that made her aware of her heritage. Beautifully illustrated by the author. Nonfiction.

Cahn, Edgar S., and David W. Hearne, editors. **Our Brother's Keeper: The Indian in White America.** New Community 1969.

The editors list and analyze the modern injustices and miseries which American Indians suffer: poverty, lack of education and health care facilities, dwindling land, loss of identity. Nonfiction.

Clark, Ann Nolan. **Medicine Man's Daughter.** FS&G 1963.

Navajo prayers and rituals play major roles in this fast-moving story of an intelligent and introspective young woman's preparation to follow in her father's respected footsteps. (See also *Journey to the People,* Viking Pr; and *Circle of Seasons,* FS&G.) Fiction.

Clark, LaVerne Harrell. **They Sang for Horses: The Impact of the Horse on Navajo and Apache Folklore.** U of Ariz Pr 1966.

A beautifully illustrated examination of the importance of horses in the lives and folklore of Navajo and Apache Indians over the past 300 years. Examined are ways of keeping horses holy, ceremonies in raiding for horses, use as wedding gifts, and burial with the dead. Mature nonfiction.

Corle, Edwin. **Fig Tree John** (© 1935). PB 1972.

Indomitable and at peace with his world, Agocho becomes defiant, bitter, and withdrawn when his wife Kai-a is brutally killed by white men, white settlers irrigate and develop the once peaceful desert surrounding his home beside the Salton Sea, and his only son N'Chai Chidn forsakes his Apache traditions for the attractions of money, flashy cars, and a white woman. Fiction.

Council on Interracial Books for Children, editors. **Chronicles of American Indian Protest.** Fawcett World 1971.

Hoping to counter some of the distortions about American Indians that have been perpetuated in history books and films, this collection of documents reveals the agony and the injustices suffered by the Indians from the sixteenth century to the present. Mature nonfiction.

Courlander, Harold. **The Fourth World of the Hopis.** Fawcett World 1971.

With the underlying belief in the interrelation of all living things, this collection of myths and legends records the life and development of the Hopi people. Mature.

Curtis, Edward S. (editors A. D. Coleman and T. C. McLuhan). **Portraits from North American Indian Life** (© 1972). A & W Visual Library 1975.

From the 1903 edition of Curtis's work, the editors have taken a selection of photographs of Indians in 1899.

Curtis, Natalie, editor. **The Indians' Book: Songs and Legends of the American Indians** (© 1923). Dover 1968.

This is really the Indians' book because it consists

entirely of the words and music of their legends and
songs. Natalie Curtis has recorded 149 of them from
eighteen tribes. Nonfiction.

David, Jay, editor. **The American Indian: The First
Victim.** Morrow 1972.

The editor has selected more than two dozen essays,
poems, published speeches, and segments from biographies of well-known Indians to illustrate, in their own
words, what it means to grow up Indian, to encounter
the white man, and to suffer and endure in the twentieth century.

Debo, Angie. **A History of the Indians of the United
States.** U of Okla Pr 1970.

American Indians before the white man, the coming of
whites, the frontier fights, the reservation system, and
contemporary Indians and their problems and hopes.
(See also *The Road to Disappearance: A History of
the Creek Indians,* U of Okla Pr.) Nonfiction.

Deloria, Vine, Jr. **Behind the Trail of Broken Treaties:
An Indian Declaration of Independence.** Dell 1974.

Probably the leading spokesman for Indian rights today, Deloria makes a strong and convincing case for a
new policy by the federal government toward Indians.
Detailing the number of treaties made and broken in
the past, Deloria insists that the U.S. must redefine
and then protect the rights of Indians. Nonfiction.

Deloria, Vine, Jr. **Custer Died for Your Sins: An Indian
Manifesto** (© 1969). Avon 1970.

In one of the most popular and influential Indian books
of the early 1970s, Deloria dispels numerous myths
and misconceptions about Indians. He sets the white
man straight with unusual wit and irony on such
topics as treaties, religion, government agencies, and
Indian humor. (See also *We Talk, You Listen: New
Tribes, New Turf,* Dell; and *The Indian Affair,* Friend
Pr.) Nonfiction.

Deloria, Vine, Jr., editor. **Of Utmost Good Faith** (©
1971). Bantam 1972.

This history of the white man's inability to treat the
Indians with compassion, charity, or fairness covers

court decisions, treaties, congressional hearings, and
political and military confrontations between Indians
and whites. Mature nonfiction.

Ellis, Mel. **Sidewalk Indian.** HR&W 1974.

Charley Nightwind, a city Indian, escapes to the forests
of a Wisconsin reservation after he is unjustly accused of killing a policeman during an Indian protest.
Fiction.

Erdoes, Richard. **The Sun Dance People: The Plains
Indians, Their Past and Present.** VinRandom 1972.

A concise history of the Indians of the Great Plains.
Nonfiction.

Fahey, John. **The Flathead Indians.** U of Okla Pr 1974.

The Flatheads (or Salish) are a little-known Indian
tribe whose land was the Bitterroot Valley in western
Montana. The Flatheads welcomed the white settlers,
accepted them, shared their lands with them, and were
finally dispossessed and destroyed by them. Mature
nonfiction.

Fall, Thomas. **The Ordeal of Running Standing** (©
1970). Bantam 1971.

Running Standing and Crosses-the-River marry. She
returns to help her Cheyenne people develop their
reservation land, while he is lured by the white man's
riches. Eventually, outwitted by the dishonest whites,
Running Standing seeks revenge. Fiction.

Fehrenbach, T. R. **Comanches: The Destruction of a
People.** Knopf 1974.

An interpretation of the history of the fierce tribe that
for sixty years was the single greatest obstacle to the
white conquest of the country. Mature nonfiction.

Fergusson, Erna. **Dancing Gods: Indian Ceremonials of
New Mexico and Arizona** (© 1931). U of NM Pr
1957.

Fergusson describes some of the history and major
ceremonial dances of the Pueblo, Hopi, Navajo, and
Apache Indians. Although the explanations are somewhat superficial at times due to the white writer's
limited access to the secrets of the ceremonies, Fergusson's personal observations are honest and recounted
with relish. Nonfiction.

Folsom, Franklin. **Red Power on the Rio Grande: The Native American Revolution of 1680.** Follett 1973.

In 1680, nearly a century before the revolution of the Americans against British rule, the Pueblo Indians, in what is now New Mexico, revolted against their Spanish rulers. This is the little-known story of that revolution, under the leadership of Popé, against forced labor, involuntary seizure of harvests, and religious persecution. Nonfiction.

Forman, James. **The Life and Death of Yellow Bird.** FS&G 1973.

The story of Yellow Bird, Indian son of General George Custer, during the years when the Plains Indians fought under Crazy Horse and Sitting Bull against the treachery and lies of the blue-coated soldiers—from the Little Big Horn to the 1890 massacre at Wounded Knee. Fiction.

Forman, James. **People of the Dream** (© 1972). Dell 1974.

When the Nez Percé tribe is ordered to leave its Wallowa Valley lands in Oregon, Chief Joseph leads his people in a desperate struggle to remain free. A poetic portrait of a leader who chooses to resist rather than to surrender as the white man usurps the land and assaults the spirit and culture of his tribe. Fiction.

Garst, Shannon. **Crazy Horse, Great Warrior of the Sioux.** HM 1950.

Crazy Horse led his Sioux people against the white men who ravaged Indian land. Nonfiction.

Gillmor, Frances, and Louisa Wade Wetherill. **Traders to the Navajos: The Story of the Wetherills of Kayenta** (© 1934). U of NM Pr 1967.

The Wetherills' life as traders in the Southwest during the early 1900s and their archaeology explorations during which they "discovered" the ruins at Mesa Verde, Betatakin, and the famous natural arch, Rainbow Bridge. Mature nonfiction.

Gooderham, Kent, editor. **I Am an Indian.** Arlington Hse 1969.

The first anthology of Indian literature to be published in Canada contains contemporary poems, stories, speeches, and essays from diverse tribes of Canadian Indians, including Ojibway, Micmac, Haida, Assiniboine, Cree, and Naskapi.

Halsell, Grace. **Bessie Yellowhair.** Morrow 1973.

By first living with Navajos on their arid, peaceful reservation and then "passing" as a Navajo maid with a white family in suburban California, Grace Halsell provides a moving account of Navajo life, Indian-white conflicts, and contemporary values. Nonfiction.

Harris, Marilyn. **Hatter Fox** (© 1973). Bantam 1974.

Manacled to a cot in an isolated cell of a girls' reformatory, Hatter Fox, an uncontrollable seventeen-year-old Navajo, asks only one thing of the young doctor who tries to help her: "Kill me!" Fiction.

Heizer, Robert F., and M. A. Whipple, editors. **The California Indians: A Source Book.** U of Cal Pr 1971.

Articles on history, archaeology, sociology, economics, urbanization, and the present status of California Indian tribes. Mature nonfiction.

Herbert, Frank. **Soul Catcher** (© 1972). Bantam 1973.

The relationship between thirteen-year-old David Marshall, a white boy from the modern world, and his kidnapper, Katsuk, a militant Indian intent on carrying out a ritual sacrifice of vengeance for all the innocent Indians previously murdered by whites. Fiction.

Hoig, Stan. **The Sand Creek Massacre.** U of Okla Pr 1961.

Less well known than Wounded Knee, the massacre of Indians at Sand Creek in Colorado was just as shameful and has been more controversial. Nonfiction.

Jayne, Mitchell F. **Old Fish Hawk** (© 1970). PB 1971.

Old Fish Hawk is the town drunk who decides to return to the wilderness where he once lived freely with his Osage people. But he must first kill a marauding bear and destroy an old killer boar for revenge. Fiction.

Jones, Charles, editor. **Look to the Mountain Top.** H M Gousha 1972.

This attractively illustrated book has articles about Indian history, art, religion, cooking, women, legal rights, and politics written by Indians such as Vine Deloria, Jr., as well as by non-Indians such as Vincent Price and Stewart Udall. Nonfiction.

Josephy, Alvin M., Jr. **The Indian Heritage of America** (© 1968). Bantam 1969.

A history of American Indians, prehistoric and modern, and their customs, origins, and cultural differences. Mature nonfiction.

Josephy, Alvin M., Jr., editor. **Red Power: The American Indians' Fight for Freedom.** McGraw 1971.

Two dozen essays, speeches, and documents by Indians and non-Indians illustrate the rise of the militant Red Power movement throughout the 1960s. The Indians speak out clearly for the right of self-determination—of their lands, programs, policies, and their very lives. Mature nonfiction.

Keegan, Marcia. **Mother Earth, Father Sky: Pueblo and Navajo Indians of the Southwest.** Grossman 1974.

A beautiful collection of full-color photographs of Navajo and Pueblo Indians of the Southwest, accompanied by ancient chants, emphasizing the wonder and harmony of the people and nature. The clarity of the colors contrasts sharply with the encroaching pollution and strip mining which threaten the area. Nonfiction.

LaFarge, Oliver. **Laughing Boy** (© 1929). NAL 1971.

An innocent young Navajo man, Laughing Boy, meets Slim Girl, a wily, beautiful, and rich young woman whose Indian ways have been bred out of her by education and corruption in the white world. Fiction.

Laubin, Reginald, and Gladys Laubin. **The Indian Tipi: Its History, Construction, and Use** (© 1957). Ballantine 1971.

All the details anyone would ever need to know about how to build, decorate, transport, and live in a tipi. From their extensive personal experiences, the authors write for both the outdoor camper and the student of Indian lore. Nonfiction.

Lawson, Marion. **Maggie Flying Bird.** Morrow 1974.

A courageous half-breed woman lives alternately with

white and Chippewa families in nineteenth-century Wisconsin. The novel offers keen insights into Indian ways, white attitudes, and personal identity. Fiction.

Lighthall, J. I. **The Indian Folk Medicine Guide** (© 1883). Popular Lib 1972.

After studying natural remedies of the Indians, J. I. Lighthall published this book in 1883 "to acquaint the people with an important and valuable knowledge of the medical action of a great many of our most common herbs, roots, barks, flowers, and leaves. . . ." Includes everything from sage and sarsaparilla to poke root and pulsatilla. Nonfiction.

Loh, Jules. **Lords of the Earth: A History of the Navajo Indians.** CCPr Macmillan 1971.

Loh examines the Navajo's attachment to the land and emphasizes the dignity and determination that have enabled the people to endure the unrelenting hardships of their world. Nonfiction.

Longstreet, Stephen. **War Cries on Horseback: The Story of the Indian Wars of the Great Plains.** Doubleday 1970.

A history of the Indians' defense of their lives and beliefs, covering fifty years of shameful warfare such as the Battle of Wounded Knee and the Sand Creek Massacre. Nonfiction.

Luger, Harriett M. **The Last Stronghold: A Story of the Modoc Indian War, 1872–1873.** A-W 1972.

Three teenage boys—Charka, a Modoc Indian; Ned, the son of white settlers; and Yankel, a Jewish immigrant soldier—and their involvement in the bloody Modoc Indian War on the California-Oregon border. Fiction.

Mails, Thomas E. **The People Called Apache.** P-H 1974.

A huge, well-documented, and profusely illustrated book about the life and customs of the Western, Chiricahua, Mescalero, and Jicarilla Apache. The author includes more than 300 photos and 200 sketches to illustrate his detailed descriptions of food, ceremonies, arts and crafts, games, ornaments, language, weapons, and religion of the Apaches. Mature nonfiction.

Marquis, Arnold. **A Guide to America's Indians: Ceremonies, Reservations, and Museums.** U of Okla Pr 1974.

This reference book provides the traveler with a panoramic view of American Indian tribes—their customs, crafts, culture, and ceremonies. Included are maps, guides to museums and other points of interest, dates of special events, plus the location of nearby campsites of each tribe in the country. Nonfiction.

Marriott, Alice, and Carol K. Rachlin. **Peyote** (© 1971). NAL 1972.

A well-written, factual account about the hallucinogen peyote—its origins, its effects, laws regarding its use, its institutional use within the Native American church. The authors vividly describe the rituals and significance that accompany the use of the drug. Nonfiction.

Matson, Emerson N. **Legends of the Great Chiefs.** Nelson 1972.

Legends of the Nisqually, Oglala Sioux, Nez Percé, Snohomish, and other tribes. Nonfiction.

McLuhan, T. C., compiler. **Touch the Earth: A Self-Portrait of Indian Existence** (© 1971). PB 1972.

An outstanding compilation of speeches and writings of numerous North American Indians. The Indians— Luther Standing Bear, Black Elk, Chief Joseph, Crazy Horse, Vine Deloria, Jr., and others—speak eloquently about the land, about the white man, and about freedom and dignity. Illustrated with more than fifty photographs by Edward S. Curtis. Nonfiction.

Means, Florence Crannell. **Our Cup Is Broken.** HM 1969.

Sarah grows up in a Hopi village and then lives with a middle-class white family. After high school and a broken love affair, she returns to the reservation. Fiction.

Miller, David Humphreys. **Custer's Fall** (© 1963). Bantam 1972.

Based on twenty years of interviews with seventy-one eyewitnesses, Miller describes the Indians' version of what really happended at the Battle of the Little Big

Horn. This authentic account dispels many of the myths about Custer's irrational and fatal attempt to attack overwhelming numbers of Sioux and Cheyenne in 1876. Nonfiction.

Momaday, N. Scott. **The Way to Rainy Mountain** (© 1969). Ballantine 1972.

Momaday, a Kiowa Indian, tells of his people: their legends, folklore, and stories; their reflections; and their beliefs and suffering. Mature nonfiction.

Moquin, Wayne, and Charles Van Doren, editors. **Great Documents in American Indian History** (© 1973). Praeger 1974.

An impressive documentary survey of American Indian life and history in the words of the people themselves. Starting with descriptions of legends and customs, this collection next examines Indian and white conflicts, broken treaties, and reservation life. The last section deals with urbanization, identity, and the "Red Power" movement of the 1960s and 70s. Mature nonfiction.

Newcomb, Charles. **Throw His Saddle Out.** Northland 1970.

Two young traders on a Navajo reservation serve as friends, counselors, and doctors to the people, as well as advocates of the Indians' social and economic welfare. Fiction.

O'Dell, Scott. **Sing Down the Moon.** HM 1970.

When Bright Morning is fifteen in 1864, soldiers force the people of her village to join other Navajos in the historic Long Walk to New Mexico. Hundreds die; others lose their spirit. Bright Morning makes plans to escape and return to her canyon with her crippled husband and their son. Fiction.

Olsen, Theodore V. **Soldier Blue** (© 1969). Dell 1970.

Originally titled *Arrow in the Sun,* this is the story of a beautiful white woman and an inept soldier who survive a Cheyenne Indian attack on a cavalry train. Fiction.

Pike, Donald G., and David Muench. **Anasazi: Ancient People of the Rock.** Am West 1974.

Over a hundred spectacular full-color photographs by

Muench and Pike's thoroughly researched text present the cultural history and enduring remains of the prehistoric Anasazi who built magnificent stone cities among the stark cliffs of the Southwest. Nonfiction.

Place, Marian T. **Retreat to the Bear Paw: The Story of the Nez Percé.** Four Winds 1969.

A vivid and moving account of the Nez Percé War during which only several hundred Indians under the leadership of Chief Joseph outmaneuvered nearly 2,000 soldiers in an unprecedented 1,700-mile retreat. Nonfiction.

Reid, William, and Adelaide de Menil. **Out of the Silence** (© 1971). Har-Row 1972.

Black and white photographs by Adelaide de Menil of totem poles of the Haida, Kwakiutl, Tlingit, and Tsimshian Indians of the Pacific Northwest, accompanied by a very brief text by William Reid about the people and the art of their finely carved poles. Nonfiction.

Reynolds, Charles R., Jr., editor. **American Indian Portraits from the Wanamaker Expedition of 1913.** Greene 1971.

A collection of Indian portraits only recently found in a file in the American Museum of Natural History. The portraits are of many tribes, but all establish the dignity of humanity. Nonfiction.

Sanchez, Thomas. **Rabbit Boss.** Ballantine 1973.

This lengthy but exceptionally well-written novel, from shifting points of view and time, takes the reader through four generations of Washo Indians in Nevada during the past century. Powerful episodes reveal the whites as thoughtless, selfish savages, while the doomed Indians struggle to survive and preserve their individuality and beliefs. Mature fiction.

Sanders, Thomas E., and Walter W. Peek, editors. **Literature of the American Indian.** Glencoe 1973.

This anthology provides a broad and representative cross section of Native American writings. In addition to legends, folktales, biographies, poems, stories, and essays of protest, the Indian editors comment on Indian life and literature. Mature.

Sandoz, Mari. **These Were the Sioux** (© 1961). Dell 1971.

The customs and ideas of the people who were the author's neighbors and playmates when she was growing up in northwestern Nebraska. This short, personal account shows the tenderness and caring within the Sioux family life as opposed to their reputation as fierce warriors. Nonfiction.

Scherer, Joanna Cohan (with Jean Burton Walker). **Indians: The Great Photographs That Reveal North American Indian Life, 1847–1929.** Crown 1974.

An extraordinary collection of photographs of American Indians made between 1847 and 1929. These unusually high-quality photographs from the Smithsonian Institution's Archives are accompanied by a brief and informative text explaining the subtle changes that occurred in Indian life as a result of the expansion of white "civilization." Nonfiction.

Schneider, Richard C. **Crafts of the North American Indians: A Craftsman's Manual.** Van Nos Reinhold 1972.

An art teacher describes and demonstrates how to make Indian tools, moccasins, drums, beadwork, baskets, and pottery. What makes this book especially valuable is that the author presents only those crafts which he himself has mastered using native materials. Nonfiction.

Sneve, Virginia Driving Hawk. **Betrayed.** Holiday 1974.

During the Santee Sioux uprising in the Dakota Territory in 1862, Indians take numerous white captives. The events culminate in the hanging of thirty-eight Indians of the Santee tribe in Mankato, Minnesota. Fiction.

Stands in Timber, John, and Margot Liberty (with Robert M. Utley). **Cheyenne Memories** (© 1967). U of Nebr Pr 1972.

Drawing upon his own experiences and interviews, John Stands in Timber writes a history of the Cheyenne people. Included here are accounts of the Ghost Dance, the Custer fight, and tribal reactions to the twentieth century. Nonfiction.

Steiner, Stan. **The New Indians** (© 1968). Dell 1969.

Using anecdotes, interviews, documents, songs, and statistics, Steiner presents the young Indians' search for identity and their impatience with the lack of justice in America. Nonfiction.

Steiner, Stan. **The Tiguas: The Lost Tribe of City Indians.** CCPr Macmillan 1972.

The incredible story of the Tiguas, an ancient tribe of Indians, thought to be extinct, who have been living and carrying on their old traditions, unknown to most of the modern world—not on some obscure reservation, but in a suburb of El Paso, Texas! Nonfiction.

Stensland, Anna Lee. **Literature by and about the American Indian: An Annotated Bibliography.** NCTE 1973.

In addition to categorizing titles according to subject matter, the author includes short biographies of twenty-five important American Indian writers and study guides of nine popular literary works. Nonfiction.

Tamarin, Alfred. **We Have Not Vanished: Eastern Indians of the United States.** Follett 1974.

Because some books imply that Indian tribes have disappeared from the eastern United States, Alfred Tamarin wrote this book to note the locations and describe the activities of more than 115,000 modern-day Native Americans who live in the states along the East Coast. Nonfiction.

Terrell, John Upton. **Apache Chronicle.** T R Crowell 1972.

Terrell traces the history of the Apaches from their first encounters with European explorers to the surrender of Geronimo 350 years later. Nonfiction.

Terrell, John Upton. **Sioux Trail**. McGraw 1974.

The history of the Sioux Nation from their first appearance in North America (possibly as early as 16,000 B.C.) to their emergence as the great horsemen and warriors of the Western plains. Nonfiction.

Tibbles, Thomas Henry, editor. **The Ponca Chiefs: An Account of the Trial of Standing Bear** (© 1880). U of Nebr Pr 1972.

In 1879 a small group of Ponca Indians defied the government by leaving the reservation and walking to their ancestral home. The trial of their chief led to the first court case in which Indians successfully challenged the federal government's complete authority over them. Nonfiction.

Turner, Frederick W., III, editor. **The Portable North American Indian Reader** (© 1973). Viking Pr 1974.

Intending to present the reader with "the traditions and the historical realities of the North American Indian," Turner has assembled a large collection of tales, poems, speeches, stories, biographies, and essays, both ancient and contemporary, which show the Indians' wisdom and perceptivity as well as their humor and obscenity.

Underhill, Ruth M. **The Navajos** (© 1956). U of Okla Pr 1971.

Once a proud tribe who ruled most of the desert Southwest, the Navajos were forced to change their lives when Kit Carson and his soldiers defeated them in 1864. Since then, the Navajos have been best known for their weaving and silversmithing. Nonfiction.

Vanderwerth, W. C., compiler. **Indian Oratory: Famous Speeches by Noted Indian Chieftains** (© 1971). Ballantine 1972.

Chief Joseph, in 1879, said: ". . . I have been asked to show you my heart." In this collection of famous speeches, Joseph and other Indian leaders such as Pontiac, Tecumseh, Cochise, and Sitting Bull show their hearts and concerns for freedom, ecology, self-determination, and peace. Nonfiction.

Vizenor, Gerald. **The Everlasting Sky: New Voices from the People Named the Chippewa.** CCPr Macmillan 1972.

Gerald Vizenor lets the *oshki anishinabe* speak for themselves—their uncertainties, their anger, their struggles, hopes, and failures. No stereotypes here, only real people—young and old—in their daily efforts to maintain their individuality and to regain or defend their cultural heritage. Nonfiction.

Vlahos, Olivia. **New World Beginnings: Indian Cultures in the Americas** (© 1970). Fawcett World 1972.

Based on anthropological readings from "bones and

stones," Vlahos describes the ancient Indian cultures in the Western Hemisphere. The cultures are examined in five groups: hunters, fishermen, gatherers, farmers, and empire builders. Nonfiction.

Waters, Frank, editor (translator Oswald White Bear Fredericks). **Book of the Hopi** (© 1963). Ballantine 1969.

Unlike his predecessors who studied the Hopi Indians, Waters let thirty-two elders of the tribe describe their creation stories, legends, and rituals to his Hopi assistant, Oswald White Bear Fredericks, who translated them into English. Waters introduces and comments on the myths, sacred narratives, and Hopi world-view. (Waters has recorded his personal experiences during his three years of living with the Hopi in *Pumpkin Seed Point: Being within the Hopi,* Swallow.) Nonfiction.

Waters, Frank. **The Man Who Killed the Deer** (© 1941). PB 1971.

Martiniano finds himself in constant trouble, trying to make sense of his white education and knowledge of white ways while living by the laws of his pueblo. He looks into himself and his two worlds, hoping to find out who he is. Fiction.

Waters, Frank. **Masked Gods: Navaho and Pueblo Ceremonialism** (© 1950). Ballantine 1973.

Waters describes the background of Navajo and Pueblo people as well as their songs, dances, and ceremonials. Waters makes interesting comparisons with Taoism and Buddhism. Mature nonfiction.

Webb, William, and Robert A. Weinstein, editors. **Dwellers at the Source: Southwestern Indian Photographs of A. C. Vroman, 1895–1905.** Grossman 1973.

A. C. Vroman's documentary photographs present unsentimental but sensitive portraits of Southwestern Indians from a time shortly after the Indians had been defeated by the U.S. Army but had not yet been overcome by missionaries, anthropologists, or tourists. Nonfiction.

Welch, James. **Winter in the Blood.** Har-Row 1974.

Both in subject matter and style, this is a superior fictional treatment of Indian life, Welch being particularly deft at creating believable characters. In the stark setting of a rural Montana ranch and its surrounding towns, the narrator describes his dissatisfied life and his search for meaning in past memories and present conflicts. Mature fiction.

Weltfish, Gene. **The Lost Universe: The Way of Life of The Pawnee** (© 1965). Ballantine 1971.

After interviewing some old tribal members, Weltfish describes what life was probably like for the Pawnee Indians during the year 1867. Through this technique he is able to describe the yearly ceremonies and activities: planting crops, hunting, cooking, making instruments, harvesting. Mature nonfiction.

Witt, Shirley Hill. **The Tuscaroras.** CCPr Macmillan 1972.

Witt conveys a picture of today's Tuscarora Indians, the last of the Indian nations to join the Iroquois Confederacy. Drawing on the past and present, the author shows the lands, the people, their activities, their religion, and their spirit. Nonfiction.

Witt, Shirley Hill, and Stan Steiner, editors. **The Way: An Anthology of American Indian Literature.** Vin-Random 1972.

This diversified anthology of American Indian writings speaks for contemporary Indians. It contains essays, documents, and newspaper articles as well as poems, legends, and stories. The writings are grouped into eight sections, including songs, education, laws, death, and prophecies of the future.

Wood, Nancy. **Hollering Sun.** S&S 1972.

A brief and poetic journey through the history and beliefs of the 1,000-year-old pueblo at Taos, New Mexico. A portrait of the present inhabitants through photographs, poems, sayings, aphorisms, and legends. Nonfiction.

Wood, Nancy. **Many Winters.** Doubleday 1974.

Writing in poetry and prose what the old men have told her, Nancy Wood presents the wisdom and philosophies of the Indians of Taos Pueblo, New Mexico. Nonfiction.

Wrone, David R., and Russell S. Nelson, Jr., editors. **Who's the Savage? A Documentary History of the Mistreatment of the Native North Americans.** Fawcett World 1973.

This collection of public documents, most of them from the federal government, reveals the long history of white savagery against American Indians. Not just the outright stealing of Indian lands, but also the barbarous, bloody, horrifying acts of decapitating and skinning Indians, mutilating pregnant women, and paying bounties for Indian skulls. Mature nonfiction.

The Zuni People (translator Alvina Quam). **The Zunis: Self-Portrayals** (© 1972). NAL 1974.

A written record of the oral literature of the Zuni Indians of New Mexico. Recounted simply and carefully by the elders from generation to generation, these forty-six stories of myths, legends, traditions, and factual experiences provide a unique narrative of the Zuni people.

BLACK EXPERIENCES

Adoff, Arnold, editor. **Black Out Loud: An Anthology of Modern Poems by Black Americans.** Macmillan 1970.

Compiled for today's youth, this collection contains poems by promising young black poets as well as established artists.

Alexander, Rae Pace, and Julius Lester, editors. **Young and Black in America.** VinRandom 1970.

Eight men and women relate what it is like to be young and black in America today through poignant accounts from their own lives. Nonfiction.

Armstrong, William. **Sounder** (© 1969). Har-Row 1972.

Sounder is the coon dog belonging to the young son of a black sharecropper living in the deep South some years ago. The boy, his family, and the coon dog are all victims, but the boy tells the story without self-pity. Fiction.

Baldwin, James, and Nikki Giovanni. **A Dialogue.** Lippincott 1973.

Two black writers talk on a London TV show. Transcripts of that show reveal what it means to be black and what it means to be human in today's world. Non-fiction.

Bonham, Frank, editor. **Cool Cat** (© 1971). Dell 1972.

Three black teenagers in a ghetto want to raise some money. Uncle Jules offers to sell them an old truck so they can do some hauling. Then they get involved in a drug ring. (See also *Nitty Gritty,* Dell.) Fiction.

Breitman, George, editor. **Malcolm X Speaks.** Ballantine 1973.

Some of the major speeches Malcolm made during the last chaotic months of his life. Mature nonfiction.

Brown, Claude. **Manchild in the Promised Land** (© 1965). NAL 1971.

A dramatic and often shocking autobiographical account of one black who succeeded in breaking out of the ghetto. Brown's graphic story of his coming of age during the 40s and 50s packs a terrific emotional wallop by vividly recreating the savagery and pathos of life in Harlem. Despite a sometimes wordy style and crude language, this book is a shattering portrayal of American life. Fiction.

Chalk, Ocania. **Pioneers of Black Sport.** Dodd 1975.

Stories of black athletes who broke down the color barriers in professional baseball, basketball, boxing, and football. Nonfiction.

Chambers, Bradford, and Rebecca Moon, editors. **Right On: An Anthology of Black Literature.** NAL 1970.

A collection of short stories and poems and articles about black people and black experiences by writers such as Claude McKay, Malcolm X, Margaret Walker, Frederick Douglass, Paul Laurence Dunbar, and Nikki Giovanni.

Chapman, Abraham, editor. **Black Voices: An Anthology of Afro-American Literature.** NAL 1968.

"Powerful prose and poetry" written by Afro-American men and women of letters. (See also *New Black Voices: An Anthology of Contemporary Afro-American Literature,* NAL.) Mature.

Chisholm, Shirley. **Shirley Chisholm: Unbought and Unbossed** (© 1970). Avon 1971.

Ms. Chisholm reminisces about her childhood, her education, and her "ever-increasing" involvement in politics. From her active involvement in a "boss-run" Brooklyn Democratic clubhouse to the New York State Assembly to the U.S. Congress, she refused and still refuses to be a "sell-out" and a "yes" person in or out of the political arena. Nonfiction.

Clarke, John Henrik, editor. **American Negro Short Stories.** Hill & Wang 1966.

Clarke presents a collection of uncynical and nonbitter stories written by well-known black writers who describe with realism and hopefulness the black experience in America. Fiction.

Cleaver, Eldridge. **Soul on Ice** (© 1968). Dell 1970.

Cleaver was sentenced to prison for possession of marijuana. In prison, he began to write to save his sanity and in the process of writing, he found himself, a better self than he had ever known. The language and ideas may offend some readers. Mature nonfiction.

Conroy, Pat. **The Water Is Wide** (© 1972). Dell 1974.

When Pat Conroy goes as a teacher to Yamacraw Island, off South Carolina, he is not prepared for the task before him. He is not prepared to cope with eighteen black children who cannot spell their names or count to five, nor with adults who fail to understand his mission or his unusual techniques. Nonfiction.

David, Jay, editor. **Growing Up Black** (© 1968). PB 1969.

Nineteen blacks write about what it means to be black in America. All true experiences, the book covers the period from slavery till now. Nonfiction.

Dorson, Richard M., editor. **American Negro Folktales** (© 1967). Fawcett World 1972.

Folklore is a representative depiction of a culture of a given people, and from the tales which are included in this outstanding collection the reader can get a telescopic view of what the overall black experience is all about. Mature fiction.

Drotning, Phillip T., and Wesley W. South, editors. **Up from the Ghetto** (© 1969). WSP 1971.

Through candid sketches, fourteen American blacks reveal how they escaped the bonds of the ghetto and racism to find their niche in American society. Nonfiction.

Ellison, Ralph. **Invisible Man** (© 1952). VinRandom 1959.

Unfairly expelled from a Southern college, an unnamed black goes north to Harlem. Exploited by Communists, he is shot during a riot and takes refuge by literally living underground. Mature fiction.

Fair, Ronald L. **We Can't Breathe.** Har-Row 1972.

An autobiographical novel of a young black, Ernie, growing up and attempting to survive in a Chicago slum ghetto during the 1930s and 40s. Fiction.

Fairbairn, Ann. **Five Smooth Stones** (© 1960). Bantam 1971.

The story of David Champlin, a young black who escapes the South by winning a scholarship to a small Ohio college. His love for a white girl, his struggles for a legal education, and his dedication to improvement of race relations through nonviolence make this exciting, often melodramatic reading. Fiction.

Folsom, Franklin. **The Life and Legend of George Mc-Junkin, Black Cowboy.** Nelson 1973.

This is an account of an extraordinary man who had a love for freedom and adventure and a thirst for living. Nonfiction.

Freedman, Frances S., editor. **The Black American Experience.** Bantam 1970.

An anthology which presents the story of the black American experience through thematically arranged literary selections written by black Americans. Fiction.

Gaines, Ernest J. **The Autobiography of Miss Jane Pittman** (© 1971). Bantam 1972.

Born and raised a slave, Jane Pittman is freed as a a young girl after the Civil War and lives to see the beginnings of black militancy and civil rights work in the 1960s. Fiction.

Goodman, Morris C., and Kenneth Clark. **A Junior History of the American Negro,** 2 vols. Fleet 1969 (Vol. I) and 1970 (Vol. II).

While the rather outmoded term "Negro" is used throughout this book, this two volume work is still current as an account of the black contribution to American history, a contribution that has been sorely neglected by historians in the past. Nonfiction.

Gregory, Dick (with Robert Lipsyte). **Nigger: An Autobiography.** PB 1964.

The black comedian turned social reformer writes about his life and why he turned from being a comedian to hunger fasts and other forms of social protest. A powerful, often bitter, and sometimes quite frank story of a significant man. (See also *The Shadow That Scares Me,* PB.) Nonfiction.

Guffy, Ossie (with Caryl Ledner). **Ossie: The Autobiography of a Black Woman** (© 1971). Bantam 1972.

A person of ordinary status reveals what life has been for her as a woman and as a black American. Nonfiction.

Guy, Rosa, editor. **Children of Longing.** HR&W 1971.

The editor compassionately presents the lives and experiences of twenty-four black youths in both the North and South who relate their hopes of becoming a part of the total scene in America. Nonfiction.

Hamilton, Virginia. **Paul Robeson: The Life and Times of a Free Black Man.** Har-Row 1974.

Paul Robeson is a singer, an actor, a former football All-American, and activist in trying to improve the lives of his black brothers and sisters. During the 1940s and 1950s Robeson turned to the Communist Party, but millions of black and white people respect him for his work and his honesty. Nonfiction.

Hamilton, Virginia, editor. **The Writings of W. E. B. Du Bois.** T Y Crowell 1975.

Du Bois was one of America's greatest black spokesmen. His cries for equality and freedom and his opposition to segregation and oppression are clear in the selections from Du Bois's speeches, articles, and letters. (See also *W. E. B. Du Bois: A Biography,* T Y Crowell.) Nonfiction.

Hansberry, Lorraine. **To Be Young, Gifted and Black: Lorraine Hansberry in Her Own Words** (© 1969). NAL 1970.

This autobiography (in play form) is "the portrait of an individual," the blueprint of a gifted artist, and "the chronicle of a rebel who celebrated the human spirit." Nonfiction.

Harris, Middleton. **The Black Book.** Random 1973.

A collection of newspaper clippings, magazine articles, sheet music covers, photographs, movie stills, and much more illustrating the black existence in America from its start to fairly recent times. Nonfiction.

Hughes, Langston, Milton Meltzer, and C. Eric Lincoln, editors. **A Pictorial History of Black Americans.** Crown 1973.

The editors present and discuss the changes within the black community since the advent of the "new" black Renaissance. Some of the added chapters deal with the civilizations of ancient Africa, Afro-Americans and Africans today, the black American in motion pictures, the arts, and literature. Nonfiction.

Hunter, Kristin. **The Soul Brothers and Sister Lou** (© 1968). Avon 1969.

Louretta Hawkins lives with her seven brothers and sisters and a very strong mother. Lou's friends are street people only interested in being tough. She believes there is more to life than this, and she and her friends start their own musical group. Fiction.

Jackson, George. **Blood in My Eye.** Bantam 1972.

George Jackson was a revolutionary black leader killed at San Quentin Prison in 1971. He proposes revolution and suggests why revolution is necessary to change the social order and structure. An angry book that will offend some readers. Mature nonfiction.

Johnson, James Weldon, and J. Rosamund Johnson. **Lift Every Voice and Sing: Words and Music.** Hawthorn 1970.

Although written at the turn of the century, this song,

often referred to as the black "national anthem," still creates a firm "bond between black Americans of today and of their past." Accompanying verse and music are fitting illustrations.

Jordan, June. **Dry Victories.** HR&W 1972.

Through photographs and dialogue between two young black Americans, Kenny and Jerome, the two distinct periods of history—the Reconstruction era and the decade of civil rights—are presented in another light. Nonfiction.

Jordan, June. **His Own Where** (© 1971). Dell 1973.

Buddy and Angela love each other, but neither of their families will accept the love. The two young people find a place of their own, a cemetery, where they can talk and make love. Fiction.

Jordan, Pat. **Black Coach.** Dodd 1971.

When a popular white coach is ousted by the Walter Williams High School Board in Burlington, North Carolina, black Jerome Evans becomes football coach of the recently integrated school. Evans is a hard man to get to know, and he has problems with players and some townspeople on his way to a generally successful first season. Nonfiction.

Kaland, William J., editor. **The Great Ones.** WSP 1970.

A collection of dramatized stories of black Americans who because of their independence rebelled against racial barriers and left a proud heritage for today's blacks. Fiction.

King, Woodie, and Ron Milner, editors. **Black Drama Anthology.** NAL 1972.

As varied as their lifestyles, their environments, and their experiences, twenty-three playwrights relate through drama "what it is and what it means to be black in the here and now of America as no white has ever really known it." Plays contained in this collection are by Imamu Amiri Baraka, Douglas Turner Ward, Ben Caldwell, Lonne Elder III, and others. Mature fiction.

Landay, Ilene, editor. **Black Film Stars: A Picture Album.** Drake Pubs 1973.

The story of thirty black actors and actresses, from

the earliest days of Hollywood to the present, who have found success and have made an indelible imprint in the medium of film. Two hundred photographs accompany the biographical sketches of Stepin Fetchit, Bill Robinson, Butterfly McQueen, Paul Robeson, Ethel Waters, James Earl Jones, Diana Ross, Diana Sands, Sidney Poitier, Cicely Tyson, and others. Nonfiction.

Leckie, William H. **The Buffalo Soldiers: A Narrative of the Negro Cavalry in the West** (© 1967). U of Okla Pr 1970.

Many people are not aware of the blacks who lived and worked on the western frontier after the Civil War. Indians called black soldiers "buffalo soldiers," a tribute to black bravery. The author writes of the buffalo soldiers, their battles and frustrations and the prejudice usually directed at them. Nonfiction.

Lerner, Gerda, editor. **Black Women in White America: A Documentary History** (© 1972). VinRandom 1973.

Selections about the meaning and status of black women in the United States from the time of slavery until now. Mature nonfiction.

Lester, Julius. **Black Folktales.** Grove 1970.

These folktales are grouped under themes such as love, origins, heroes and people. The fifteen tales have been revised from original sources to provide lively reading. Fiction.

Lichello, Robert. **Pioneer in Blood Plasma: Dr. Charles Richard Drew.** Messner 1968.

Dr. Drew was an athlete who became a scientist and surgeon famous for his discovery of blood plasma during World War II. Nonfiction.

Lindenmeyer, Otto. **Black History: Lost, Stolen or Strayed.** Avon 1970.

A brief history of the black people in the United States, the cowboys, the slaves, the revolutionaries. The Hollywood image of the black man, the African impact, the political changes in America, all are used to illustrate the past, the present, and the future of blacks in America. Nonfiction.

Lockwood, Lee. **Conversation with Eldridge Cleaver—Algiers.** Dell 1970.

In this interview with Eldridge Cleaver, then a political exile, readers get an insight into the philosophy, the political position, and the basic ideology of a man who has traveled extensively throughout the world in quest of answers and possible solutions to the problems which he and other black Americans face. Mature nonfiction.

Malcolm X (editor George Breitman). **Malcolm X Speaks.** Grove 1965.

Speeches, interviews, and letters of one of the foremost leaders of the black revolution. Nonfiction.

Malcolm X and Alex Haley. **The Autobiography of Malcolm X** (© 1965). Ballantine 1973.

In sometimes frank language, the authors tell of the hoodlum, thief, and dope peddler who became one of the leaders of the black Muslims. This man, who at first hated whites, later saw hope for bringing blacks and whites together. Mature nonfiction.

Mead, Margaret, and James Baldwin. **A Rap on Race** (© 1971). Dell 1972.

A unique discussion between Margaret Mead and James Baldwin on one of the most pressing problems facing the world today—race and society. Mature nonfiction.

Meriwether, Louise. **Daddy Was a Number Runner** (© 1970). Pyramid Pubns 1971.

A twelve-year-old girl and her family live in Harlem. The girl knows the evil and the strength of the area and encounters fear and despair and love. Fiction.

Miller, Warren. **The Cool World** (© 1959). Fawcett World 1969.

A very frank and often bitter picture of New York's Harlem ghetto and the horrors of growing up and staying alive told through the experiences of one young man. The ugliness of some of the incidents demands frank language which may offend some readers. Mature fiction.

Morrison, Toni. **Sula.** Knopf 1974.

Sula and Nel are childhood friends who live in the

Bottom, land relegated to blacks. Sula leaves for ten years and when she reappears, she breaks up Nel's marriage. Fiction.

Newton, Huey P. (with Herman Blake). **Revolutionary Suicide.** HarBraceJ 1973.

Huey P. Newton's autobiographical account emphasizes influences which contributed to his leadership in the black community: his father, who gave him a sense of dignity and pride; and his brother Melvin, who awakened a love of learning that led Huey, almost illiterate at eighteen, to teach himself to read. Mature nonfiction.

Owens, Jesse (with Paul Neimark). **Blackthink: My Life As Black Man and White Man** (© 1970). PB 1971.

Jesse Owens, hero of the 1936 Olympics, writes a frank and honest story of his life, from his youth to the Olympics. He describes how it feels to be a hero patronized by whites and his struggle against bigotry in our country. Nonfiction.

Parks, Gordon. **A Choice of Weapons.** Berkley Pub 1966.

Parks describes his early life on a Kansas farm, his later life on the edge of crime, and how and why he made the choice to become what he became, a writer, photographer, and thinker. Nonfiction.

Parks, Gordon. **The Learning Tree** (© 1963). Fawcett World 1974.

A frank autobiographical novel of young Newt Winger, a young black man faced with prejudice while growing up in rural Kansas. Fiction.

Patterson, Lindsay, editor. **Black Theater.** NAL 1971.

A collection of notable dramatic expressions and experiences as seen through the eyes of eleven of America's foremost black playwrights. In this anthology are plays by Arna Bontemps, Alice Childress, Langston Hughes, Lorraine Hansberry, Ossie Davis, Ed Bullins, and others.

Rosengarten, Theodore. **All God's Dangers: The Life of Nate Shaw.** Knopf 1974.

The author tape-recorded and edited Nate Shaw's story

of his eighty-five years as an Alabama sharecropper and tenant farmer. In the 1930s Shaw joined the Alabama sharecropper's union to fight cheating landlords and their allies and spent twelve years in prison for shooting at law officers. Mature nonfiction.

Sellers, Cleveland (with Robert Terrell). **The River of No Return: The Autobiography of a Black Militant and the Life and Death of SNCC.** Morrow 1973.

Cleveland Sellers was raised in a small South Carolina town. He knew little about the white world, but he learned about it in the 1960s when he became involved with the Student Nonviolent Coordinating Committee (SNCC). Nonfiction.

Sterling, Dorothy. **Tear Down the Walls! A History of the Black Revolution in the United States.** NAL 1970.

The story of a great people, their place in and their contribution to America, their 200-year struggle for equality and survival, and their foes and allies, the white Americans. "It is the story of a people who decided to make history out of their lives." Mature nonfiction.

Watkins, Mel, and Jay David, editors. **To Be a Black Woman: Portraits in Fact and Fiction.** Morrow 1970.

These literary excerpts reflect and portray the vast experiences of the black woman in America.

Young, Al. **Who Is Angelina?** HR&W 1975.

A fortuneteller tells black Angelina Green that she is "lost" and will meet a man soon. Angelina is "lost" and confused, and in Mexico she does meet a smuggler of artifacts from ancient Indian ruins. Fiction.

CHICANO EXPERIENCES

Acosta, Oscar Zeta. **The Revolt of the Cockroach People.** Bantam 1973.

The Chicanos of Los Angeles fight the Anglo-dominated churches, courts, and government. They're led by an angry activist named Buffalo Z. Brown, whose exploits with sex and drugs are depicted as openly and honestly as are his battles in court. Mature fiction.

Acuña, Rudolfo. **Occupied America: The Chicano's Struggle for Liberation.** Canfield Pr 1972.

The history of Mexican-Americans in the United States is a record of injustice and discrimination, and the author suggests how and why some changes can be effected. Mature nonfiction.

Alford, Harold J. **The Proud Peoples: The Heritage and Culture of Spanish-Speaking Peoples in the United States** (© 1972). NAL 1973.

Filling many of the gaps in traditional American history books, Alford presents a compact history of the Spanish-speaking people of the country, from the earliest Spanish explorers and settlers to present-day migrants and militants. Sixty short biographies are also included. Mature nonfiction.

Barrio, Raymond. **The Plum Plum Pickers.** Har-Row 1969.

The desperate lives and oppressive living conditions of Mexican migrant farm laborers in California are seen in the experiences of Manuel and Lupe Gutierrez and the operators of the Western Grande fruit plantation. Fiction.

Bonham, Frank. **Viva Chicano** (© 1970). Dell 1971.

Bonham captures the frustration, uncertainty, and hardships of a young Mexican-American, Keeney Durán, as he tries to stay out of trouble and find some cultural identity in a Los Angeles barrio. Fiction.

Castro, Tony. **Chicano Power: The Emergence of Mexican America.** Sat Rev Pr 1974.

Castro reviews the realities and dreams of the Chicano movement with particular attention to its recent past and present leadership under men like Corky Gonzales, Cesar Chavez, and Lopez Tijerina. In doing this, he discusses the role of the Chicano movement in recent political campaigns and notes how the movement has been generally ineffective. Nonfiction.

Colman, Hila. **Chicano Girl.** Morrow 1973.

Donna Martinez, a Chicano girl from a small village in Arizona, leaves her village and becomes bitter and disillusioned when she discovers the realities of the world outside her home. Fiction.

Cox, William R. **Chicano Cruz.** Bantam 1972.

Mando, the proud Chicano, Sandy Roosevelt, the determined black, Gil Jones, the rich kid, and Jack Kelly, the middle-class white, learn the necessity of teamwork off the field as well as on it. Fiction.

Coy, Harold. **The Mexicans.** Little 1970.

Although it is not a book about Chicanos in the U.S., this history of the Mexican people provides a better understanding of the culture from which many Mexican-Americans have come. Nonfiction.

Gardner, Richard. **¡Grito! Reies Tijerina and the New Mexico Land Grant War of 1967** (© 1970). Har-Row 1971.

An account of one of the most important political events in contemporary Mexican-American history and one of the least known outside of the southwestern United States—the events relating to the New Mexico Land Grant of 1832 and Reies Tijerina's raid on the Tierra Amarilla courthouse in 1967. Nonfiction.

Gonzales, Rodolfo. **I Am Joaquín / Yo Soy Joaquín.** Bantam 1972.

Printed in both English and Spanish and lavishly illustrated with photographs, the long poem traces the colorful history of the Mexican-Americans from the Spanish conquistadores and Aztec princes to the present-day struggles of La Raza. Mature.

González, Nancie L. **The Spanish-Americans of New Mexico: A Heritage of Pride.** U of NM Pr 1967.

The author traces the colorful history of Spanish-speaking people in New Mexico from 1598 to the present, focusing mainly on problems of urbanization and maintaining the Spanish cultural heritage in the face of the dominant Anglo culture. Well-documented. Mature nonfiction.

Harth, Dorothy E., and Lewis M. Baldwin, editors. **Voices of Aztlan: Chicano Literature of Today.** NAL 1974.

An anthology of contemporary Mexican-American literature, including eight short stories, four excerpts from Chicano novels, twenty-two poems, and three plays by Luis Valdez that were written for the *Teatro Campesino.*

Ludwig, Edward W., and James Santibanez, editors. **The Chicanos: Mexican American Voices.** Penguin 1971.

A collection of articles, fiction, and poetry about Chicanos and Chicano life today. Topics covered include Chicano history, prisons, the barrio, Cesar Chavez, and religion. Mature.

Martinez, Al, editor. **Rising Voices.** NAL 1974.

Brief biographies of fifty-two outstanding Spanish-speaking Americans, including Senator Joseph Montoya, singer Vikki Carr, actor Anthony Quinn, judge Harold Medina, Dr. Antonio Gasset, quarterback Jim Plunkett, golfer Lee Treviño, former prisoner-of-war Lt. Commander Everett Alvarez, Jr., labor leader Cesar Chavez, and TV journalist Geraldo Rivera. Nonfiction.

Martínez, Elizabeth Sutherland, and Enriqueta Vásquez. **Viva La Raza: The Struggle of the Mexican American People.** Doubleday 1974.

Two women tell the story of their people, the treatment of Mexican-Americans as strangers in their own land, and their vision of a growing nation of people. Nonfiction.

Matthiessen, Peter. **Sal Si Puedes: Cesar Chavez and the New American Revolution** (© 1969). Dell 1973.

From his encounters with Cesar Chavez and various incidents associated with Chavez's nonviolent battle for the rights of agricultural workers, Matthiessen presents a personal as well as a historical narrative portrait of *La Causa*. Nonfiction.

McWilliams, Carey. **North from Mexico: The Spanish Speaking People of the United States** (© 1949). Greenwood 1968.

First published in 1949, this history of the Mexican-Americans in the Southwest still ranks as authoritative and popular. Mature nonfiction.

Meier, Matt S., and Feliciano Rivera, editors. **Readings on La Raza: The Twentieth Century.** Hill & Wang 1974.

A well-structured collection of nearly fifty essays by various writers—from Carey McWilliams to Ruben Salazar and Ernesto Galarza—highlighting the progress of the Mexican-American *Raza* during the twentieth century, from the immigrations from Mexico to Chicano militancy (See also *The Chicanos: A History of Mexican Americans,* Hill & Wang.) Nonfiction.

Moquin, Wayne, and Charles Van Doren, editors. **A Documentary History of the Mexican Americans** (© 1971). Bantam 1972.

From the early coming of the Spanish in the sixteenth century until the problems of the Chicano today, the editors cover problems of historical events, religion, education, migration, immigration, and economic strife. Mature nonfiction.

O'Dell, Scott. **Child of Fire.** HM 1974.

A slightly offbeat story involving bullfighting, drug smuggling, machismo, cock fighting, and Mexican-American history as seen through the eyes of a Southern California parole officer and the two Chicano gang leaders he supervises. Fiction.

Ortego, Philip D., editor. **We Are Chicanos: An Anthology of Mexican-American Literature.** WSP 1973.

A collection of modern and contemporary poetry, fiction, and essays by Mexican-American writers reflecting history, culture, politics, and emerging power. Mature.

Pillsbury, Dorothy L. **Star over Adobe.** U of NM Pr 1963.

A unified collection of thirty-five short stories whose touching and lighthearted incidents reveal the human nature of people from three cultures—Pueblo Indian, Mexican-American, and Anglo—around Santa Fe, New Mexico, during the Christmas season. Fiction.

Pitrone, Jean Maddern. **Chavez: Man of the Migrants.** Pyramid Pubns 1971.

A biography of Cesar Chavez emphasizing the events surrounding the historic boycott of California grape growers in the middle to late 1960s as Chavez fought quietly for justice for field laborers. Nonfiction.

Prago, Albert. **Strangers in Their Own Land: A History of Mexican Americans.** Four Winds 1973.

Starting with the Spanish penetrations of Columbus and Cortez into the "New World," Prago traces the turbulent history of Mexican-Americans, pointing out distortions and omissions in Anglo-oriented histories and focusing on Mexican leaders from Juarez and Pancho Villa in the past to Cesar Chavez and Corky Gonzalez in the present. Nonfiction.

Rendon, Armando B. (editor S. D. Stewart). **Chicano Manifesto.** Macmillan 1971.

Rendon speaks strongly and authoritatively against Anglo oppression and for acceptance of Chicano identity—for his way of life, for his culture, and for his language. Noting numerous incidents of both national and local significance, Rendon speaks to Anglos as well as to Chicanos about "a new day and a new world." Mature nonfiction.

Romano-V, Octavio I., and Herminio Rios, editors. **El Espejo, the Mirror: Selected Chicano Literature** (© 1969). Quinto Sol Pubns 1972.

The first anthology of Mexican-American writings prepared entirely by Mexican-Americans, parts of which are written in Spanish as well as English. The book includes a play, numerous poems, and several stories about the Chicano experience, many of them reflecting the militancy of the late 1960s. Mature.

Rulfo, Juan (translator Lysander Kemp). **Pedro Páramo: A Novel of Mexico.** Grove 1959.

A young man, after his mother's death, searches for his missing father in a remote Mexican village. Mature fiction.

Salinas, Luis Omar, and Lillian Faderman, editors. **From the Barrio: A Chicano Anthology.** Canfield Pr 1973.

With vibrant speech and earthy language, the Chicano poets, dramatists, essayists, and fiction writers in this anthology speak out strongly for *chicanismo*. Mature.

Simmen, Edward, editor. **The Chicano: From Caricature to Self-Portrait.** NAL 1971.

A group of short stories about Mexican-Americans, starting with stereotypes from the late nineteenth century and progressing to realistic views of the 1960s and 1970s. Included in the unique collection are stories by Bret Harte, Amado Múro, Jack London, Philip D. Ortego, John Steinbeck, Ray Bradbury, and Nick C. Vaca. Fiction.

Simmen, Edward, editor. **Pain and Promise: The Chicano Today.** NAL 1972.

A balanced examination—both objective and subjective

—of the culture, problems, and accomplishments of contemporary Chicanos. Relying on a wide variety of sources, both white and Chicano, these thirty-two essays were selected from publications as diverse as the *Nation, Newsweek,* and *Sociology and Social Research* to *Con Safos* and *El Grito.* Nonfiction.

Steiner, Stan. **La Raza: The Mexican Americans.** Har-Row 1970.

A vivid, moving account of Mexican-American life in the United States. Steiner does not preach. Instead, he tells the stories of people—real people—and makes the culture, the concerns, the anguish, and the joys of the people live. Nonfiction.

Summers, James. **You Can't Make It by Bus.** Westminster 1969.

Paul Guevara finds himself in the city, where he is not accepted as a first-class citizen, and he is torn between his conservative father and his revolutionary Chicano friends. Fiction.

Terzian, James P., and Kathryn Cramer. **Mighty Hard Road: The Story of Cesar Chavez.** PB 1970.

A brief biography of Chavez, from his early days as a poorly paid fieldhand to his efforts to organize and bring power to the United Farm Workers union. Nonfiction.

Valdez, Luis, and Stan Steiner, editors. **Aztlan: An Anthology of Mexican American Literature.** VinRandom 1972.

A collection of material covering the origins of Mexican-Americans and their problems, both past and present. Mature.

Vasquez, Richard. **Chicano** (©1970). Avon 1971.

The history of the Sandoval family, from a nondescript life in Mexico to the barrios of East Los Angeles, and their search for the good life and their cultural identity. Fiction.

Villarreal, José Antonio. **Pocho** (© 1959). Doubleday 1970.

A young Mexican grows up during the Depression and learns how to survive in a white world. Mature fiction.

Villasenor, Edmund. **Macho!** Bantam 1973.

Roberto Garcia, eldest son of a poor Mexican family, tries to escape the poverty of his village by illegally entering the United States. Fiction.

Waters, Frank. **People of the Valley.** Swallow 1941.

The story of Maria del Valle who, though raised with goats, grows to be a wise and influential woman among the people who live quietly in the isolation of the Sangre de Cristo mountains as the machinery of modern American "progress" moves in. Mature fiction.

OTHER ETHNIC EXPERIENCES

Chapman, Abraham, editor. **Jewish American Literature: An Anthology.** NAL 1974.

An anthology of fiction, autobiography, poetry, and essays by writers like Dorothy Parker, Bernard Malamud, Philip Roth, David Ignatow, Denise Levertov, and Elie Wiesel about the Jewish heritage and experience. Mature.

Colman, Hila. **A Girl from Puerto Rico.** Morrow 1961.

A teenage daughter convinces her mother to move to the United States where life will be better. However, the family quickly feels the constraints of living in New York's Spanish ghetto. Fiction.

David, Jay, editor. **Growing Up Jewish.** Morrow 1969.

This collection of autobiographical sketches includes selections by Harry Golden, Anne Frank, Edna Ferber, and Alfred Kazin. The recurring theme is the pattern of Jewish family life. Nonfiction.

Hosokawa, Bill. **Nisei: The Quiet Americans.** Morrow 1969.

Japanese-Americans have been a part of the United States for generations, but the stereotyped image of the Japanese and their internment during World War II make clear how poorly they have been understood. Nonfiction.

Houston, Jeanne W., and James D. Houston. **Farewell to Manzanar.** HM 1973.

During World War II a community called Manzanar was hastily created in the east Sierras to house thousands of Japanese-American internees. Jeanne Wakatuski, a seven-year-old at the time, recalls with vivid observations the fear, frustration, and bewilderment experienced by her family. Nonfiction.

Hubmann, Franz, editor. **The Jewish Family Album.** Little 1975.

More than 300 photographs from 1850 to 1945 taken in Russia, Poland, and America illustrating Jewish life. Nonfiction.

Mangione, Jerre. **Mount Allegro.** Crown 1972.

Twelve-year-old Gerry Amoroso is born an American but reared by Sicilian parents who act as though they had never left their homeland. Living in two worlds, Gerry tries to cope with the values of his family and the values expressed by Americans outside his family. Fiction.

Matilla, Alfredo, and Ivan Silen, editors. **The Puerto Rican Poets.** Bantam 1972.

A bilingual anthology (a poem is given in Spanish on one page and in English on the opposite) of Puerto Rican poets, a few before 1955 but the majority by contemporary poets.

Matsuoka, Jack. **Camp II, Block 211: Daily Life in an Internment Camp.** Japan Pubns 1974.

A book of cartoons, from funny to bitter, picturing the life of Japanese-American interned by the government during World War II. Nonfiction.

Means, Florence Crannell. **The Moved-Outers.** HM 1945.

The author present the moving story of the O'Haras, a Japanese-American family prior to and during its relocation following the bombing of Pearl Harbor during World War II. Fiction.

Metzker, Isaac, editor. **A Bintel Brief.** Ballantine 1971.

This volume presents a realistic portrait of New York City Jews and their problems of assimilation. Nonfiction.

Nee, Victor G. and Brett de Bary Nee. **Longtime Californ': A Documentary Study of an American Chinatown.** Pantheon 1973.

The story of Chinatown in San Francisco, the people who live there, their families and societies. Mature nonfiction.

Nuligak (editor and translator Maurice Metayer). **I Nuligak.** PB 1966.

The autobiography of Nuligak, an Eskimo born around 1895. Nuligak very early learns the harsh life of the Arctic cold, hunting caribou for survival and fighting epidemics that wipe out entire villages. Nonfiction.

Porter, Jack N., and Peter Dreier, editors. **Jewish Radicalism: A Selected Anthology.** Grove 1973.

This volume contains selections by forty writers who examine the oppression of Jews in the Soviet Union and the concerns of younger Jews who are vitally interested in their heritage and social questions. Mature nonfiction.

Ruesch, Hans. **Back to the Top of the World.** Scribner 1973.

One nomadic Polar Eskimo family's head-on cultural conflict with the white man's values. Allows the reader to see the world from the Eskimo's point of view, a world in which the struggle for survival is the primary concern. Fiction.

Soto, Pedro J. **Hot Land, Cold Season.** Dell 1973.

A revealing look at Puerto Rican life both in Puerto Rico and in the United States. Jacinto, torn in his allegiance, his identity, and his language, searches for a place to belong. Fiction.

Thomas, Piri. **Down These Mean Streets** (© 1967). NAL 1971.

Thomas speaks from personal experiences as a youth growing up in Spanish Harlem. The eldest of seven children, Thomas recalls his years in prison and his fight for rehabilitation as a step in regaining his manhood. Some readers may find situations and language distasteful. Mature nonfiction.

Thomas, Piri. **Seven Long Times.** Praeger 1974.

Thomas recounts his arrest, conviction, and seven years in jail for armed robbery and felonious assault during the 1950s. He hates the racism and insensitivity around him, but he is able to find a safety valve for his emotions in his reading and especially in his writing. Some readers may object to both situations and language. Mature nonfiction.

Tuck, Jay N., and Norma G. Vergara. **Heroes of Puerto Rico.** Fleet 1969.

The authors present a historical treatise on Puerto Rico through the eyes and words of this country's famous individuals who struggled for the freedom and dignity of their people. Nonfiction.

Yoshida, Jim (with Bill Hosokawa). **The Two Worlds of Jim Yoshida.** Morrow 1972.

Born in Seattle, Washington, of Japanese-American parents, Jim and his sisters were taken to Japan following the death of their father; they were trapped there when World War II started. Forced to serve in the Japanese Army, Jim lost his American citizenship. This is his own account of serving in two wars and his attempt to regain his American citizenship. Nonfiction.

COLLECTED ETHNIC EXPERIENCES

Baron, Virginia Olsen, editor. **Here I Am!** (© 1969). Bantam 1971.

Through the medium of poetry, with accompanying photographs, young Americans from various minority groups—black, Cuban, Eskimo, Puerto Rican, Native American, Japanese, and Chinese—speak out for themselves, revealing their innermost joys, dreams, aspirations, sorrows, and sometimes anger.

Jacobs, Paul, and Saul Landau (with Eve Pell). **To Serve the Devil,** 2 vols. VinRandom 1971.

A history of the mistreatment of American racial minorities—Indians, blacks, Chicanos, Hawaiians, Chinese, Japanese, and Puerto Ricans. Mature nonfiction.

Light, Ivan H. **Ethnic Enterprise in America: Business and Welfare among Chinese, Japanese and Blacks.** U of Cal Pr 1972.

Light has written a satisfying book on the perplexing problem of minority business enterprise in three ethnic communities. They are the black, Chinese, and Japanese communities. The work contributes to the understanding of both the sociology of ethnicity and the sociology of business enterprise. Nonfiction.

Lowenfels, Walter, editor. **From the Belly of the Shark.** VinRandom 1973.

Poems by Chicano, Indian, Puerto Rican, Eskimo, black, and Hawaiian writers appear here for the first time. Lowenfels states: "[The poets] have their own way of speaking, their own music and cultural patterns." Mature.

Murphy, Sharon. **Other Voices: Black, Chicano, and American Indian Press.** Pflaum-Standard 1974.

A history and description of black, Chicano, and Indian newspapers, minority personalities in the media, and communications ideas. Mature nonfiction.

Rothenberg, Jerome, and George Quasha, editors. **America a Prophecy** (© 1973). VinRandom 1974.

A new reading of poetry from pre-Columbian times to the present, this volume includes selections from American Indian, black, Asian, and Chicano cultures. Represented are such writers as John Cage, William Faulkner, Eugene Jolas, William Carlos Williams, Langston Hughes, and Jose Garcia Villa. Mature.

Selvin, David. **The Other San Francisco.** Seabury 1969.

An account of contributions of various ethnic groups to the building of this famous West Coast city. Nonfiction.

Turner, Mary, editor. **We, Too, Belong: An Anthology about Minorities in America.** Dell 1969.

Short stories, poetry, and nonfiction about many minorities, their hopes, dreams, fears, and realities.

Wand, David Hsin-Fu, editor. **Asian American Heritage: An Anthology of Prose and Poetry.** WSP 1974.

A collection of stories, poetry, and essays of people with an Asian heritage. The book covers almost every Asian nationality and has a helpful bibliography for further reading.

Wheeler, Thomas C., editor. **The Immigrant Experience: The Anguish of Becoming American.** Penguin 1971.

Brief articles and historical sketches about the problems of becoming citizens by Irish, Italians, Norwegians, Puerto Ricans, Chinese, Polish, blacks, and Jews. Nonfiction.

URBAN LIFE, URBAN CONCERNS

Bell, Gwen, and Jacqueline Tyrwhitt, editors. **Human Identity in the Urban Environment** (© 1972). Penguin 1973.

Writers including W. H. Auden, Buckminster Fuller, Arnold Toynbee, and Margaret Mead speak to the question: "How are persons to remain human in the coming wilderness of steel, concrete and tarmac?" Mature nonfiction.

Bettmann, Otto L. **The Good Old Days—They Were Terrible.** Random 1974.

Disturbed by the nostalgia for the past of the last few years, the author proves that the past was not a happy time. The air was polluted years ago, traffic was dangerous, housing was inadequate, crime was common, health standards were terrible, and working conditions were disgraceful. Many illustrations. Nonfiction.

Burke, Carl F., editor. **Treat Me Cool, Lord.** Assn Pr 1968.

A collection of brief and simple prayers by young people who composed them while in jail, in detention homes, and in summer camps for disadvantaged youth. Expressed in the kids' own—sometimes frank—language.

Cahill, Tom, and Susan Cahill, editors. **Big City Stories by Modern American Writers.** Bantam 1971.

Moving from big city ghetto tenements to high-rise apartments, authors such as James Baldwin, Bernard Malamud, Nelson Algren, and Jack Kerouac describe how it is to live in these cities, including methods of survival. Fiction.

Childress, Alice. **A Hero Ain't Nothin' But a Sandwich** (© 1973). Avon 1974.

Ten people, including his mother, grandmother, stepfather, friends, and teachers, tell the story of Benjie Johnson, a thirteen-year-old black boy well on his way to being hooked on heroin. Fiction.

Clarke, Robin, and Geoffrey Hindley. **The Challenge of the Primitives.** McGraw 1975.

Primitive cultures, the authors claim, offer alternatives to the urban-industrial organization of the modern state, which they claim can last only another two centuries. Mature nonfiction.

Cook, Ann, Marilyn Gittell, and Herb Mack. **City Life, 1865–1900: Views of Urban America.** Praeger 1973.

Contemporary sources from 1865 to 1900, such as pictures, magazine articles, newspaper stories, and advertisements, give a picture of the reality of city life, the smells and the bustle, the filth and the poverty, the pleasures and the dangers. Nonfiction.

Dales, Hy, and Joanna Matturri, editors. **Inner City Reflections in Black and White.** WSP 1973.

Impressions and reflections of life in the inner city are vividly revealed through a collection of visuals by young photographers who live it. Nonfiction.

Fried, Joseph P. **Housing Crisis USA** (© 1971). Penguin 1972.

The author discusses the need for more and better housing for all Americans. Mature nonfiction.

Georgakas, Dan, and Marvin Surkin. **Detroit: I Do Mind Dying.** St Martin 1974.

After a violent urban rebellion in the summer of 1967, Detroit's citizens organized to make their grievances against industries, unions, and police felt. Nonfiction.

Halacy, D. S., Jr. **Your City Tomorrow.** Schol Bk Serv 1973.

This book examines the reasons for cities throughout history and proposes some solutions for relieving the polluted environment and improving the quality of modern urban life. Nonfiction.

Heizer, Robert F., and Alan F. Almquist. **The Other Californians.** U of Cal Pr 1971.

The authors describe little-known facts about California history, especially as it pertains to several identifiable ethnic groups, such as Mexican, Chinese, Japanese, and black. The two anthropologists document official and general public attitudes toward these groups from the eighteenth century to the early years of the twentieth. Nonfiction.

Hellman, Hal. **The City in the World of the Future.** M Evans 1970.

The author discusses the nature of the city and city living and suggests some aspects of the city in the years to come. Nonfiction.

Jordan, June, and Terri Bush, editors. **The Voice of the Children** (© 1970). PB 1974.

What would happen if twenty-six ghetto kids from New York City were brought together in a writing workshop to express their ambitions, their frustrations, and their joys? Well, it was done, and the resulting poetry is full of surprises.

Joseph, Stephen M., editor. **The Me Nobody Knows: Children's Voices from the Ghetto** (© 1969). Avon 1972.

An anthology of prose and poetry by young people from the ghetto who write about their world, their joys, sorrows, and problems. Often moving, with occasional use of words that may offend some people.

Larrick, Nancy, editor. **I Heard a Scream in the Street: Poems by Young People in the City** (© 1970). Dell 1972.

Young people from the inner city write poems about their lives—the sights and sounds and smells and violence that affect them.

Lens, Sidney. **Poverty, Yesterday and Today.** T Y Crowell 1973.

Poverty and the conditions leading to poverty have plagued humanity for hundreds of years. The author describes some conditions of poverty and some attempts made to alter them. Nonfiction.

Lipsyte, Robert. **The Contender** (© 1967). Bantam 1969.

Alfred, a black seventeen-year-old dropout, wants to get out of the ghetto, so he becomes a prizefighter. Fiction.

Liston, Robert A. **Downtown—Our Challenging Urban Problems** (© 1965). Dell 1969.

Liston writes with understanding and deep concern for those persons who live in America's cities. He believes that social problems in the cities will only be solved by those who live there. Nonfiction.

Meltzer, Milton, and Bernard Cole. **The Eye of Conscience: Photographers and Social Change.** Follett 1974.

This volume contains more than 100 photographs by noted photographers, past and present, who used their cameras for the benefit of others. Included are biographical sketches of the photographers and a pictorial perspective of social change in America. Nonfiction.

Michaels, Leonard. **Going Places.** NAL 1969.

Michaels's collection includes stories whose themes center around life in urban America's big city—New York. Students will find his stories present a kaleidoscopic pattern of human relationships. Mature fiction.

Michelsohn, David Reuben. **Housing in Tomorrow's World.** Messner 1973.

Good public housing for our citizens has been the aim of the government for years. The author describes some ways of meeting the housing problem without ruining the environment. Nonfiction.

Mohr, Nicholasa. **Nilda.** Har-Row 1973.

Spanish Harlem is the setting for this story of Nilda, a first generation Puerto Rican growing up in New York City. The author portrays the pleasures, pains, sorrows, and joys that Nilda experiences as she copes with her environment. Fiction.

Moquin, Wayne, and Charles Van Doren, editors. **A Documentary History of the Italian Americans.** Praeger 1974.

This anthology indicates the variety of Italian-American life through newspapers, magazines, letters, parish and organizational papers, and other documents which highlight the struggle and success of the Italians in America. Nonfiction.

Norwood, Christopher. **About Paterson.** Sat Rev Pr 1974.

Founded in 1792 by Alexander Hamilton, Paterson, New Jersey, soon became a center of textile manufacturing more often than not run by city bosses. In 1966, the political machine was ousted and Mayor Lawrence F. Kramer began the fight to remake the town. Mature nonfiction.

Platt, Kin. **Headman.** Morrow 1975.

Owen Kirby, tough but alone, wanders into the wrong territory in ghetto Los Angeles and nearly gets himself killed. Picked up because of the fight, he is sent to a work camp where he learns about work and hope and maybe even a future. Then he returns to his home and finds that escaping the world of the ghetto is impossible. Fiction.

Richardson, Harry W. **Urban Economics.** Penguin 1972.

The author examines key economic problems of the city, such as location, rent and land values, growth and urban renewal. Mature nonfiction.

Smith, Dennis. **Report from Engine Co. 82.** PB 1972.

A personal account of typical events in one of the world's busiest fire stations in the black ghetto of the Bronx. Smith, an eight-year veteran, portrays what it's like to be a fireman—its excitements, dangers, and everyday demands. Nonfiction.

UTOPIAS AND COMMUNES

Apsler, Alfred. **Communes through the Ages: The Search for Utopia.** Messner 1974.

A brief history of the development of communes and why people seem to need them. Different groups like Oneida and the Shakers, modern communes, and the problems of living in communes are discussed. Nonfiction.

Bellamy, Edward. **Looking Backward** (© 1888). NAL 1960.

Julian West falls asleep in the year 1887 and wakes up in the year 2000. In his narrative he describes a world of peace and plenty, a "perfect society" in which no social classes exist, where there is equality of income, and where production is in the hands of the state. Fiction.

Brand, Millen. **Fields of Peace: A Pennsylvania German Album** (© 1970). Dutton 1973.

A documentary of the predominantly German people who live in Pennsylvania. The author takes a loving look at the Amish, Mennonites, Moravians, Catholics, and Lutherans, as well as others who live a primarily rural life on beautifully cultivated land. Nonfiction.

Butler, Samuel. **Erewhon** (© 1872). NAL 1961.

With the narrative set in the imaginary world of Erewhon, Samuel Butler satirizes institutions and practices such as evolution, medicine, education, and justice. Fiction.

Cohen, Daniel. **Not of the World: A History of the Commune in America.** Follett 1974.

Although many persons believe that communal living is new and revolutionary, the author shows how many types of communes, from the Dutch Labadists to the contemporary Children of God, have been part of the American movement to create utopias in the new world. Nonfiction.

Colman, Hila. **The Family and the Fugitive.** Morrow 1972.

Five young people attempt to set up communal living in the countryside of Massachusetts and establish a coffee house. They take in a young woman who is wanted by the F.B.I. for protesting the draft. Although the commune does not fully succeed, they learn that traditional values are also important. Fiction.

Connolly, Edward. **Deer Run** (© 1971). Berkley Pub 1973.

A group of young people establish a communal farm and discover what it means to be outsiders as the nearby townspeople first show suspicion and fear which rapidly becomes antagonism. Fiction.

De Ropp, Robert S. **Church of the Earth: The Ecology of a Creative Community.** Dell 1974.

The author describes how a "creative community" was founded in Sonoma County, California. The journal begins with the building of the temple and includes the routine of the community, called the Church of the Earth, from farming, bee-keeping, fishing, and wine-making to the development of crafts to bring in income. Nonfiction.

Faber, Doris. **The Perfect Life: The Shakers in America.** FS&G 1974.

The history of the Shakers in America is traced from pre-Revolutionary days to the present. The author attempts to analyze present-day interest in the group, as well as to speculate about reasons for the successes and failures of the sect. Nonfiction.

France, Anatole (translator Belle Notkin Burke). **Penguin Island** (© 1908). NAL 1968.

Mistakenly baptized by a nearly blind old priest, a tribe of penguins is transformed into human beings. Their story provides an allegorical framework for a satirical attack upon French history in particular and all humanity in general. The author's chief targets are the Church, the institution of private property, and the politics of power. Fiction.

Gerber, Richard. **Utopian Fantasy** (© 1955). McGraw 1973.

A study of English utopian fantasies from the end of the nineteenth century to the present. Included are appendices listing utopian constructs from 1901 to 1971. Mature nonfiction.

Hall, Lynn. **Too Near the Sun** (© 1970). Dell 1972.

Armel's brother has left Icaria, a small nineteenth-century Iowa commune, and Armel's family cannot understand why anyone would want to leave a perfect society. Then Armel begins to detect the rigid restrictions of Icaria and begins to question the wisdom of the elders. Fiction.

Hedgepeth, William, and Dennis Stock. **The Alternative: Communal Life in New America.** Macmillan 1970.

New Buffalo, Messiah's World, Land of Oz, and Hog Farm—just four of the growing number of communes populated by groups of Americans (not all of them young people) who seek a way of life they think we once had. Nonfiction.

Hilton, James. **Lost Horizon** (© 1922). PB 1939.

Three men and a woman, escaping a revolution, crash-land in a plane on a high plateau in Tibet. They are rescued and brought to a Buddhist lamasery and village called Shangri-la, in the valley of the Blue Moon. There they encounter a utopian civilization practicing the Greek concept of moderation. Fiction.

Hoover, Helen. **The Gift of the Deer.** Knopf 1966.

Living in the wilderness of northeastern Minnesota, the Hoovers establish a harmonious relationship with all of nature. They befriend a family of whitetail deer and observe the living habits of a variety of wild animals. Nonfiction.

Horwitz, Elinor Lander. **Communes in America: The Place Just Right.** Lippincott 1972.

The author describes literary utopias and then surveys several collective settlements in the United States, such as the Shakers, New Harmony, Brook Farm, and others, and compares them with contemporary communes which continue the tradition of "the place just right." Nonfiction.

Howells, William Dean. **A Traveler from Altruria** (© 1894). Hill & Wang 1957.

Mr. Homos, a visitor from utopian Altruria, visits America during the great depression of 1893. Through his questions, he uncovers a number of disquieting elements in American culture and society. Fiction.

Huxley, Aldous. **Brave New World** (© 1932). Har-Row 1969.

In the brave new world of 632 After Ford (as time is reckoned in the future), babies are turned out through mass production, people are given the drug soma to keep them happy, individualism is discouraged, and people are conditioned for their roles in life. Then a young man comes from the Savage Reservation and challenges many beliefs of the brave new world. A devastating satire. Fiction.

Kinkade, Kathleen. **A Walden Two Experiment: The First Five Years of Twin Oaks Community.** Morrow 1973.

One of the founders of the Twin Oaks community writes about the reason for establishing the commune, the people it attracted, and the problems that arose. Nonfiction.

Koestler, Arthur. **Darkness at Noon** (© 1941). Bantam 1970.

An aging revolutionary is imprisoned by the party he has served all his life. The party asks him to confess his part in some anti-party crimes, and as he waits to be tortured, he relives his life as a member of a totalitarian society. Fiction.

Lawson, Donna. **Brothers and Sisters All Over This Land: America's First Communes.** Praeger 1972.

The author surveys several early American communes, such as the Amana community, Oneida, Brook Farm, Shakers, and later ones, like Father Divine's establishment in Harlem during the Depression. Nonfiction.

More, Sir Thomas (translator Peter K. Marshall). **Utopia.** PB 1965.

More wrote this picture of a perfect world in 1516 as a satire on Elizabethan England, but it has influenced writers and political thinkers ever since then. More coined the word "utopia" from Greek words which mean "no place," meaning that no ideal society like *Utopia* existed. Mature fiction.

Muncy, Raymond Lee. **Sex and Marriage in Utopian Communities: 19th Century America.** Penguin 1973.

Choosing from among some 500 utopian communities existing in nineteenth-century America, the author looks closely at the forms of marriage and family life within these communes. Nonfiction.

Mungo, Raymond. **Total Loss Farm: A Year in the Life.** Bantam 1970.

The author, having lived with some friends on a farm in Vermont, celebrates the simple life, but notes that many people cannot adapt to the life of a commune. He points out some of the problems that many have found in living such a life. Nonfiction.

O'Neill, David P. **The Book of Rewi.** Seabury 1975.

Six young people are shipwrecked on a South Pacific island and begin to develop their own society. Fiction.

Orwell, George. **1984** (© 1948). NAL 1971.

It is 1984 and a benevolent dictatorship, called Big Brother, rules the world where Winston Smith works. People are indoctrinated to believe that sex is bad; in fact, anything is bad which takes the attention and devotion of people away from Big Brother. Winston finds some forgotten but deep feelings of passion and love for a girl and joins the underground. Fiction.

Plato (editor Charles Bakewell and translator Benjamin Jowett). **The Republic.** Scribner 1928.

The great Greek philosopher of the fifth century B.C. seeks the definition of justice through the conversation of Socrates and a group of young men, who together develop the organization of the ideal community. Mature nonfiction.

Richards, Jerry. **The Good Life.** NAL 1973.

From a large number of sources, the editor has collected descriptions of various communal experiments from the 1800s to today. Nonfiction.

Stiller, Richard. **Commune on the Frontier: The Story of Frances Wright.** T Y Crowell 1972.

Frances Wright organized a unique commune, published a radical newspaper, criticized organized religion, opposed marriage as a threat to women's freedom, and preached racial brotherhood—all more than 140 years ago. Her motto: "The mind has no sex." Nonfiction.

Wizansky, Richard, editor. **Home Comfort: Life on Total Loss Farm.** NAL 1973.

From philosophy to recipes, life on Total Loss Farm in Vermont is described by persons who came from all walks of life to live harmoniously with nature and the land. Nonfiction.

Yambura, Barbara S. (with Eunice W. Bodine). **A Change and a Parting: My Story of Amana.** Iowa St U Pr 1960.

For seventy-five years, the Society of True Inspirationists flourished in Amana, Iowa. From the view of one who was born and raised among this religious-communal society, the beliefs and customs of the "ideal community" are portrayed. Nonfiction.

POLITICS, THE LAW, AND HUMANITY

Aymar, Brandt, and Edward Sagarin. **Laws and Trials That Created History.** Crown 1974.

Accounts of twenty-four trials which have been turning points in history, including those of Socrates, Joan of Arc, Galileo, Sacco and Vanzetti, Angela Davis, and the Chicago Seven. Generously illustrated.

Bailey, F. Lee (with John Greenya). **For the Defense.** Atheneum 1975.

One of America's greatest and most famous defense attorneys tells about his criminal law practice, his trials, and his clients, among them Captain Ernest Medina of My Lai Vietnam War fame and black militant Sonny Carson.

Baker, Leonard. **John Marshall: A Life in Law.** Macmillan 1974.

John Marshall was chief justice of the United States Supreme Court from 1801 to 1835. His principles, love of country, and legal brilliance made the Supreme Court the interpreter of the Constitution and truly the "high court of the land." Mature.

Barth, Alan. **Prophets with Honor: Great Dissents and Great Dissenters in the Supreme Court.** Knopf 1974.

The author discusses the nature and use of dissent in the U.S. Supreme Court and devotes separate chapters to six important dissents, from John Marshall Harlan's 1896 dissent on separate but equal facilities for blacks in *Plessy* v. *Ferguson* to William O. Douglas's 1951 dissent on freedom of speech in *Dennis* v. *United States.* Mature.

Black, Hugo, Jr. **My Father: A Remembrance.** Random 1975.

The author's father was Hugo Black, justice of the United States Supreme Court. The elder Black was a Southerner, a member at one time of the Ku Klux Klan, but he became one of the great liberal justices of all time.

Boyer, Paul S. **Purity in Print: The Vice Society Movement and Book Censorship in America.** Scribner 1968.

The pressures for book censorship increased from the

nineteenth century to the 1930s, particularly because of Anthony Comstock, America's chief unofficial censor for years. Mature.

Carter, Joseph. **Freedom to Know.** Parents 1974.

Freedom to know the truth through books and newspapers and television is basic to our lives. The author analyzes how propaganda and censorship and political chicanery have caused problems in letting us exercise the freedom to know.

Clancy, Paul R. **Just a Country Lawyer: A Biography of Senator Sam Ervin.** Ind U Pr 1974.

The life of the North Carolina senator covers his early work as lawyer and judge, but probably the most interesting parts are devoted to his great influence in Congress and his chairmanship of the committee investigating Watergate.

Clor, Harry M. **Obscenity and Public Morality: Censorship in a Liberal Society** (© 1969). U of Chicago Pr 1971.

Attorney Clor believes that obscenity must be legally controlled and a philosophy of censorship developed to serve the public interest. Mature.

Coughlin, George G. **Your Introduction to Law.** B&N 1967.

An overview of the legal profession and the American court system. Contracts, wills, criminal law, patents, divorce, and many other aspects of law are briefly introduced to give an idea of the nature, purpose, and difficulty of legal rules.

Deming, Richard. **Man against Man: Civil Law at Work** (© 1972). Dell 1974.

A history of civil law from its origins to today with chapters on different kinds of civil cases. Useful glossary.

Deming, Richard. **Man and Society: Criminal Law at Work** (© 1970). Dell 1974.

Criminal law, the author notes, "defines crimes and fixes penalties." He gives the origins of modern-day criminal law and shows how it works in the courts.

Dorman, Michael. **Under 21: A Young People's Guide to Legal Rights** (© 1970). Dell 1971.

The rights of young people in almost every area of life are examined.

Dorsen, Norman, editor. **The Rights of Americans: What They Are, What They Should Be** (© 1970). VinRandom 1972.

Essays commemorating the fiftieth anniversary of the American Civil Liberties Union all dealing with our basic rights, such as the right to vote, the right to legal services, the right to housing, and the rights of women.

Farson, Richard. **Birthrights: A Bill of Rights for Children.** Macmillan 1974.

Farson, a psychologist, discusses a number of human rights he believes should be granted to children, including the right to a single set of rules for behavior of adults and children; the right to choose their own homes; freedom from physical punishment; and the right to political power.

Fleming, Alice. **Trials That Made Headlines.** St Martin 1973.

Ten landmark trials that have helped to shape our legal system, from the Boston Massacre Trial to the Nuremburg Trials.

Forman, James D. **Law and Disorder.** Nelson 1972.

A history of the creation of law, change in legal systems, the rights granted us under our system of law, and a look at the future of the law.

Fribourg, Marjorie G. **The Bill of Rights** (© 1967). Avon 1969.

Though it is more than 150 years old, the Bill of Rights has frequently been reinterpreted to guarantee our basic civil rights as times and conditions change.

Gaylin, Willard. **Partial Justice: A Study of Bias in Sentencing.** Knopf 1974.

A major cause of attacks on the American court system has been the discrepancy in sentences given different persons for the same crimes. The author interviews four judges in depth about this problem.

Gillers, Stephen. **Getting Justice: The Rights of People** (© 1971). NAL 1973.

The rights of all American citizens when arrested, wiretapped, or arraigned.

Goodman, Elaine, and Walter Goodman. **The Rights of the People: The Major Decisions of the Warren Court.** FS&G 1971.

The authors review major Supreme Court decisions from Earl Warren's appointment as chief justice in 1953 until his retirement in 1969.

Habenstreit, Barbara. **Changing America and the Supreme Court.** Messner 1974.

The history of the origin of the United States Supreme Court, the changes that have taken place, the court battles, and the personalities of the judges.

Habenstreit, Barbara. **Eternal Vigilance: The American Civil Liberties Union in Action.** Messner 1973.

The ACLU has devoted its energies for better than fifty years to protecting the constitutional rights of all citizens of whatever political belief. The author recounts some of the controversies the ACLU has been involved in.

Harrison, Eddie, and Alfred V. J. Prather. **No Time for Dying.** P-H 1973.

Eddie Harrison made some serious mistakes, but he insisted that he did not murder Cider George. He felt victimized by the white establishment and this book details the story of his arrest and conviction, and the final resolution of the case.

Heaps, Willard A. **Juvenile Justice.** Seabury 1974.

The number of juveniles arrested for crimes has risen to more than two million annually. The kinds of crimes, the juvenile justice system, probation, and sentences are discussed.

Hiebert, Ray, Robert Jones, Ernest Lotito, and John Lorenz, editors. **The Political Image Merchants: Strategies in the New Politics.** Acropolis 1971.

Brief sections by politicians and political commentators on the coming roles of television, survey research

and polling, and computers in creating new kinds of
politics and politicans.

Hoopes, Roy. **Getting with Politics: A Guide to Political Action for Young People** (© 1968). Dell 1969.

A guide to the nature of politics, working at the precinct level, differences in political parties, and voting.

Hoyt, Olga G., and Edwin P. Hoyt. **Censorship in America.** Seabury 1970.

Since humans first spoke or thought or wrote or acted,
others (censors) have objected to something about the
words or thoughts or actions. The authors tell the
story of the censor in our country, the reasons some
people believe in censorship, the reasons other people
fear the censor and thought control.

Iannuzzi, John Nicholas. **Courthouse.** Doubleday 1975.

Marc Conte, a thirty-two-year-old New York lawyer,
firmly believes in the ideals of American justice, but
the judicial system he encounters in three cases makes
him begin to question just how fair the system really
is. Fiction.

LeMond, Alan, and Ron Fry. **No Place to Hide.** St Martin 1975.

A description of surveillance devices like "bugs" and
wiretaps which diminish our chances for privacy today.
The book has frightening implications about the kind
of world we now have, a world that we have made.

Levy, Elizabeth. **Lawyers for the People.** Knopf 1974.

Job sketches on nine young lawyers who have chosen
to represent people who might otherwise be too poor
or unorganized to obtain legal services. Their clients:
the poor, juveniles, prisoners, radicals, consumers.

Lewis, Anthony. **Gideon's Trumpet.** VinRandom 1964.

A four-time loser in a Florida prison writes his own
legal appeal to the United States Supreme Court. The
court did look into his case and in the process evolved
a major legal principle.

Liston, Robert A. **Politics from Precinct to Presidency.**
Dell 1970.

What goes on in front of the public and what takes

place behind the political scenes from local politics to national elections.

Liston, Robert A. **Who Really Runs America?** Doubleday 1974.

The federal government and how and why it works as it does, from elective officers and appointive personnel to judges and lobbyists.

Meltzer, Milton. **The Right to Remain Silent.** HarBraceJ 1972.

Stories of men and women throughout history who have suffered torment, even death, in defending their right to remain silent. Settings include the Inquisition, Puritan England, and the McCarthy era.

Miller, Arthur R. **The Assault on Privacy: Computers, Data Banks, and Dossiers.** NAL 1971.

The development of modern technology has led to electronic threats to our privacy through data banks, computers, and wiretapping. Mature.

Murphy, Patrick T. **Our Kindly Parent—The State.** Viking Pr 1974.

Murphy's work in the juvenile office of Legal Aid convinced him that the state, acting as guardian, controlled the lives and destinies of many thousands of young people guilty of nothing more serious than running away from home. He and others have battled to change the juvenile justice system.

Murray, Robert K. **The 103rd Ballot: The Democrats and the Disaster in Madison Square Garden.** Har-Row 1976.

The 1924 Democratic convention lasted more than two weeks and 102 ballots before a presidential nominee was selected. The raucous, divisive events of the convention are vividly told and its long-term effects assessed.

Neier, Aryeh. **Dossier: The Secret Files They Keep on You.** Stein & Day 1974.

The executive secretary of the American Civil Liberties Union documents the data kept on citizens in credit bureau, Defense Department, F.B.I., school, police, and hospital files. He worries that much data are false or inaccurate yet citizens often do not know what is in these files or how the files can damage their lives. Mature.

Nizer, Louis. **My Life in Court** (© 1961). Pyramid Pubns 1972.

A famous trial lawyer tells about the cases he's been involved with, how lawyers plan strategy, how they gather and present evidence, and what happens in a real (not TV) trial.

Noble, Iris. **Clarence Darrow: Defense Attorney.** Messner 1958.

Darrow made himself unpopular by defending unpopular causes and unpopular clients. Three of his major cases involved "Big Bill" Haywood, a union leader accused of murder; Nathan Leopold and Richard Loeb, accused of killing a young boy; and John T. Scopes, accused of teaching evolution.

Reitman, Alan, editor. **The Pulse of Freedom: American Liberties, 1920–1970s.** Norton 1975.

A history of civil liberties in the United States from 1920 until the present: the famous Scopes "monkey" trial, civil liberties problems in World War II, the McCarthy era, and student protests. Mature.

Rembar, Charles. **The End of Obscenity.** Bantam 1968.

An attorney opposed to censorship fights in court to save three books, the most famous being *Lady Chatterly's Lover*. Mature nonfiction.

Rembar, Charles. **Perspective.** Arbor Hse 1975.

Lawyer Rembar looks into several constitutional cases which have become legal landmarks.

Rintels, David W. **Clarence Darrow.** Doubleday 1975.

A play written for one actor who portrays Clarence Darrow from his earliest days through his attempts to win fair wages and fair hours for workmen.

Schultz, John. **Motion Will Be Denied: A New Report on the Chicago Conspiracy Trial.** Morrow 1972.

During 1969–1970, the government charged eight people with conspiracy and with inciting riot during the

1968 Democratic Convention in Chicago. The defendants, the judge, the jurors, and the implications of the trial form the drama of the book.

Strouse, Jean. **Up Against the Law: The Legal Rights of People under 21.** NAL 1970.

Questions and answers about the legal rights of young people in many areas—school, marriage, sex, drugs, contracts, the draft, etc.

Switzer, Ellen. **There Ought to Be a Law! How Laws Are Made and Broken.** Atheneum 1974.

A brief explanation of how laws are made with examples of a bill not yet law (gun legislation), why some laws do not work (prohibition), and municipal codes and regulations.

Whalen, Charles W., Jr. **Your Right to Know.** VinRandom 1973.

The author contends that journalists will be unable to dig out and present news unless they are legally protected from having to reveal their sources of information.

Wilhelmsen, Frederick D., and Jane Bret. **Telepolitics.** Tundra Bks 1972.

The authors believe that television has created a new kind of citizen with a new kind of politics. They feel that television has made people more impatient, violent, and intolerant, and those characteristics will likely change democracy as we know it. Mature.

Wilkinson, J. Harvie, III. **Serving Justice: A Supreme Court Clerk's View.** Charterhouse 1974.

Wilkinson served as law clerk to Supreme Court Justice Louis Powell. He gives sketches of the different justices, their responsibilities and philosophies, and recent court decisions.

Wise, David. **The Politics of Lying: Government Deception, Secrecy and Power.** VinRandom 1973.

Wise documents charges that administrations under Eisenhower to Nixon have engaged in political lying and deception. Mature.

Zei, Alki (translator Edward Fenton). **Wildcat under Glass** (© 1968). Dell 1975.

In 1936 a fascist dictatorship comes to Greece. The lives of Melia and her family are dramatically changed under the dictatorship. Fiction.

Zinn, Howard, editor. **Justice in Everyday Life: The Way It Really Works.** Morrow 1974.

While everyone is supposed to have the same basic civil rights, some people have to fight harder for equal treatment. Civil liberties in the courts, prison, housing, work, and schools are discussed.

THE UNITED STATES

A. *Till the Civil War*

Abodaher, David J. **Warrior on Two Continents: Thaddeus Kosciuszko.** Messner 1968.

Kosciuszko fought bravely for liberty in the American colonies and in his native Poland, where he led an uprising against imperial Russia. Thomas Jefferson called him "as pure a son of liberty as I have ever known." Nonfiction.

Alderman, Clifford Lindsey. **The Devil's Shadow: The Story of Witchcraft in Massachusetts.** Messner 1967.

The dullness of life in Salem Village, Massachusetts, and the repressive character of the Puritan religion combined with the ignorance of the citizens to create the mass hysteria which resulted in the Salem Witch Trials. The devil's shadow lingered over Salem for one year, during which hundreds were unjustly imprisoned and twenty were executed as witches. Nonfiction.

Alderman, Clifford Lindsey. **Gathering Storm: The Story of the Green Mountain Boys.** Messner 1970.

During the Revolutionary War, the Green Mountain Boys of Vermont, led by Ethan Allen, attacked Fort Ticonderoga and captured guns that helped win the Battle of Boston and made invasion into Canada possible. Nonfiction.

Alderman, Clifford Lindsey. **The War We Could Have Lost.** Four Winds 1974.

The British should have won the American Revolutionary War. They had more money than the colonies, more and better trained troops, and plenty of supplies and ammunition. Alderman writes of the blunders that cost them important victories. Nonfiction.

Aldrich, Bess Streeter. **A Lantern in Her Hand** (© 1928). Tempo G&D n.d.

As a young bride Abbie Deal moves west to frontier Nebraska. There she encourages her children to pursue ambitions that once were her own. Fiction.

Asimov, Isaac. **The Birth of the United States, 1763–1816.** HM 1974.

A history of the founding and growth of our country from the Treaty of Paris in 1763 till the end of the War of 1812. Nonfiction.

Bowen, Catherine Drinker. **The Most Dangerous Man in America: Scenes from the Life of Benjamin Franklin.** Little 1974.

Five scenes from the life of Franklin, whom the crowned heads of England and many others in Europe saw as the most dangerous man in America two hundred years ago. The scenes dramatize Franklin's progress from satiric columnist to inventor to diplomat and revolutionary. Mature nonfiction.

Brand, Oscar. **Songs of '76: A Folksinger's History of the Revolution.** M Evans 1972.

More than sixty songs which present the American Revolution as the folk balladeer sang it: ". . . a compendium of music and verses, patriotic and treasonous, sung both by the rebels and the adherents of His Royal Majesty George III." Guitar accompaniment and historic commentary, too. Nonfiction.

Bristow, Gwen. **Celia Garth** (© 1959). Popular Lib 1969.

At the request of Francis Marion, the Swamp Fox, Celia Garth returns to British-held Charleston to spy for the rebels. Fiction.

Brockway, Edith. **Land beyond the Rivers.** Westminster 1966.

In 1754 young Alan Pepperill sees service with George Washington, battles with the French, and is captured by Indians. Fiction.

Brodie, Fawn M. **Thomas Jefferson: An Intimate History** (© 1974). Bantam 1975.

The emotional side of Jefferson, rather than the intellectual side, is the focus of this long biography of the great American president. His love affairs and his feelings about race and religion make him seem more human than he usually appears in history books. Mature nonfiction.

Cable, Mary. **Black Odyssey: The Case of the Slave Ship "Amistad."** Viking Pr 1971.

In 1839, at Long Island, thirty-nine ill and starving black men were taken from the slave ship *Amistad,* which they had controlled since killing the captain. Three years later, after bitter struggles between American slaveholders and abolitionists, the freed "Amistads" set sail for their homes, taking with them America's first missionaries to West Africa. (See also the 1976 National Book Award for history, David B. Davis, *The Problem of Slavery in the Age of Revolution: 1770–1823,* Cornell U Pr.) Nonfiction.

Cannon, Le Grand, Jr. **Look to the Mountain** (© 1942). Bantam 1971.

Hoping to build a home and a future for their children, Whit and Melissa face the hostile British and the rigors of the New Hampshire wilderness. Fiction.

Carmer, Carl. **The Hudson** (© 1939). HR&W 1974.

The Hudson River serves as a background to history unfolding as people from many different backgrounds come to settle along its banks during the early days of this country. Nonfiction.

Caudill, Rebecca. **Tree of Freedom.** Viking Pr 1949.

When each family member is allowed to choose one possession to take to their new home in Kentucky, Stephanie takes an apple seed to start her "tree of freedom." Story of the Venables' homesteading experiences in the late eighteenth century. Fiction.

Clapp, Patricia. **Constance: A Story of Early Plymouth.** Lothrop 1968.

Constance dislikes her life in Plymouth Colony from the moment she steps from the Mayflower. This book, her journal, is an account of her growing love for her new home and for the young man she marries. Fiction.

Clarke, Mary Stetson. **The Limner's Daughter.** Viking Pr 1967.

Shortly after Amity Lyte, her father, and her little brother go to live with her great-aunt Keziah in 1805, Amity converts the family home to an inn and unravels the mystery which makes them so unwelcome in Woburn, Massachusetts. Fiction.

Clifford, Eth. **Search for the Crescent Moon.** HM 1973.

In 1840 Tobias Bright and his Quaker grandfather seek the old man's twin sister, who was kidnapped by Delaware Indians when they were children. Fiction.

Colby, Jean Poindexter. **Lexington and Concord, 1775: What Really Happened.** Hastings 1975.

Colby's account of that April day in 1775 when Massachusetts colonists challenged the power of the British crown is drawn from letters, diaries, and eyewitness reports which emphasize little-known incidents. Original photographs and old prints and maps complement the text. Nonfiction.

Collier, Peter. **When Shall They Rest? The Cherokees' Long Struggle with America** (© 1973). Dell 1975.

The Cherokee, a fiercely independent nation, dropped their weapons and picked up the plowshare offered them by white men and developed a model republic. Nevertheless, they were driven from their Georgia land in 1838, and one quarter of them perished along their Trail of Tears to Oklahoma. Nonfiction.

Constiner, Merle. **Sumatra Alley.** Nelson 1971.

Approached by a threatening British agent who wants him to spy on the Sons of Liberty, young Brad Agnew becomes entangled in the dangerous game of counterspying as he tries to discover the leader of the revolutionaries in his neighborhood, Sumatra Alley. Fiction.

Croy, Homer. **Jesse James Was My Neighbor.** Hawthorn 1949.

A neighbor recalls the days when Jesse and Frank James were just the boys next door! Nonfiction.

Eaton, Jeanette. **Narcissa Whitman: Pioneer of Oregon.**
HarBraceJ 1941.

Whitman was one of the first white women to cross the
continent when, in 1836, she traveled with her new husband from New York to Oregon where they hoped to
educate the Indians. Nonfiction.

Edmonds, Walter D. **Drums along the Mohawk** (©
1936). Bantam 1951.

The hardy settlers of the Mohawk Valley fight both
British regulars and Iroquois Indians during the war
for independence. Fiction.

Fast, Howard. **April Morning** (© 1961). Bantam 1962.

Adam Cooper learns what growing up means when his
father is killed by British soldiers at the start of the
Revolutionary War. Fiction.

Fast, Howard. **The Hessian.** Morrow 1972.

A young Hessian soldier escapes from Connecticut
townsmen who have ambushed and destroyed his de-
tachment. Asked to treat the young man's wounds,
Dr. Feversham must decide whether he will aid the
enemy soldier or reveal his location to vengeful citizens. Fiction.

Finney, Gertrude E. **Is This My Love?** McKay 1956.

Beatrice Whitcliff and her friend Jennifer, who arrive
on a boat carrying brides for settlers in the colonies,
find life in the new land strange and crude. Fiction.

Forbes, Esther. **Johnny Tremain.** HM 1943.

Though Johnny's prospects as a silversmith dim when
he injures his hand, he finds that he can still play an
important role in the Revolutionary War. Fiction.

Forbes, Esther. **Paul Revere and the World He Lived
In.** HM 1942.

The Pulitzer Prize-winning biography of the patriot,
silversmith, and soldier. Nonfiction.

Foster, Genevieve. **The World of William Penn.** Scribner 1973.

Foster offers not only a biographical account of sensible, peace-loving William Penn, first governor of
Pennsylvania, but sketches of personalities and his-

torical events which significantly affected the world in which Penn lived. Nonfiction.

Gerson, Noel B. **Survival: Jamestown, First English Colony in America.** Messner 1967.

Indians, nature, and their own disunity—all were threats to the survival of the 150 men who settled Jamestown in 1606. For leadership they looked to Captain John Smith. Nonfiction.

Gibbs, Alonzo. **The Fields Breathe Sweet.** Lothrop 1963.

Two men care for Gretje—a lighthearted, wandering shoemaker and a Quaker devoted to the cause of religious freedom. At eighteen she must decide whether to marry one of them or to remain with her family. Fiction.

Giles, Janice Holt. **Johnny Osage** (© 1960). Paperback Lib 1972.

Johnny, an Osage Indian, tries to arrange a truce between his people and the Cherokee Indians in Oklahoma in the 1820s. Fiction.

Green, Margaret. **Radical of the Revolution: Samuel Adams.** Messner 1971.

Adams was "a firebrand who preached rebellion against authority, sided with the poor and oppressed against wealth and power and suffered years of mockery, hardship and seeming failure." He was, however, the man who kept the revolutionary flame alive. Nonfiction.

Griswold, Wesley S. **The Night the Revolution Began.** Greene 1972.

The Boston Tea Party on December 16, 1773, followed a series of protests by colonists and ignited the Revolutionary War. Nonfiction.

Gutheim, Frederick. **The Potomac** (© 1949). HR&W 1974.

The role of this river in the early history of the United States and its function in bringing together people of opposite cultures, the aristocrats and the farmers, as they settle on both sides of its banks. Nonfiction.

Haynes, Betsy. **Spies on the Devil's Belt.** Nelson 1974.

When Jonathan runs errands for his captain, he uses

the opportunity to spy on the British, a risk which nearly costs him his life. Fiction.

Hickman, Janet. **The Valley of the Shadow.** Macmillan 1974.

Tobias, a thirteen-year-old Delaware Indian boy, tells of life in the Moravian towns of the Ohio country during the Revolutionary War. Fiction.

Hofstadter, Richard. **America at 1750** (© 1971). Vin-Random 1973.

American colonial society, its religions, its slavery, its values, and its problems only two decades before the Revolutionary War. Mature nonfiction.

Jackson, Shirley. **The Witchcraft of Salem Village.** Random 1956.

In order to cover the traces of their playing sinful black magic games, several young girls in Puritan Salem Village, Massachusetts, accuse townspeople of being witches in 1692. Their foolishness results in the unjust executions of twenty citizens and the eventual destruction of the village. Fiction.

Ketchum, Richard M. **Decisive Day: The Battle for Bunker Hill.** Doubleday 1974.

A well-illustrated record of what led up to the battle of Bunker Hill and what came out of it. Nonfiction.

Lancaster, Bruce, and J. H. Plumb. **The American Heritage Book of the Revolution.** Dell 1963.

A concise and authoritative account of our country's struggle for independence, a struggle which we nearly lost. Mature nonfiction.

Meltzer, Milton. **Hunted Like a Wolf: The Story of the Seminole War.** FS&G 1972.

The Seminoles and the black fugitives who sought refuge with them fought valiantly to keep their freedom and their Florida land. The Seminole War (1835–42) was the longest, bloodiest, and most costly Indian war in America's history. Nonfiction.

Miller, Lillian B. **In the Minds and Hearts of the People: Prologue to the American Revolution, 1760–1774.** NYGS 1974.

The events that led up to the Revolutionary War,

with many contemporary illustrations and paintings. Nonfiction.

Molloy, Anne. **The Years before the Mayflower: The Pilgrims in Holland.** Hastings 1972.

Seeking religious freedom, a small group of Pilgrims left Britain in 1608 and settled in Holland. They remained there twelve years before arranging to travel to the New World. Nonfiction.

Morison, Samuel E. **Christopher Columbus, Mariner** (© 1955). NAL 1956.

Vivid and lively narrative of Columbus's life and voyages includes descriptions of fifteenth-century navigational methods and the routes Columbus followed. Nonfiction.

Nolan, Jeannette Covert. **Benedict Arnold, Traitor to His Country.** Messner 1956.

Though his motives were selfish, Arnold became a hero of the American Revolution. Later, greedy for money, he agreed to give the British information which might have led to the capture of West Point, the betrayal of George Washington, and the loss of independence for the American colonists. Nonfiction.

North, Sterling. **Captured by the Mohawks.** HM 1960.

After they murder and scalp his two companions, the Mohawks capture sixteen-year-old Pierre Radisson. Radisson accompanies his captors on war parties and, later, is the first to explore Lake Superior to its western limits and to visit the villages of the Dakota Sioux. Nonfiction.

Parkman, Francis. **The Oregon Trail** (© 1849). NAL 1972.

Journal of a young Easterner who set out to explore the uncivilized West in 1846, his experiences with Indians, outlaws, trappers, settlers, and fellow adventurers. Nonfiction.

Peck, Robert Newton. **Fawn.** Little 1975.

Fawn, a seventeen-year-old boy, grew up among his mother's Mohawk people. After refusing to join his French father in defending Fort Carillon, he runs off into the woods alone and gradually comes to understand the man. Fiction.

The People's Bicentennial Commission, editors. **Voices of the American Revolution.** Bantam 1974.

A brief review of events leading to the signing of the Declaration of Independence, followed by excerpts from documents of the period—"voices of the American Revolution." Generously illustrated with reprints of authentic portraits, sketches, and cartoons. Mature nonfiction.

Petry, Ann. **Tituba of Salem Village.** T Y Crowell 1964.

After leaving her native Barbados and coming to serve her new owner in New England, Tituba is accused of being a witch. A fully documented and suspenseful account of the Salem witchcraft era. Fiction.

Reeder, Red. **Bold Leaders of the Revolutionary War.** Little 1973.

A gallery of twelve men and women whose daring exploits during the American Revolution still capture the imagination. Includes stories of a woman who enlisted disguised as a man and of a man who spied for the British. Nonfiction.

Richter, Conrad. **The Light in the Forest** (© 1953). Bantam 1963.

True Son, a white boy kidnapped and reared by Indians, rebels when he is returned to the settlement. Fiction.

Robinson, Barbara. **Trace through the Forest.** Lothrop 1965.

Jim Fraley tells of his adventures as the only boy to accompany Colonel Zane and his men as they blazed the Ohio trail in 1796. His father and his brother, who went to Ohio to find farm land a year earlier, have not yet returned. Jim vows to find them and to bring them back. Fiction.

Rouse, Parke, Jr. **Planters and Pioneers: Life in Colonial Virginia.** Hastings 1968.

The life and work of Virginia citizens, 1607–1789: the churches, the plantations, arts and entertainment, outdoor life, education, houses, roads, and inns. Mature nonfiction.

Schellie, Don. **Me, Cholay & Co.** Four Winds 1973.

When Cholay's little sister is kidnapped during a raid on their Apache village, he and his friend Josh Thane prepare to steal her back from the Papago Indians. Based on a historical incident which occurred in the Arizona Territory in 1850. Fiction.

Scott, John Anthony, and Milton Meltzer. **Fanny Kemble's America.** T Y Crowell 1973.

When a brilliant young English actress toured America in 1832, she fell in love with and married the owner of Georgia's largest plantation. A free spirit, she was deeply distressed to find that her husband owned 700 slaves and was determined to control her life as well. Nonfiction.

Sirkis, Nancy, and Ellwood Parry. **Reflections of 1776: The Colonies Revisited.** Viking Pr 1974.

The history of colonial America reflected in photographs of the homes people lived in, their houses of worship, and the shops, markets, and inns where they gathered. The text relates architecture of various regions to the ways in which people lived. Nonfiction.

Speare, Elizabeth George. **The Witch of Blackbird Pond.** HM 1958.

Kit Tyler's friendship with a lonely old Quaker woman, who Connecticut neighbors think is a witch, results in Kit standing trial for witchcraft. (See also *Calico Captive,* HM.) Fiction.

Vidal, Gore. **Burr** (© 1973). Bantam 1974.

Aaron Burr is often called a traitor and a murderer, but Vidal's novel pictures him as a man of great charm and intelligence whose influence and ability have been underrated. Fiction.

West, Jessamyn. **The Massacre at Fall Creek.** HarBraceJ 1975.

White men murder Indians in 1824 Indiana and are surprisingly (for that time) brought to trial. The men slowly grasp the humanity of the Indians and the horror of their deed. Fiction.

Wibberley, Leonard. **Man of Liberty: A Life of Thomas Jefferson.** FS&G 1968.

Wibberley depicts Jefferson "as farmer, as worried provider for a huge household, and worried President in a hostile world." Nonfiction.

Wibberley, Leonard. **Red Pawns.** FS&G 1973.

Manly Treegate, eighteen, and his younger brother Peter travel to the Northwest in 1811 to aid the militia in its battle with Tecumseh's forces, the "red pawns," in what became America's second war with England, the War of 1812. (See also *Leopard's Prey,* FS&G.) Fiction.

Wood, James Playsted. **The People of Concord.** Seabury 1970.

Henry David Thoreau called Concord, Massachusetts, his "university." Wood describes the intertwining lives of writers who, like Thoreau, drew inspiration from their beloved village: Ralph Waldo Emerson, Nathaniel Hawthorne, and Louisa May Alcott. Nonfiction.

Young, Bob, and Jan Young. **54–40 or Fight! The Story of the Oregon Territory.** Messner 1967.

The United States and Britain were near war in 1846 over fur-rich disputed territory which lay between northern California and Alaska. Britain's Hudson's Bay Company fought hard to keep out American fur traders. Nonfiction.

B. About the Civil War

Bacon, Margaret Hope. **Rebellion at Christiana.** Crown 1974.

A Maryland slaveholder is killed in Christiana, Pennsylvania, in 1851 when he attempts to capture some runaway slaves whose leader is William Parker, himself an escaped slave. That incident and subsequent trials made the Fugitive Slave Law ineffectual and thus confirmed attitudes of a growing number of antislavery groups. Nonfiction.

Blassingame, Wyatt. **William Tecumseh Sherman: Defender of the Union.** P-H 1970.

Though he did not have strong feelings about slavery, General Sherman was a fanatic about preservation of the Union. In order to preserve it, he spilled oceans of blood and set fire to Atlanta—necessary tasks which the general loathed. Nonfiction.

Buckmaster, Henrietta. **Flight to Freedom: The Story of the Underground Railroad** (© 1958). Dell 1968.

The Underground Railroad had no tracks, no tunnels. Instead, it consisted of the combined efforts of dedicated people who risked life and reputation in order to assist the movement of slaves toward freedom. Nonfiction.

Crane, William D. **Patriotic Rebel: John C. Calhoun.** Messner 1972.

As representative, senator, secretary of state, and vice-president, Calhoun struggled to reconcile the interests of his native South with the needs of the federal government during the decades preceding the Civil War. Ironically, his leadership drew the South toward the disaster he dreaded and tried so hard to avoid. Nonfiction.

Douty, Esther M. **Forten the Sailmaker**. Rand 1968.

James Forten, a free black man, owned the leading sail-making establishment in Philadelphia and contributed his wealth and his effort to the cause of freeing slaves. Nonfiction.

Emery, Guy. **Robert E. Lee.** Messner 1951.

At the opening of the Civil War, Lee was asked to accept President Lincoln's appointment as commander of the U.S. Army and thus to choose between two deep loyalties—his country and his family. His performance as commander of the Confederate defense earned him the admiration and respect of even his Northern opponents. Nonfiction.

Foster, John. **Rebel Sea Raider: The Story of Raphael Semmes.** Morrow 1965.

Convinced that the South had a right to secede from the Union, Semmes took charge of the Confederacy's only ship in 1861. In 1862 he took command of the CSS *Alabama* and made naval history, nearly destroying the American merchant marine. Nonfiction.

Genovese, Eugene D. **Roll, Jordan, Roll: The World the Slaves Made.** Pantheon 1974.

Using slave narratives, family papers, and other documents, Genovese constructs an exhaustive portrait of slavery and American slave culture. He systematically puts to rest many myths (for example, the powerful master and the happy "mammy") and examines such aspects of slave life as weddings, religion, Afro-American language, clothing, and work. Mature nonfiction.

Haynes, Betsy. **Cowslip.** Nelson 1973.

In 1861 Cowslip is sold to Colonel Sprague and goes to care for his children. Her friends are Job, an educated slave who had once been free, and Reba, who is killed when she tries to run away. Cowslip's growing determination to be free is fed by her realization that "I'm a human person, and I got dignity." Fiction.

Jones, Katherine M., and John Egle, editors. **Heroines of Dixie: The Spring of High Hopes.** Ballantine 1974.

The first three years of the Civil War as seen through the eyes of Southern women and recorded in their letters and diaries. Nonfiction.

Lester, Julius. **To Be a Slave** (© 1968). Dell 1970.

In order to "tell it like it was," Lester uses unpublished primary sources to assemble these vivid excerpts of firsthand experiences and narratives which communicate what it was like to be a slave. Nonfiction.

McCague, James. **The Second Rebellion: The Story of the New York City Draft Riots of 1863.** Dial 1968.

A day-by-day account of the five days of bloody rioting in New York City in July 1863, triggered by the nation's first draft act. Analyzes causes for the rebellion in the events, personalities, and social attitudes of the day. Mature nonfiction.

Mitchell, Margaret. **Gone with the Wind** (© 1936). Avon 1974.

Scarlett O'Hara fascinated many men, among them Rhett Butler, who loved her. Her willingness to play with love and other people's lives is the central theme of this picture of the Civil War period. Fiction.

Mitgang, Herbert. **The Fiery Trial: A Life of Lincoln.** Viking Pr 1974.

A biography of the great Civil War president and an

analysis of the political and historical causes that involved Lincoln in the life and death struggle to save the Union. Nonfiction.

Pitkin, Thomas M., editor. **Grant the Soldier.** Acropolis 1965.

This collection of anecdotes is written by people who knew Ulysses S. Grant, supplemented by excerpts from Grant's own memoirs. The purpose of the book is to close the debate over whether Grant was a fine military leader or an inferior one. Nonfiction.

Walker, Margaret. **Jubilee** (© 1966). Bantam 1967.

Vyry is the daughter of a plantation owner and his black mistress. The story centers on her life as a slave and her attempt to keep her family together after the Civil War. Fiction.

Werstein, Irving. **The Many Faces of the Civil War.** Messner 1961.

A comprehensive account of a war in which brother fought brother: the personalities and their deeds, the causes of the war, the emotional impact of the war on the people who fought and endured it. Nonfiction.

Young, Bob, and Jan Young. **Reluctant Warrior: Ulysses S. Grant.** Messner 1971.

Though he hated war and did not want to be a soldier, Grant became the most famous general of his time. Because he scorned politics and was not well prepared for his role as politician, he became a president whose name is firmly linked to the scandal and corruption characteristic of his administration. Nonfiction.

C. *Since the Civil War*

Agee, James, and Walker Evans. **Let Us Now Praise Famous Men** (© 1941). Ballantine 1974.

Evans's pictures and Agee's words convey the feeling of what the American Depression of the 1930s did to the hearts and minds of men and women. Nonfiction.

Anderson, Peggy. **The Daughters.** St Martin 1974.

Many people do not react kindly to the Daughters of the American Revolution (DAR), but the author's research and interviews suggest that the DAR stereotype is not entirely fair. Nonfiction.

Archer, Jules. **The Plot to Seize the White House.** Hawthorn 1973.

In July 1933, veterans camped in Washington, D.C., trying to get some money for themselves and their families. General Smedley Darlington Butler led the administration forces. This book explains how and why the veterans' rebellion began and what became of it. Nonfiction.

Archer, Jules. **Strikes, Bombs, and Bullets: Big Bill Haywood and the IWW.** Messner 1972.

Haywood, founder of the Industrial Workers of the World (IWW), preached violence to workers to answer the antiunion activities and violence of factory and mine owners. His life parallels the rise in unionism prior to World War I. Nonfiction.

Archer, Jules. **Watergate: America in Crisis.** T Y Crowell 1975.

A history of the undercover operation that led to the Watergate break-in on June 18, 1972, and the political and legal issues that came out of Watergate. Nonfiction.

Baker, Marilyn (with Sally Brompton). **Exclusive! The Inside Story of Patricia Hearst and the SLA.** Macmillan 1974.

Baker gives an inside account of her investigation of the Symbionese Liberation Army (SLA) and the Patty Hearst kidnapping, which she covered as a reporter for a public television station in San Francisco. Nonfiction.

Baldwin, James. **Nobody Knows My Name.** Dell 1961.

A major black writer discusses his return to America from a self-imposed exile in Europe, desegregation, what blacks want and what whites are apparently ready to grant them, and where America seems to be heading. Nonfiction.

Baldwin, James. **Notes of a Native Son** (© 1955). Beacon Pr 1957.

Baldwin writes, ". . . The only real concern of the artist [is] to recreate out of the disorder of life that order which is art," and Baldwin tries to make order and sense out of his experiences in Harlem and the South and the black experience generally. Nonfiction.

Beichman, Arnold. **Nine Lies about America** (© 1972). PB 1973.

The author refutes nine lies he has heard about the United States, among them statements that Americans are only interested in material possessions, that the United States is fascist, and that a revolution is needed to change America's social structure. Nonfiction.

Bernstein, Carl, and Bob Woodward. **All the President's Men.** S&S 1974.

Two reporters from the *Washington Post* who broke open the Watergate story tell how they first uncovered this information and began to put the pieces together. Frank language and honest emotions by the president, his men, and the two reporters come across in this book. Nonfiction.

Breslin, Jimmy. **How the Good Guys Finally Won: Notes from an Impeachment Summer.** Viking Pr 1975.

Breslin's study of power is built around Representative Thomas (Tip) P. O'Neill, Democratic majority leader from Massachusetts, and his role in the impeachment proceedings against former President Nixon. Nonfiction.

Bryan, John. **This Soldier Still at War.** HarBraceJ 1975.

Joseph Remiro went to Vietnam and after leaving the service joined the flower children in San Francisco's Haight-Ashbury. Then he became a member of the Symbionese Liberation Army (SLA) and was tried for the murder of Marcus Foster, the Oakland, California, school superintendent. Nonfiction.

Buckley, William F., Jr. **Cruising Speed: A Documentary** (© 1971). Bantam 1972.

A journal of one week in which the conservative writer comments on America, Dick Gregory, Richard Nixon, the *National Review,* economics, and just about anything else he cares to. Mature nonfiction.

Bugliosi, Vincent (with Curt Gentry). **Helter Skelter: The True Story of the Manson Murders.** Norton 1974.

On the night of August 9, 1969, actress Sharon Tate and four friends were brutally murdered in Hollywood. Charles Manson and members of his "family" were tracked down, brought to trial, and convicted. A frank picture of a horrifying crime, its victims and its perpetrators. Mature nonfiction.

Caidin, Martin. **When War Comes.** Morrow 1972.

A frightening warning about the possibility of war to come and an even more frightening picture of what will happen to humanity should war occur. Nonfiction.

Collier, Peter, and David Horowitz. **The Rockefellers: An American Dynasty.** HR&W 1976.

Benefiting from access to family records and candid interviews with family members, Collier and Horowitz have put together a remarkable account of four generations of a wealthy and powerful family. Mature nonfiction.

Cooke, Alistair. **America.** Knopf 1973.

Cooke was born in England but became an American citizen in 1941. He records his life-long love affair with our country through a well-illustrated history from the Revolutionary War until the present. Nonfiction.

Daniels, Jonathan. **White House Witness: 1942–1945.** Doubleday 1975.

Daniels worked in the administration of President Franklin Roosevelt during World War II. His book, written from a diary he kept, reveals many of the intrigues that surround men in power. Nonfiction.

Davis, Angela. **Angela Davis: An Autobiography.** Random 1974.

A political book about the treatment accorded Davis, an avowed and dedicated Communist, in various jails and courtrooms. Includes details about her earlier life. Biased and may offend many readers but worth reading for its insights into the mind of a brilliant woman. Nonfiction.

Dobler, Bruce. **Icepick: A Novel about Life and Death in a Maximum Security Prison.** Little 1974.

This apparently accurate, well-researched account of penitentiary life should be of interest to anyone who wants to know about the raw, emotional side of that existence. Fiction.

Drew, Elizabeth. **Washington Journal: The Events of 1973–1974.** Random 1975.

The author, an experienced Washington journalist, chronicles in detail the Watergate crisis from September 1973 through August 1974. Nonfiction.

Ellsberg, Daniel. **Papers on the War** (© 1971). PB 1972.

This book collects reports, book reviews, articles, and miscellaneous short pieces, originally written between 1965 and 1971, which the author claims give evidence of misguided government decision-making during the Vietnam War. Nonfiction.

Fager, Charles E. **Selma, 1965: The Town Where the South Was Changed.** Scribner 1974.

Selma, Alabama, was chosen as the site of a 1965 demonstration to achieve voting rights for blacks. The sheriff and most of the white establishment opposed the demonstration. This history records the violence, emotionalism, and ultimate victory of justice. Nonfiction.

Ferber, Edna. **Cimarron** (© 1930). Doubleday 1951.

Yancy Cravat takes part in the rush of homesteaders into Oklahoma in 1889. When adventure calls, he leaves his wife with the responsibility for running his newspaper and raising their son. Fiction.

Feuerlicht, Roberta Strauss. **Joe McCarthy and McCarthyism: The Hate That Haunts America.** McGraw 1972.

Today the word "McCarthyism" stands for smear attacks, unsupported accusations, personal vilification, and crimes against civil liberties committed in the name of anticommunism. Who was McCarthy, who sowed so much hate in America? Who must bear the responsibility for the prosperity of his attitudes? Mature nonfiction.

Fischer, John. **Vital Signs, U.S.A.** Har-Row 1975.

The author argues that things are getting accomplished in the United States: he cites progress toward better living conditions in Seattle, a new kind of urban renewal in Minneapolis, and other signs of genuine progress in many areas of the country. Nonfiction.

Griffin, John Howard. **Black Like Me.** NAL 1961.

Medically aided to make his skin appear black, Griffin traveled in the deep South to find what it is to be part of a minority. Treated as a black, he found himself degraded and treated spitefully, unfairly, and bitterly by whites. Nonfiction.

Gutman, Judith Mara. **Is America Used Up?** Bantam 1973.

Both text and many photographs note the rise of the American "Dream," what changed it during our history, and where the American "Dream" is today. Sometimes angry, the book offers hope. Nonfiction.

Haddix, Cecille, editor. **Who Speaks For Appalachia?** PB 1975.

A collection of stories and poems about the Applachian Mountains and its people by authors like Robert Penn Warren, Thomas Wolfe, James Agee, Jesse Stuart, and O. Henry. Fiction.

Handsfield, Leicester, and Harriet Handsfield, editors. **Dick's Encyclopedia of Practical Receipts and Processes.** Funk & W 1975.

This is a reissue of an 1870 encyclopedia with over 6,400 "receipts" and processes. It presents a unique, informative, and amusing look into the do-it-yourself methods of yesteryear: how to make ginger pop, test gold on silver, the best way to wash a white dog, etc. Nonfiction.

Hunt, Irene. **No Promises in the Wind** (© 1970). Tempo G&D 1973.

Two boys leave Depression-time Chicago during the 1930s and seek love and financial help wandering around the Midwest. Fiction.

Jensen, Oliver, and the *American Heritage* Editors. **American Album.** Ballantine 1968.

The face of yesterday just as it was, reflected in 226 rare photographs collected by the editors of *American Heritage* magazine. Nonfiction.

Kalb, Marvin, and Bernard Kalb. **Kissinger.** Little 1974.

Born in Germany, Henry Kissinger came to the United

States when he was young, graduated from Harvard, ultimately became a close adviser to several presidents, and has been secretary of state under Presidents Nixon and Ford. Mature nonfiction.

Keniston, Kenneth. **The Uncommitted** (© 1965). Dell 1970.

A frank, well-documented discussion of the alienation felt by the youth of the 1950s. Mature nonfiction.

Lane, Rose Wilder. **Let the Hurricane Roar.** McKay 1933.

Shortly after they are married, Charles takes Caroline to the Dakota Territory of the late nineteenth century, where they build their home on a lonely stretch of prairie and battle the elements in order to sustain it. Fiction.

Liston, Robert A. **The United States and the Soviet Union: A Background Book on the Struggle for Power.** Parents 1973.

Taking an objective view of U.S.-Soviet relations of the past fifty years, the author sees the antagonisms that have existed between the two powers as being the result of each nation's "misperception" of the other. Nonfiction.

Liston, Robert A. **Violence in America.** Messner 1974.

Examining violence in the United States today, the author devotes several chapters to the history of violence; the remainder of the book investigates violence in today's society, the causes, and some suggested remedies. Nonfiction.

Lukas, J. Anthony. **Don't Shoot—We Are Your Children** (© 1971). Dell 1972.

This documentary of the 1960s explores the lives of ten young people involved in the youthful revolution of the time. Each of the ten had apparently rejected the lifestyle of parents and had created a new way of living. Nonfiction.

Maas, Peter. **Serpico** (© 1973). Bantam 1974.

Frank Serpico, New York City policeman, set out to uncover and battle police corruption of all kinds. He was an enigma to some policemen and enemy to others who did everything they could to stop him and his work. Nonfiction.

Magruder, Jeb Stuart. **An American Life: One Man's Road to Watergate.** Atheneum 1974.

Magruder joined former President Nixon's staff in 1969. Later in 1972 he served as deputy director of the Committee to Re-Elect the President and became involved in the Watergate cover-up, which eventually led to a prison term. Nonfiction.

Manchester, William. **The Glory and the Dream: A Narrative History of America, 1932–1972,** 2 vols. Little 1974.

A mammoth history of the last forty years in the United States with comments on or stories about politicians, cars, films, and almost everything else. Mature nonfiction.

Mankiewicz, Frank. **U.S. v. Richard M. Nixon: The Final Crisis.** Quadrangle 1975.

Comments on the role of the press, the special prosecutor's office, and the House of Representatives' Judiciary Committee in the Watergate investigations. Nonfiction.

Maynard, Joyce. **Looking Back: A Chronicle of Growing Old in the Sixties** (© 1973). Avon 1974.

Nineteen-year-old Maynard recalls the 1960s when she was growing up: civil rights marches, President Kennedy's assassination, sex, miniskirts, and other ideas and incidents of her adolescence. Nonfiction.

McCarry, Charles. **Citizen Nader.** Sat Rev Pr 1972.

The life of a man who has been one of the most influential, aggressive, and significant protectors of this nation's consumers. Nonfiction.

Meeropol, Robert, and Michael Meeropol. **We Are Your Sons: The Legacy of Ethel and Julius Rosenberg.** HM 1975.

On July 17, 1950, the lives of Ethel and Julius Rosenberg and their two sons were changed forever when Julius was arrested as a Russian spy. Later, Ethel was arrested and the two were charged with conspiracy to commit espionage. They were found guilty; on June

19, 1953, they were executed. Their sons, Robert and Michael, were adopted by Anne and Abel Meeropol. Nonfiction.

Miles, Robert, editor. **Searching for Ourselves.** Bantam 1973.

A collection of essays on America and Americans today, what we are, who we are, and where we seem to be going, from authors like Marya Mannes, Eldridge Cleaver, John Holt, Pauline Kael, and Tom Wolfe. Mature nonfiction.

Miller, Merle. **Plain Speaking: An Oral Biography of Harry S Truman** (© 1973). Berkley Pub 1974.

Miller tape-recorded the words of President Truman about his childhood, his political life, his presidency, and the major national and world figures he had known. Nonfiction.

Mitford, Jessica. **Kind and Usual Punishment: The Prison Business** (© 1973). VinRandom 1974.

Case studies, statistics, anecdotes, and comments by prisoners and prison authorities are used to make a case against retaining the kinds of prisons we presently have in the United States. Nonfiction.

Moody, Anne. **Coming of Age in Mississippi** (© 1968). Dell 1970.

The author recounts her childhood and adolescence in the South, the poverty of blacks and the threats to blacks who tried to change the system. She also discusses her involvement with CORE and the NAACP. Nonfiction.

Moyers, Bill. **Listening to America** (© 1971). Dell 1972.

A former special assistant to President Johnson traveled throughout America and recorded the moods and humor and concerns of people from Ohio, Wyoming, Texas, Kansas, Connecticut, North Carolina, and many other states. Nonfiction.

O'Neill, William L. **Coming Apart: An Informal History of America in the 1960's** (© 1971). Quadrangle 1973.

The last decade, from the Eisenhower administration until 1969. Sections on Ralph Nader, sports, Cesar Chavez, religion, motorcyclists, the death of President

Kennedy, civil rights, women's liberation, and many other contemporary topics and issues. Mature nonfiction.

Paradis, Adrian A. **Inflation in Action.** Messner 1974.

A concise discussion of the most important causes of inflation, various means used to control it, and the ways it has affected people from ancient times to the present day. Nonfiction.

Rather, Dan, and Gary Paul Gates. **The Palace Guard.** Har-Row 1974.

Former President Nixon brought many honest and dedicated people with him when he assumed office in 1968, but more and more he turned to people who became powerful and cared more about the Nixon administration than they did the country. The Watergate burglary and cover-up stemmed from some of those powerful men. Nonfiction.

Rölvaag, O. E. **Giants in the Earth: A Saga of the Prairie.** Har-Row 1927.

Per Hansa finds challenge for his energy and his optimism when he brings his family from Norway to settle in the Dakota Territory. His wife Beret, overcome by loneliness and fear, yields to the dark spirits of the prairie and withdraws from life. Mature fiction.

Rosenthal, Abraham M. **Thirty-eight Witnesses.** McGraw 1964.

Kitty Genovese was attacked and stabbed repeatedly as she tried to get to her New York City home. Although thirty-eight people heard or saw what went on, all refused to become involved. Nonfiction.

Safire, William. **Before the Fall: An Inside View of the Pre-Watergate White House.** Doubleday 1975.

Safire was hired by former President Nixon as a speech writer. He reports on his years at the White House, the president and his advisors, and some of the people and events that led to Watergate. Mature nonfiction.

Smith, Sam. **Captive Capital: Colonial Life in Modern Washington.** Ind U Pr 1974.

Smith gives an insider's view of life in the nation's capital. He provides the background for understanding the residents' position as they struggle to gain the same full constitutional rights as other Americans. Nonfiction.

Stern, Susan. **With the Weathermen: The Personal Journal of a Revolutionary Woman.** Doubleday 1975.

Stern joined the radical and revolutionary Weathermen and soon became one of the group's most important members. Nonfiction.

Summers, Mark W. **A Student Cartoonist's View of Great Figures in American History.** PB 1972.

"Millard Fillmore needs a face if he is to become more than an abstraction. A caricature . . . does more than present a portrait: it provides the reader with a sense of the character's personality." Over 100 caricatures and biographical sketches. Nonfiction.

Sussman, Barry. **The Great Cover-Up: Nixon and the Scandal of Watergate.** NAL 1974.

Sussman, an editor of the *Washington Post,* was part of the team which helped uncover the Watergate break-in leading to Nixon's resignation. Nonfiction.

Terkel, Studs. **Working.** Pantheon 1974.

Candid views of American workers concerning the jobs they have and the lives they lead, expressed in their own words. Read one interview or ten or a hundred: actor, barber, bar pianist, spot welder, domestic, jockey, priest. Some frank language. (See also *Division Street: America,* Avon.) Nonfiction.

Truman, Harry S. **Memoirs,** 2 vols. (© 1955). NAL 1965.

Truman's poignant and candid account of his first years as president of the United States gives an enlightening and human view of the highest political office in the U.S. The story begins in 1945 with the death of President Roosevelt and ends with the atomic age. Nonfiction.

Truman, Margaret. **Harry S Truman** (© 1973). PB 1974.

Margaret Truman's story of her father is rich in family and personal detail. She relates her father's involvement in and instigation of many major historical events. The book is almost a history of the American Dream in our time. Mature nonfiction.

Ullman, James Ramsey. **Down the Colorado with Major Powell.** HM 1960.

Major John Wesley Powell, later to become the foremost explorer of the West, began a charting expedition of the turbulent and treacherous Colorado River with nine other adventurers in early 1869. Months later, six men completed the hazardous journey, emerging with the first maps of that new land. Nonfiction.

U.S. News & World Report Editors. **Good Things about the U.S. Today.** Macmillan 1970.

The editors of *U.S. News & World Report* believe that the media have overemphasized the violence, corruption, race problems, and other ills of America. They assemble a report of the positive progress in medicine, science, education, fine arts, and other areas to indicate that the United States is still a great place to live. Nonfiction.

Utley, Robert M. **Frontier Regulars: The United States Army and the Indian, 1866–1891.** Macmillan 1974.

Based mostly on military and Congressional records and on accounts by whites, with comparatively few Indian sources, Utley presents his analysis of the U.S. Army's campaign against the Indians from 1866 to the Battle of Wounded Knee in 1890, during which time all organized Indian resistance to white expansion was crushed. Mature nonfiction.

Wattenberg, Ben J. **The Real America.** Doubleday 1974.

Wattenberg examines data of all kinds to determine what Americans are like and what we believe. He arrives at some generally optimistic conclusions. Mature nonfiction.

White, Theodore H. **Breach of Faith: The Fall of Richard Nixon.** Atheneum 1975.

Beginning with the July 24, 1974, Supreme Court decision that Nixon could no longer refuse the Watergate tape recordings to Special Prosecutor Leon Jaworski, White retraces the events of the election year 1972 that led up to the fall of the president. Mature nonfiction.

Wicker, Tom. **A Time to Die.** Quadrangle 1975.

During the Attica (New York) prison riot in September 1971, the convicts invited *New York Times* reporter-columnist Wicker to be an observer. The deaths, prison conditions, anger, and frustrations are all movingly described. Mature nonfiction.

Wilkes, Paul. **Trying Out the Dream: A Year in the Life of an American Family.** Lippincott 1975.

Searching for the "average American family," the author finds one family—the Neumeyers—which fits the census description of an "average" family. Wilkes describes the members of the family, their problems, and their search for the American Dream. Nonfiction.

Wolfson, Victor. **The Man Who Cared: A Life of Harry S Truman.** FS&G 1966.

Truman entered politics after an unsuccessful try at business. After becoming president, he faced many crises, among them dropping the atomic bomb on Hiroshima during World War II. Nonfiction.

Wright, Theon. **The Disenchanted Isles: The Story of the Second Rebellion in Hawaii.** Dial 1972.

Hawaiian Queen Liliuokalani was in her chambers on January 17, 1893, when U.S. troops landed in Honolulu. The troops and Sanford Dole, leader of the island "revolutionaries," forced her to abdicate, which led to the eventual annexation of the islands to the United States. Nonfiction.

THE THIRD WORLD YESTERDAY

Achebe, Chinua. **Things Fall Apart** (© 1959). Fawcett World 1969.

An African man of the Ibo tribe has dreams of getting ahead and gaining power in his society. Then the white man enters Africa, destroying customs and a whole way of life. Fiction.

Azuela, Mariano (translator E. Munguía, Jr.). **The Underdogs.** NAL 1962.

Demetrio Macías, a young, immature, and peace-loving Indian, is forced to take the side of the rebels to protect his family. He proves his courage and becomes a general in this novel of the Mexican Revolution. Fiction.

Birch, Cyril, editor. **Anthology of Chinese Literature.** Grove 1972.

This volume represents the first true English anthology of Chinese literature. The reader will find famous Chinese drinking poems, cynical love stories, and lyrical religious tracts. Mature.

Block, Irvin. **The Lives of Pearl Buck: A Tale of China and America.** T Y Crowell 1973.

A warm and affectionate portrait of the first American woman to win the Nobel Prize for literature. Nonfiction.

Bloodworth, Dennis. **The Chinese Looking Glass** (© 1967). Dell 1969.

This book traces China through more than 3,000 years of history in a manner made more credible by the author's personal experiences. Nonfiction.

Bownas, Geoffrey, and Anthony Thwaite, editors and translators. **The Penguin Book of Japanese Verse.** Penguin 1964.

A chronological survey of Japanese poetry from about the third century until the present. Classic Japanese verse forms like haiku and *tanka* are represented as well as forms usually associated with Western poetry.

Brandon, James R., editor. **Traditional Asian Plays.** Hill & Wang 1972.

Included in the six plays are Indian Sanskrit drama, Thai dance-drama, Japanese Noh and Kabuki, and Chinese opera.

Brown, J. P. S. **The Forests of the Night.** Dial 1974.

Adán has chosen to fight for survival for himself and his family in the Mexican Sierras. His greatest challenge is a killer jaguar. Fiction.

Clavell, James. **Shōgun.** Atheneum 1975.

In feudal Japan of 1600 the Lord Protector of Japan dies, leaving his seven-year-old son to be raised by five warlords. All five vie to become the military dictator. Then a British ship's pilot is captured and becomes their political pawn. Mature fiction.

Coleman, Eleanor S. **The Cross and the Sword of Cortes.** S&S 1968.

A priest accompanies Cortes in his efforts to conquer the Aztecs and yet preserve their civilization. Nonfiction.

Coolidge, Olivia. **Gandhi.** HM 1971.

Mahatma, "Great Soul," spent his life attempting to bring India together. Gandhi was many things—patriot, revolutionary, reformer, doctor, statesman—and Coolidge brings out his strengths and weaknesses. Nonfiction.

De Treviño, Elizabeth B. **Juárez, Man of Law.** FS&G 1974.

Benito Juárez, an Indian born in Mexico in 1806, toiled as a shepherd and a servant until his superior intelligence was recognized. His journey takes him from this beginning to the presidency of Mexico. Nonfiction.

Downs, Ray F., editor. **Japan Yesterday and Today** (© 1969). Bantam 1970.

Japan's growth is traced from a mere series of mountainous islands to its status as a twentieth-century economic power. Nonfiction.

Eberhard, Wolfram, editor and translator. **Folktales of China.** U of Chicago Pr 1965.

Urban and rural Chinese tales of love, creation, and supernatural powers.

Esterer, Arnulf K., and Louise A. Esterer. **Sun Yat-sen, China's Great Champion.** Messner 1970.

Sun Yat-sen, a gentle, modest, untiring doctor, dedicated his life to abolishing the corrupt Manchu dynasty and restoring China to its former greatness. Nonfiction.

Feldmann, Susan, editor. **African Myths and Tales** (© 1963). Dell 1970.

Legends, myths, and stories involving religion, death, and adventure told by African tribes.

Fuentes, Carlos (translator Sam Hileman). **The Death of Artemio Cruz.** FS&G 1964.

The history of modern Mexico is revealed through the life of Artemio Cruz. Fiction.

Fuja, Abayomi, compiler. **Fourteen Hundred Cowries and Other African Tales** (© 1962). WSP 1973.

Tales of the Yoruba people of West Africa written and told in the ancient tradition yet applicable to contemporary life.

Gosfield, Frank, and Bernhardt J. Hurwood. **Korea: Land of the Thirty-eighth Parallel.** Parents 1968.

About half of this book is the history of Korea from its origin 5,000 years ago to the seizure of the USS *Pueblo* in 1968. The other half is a unique collection of documents that figure in the history of this divided Asian nation. Nonfiction.

Hellerman, Leon, and Alan L. Stein, editors. **China: Selected Readings on the Middle Kingdom.** WSP 1971.

These legends, letters, and poems may help to explain the paradox of China to the Western mind.

Hersey, John. **A Single Pebble** (© 1956). Bantam 1968.

A cocky young American engineer travels up the Yangtze River in China to see whether it is possible to build a power project in one of the river gorges. In the process, the young man learns much about old and new China and even more about himself. Fiction.

Hirschfeld, Burt. **Fifty-five Days of Terror: The Story of the Boxer Rebellion.** Messner 1964.

The famous Boxer Rebellion of June 1900, when a fanatical Chinese army trapped the diplomatic envoys of eleven countries behind the walls of Peking. Nonfiction.

Hookman, Hilda. **A Short History of China** (© 1969). NAL 1972.

Beginning with the Shang farmers of the sixteenth century B.C., this history traces China to the time of Mao. Illustrated with photos, drawings, and maps, this book depicts the major facets of China's political, social, and cultural life. Nonfiction.

Jordan, A. C. **Tales from Southern Africa.** U of Cal Pr 1973.

Thirteen Xhosa tales from South Africa translated

from the oral tradition relate some of the distinctive features of Xhosa customs and life.

Keene, Donald, editor. **Anthology of Japanese Literature** (© 1955). Grove 1956.

Japanese literature from its very earliest times to the mid-nineteenth century. Scenes from famous Noh plays, poetry, and seventeenth-century novels are included. Mature.

Keene, Donald. **Japanese Literature: An Introduction for Western Readers.** Grove 1955.

A classic introduction for the Western reader by an expert on Eastern literature dealing with theatre, novels, and poetry as well as the Western influence on Japanese literature. Nonfiction.

Kennedy, Malcolm D. **A Short History of Japan.** NAL 1963.

The cultural and political development of Japan, from its legendary origin in 660 B.C. to its position in the cold war. Mature nonfiction.

Lattimore, Owen, and Eleanor Lattimore, editors. **Silks, Spices, and Empires** (© 1968). Dell 1971.

Subtitled "Asia through the Eyes of Its Discoverers," this book is a collection of excerpts from the writing of those who explored Asia. China, Japan, Tibet, and Siberia are some of the locales whose early history is discussed in this informative travel/history book. Nonfiction.

Lum, Peter. **Six Centuries in East Asia.** S G Phillips 1973.

The history of East Asia, China, Japan, and Korea during the last 600 years until the fall of the last Chinese dynasty and the beginning of the Chinese Republic in 1912. Nonfiction.

Malraux, André. **Man's Fate** (© 1934). VinRandom 1969.

In 1927 China was badly divided. Malraux's psychological novel is based on the Shanghai Insurrection of 1927 and probes ideologies, conspiracy, betrayal, and free will vs. fate. Fiction.

Meltzer, Milton. **Bound for the Rio Grande: The Mexican Struggle.** Knopf 1974.

Letters, diaries, maps, songs, illustrations, and other original documents provide a new look at the political and social decay that led to Mexico's defeat in the 1846–1847 war with the United States and the problems that the U.S. faced when it took the vast territory north of the Rio Grande River. Nonfiction.

Mitchison, Naomi. **African Heroes.** FS&G 1968.

This book recounts eleven tales of African heroes, some semilegendary, up to the time of Cetshwayo, the last great warrior king of the Zulu, who died after defeat by the British. Nonfiction.

Moore, Clark D., and Ann Dunbar, editors. **Africa Yesterday and Today.** Bantam 1968.

The peoples and lands of Africa yesterday and the emerging nations and their economics, agriculture, and politics today; includes an overview of the future of African nations. Mature nonfiction.

Moore, Clark D., and Daniel Eldridge, editors. **India Yesterday and Today.** Praeger 1970.

India's distinct culture, the impact of British rule, the resulting struggle for independence, and India's way of dealing with contemporary problems. Nonfiction.

Nguyen Du, and Huynh-Sanh. **The Tale of Kieu: The Classic Vietnamese Verse Story.** VinRandom 1973.

This long, narrative poem is the best-known and best-loved poem in Vietnamese literature. Taking place in the early 1800s, it tells of the love affair, separation, and ultimate reunion of Thuy Kieu and Kim Trong.

Nolen, Barbara, editor. **Mexico Is People: Land of Three Cultures.** Scribner 1973.

Using documents, diaries, legends, and many firsthand accounts of the beginnings and development of a civilization, the author focuses on Indian, Spanish, and Mestigo cultures to help the reader understand the people of Mexico. Nonfiction.

Payne, Robert, editor. **The White Pony: An Anthology of Chinese Poetry.** NAL 1947.

Chinese poetry from the earliest times to the present

day. Payne includes brief introductions to the selections as well as short notes to provide a clear understanding of the material.

Reines, Bernard. **A People's Hero: Rizal of the Philippines.** Praeger 1971.

A political rebel, José Rizal was executed in 1896 at the age of thirty-five by the Spanish, who had controlled the Philippines for 200 years. Rizal, an ardent opponent of Spanish colonial oppression, was "the father of his country." Nonfiction.

Renault, Mary. **The Persian Boy** (© 1972). Bantam 1974.

Ten-year-old Bagoas was sold as a slave after his family was murdered and his father's property sold. His fortunes improve when he is sold first to Darius, the Persian king, and then given to the conqueror of Persia, Alexander the Great. The love affair between these two young men lasts until Alexander's death. (See also *The Mask of Apollo,* Bantam; and *The King Must Die,* Bantam.) Fiction.

Rink, Paul. **The Land Divided, the World United: The Story of the Panama Canal.** Messner 1963.

People's thirst for adventure, their bravery, greed, desire for victory over nature, and heroic qualities are all present in this story of the building of the Panama Canal. Nonfiction.

Rink, Paul. **Soldier of the Andes: José de San Martín.** Messner 1971.

San Martín fought against the Spanish Army that trained him, became a general, and led an army in pursuit of liberty for the South American continent. Nonfiction.

Roberts, John G. **Black Ship and Rising Sun.** Messner 1971.

After Commodore Perry's visit of 1854, Japan was plunged into civil strife over the question of isolationism. Emperor Meiji set out to learn the ways of the West without giving up Japanese identity. Nonfiction.

Ronning, Chester. **A Memoir of China in Revolution.** Pantheon 1974.

A history of China from the Boxer Rebellion until the

contemporary People's Republic. Many illustrations. Nonfiction.

Rugoff, Milton, and L. Carrington Goodrich. **Marco Polo's Adventures in China.** Am Heritage 1964.

Marco Polo traveled to China two centuries before Columbus left for the New World. A fascinating account of thirteenth-century China and the trader who told the world of its many early monumental discoveries. Nonfiction.

Shah, Idries. **Thinkers of the East.** Penguin 1972.

A collection of anecdotes and "parables in action" illustrating the practical thought of the Eastern dervish teachers (instructors in devotional exercises) and offering insights into the thinking of the East. Nonfiction.

Trupin, James E. **West Africa: A Background Book from Ancient Kingdoms to Modern Times.** Parents 1971.

The author gives the history of western Africa, from ancient Ghana to the emerging nations today. Nonfiction.

Van Over, Raymond, editor. **A Treasury of Chinese Literature.** Fawcett World 1972.

Chinese literature from 2,500 years of an unbroken cultural tradition; the stories, folktales, fables, and parables contained in this volume represent some of the best of this tradition.

Varley, H. Paul. **Samurai.** Dell 1971.

A brief portrait of the samurai, the warrior caste responsible for Japan's feudal militaristic tradition. Their code of honor and fearlessness in the face of death influenced Japan well into this century. Nonfiction.

Villas-Boas, Claudio, and Orlando Villas-Boas. **Xingu: The Indians, Their Myths** (© 1970). FS&G 1974.

Thirty-one myths accompany a historical account of the past and present culture of the fifteen tribes of the Upper Xingu region of Brazil. Nonfiction.

Wilson, Dick. **Anatomy of China.** NAL 1969.

Wilson considers the main elements in Chinese cultural, social, and political life as well as the national economy and China's international relations. Nonfiction.

Womack, John, Jr. **Zapata and the Mexican Revolution** (© 1968). VinRandom 1970.

Because the people of the small state of Morelos were not willing to move from their cherished land, they became involved in the Mexican Revolution in the early twentieth century. Emiliano Zapata was one of their most famous leaders. Nonfiction.

THE THIRD WORLD, TODAY AND TOMORROW

Archer, Jules. **Mao Tse-tung** (© 1972). WSP 1973.

Chairman Mao is portrayed as a Chinese patriot first and a Communist second, from his days as a strongminded youth to the time of his dealings with the Nixon administration. Nonfiction.

Archer, Jules. **Mexico and the United States.** Hawthorn 1973.

A brief history of Old Mexico and a look at current relations between Mexico and United States sets the stage for a discussion of the various conflicts, compromises, and cooperative efforts between these countries from colonial times to the present. Nonfiction.

Biocca, Ettore (translator Dennis Rhodes). **Yanoáma: The Narrative of a White Girl Kidnapped by Amazonian Indians.** Dutton 1971.

Helena Valero, an eleven-year-old Spanish girl, was kidnapped by Indians of the Upper Amazon and kept captive for twenty years. Nonfiction.

Brilliant, Moshe. **Portrait of Israel.** Am Heritage 1970.

A concise encyclopedia of Israeli society, culture, religion, habits, and mores, treated in a semihistorical perspective. Nonfiction.

Brooks, Charlotte K., editor. **African Rhythms: Selected Stories and Poems.** WSP 1974.

Through a collection of well-selected stories, poems, and photographic essays by and about Africans, the reader receives a panoramic view of African culture.

Burns, E. Bradford. **Latin America: A Concise Interpretive History.** P-H 1972.

The history of Latin America serves as a background for a discussion of change and the turmoil that change has brought to Latin America today. Nonfiction.

Cartey, Wilfred, editor. **Palaver: Modern African Writings.** Nelson 1970.

A diverse anthology of twentieth-century writers who have maintained their cultural heritage in spite of their international recognition.

Cone, Molly. **Dance Around the Fire.** HM 1974.

Unlike many adolescents who turn away from religion, Joanne Rueben is determined to find the true meaning of Judaism. The arising difficulties with her non-religious family and her own religious beliefs lead to Joanne's symbolic "exodus" to Israel. Fiction.

David, Jay, and Helise Harrington, editors. **Growing Up African.** Morrow 1971.

A collection of thirty-five biographical selections chronicling the childhood experiences of youngsters who recount their discoveries and awareness in tribal, colonial, and independent Africa. Nonfiction.

Davidson, Basil. **Black Star: A View of the Life and Times of Kwame Nkrumah.** Praeger 1974.

This biography captures the life and times of the first prime minister of Ghana, the first African colony to achieve political independence. Nonfiction.

Debray, Régis, and Salvador Allende. **The Chilean Revolution.** VinRandom 1971.

The three sections of this book include an essay on the history and politics of Chile, conversations with the late President Allende, and a postscript by Allende, who was killed in a military takeover of the government. Nonfiction.

De Jesus, Carolina Maria (translator David St. Clair). **Child of the Dark: The Diary of Carolina Maria De Jesus** (© 1962). NAL 1964.

A Brazilian mother tells of the struggles to keep her-

self and her three children alive in the slums of São
Paulo. Nonfiction.

Dobson, Christopher (editor H. W. Griffin). **Black September: Its Short, Violent History.** Macmillan 1974.

This account of the Black September movement points
out the futility of the violence that this group of Arab
terrorists created. From November 28, 1971, until August 10, 1973, the terrorists killed innocent people in
an attempt to frighten and overcome their enemy, the
state of Israel. Nonfiction.

Ellis, Harry B. **Israel: One Land, Two Peoples.** T Y
Crowell 1972.

The problem of the relationship between Palestinians
and Israelis and the uneasy peace in Israel is the subject of this book. Nonfiction.

Elon, Amos. **The Israelis: Founders and Sons** (© 1971).
Bantam 1972.

A history and analysis of Israel—the founders, builders, and workers. The author discusses the problems
of the country and the likely conflicts during the next
few years. Nonfiction.

Elon, Amos, and Sana Hassan. **Between Enemies: A
Compassionate Dialogue between an Israeli and an
Arab.** Random 1974.

Elon, an Israeli, and Hassan, an Egyptian, met in
1974 and began a series of conversations about their
countries and the politics and emotions which have
caused problems for centuries. Nonfiction.

Flender, Harold, editor. **The Kids Who Went to Israel.**
WSP 1973.

First-person accounts by fifteen teenagers who emi-
grated to Israel from points throughout the world, including the U.S.S.R., Iraq, India, Japan, and the
United States. Nonfiction.

Forman, James. **My Enemy, My Brother** (© 1969).
Schol Bk Serv 1972.

A young survivor of the Nazi persecution of Warsaw
Jews goes to the promised land of Israel. Fiction.

Franz, Carl. **The People's Guide to Mexico.** John Muir 1972.

All of the information that the traveler to Mexico needs to get along is included in this comprehensive travel guide. Nonfiction.

Galston, Arthur W. (with Jean S. Savage). **Daily Life in People's China.** T Y Crowell 1973.

This informal account of a 1972 visit to China examines many key aspects of Chinese life. Galston spent most of his visit in a commune but reports equally well his impressions of factories, cities, and schools. Nonfiction.

Gilio, Maria Esther (translator Anne Edmondson). **The Tupamaro Guerrillas** (© 1970). Ballantine 1973.

The establishment and activities of a South American guerrilla movement—active in Uruguay, Argentina, and Chile—and the people involved show what can happen to nations undergoing economic, political, and social problems. Nonfiction.

Groussard, Serge (translator Harold Salemson). **The Blood of Israel: The Massacre of the Israeli Athletes, the Olympics 1972.** Morrow 1975.

On September 5, 1972, terrorists invaded the quarters of Israeli athletes at the Munich Olympic Games. The author investigates the events and suggests who was really responsible for the death of eleven Israeli athletes and coaches. Nonfiction.

Keene, Donald, editor. **Modern Japanese Literature.** Grove 1956.

Some of the selections the reader will find include "Growing-Up," a lyrical story of preadolescence, and Natsume's amusing story, "Botchan." Mature fiction.

Lange, Suzanne. **The Year.** S G Phillips 1970.

Ann Sanger has trouble adjusting to the self-discipline and tolerance of an Israeli kibbutz, partly because it seems foreign to her Texas upbringing. Fiction.

Laqueur, Walter, editor. **The Israel-Arab Reader** (© 1969). Bantam 1970.

Forty-two documents about the Near East crisis from 1882 to the present are followed by statements from both Arabs and Israelis about Arab-Israel wars, what led up to them, and the problems that must be solved if peace is ever to come to the region. Mature nonfiction.

Lazo, Mario. **American Policy Failures in Cuba** (© 1968). Twin Circle 1970.

The author, a highly respected Latin American lawyer, tells why Cuba became a Communist stronghold and why Communism has become so influential in the Caribbean. Nonfiction.

Livingston, James T., editor. **Caribbean Rhythms: The Emerging English Literature of the West Indies.** WSP 1974.

The rhythms of the Caribbean are seen in these stories, poems, essays, and plays that reflect the beauty of life in these tropical lands.

MacLaine, Shirley. **You Can Get There from Here.** Norton 1975.

The movie star was invited by the Chinese to head a delegation of a dozen women to visit the People's Republic of China. She reports the illnesses they had and the problems they faced, but most of all, she reports the profound cultural differences between the Chinese and their visitors. Nonfiction.

Mao Tse-tung (editor Anne Fremantle). **Mao Tse-tung: An Anthology of his Writings.** NAL 1971.

A number of Mao's writings, from 1926 until contemporary times, about philosophy and warfare. Mature nonfiction.

Markward, Edris, and Leslie Alexander Lacy, editors. **Contemporary African Literature.** Random 1972.

A diverse yet representative collection of African literature, written from the perspective of the African writer, portraying the differences and similarities of literary types, styles, subject matter, and various cultures and regions of the vast continent of Africa. Mature.

Marshall, Andrew. **Brazil.** Walker & Co 1966.

The political, social, and cultural life of this Third World power sets the stage for an analysis of current Brazilian problems. Nonfiction.

Matthew, Helen G., editor. **Asia in the Modern World.** NAL 1963.

Individual Asian countries are discussed in terms of their past history and culture and the revolutionary changes that are transforming them into modern states. Nonfiction.

Milton, Daniel L., and William Clifford, editors. **A Treasury of Modern Asian Stories** (© 1961). NAL 1971.

These stories from Asia transcend the barriers of language and culture to communicate turmoil and change through the literature of despair, love, childbirth, hatred, and humor. Fiction.

Mphahlele, Ezekiel. **The African Image.** Praeger 1974.

The author examines the image, personality, and the past and future of Africa; also included is a section on African literature. Mature nonfiction.

Mphahlele, Ezekiel, editor. **African Writing Today.** Penguin 1967.

Included in this volume of the poetry and prose of black Africa are some works that are published here for the first time. Mature.

Nolen, Barbara, editor. **Africa Is Thunder and Wonder.** Scribner 1972.

This collection of African poetry and short stories provides a sampling of works by major modern African writers. Thematic divisions are aids in understanding African life and culture.

Parker, Richard. **Three by Mistake.** Nelson 1974.

Simon Farid invites some school friends home with him one Friday. As they approach the house, they are ambushed, tied, and gagged by Arab terrorists. The children hear the arguments of the terrorists as they use the youngsters as hostages to free some guerrilla hijackers. Fiction.

Paz, Octavio (translator Lysander Kemp). **The Other Mexico: Critique of the Pyramid.** Grove 1972.

The pyramids and their symbolic influence are examined in this historical and philosophical essay about modern Mexico's politics, history, and culture. (See also *The Labyrinth of Solitude,* Grove.) Nonfiction.

Perl, Lila. **East Africa: Kenya, Tanzania, Uganda.** Morrow 1973.

An in-depth view of the past, present, and future of the three nations (Kenya, Tanzania, and Uganda) which comprise the territory of East Africa. Mature nonfiction.

Raswan, Carl R. **Drinkers of the Wind.** FS&G 1942.

The author's quest for the perfect Arabian stallion begins during his childhood in Austria. Once Raswan reaches Egypt as a young man, he befriends the Bedouins of Saudi Arabia. His travels through the Arabian desert with his new friends are described in detail. Nonfiction.

Rice, Edward. **Mother India's Children.** Pantheon 1971.

A time and culture are captured in this book of twenty informal interviews with young people of India. Through words and photographs, this book examines today's Indian adolescents and records their answers to many questions. Nonfiction.

Rosenblum, Morris. **Heroes of Israel.** Fleet 1972.

Rosenblum sets the tone by describing the land of Israel. Included in this volume are profiles of famous Israelis such as David Ben-Gurion, Golda Meir, Chaim Weizmann, and Moshe Dayan. Nonfiction.

Salkey, Andrew, editor. **Island Voices: Stories from the West Indies.** Liveright 1970.

The superstitions, the tragedies, the humor, the fantasies, and the resentments of the inhabitants of the West Indies are revealed in the dialects of the islands in these stories told by native writers. Fiction.

Scott-Stokes, Henry. **The Life and Death of Yukio Mishima.** FS&G 1974.

Mishima was a famous but enigmatic Japanese novelist and playwright. At the age of forty-five he committed suicide by hara-kiri. Nonfiction.

Shimer, Dorothy Blair, editor. **Voices of Modern Asia.** NAL 1973.

Short stories, poetry, and essays by Asian writers

revealing the psychology and philosophy of modern Asia. (See also *The Mentor Book of Modern Asian Literature,* NAL.)

Smith, Edith Hutchins. **El Tigre!** Blair 1956.

The author brings Mexican villagers to life in short stories that vividly and warmly capture the Mexican way of life. Fiction.

Taylor, Alice, editor. **Focus on South America.** Praeger 1973.

The changes in lifestyle and the economic, social, and political factors that are operating in each of the nations and in South America as a whole. Nonfiction.

Traven, B. **General from the Jungle.** Hill & Wang 1973.

The army is the real protagonist in this novel of guerrilla warfare in one of the southern states of Mexico. Fiction.

Turnbull, Colin M. **The Mountain People.** S&S 1972.

Ousted by the government from their native hunting area, an African mountain tribe called the Ik has in only three generations deteriorated from a cooperative to a hostile group whose members distrust each other and compete to survive. (See also *The Forest People: A Study of the Pygmies of the Congo,* S&S; and *The Lonely African,* S&S.) Nonfiction.

Uris, Leon. **Exodus** (© 1958). Bantam 1969.

This story of the founding of Israel chronicles the human struggle for freedom. Along with its accounts of war and suffering, it includes the love story of a Jewish leader and an American nurse. Fiction.

van der Post, Laurens. **A Story Like the Wind.** Morrow 1972.

Francois Joubert, a thirteen-year-old boy, lives on Hunter's Drift, a farm in South Africa. Through the teachings of his father, an exile from the racist South African government, and from the experiences and teachings of Bamuthi, a Matabele herdsman, and Mopani Theron, a hunter whose name is a legend throughout Africa, Francois learns to make his way and survive in the bush. Fiction.

Warren, Fred (with Lee Warren). **The Music of Africa.**
P-H 1970.

Africa is just now being recognized as having made
important contributions to music. The range of African musical forms and instruments and the place of
music in the lives of Africans are discussed. Nonfiction.

Warren, Lee. **The Dance of Africa—An Introduction.**
P-H 1972.

African dance and its relationship to and influence on
the cultures and subcultures of Africa's inhabitants.
Nonfiction.

White, Jo Ann, editor. **Impact: Asian Views of the
West.** Messner 1971.

From the earliest contacts of the Orient with the West
until modern times, contemporary reporters discuss the
influence of the West on Asia and what Asia thought
and thinks of the West. Nonfiction.

Williams, Byron. **Puerto Rico: Commonwealth, State,
or Nation?** Parents 1972.

The history of Puerto Rico and the story of its people.
Nonfiction.

Wilson, Dick. **Asia Awakes: A Continent in Transition**
(© 1970). NAL 1971.

A comprehensive study of the emerging nations of
Asia—cultural conflicts, wars, politics, agriculture, and
economics, and the roles of the Soviet Union and the
United States in the future of Asia. Mature nonfiction.

WAR

Alderman, Clifford Lindsey. **Liberty! Equality! Frater-
nity! The Story of the French Revolution.** Messner
1965.

The glories and tragedies of the French Revolution
are told in this brief account. The revolution of 1789
abolished the monarchy, led to the bloody Reign of
Terror, and irrevocably changed the history of France.
Nonfiction.

Arden, John. **Serjeant Musgrave's Dance.** Grove 1960.

Serjeant Musgrave and three of his men come into a

small village in northern England. The coal miners
are on strike and first believe the soldiers have been
sent to break the strike. They are then led to believe
the soldiers are on a recruiting drive. But Serjeant
Musgrave's mission is much different. Mature fiction.

Arnold-Forster, Mark. **The World at War.** NAL 1973.

A series of accounts of individual campaigns during
World War II, beginning with the Nazi buildup in
Germany and concluding with the fall of the Axis
powers. Nonfiction.

Benchley, Nathaniel. **Bright Candles: A Novel of the
Danish Resistance.** Har-Row 1974.

In 1940, Jens Hansen is sixteen years old; it is also
the year the Germans occupy Denmark. From that
year until liberation, Jens is involved in increasingly
dangerous sabotage work, helping fellow Danes resist
the occupation. Fiction.

Blair, Clay, Jr. **Silent Victory: The U.S. Submarine
War against Japan.** Lippincott 1975.

After one chapter on events leading up to the entry of
the U.S. in World War II, the author relates the activities of submarine warfare from Pearl Harbor to the
surrender of Japan. Using thousands of sources, he
has written a detailed account of how submarines contributed to the victory in the Pacific. Nonfiction.

Boom, Corrie ten (with John and Elizabeth Sherrill).
The Hiding Place (© 1971). Bantam 1974.

Put in a German concentration camp during World
War II because she protected Jews, the author found
solace in religion, which protected her during the war
and protects her even now. (See also *A Prisoner and
Yet . . .*, Chr Lit.) Nonfiction.

Boulle, Pierre. **The Bridge over the River Kwai** (©
1954). Bantam 1970.

When his troops are confined to a Japanese prisoner-
of-war camp, Colonel Nicholson proves he is a disci-
plinarian and perfectionist by leading his men in the
building of a railroad bridge over the River Kwai.
However, the military value of the bridge to the Japanese and Nicholson's harsh leadership causes dissen-
sion among his men.

Burdick, Eugene, and Harvey Wheeler. **Fail-Safe.** Mc-Graw 1962.

Fail-safe is the name given to the complex machinery designed to prevent the accidental nuclear bombing of an enemy. How this machinery does fail, leading to thermonuclear destruction, is compellingly narrated. Fiction.

Caidin, Martin. **The Last Dogfight.** HM 1974.

U.S. Air Force Captain Mitch Ross is an ace in the air but a mystery to his men when he is not flying. His counterpart in the Japanese Air Force is Shigura Tanimoto. Though they admire and respect each other, inevitably they meet in an air duel over the Pacific during World War II. Fiction.

Calvocoressi, Peter, and Guy Wint. **Total War: The Story of World War II,** 2 vols. Ballantine 1972.

A detailed history of World War II—its background, generals, battles, and campaigns. Illustrated with many photographs. Nonfiction.

Carter, Ross S. **Those Devils in Baggy Pants** (© 1951). NAL 1971.

One of three surviving members of the original paratroop platoon of the Eighty-second Airborne Division, the author narrates the unit's many battles, from North Africa to the Battle of the Bulge, in World War II. Nonfiction.

Chambliss, William C. **The Silent Service.** NAL 1959.

Six true stories of submarines and their crews in the Pacific during World War II illustrate how the submariners were instrumental in deciding battles against the Japanese Navy. Nonfiction.

Collins, Larry, and Dominique Lapierre. **Is Paris Burning?** (© 1965). PB 1973.

The authors detail how and when Paris was liberated from German occupation in 1944. Hitler had ordered the city to be completely destroyed; how it was saved and how the Gaullists and Communists differed politically in the saving of the city are detailed. Nonfiction.

Davidowicz, Lucy S. **The War against the Jews, 1933–1945.** HR&W 1975.

The author tries to answer three questions. First, why

did a modern country like Germany systematically murder a people just because they were Jews? Second, why did the Jews allow this to happen to themselves? Third, why did the world allow this to happen without making any efforts to stop the mass murders? Mature nonfiction.

Degens, T. **Transport 7-41-R.** Viking Pr 1974.

A thirteen-year-old German girl discovers in the aftermath of the Nazi defeat the importance of caring for others by helping an old man conceal his wife's death from other evacuees aboard their train so he may fulfill his promise to bury her in Cologne, her native city. Fiction.

Deighton, Len. **Declarations of War** (© 1971). Panther 1973.

Thirteen short stories, ranging in time from Roman battles through World War I and Vietnam, each focusing on individuals who face death. Fiction.

Dowd, David L., and *Horizon* Magazine Editors. **The French Revolution.** Am Heritage 1965.

With paintings and drawings from the eighteenth century, this short history tells the story of the causes and effects of the French Revolution, from before the fall of the Bastille to Napoleon. Nonfiction.

Dunn, Mary Lois. **The Man in the Box: A Story from Vietnam** (© 1968). Dell 1975.

Chau Li had watched his father being put into a torture box by the Viet Cong, but he was too little to stop them and his father died. Now he sees an American soldier being put in a similar box, and he knows he must do everything he can to save him. Fiction.

Forman, James. **Code Name Valkyrie.** S G Phillips 1973.

In 1943, while German Colonel Claus von Stauffenberg lay in a hospital reviewing the reasons why he was there, he conceived a plan to assassinate Adolf Hitler. Nonfiction.

Forman, James. **Horses of Anger.** FS&G 1967.

Hans Amann, a German boy serving as a Nazi gunner close to the end of World War II, witnesses the loss of spirit in his family, himself, and his close friends when they experience adversity and fear in their own country. Fiction.

Forman, James. **Ring the Judas Bell.** FS&G 1965.
Captured when the Communists are trying to take over Greece, Nicholas and his sister are taken to a prison camp in Albania. Fiction.

Forsyth, Frederick. **The Dogs of War.** Viking Pr 1974.
A mercenary hired by a British financier sets out to overthrow an African dictatorship, and the details of his planning and the violence of his attempt are given in documentary style. (See also *The Odessa File,* Bantam.) Mature fiction.

Franks, Lucinda. **Waiting Out a War.** Coward 1974.
In 1967, draftee John Picciano deserted the army and fled to Canada and then Sweden. His decision involved and affected many people, most of all his family. Nonfiction.

Friedman, Leon. **The Wise Minority.** Dial 1971.
Civil disobedience and draft resistance have been part of our history since the Revolutionary War, beginning with the Whiskey Rebellion in 1794 and concluding with the Vietnam War. Nonfiction.

Gallagher, Thomas. **Assault in Norway.** HarBraceJ 1975.
Nazi Germany was ahead of any Allied country in developing the atomic bomb. But in 1942, a small group of Norwegian commandoes destroyed Germany's nuclear production facility at Vemork in Nazi-occupied Norway. This daring raid halted Germany's development of the bomb. Nonfiction.

Giles, Janice Holt. **The Damned Engineers.** HM 1970.
In 1944–45, the German Army launched a desperate winter offensive to drive back the Allied forces approaching the German frontier. The 291st Engineer Combat Battalion was the only force in Hitler's way. Nonfiction.

Graham, Gail. **Cross-Fire: A Vietnam Novel.** Pantheon 1972.
Separated from his company in Vietnam, Harry meets

the only surviving members of a bombed-out village,
a young girl and her two younger brothers. Though
he does not know Vietnamese and they do not know
English, they communicate well enough to begin their
trek toward a Catholic mission and then Saigon. Fiction.

Grant, Zalin. **Survivors.** Norton 1975.

Nine American soldiers, captured in Vietnam, tell about
their daily lives in their jungle prison, the confusion
and the terrors. Nonfiction.

Greene, Bette. **Summer of My German Soldier.** Dial
1973.

The only child of a Jewish family living in a small
Arkansas town during World War II, Patty Bergen
aids a German soldier who has escaped from a nearby
internment camp. Despite the realities of war and
politics which make her actions shocking to her parents, Patty is motivated by the soldier's warmth and
his insistence that she is indeed a "person of value."
Fiction.

Grunberger, Richard. **Hitler's SS** (© 1971). Dell 1972.

A sketch of all phases of the Nazi *Schutzstaffel* (the
SS or "Blackshirts"), from its inception in the 1920s
through the end of World War II. Commanded by
Heinrich Himmler, the SS carried out the extermination of Jews and others in Germany and in territory
occupied by Germany during the war. Nonfiction.

Hahn, Thich N. (translator Helen Coutant). **The Cry of
Vietnam** (© 1968). Unicorn Pr 1971.

Written by a Vietnamese, these poems cry out the anguish and despair over the years of appalling bloodshed
in Vietnam. But still the poet can express his love
for humanity. Vivid drawings reflect the emotions in
the poems.

Haldeman, Joe W. **War Year.** HR&W 1972.

In the language of a soldier in the field, John Farmer
relates his training as a combat engineer, his duties
both on the front lines and in the rear, and the many
battles in the highlands of Vietnam. Fiction.

Hermanns, William. **The Holocaust.** Har-Row 1972.

A young, patriotic German volunteers for World War
I. Shortly he finds himself in the mud and death of
the battle of Verdun, the bloodiest battle in history.
Nonfiction.

Hersh, Seymour M. **My Lai 4: A Report on the Massacre and Its Aftermath.** Random 1970.

On March 16, 1968, American soldiers entered My Lai
4, a small village in Vietnam, and killed the inhabitants. Hersh reviews the events of the killing and the
legal battles and trials that came out of it. Nonfiction.

Höhne, Heinz, and Hermann Zolling. **The General Was
a Spy.** Bantam 1972.

General Reinhard Gehlen was Hitler's chief of Intelligence for Russian operations, but in 1945 he became
an important operative for the American C.I.A. Nonfiction.

Horne, Alistair. **Death of a Generation: Neuve Chapelle
to Verdun and the Somme.** Am Heritage 1970.

In one year during World War I, two major battles
were fought between the Allies and the Germans. In
those two battles, the Germans lost over 700,000 men,
the French over 500,000, and the British over 400,000.
Nonfiction.

Huberman, Edward, and Elizabeth Huberman, editors.
War: An Anthology. WSP 1969.

This collection of poems, short stories, and essays, none
of which glorify war, contains material from a wide
variety of times and places. Regardless of the time in
which each work was written, each still speaks about
today's situations.

Janssen, Pierre (translator William R. Tyler). **A Moment of Silence.** Atheneum 1970.

At 8:00 p.m. every May 4, the entire country of the
Netherlands becomes silent in tribute to the many
Dutch who died in World War II during the German
occupation. Commenting on the photographs of me-
morials throughout Holland, the author expresses the
need for freedom. Nonfiction.

Jarman, T. L. **The Rise and Fall of Nazi Germany** (© 1956). NAL 1961.

This chronicle of the Third Reich offers a well-rounded account without an overabundance of facts and analysis. Mature nonfiction.

John, Otto (translator Richard Barry). **Twice Through the Lines: The Autobiography of Otto John.** Har-Row 1973.

Dr. John, the last survivor of the conspiracy to assassinate Hitler, gained attention when he disappeared in Berlin in 1954. Had he become a spy for Russia or was he a double agent? Nonfiction.

Johnston, Jennifer. **How Many Miles to Babylon?** Doubleday 1974.

Wellborn Alexander Moore is a friend of peasant-born Jerry Crowe. When World War I erupts, both boys enlist. Crowe deserts and is sentenced to die, and Moore is put in command of the firing squad. Fiction.

Kosinski, Jerzy. **The Painted Bird** (© 1965). Bantam 1972.

A young Jewish boy is separated from his parents at the beginning of World War II and begins four years of wandering through Eastern Europe. He is a victim, observer, and miraculous survivor of the many forms of evil that humans are capable of when war strips away or perverts the usual restraints of the community. Mature fiction.

Lang, Daniel. **Casualties of War.** McGraw 1969.

In November 1966, five American soldiers were on patrol in Vietnam. Four of them kidnapped, raped, and murdered Phan Thi Mao, a young Vietnamese girl. One reported the crime to army officials and the four were court-martialed, but the questions of how and why are disturbingly brought out. Nonfiction.

Leckie, Robert. **The Wars of America.** Har-Row 1968.

From 1609, when Champlain fought against the Iroquois Indians, to the present, America has been in numerous wars. The author outlines and relates them to social, economic, and political factors and looks at some of the personal aspects of wars. Nonfiction.

Lifton, Betty Jean. **Return to Hiroshima.** Atheneum 1970.

On August 6, 1945, the atomic bomb was dropped on Hiroshima. In prose and black and white photographs, this book illustrates how the city and some of its people have survived since that day of holocaust. Non-fiction.

Lifton, Betty Jean, and Thomas C. Fox. **Children of Vietnam.** Atheneum 1972.

In any modern war, civilians suffer, perhaps more than the combatants. Of civilians, children suffer most of all because they do not understand. This book looks at children in prose and with pictures to see how they suffer and endure war. Nonfiction.

Lord, Walter. **Incredible Victory.** Har-Row 1967.

In June 1942, American forces in the South Pacific were outclassed in equipment and men by the Japanese. But at the battle of Midway, the American Navy and Army defeated the superior Japanese forces, leading to the reversal of Japanese dominance in the Pacific. Nonfiction.

March, William. **Company K** (© 1933). Hill & Wang 1957.

Sketches of the men of Company K of the American Army during World War I are woven together to reveal courage, stupidity, loneliness, irony, and, at times, bitter humor. The war is shown from the point of view of men who were there. Fiction.

Mee, Charles L., Jr. **Meeting at Potsdam.** M Evans 1975.

During summer 1945, President Harry Truman, Prime Minister Winston Churchill, and Premier Josef Stalin met in Potsdam, Germany, to determine national boundaries and the conditions that would prevail in Europe after Germany had been defeated. Nonfiction.

Meissner, Hans (translator Erica Pomerans). **Duel in the Snow.** Morrow 1972.

In June 1942, the Japanese capture an island in the American Aleutians and parachute guerrillas into nearby Alaska. American scouts are sent on a mission to destroy the Japanese. Fiction.

Monsarrat, Nicholas (editors Harry Shefter et al.). **The Cruel Sea** (© 1951). WSP 1964.

Lieutenant Commander Ericson takes command of a corvette assigned to escort supply ships across the Atlantic during the early days of World War II. After this ship is torpedoed, he takes command of a larger one, a frigate. Fiction.

Morris, Marjorie, and Don Sauers. **And/Or: Antonyms for Our Age.** Har-Row 1967.

By using contrasting black and white photographs, the authors illuminate the contrasts of peace and war, love and hate, joy and grief, hope and despair. Nonfiction.

Nagatsuka, Ruyji (translator Nina Rootes). **I Was a Kamikaze.** Macmillan 1974.

The author, a former student of French literature, volunteered for the Japanese Air Force. He then became one of those asked to volunteer for suicide missions—the kamikaze, "knights of the divine winds." The training he received and his thoughts during his training are detailed. Nonfiction.

O'Brien, Tim. **If I Die in a Combat Zone, Box Me Up & Send Me Home** (© 1973). Dell 1974.

Questioning the rightness of the Vietnam War and his own ability and courage, the author kept a journal of his experience in the army and in Vietnam. Nonfiction.

Onoda, Hiroo. **No Surrender: My Thirty-Year War.** Kodansha 1974.

In 1944 Second Lieutenant Hiroo Onoda was ordered by the Japanese Army to conduct guerrilla warfare on the Philippine island of Lubang. In 1974 he surrendered after thirty years of battle against the enemy and the elements. Nonfiction.

Orrmont, Arthur. **Requiem for War: The Life of Wilfred Owen.** Four Winds 1972.

The life of Wilfred Owen, British poet and soldier, to his death in battle only one week before the armistice that ended World War I. Nonfiction.

O'Sullivan, P. Michael. **Patriot Graves: Resistance in Ireland.** Follett 1972.

The author first gives a brief history of Ireland that

provides a better understanding of the Irish Republican Movement and the attempt to make Northern Ireland part of the Irish Republic. Politics rather than religion seems to be the impulse behind the fighting. Many interviews with contemporary leaders and citizens stress an independent Ireland. Nonfiction.

Procktor, Richard. **Nazi Germany: The Origins and Collapse of the Third Reich** (© 1970). HR&W 1973.

A detailed picture of the Hitler nightmare. Nonfiction.

Remarque, Erich Marie (translator A. W. Wheen). **All Quiet on the Western Front.** Little 1929.

Paul Baumer enlists in the German Army during World War I after graduating from school, urged on by the ideas of teachers and friends in his small town. He finds that the war reduces men to fighting for mere survival. Fiction.

Reynolds, Quentin. **70,000 to 1.** Pyramid Pubns 1946.

During World War II, an American soldier is alone on a Japanese-controlled island. His terrifying story is told in a novel-like fashion. Nonfiction.

Richter, Hans Peter (translator Edite Kroll). **Friedrich** (© 1970). Dell 1973.

A first-person account of a German boy whose best friend Friedrich, member of a prosperous Jewish family, undergoes radical change through the years 1925–42. Fiction.

Robinson, Derek. **Goshawk Squadron** (© 1972). Viking Pr 1973.

A bitter and cynical story of British fliers in World War I. The men of Goshawk Squadron of the Royal Flying Corps passionately hate their commander, Major Stanley Woolley, who bullies them into action. Fiction.

Russ, Martin. **Line of Departure: Tarawa.** Doubleday 1975.

Tarawa, one of the atolls of the Gilbert Islands in the Pacific, was heavily fortified by the Japanese during World War II, but, in one of the fiercest battles of the war, the American Marines took the atoll despite enormous losses. Nonfiction.

Ryan, Cornelius. **A Bridge Too Far.** S&S 1974.

In a campaign planned by Field Marshall Sir Bernard Montgomery, the Allies attempted to shorten World War II by capturing the crucial bridge across the Rhine at Arnhem. Nonfiction.

Ryss, Yevgeny (translator Bonnie Carey). **Search behind the Lines.** Morrow 1974.

When the World War II German invasion of the U.S.S.R. comes, Kolya and Lena, the daughter of a famous Soviet general, flee their small village and live with Kolya's grandfather deep in the woods. Fiction.

Sack, John. **The Man-Eating Machine.** FS&G 1973.

Four men fight in Vietnam and return home to a changed America. Their stories, the most famous being that of Lieutenant Calley, are a satiric indictment of much of contemporary life. Nonfiction.

Sajer, Guy (translator Lily Emmet). **The Forgotten Soldier.** Har-Row 1971.

This autobiography shows the fighting person's side of World War II. Joining the German Army at sixteen and later surviving the disasters of the Russian front, the author brings to life the horror of war. Mature nonfiction.

Salisbury, Harrison E. **The 900 Days: The Siege of Leningrad.** Har-Row 1969.

For 900 days the Germans held Russian forces and civilians under siege at Leningrad, the longest siege of a city since Biblical days. During this time, over one million people died. The Russian military blundered, but the Russian people endured. Mature nonfiction.

Schoenberner, Gerhard (translator Susan Sweet). **The Yellow Star: The Persecution of the Jews in Europe, 1933–1945** (© 1960). Bantam 1973.

An unrelenting photographic documentation of the supreme nightmare of our time: the imprisonment and extermination of European Jewry. The horrifying nature of some photographs may be unsettling to some readers. Mature nonfiction.

Shaw, Robert. **The Man in the Glass Booth** (© 1968). Grove 1969.

Arthur Goldman is mistaken by Israeli agents for Colonel Adolf Karl Dorff, a German Nazi accused of committing atrocities against the Jews in World War II. When his trial begins, he does not reveal the mistake but plays the role of Dorff and adopts his anti-Semitic attitude. Mature.

Smith, R. Harris. **OSS: The Secret History of America's First Central Intelligence Agency** (© 1972). Dell 1973.

The U.S. Office of Strategic Services (OSS) began in World War II as the chief agency of U.S. intelligence. The author, a former C.I.A. worker, interviewed 200 former OSS employees to compile this history. Nonfiction.

Solzhenitsyn, Alexander (translator Michael Glenny). **August 1914** (© 1972). Bantam 1974.

Set in Russia during World War I, Solzhenitsyn's story presents a cross section of attitudes, social classes, and scenes ranging from the strategies of armies to the fear of the individual soldier in a trench under shellfire. Mature fiction.

Southall, Ivan. **Seventeen Seconds.** Macmillan 1974.

A band of Australian soldiers was trained in World War II to disarm and dismantle German bombs and missiles dropped on England. Their exploits and dangers often averted disaster for whole city blocks. Nonfiction.

Thayer, Charles W. **Guerrilla.** Har-Row 1963.

From long experience in diplomacy and warfare, the author discusses the underground guerrilla movements in many countries and some of the reasons why guerrilla warfare is effective in this nuclear age. Nonfiction.

Toland, John. **Battle: The Story of the Bulge.** NAL 1959.

In the winter of 1944, the German Army launched a counterattack against the Allied Armies along the Ardennes front. The Belgian town of Bastogne at one

time was completely surrounded by German troops.
The Allies fought back and eventually defeated the
Germans in one of the most important campaigns of
World War II. Nonfiction.

Tolstoy, Leo (translator Rosemary Edmonds). **War and
Peace.** Penguin 1969.

A panoramic 1865 novel set in Russia during the early
nineteenth century when Napoleon was preparing to
attack. Pierre Bejuhov and his friend Andrey Bolko-
vsky both find the young Natasha fascinating, and
Andrey offers to marry her. Though she loves Andrey,
she is foolishly attracted to another man and runs off
with him only to find he has deceived her and is already married. Napoleon's approach to Moscow even
further disrupts all their lives. Mature fiction.

Trumbo, Dalton. **Johnny Got His Gun** (© 1939). Bantam 1970.

Published before World War II but only gaining recognition in the 1960s, this unflinching antiwar novel
is about Johnny, his entrance into the war, and his
life-in-death as a hopeless vegetable in a veterans hospital. Mature fiction.

Tuchman, Barbara. **The Guns of August** (© 1962). Dell
1971.

The dramatic beginning of the long and bloody struggle of World War I is told in this Pulitzer Prize-winning account of August 1914. Mature nonfiction.

Tunis, John R. **His Enemy, His Friend.** Avon 1967.

In 1944, a German sergeant has his harmonious relationship with a French village ruined when he is ordered to arrest and shoot some hostages. Years later,
the much older German is a member of a soccer team
playing a French team. One member of the French
team is the son of one of the murdered hostages.
Fiction.

Tute, Warren, John Costello, and Terry Hughes. **D-Day.**
Macmillan 1974.

A lavishly illustrated history of the events that led up
to D-Day in World War II. Nonfiction.

Uris, Leon. **Mila 18** (© 1961). Bantam 1970.

The persecution and mass execution of Polish Jews is

the background for the epic struggle of the Jewish forces in the Warsaw ghetto whose efforts held the Germans at bay for almost a month and a half during World War II. Fiction.

Uris, Leon. **QB VII** (© 1970). Bantam 1972.

Abraham Cady believes that Sir Adam Kelno was a sadistic doctor working with the Nazis in a concentration camp. Cady accuses Kelno in a book, and Kelno sues Cady for libel, a legal battle to be heard in the Queen's Bench Courtroom Number 7. Fiction.

Wakin, Edward. **Black Fighting Men in U.S. History.** Lothrop 1971.

From Crispus Attucks, a black man who was the first man killed in the American Revolution, to Colonel Daniel James, Jr., who fought in both the Korean War and Vietnam, the lives of black men are sketched out and their contributions to the wars of the U.S. are narrated. Nonfiction.

West, F. J., Jr. **The Village.** Har-Row 1972.

During the Vietnam War, twelve American Marines volunteered to live and fight side by side with twelve Vietnamese in the tiny provincial village of Binh Nghia. Nonfiction.

Westheimer, David. **Von Ryan's Express** (© 1964). NAL n.d.

Colonel Joseph Ryan is captured by Italians after his plane is shot down. He is brought to a prisoner-of-war camp where he quickly brings the prisoners into better shape. After the Germans place the prisoners on a train bound for Germany, Ryan leads them in their escape to Switzerland. Fiction.

Wiesel, Elie. **Night, Dawn, the Accident.** Hill & Wang 1972.

The first work in this collection tells the true story of a young Jewish boy taken with his family from their home to the Nazi extermination camps of Auschwitz and Buchenwald. The second, a short novel, narrates how the survivor of the Nazi camps has become a member of the underground in British-controlled Palestine. The third has the narrator living in New York and almost killed in an automobile accident.

Wilhelm, Maria. **For the Glory of France: The Story of the French Resistance.** Messner 1968.

In 1940 France surrendered to Nazi Germany. From then until the liberation, Resistance groups fought underground against the invaders. Many men and women became heroes as they courageously defied their enemy—and often died. Nonfiction.

Wilkinson, Burke, editor. **Cry Sabotage: True Stories of Twentieth-Century Saboteurs.** Bradbury Pr 1972.

Brief accounts of saboteurs and their work, from the sinking of the battleship *Maine* in 1895, which led to the Spanish-American War, to the British-Irish Republican Army struggle in the early 1970s. Nonfiction.

Williams, Eric. **The Wooden Horse.** Dell 1958.

In a German prison camp, two British officers and their fellow prisoners make a wooden horse in their attempt to escape. Nonfiction.

Willwerth, James. **Eye in the Last Storm.** Grossman 1972.

A reporter for *Time* magazine reports the Vietnam stories that never made the headlines—the personal conflicts, the brutality, the bombings, the night life, and the deaths. Nonfiction.

Winterbotham, F. W. **The Ultra Secret.** Har-Row 1974.

The story of how the British cracked the German military's communication code with a machine called "Enigma." The book also documents the invaluable information that the machine provided during World War II. Nonfiction.

Wojciechowska, Maia. **Till the Break of Day.** Har-BraceJ 1972.

Wojciechowska, author of several award-winning books, tells the story of how she and her family fled their estate in Poland at the outbreak of World War II and traveled across France during the Nazi occupation. Nonfiction.

Woodham-Smith, Cecil. **The Reason Why** (© 1953). McGraw 1971.

The charge of the English Light Cavalry Brigade against Russian artillery in the 1854 Crimean War, one of the bravest and most senseless acts in military history, is here examined as history, not legend. Nonfiction.

Wouk, Herman. **The Caine Mutiny** (© 1954). PB 1973.

Captain Queeg is put in command of the USS *Caine* for operation in the Pacific against the Japanese. A number of incidents occur on board until finally, during a typhoon, the officers of the ship decide that the captain is incapable of further command and join in mutiny against him. Fiction.

Zassenhaus, Hiltgunt. **Walls: Resisting the Third Reich—One Woman's Story.** Beacon Pr 1974.

Seventeen when Hitler came into power, the author refused to become a Nazi. She fought Hitler during World War II by accepting a job as a mail censor and then working secretly with the Swedish Red Cross to smuggle food into German prisons. Nonfiction.

Ziemian, Joseph (translator Janina David). **The Cigarette Sellers of Three Crosses Square** (© 1970). Lerner Pubns 1975.

Few Jews survived confinement in the Warsaw ghetto during World War II. Those who did were the children whose daring and resourcefulness are depicted by a member of the Jewish Underground who aided them. Nonfiction.

OUR LANGUAGES

Asimov, Isaac. **Words of Science** (© 1959). NAL 1969.

From "Absolute Zero" to "Zodiac," Asimov traces some 1,500 scientific terms through history from their simple roots to their complicated usages today. (See also *Words from the Myths,* NAL.)

Auden, W. H., and Louis Kronenberger, editors. **The Viking Book of Aphorisms** (© 1962). Viking Pr 1966.

An aphorism is a general truth expressed succinctly that makes a wise, if often ironic, comment on human behavior. This anthology contains more than 3,000 aphorisms by 450 different authors. The collection is divided into such categories as history, love, marriage, and friendship.

Barnhart, Clarence L., Sol Steinmetz, and Robert K. Barnhart, editors. **The Barnhart Dictionary of New English since 1963.** Har-Row 1973.

This is a record of many recent terms required and created by our scientific researchers and achievements, our technical and cultural activities, and our social and personal lives. Each of the 5,000 entries receives the standard dictionary treatment.

Black, Max. **The Labyrinth of Language** (© 1968). NAL 1969.

A survey of modern linguistic analysis that explores the inner workings of language, from basic sounds to complex grammar, as well as the elusive concept of meaning.

Bombaugh, C. C. (editor Martin Gardner). **Oddities and Curiosities of Words and Literature.** Dover 1961.

An abridgement of a book originally published in 1874, this collection will delight anyone interested in what has been done with the English language. There are plenty of puns, puzzles, and palindromes, not to mention shape poems, riddles, unusual names, hoaxes, and frauds.

Burgess, Anthony. **Language Made Plain** (© 1964). T Y Crowell 1969.

A good introduction to the mechanics and psychology of language by a popular novelist. Beginning with language in general, Burgess discusses the ideas of sound and the alphabet. In his section on languages he discusses language families and the development of English.

Chaneles, Sol, and Jerome Snyder. **That Pestilent Cosmetic Rhetoric.** Grossman 1972.

A delightfully instructive explanation of some familiar —and some unfamiliar—rhetorical devices. The tricks of the verbal trade are named, defined, and shown in action with quotations from Shaw to Nixon.

Chase, Stuart. **Danger—Men Talking!** Parents 1969.

Language, the author notes, can be used to clear up meaning or obscure it. He comments on the tools of language, how to analyze language, and the dangers one needs to watch for in using language or in hearing the language of others.

Davis, Flora. **Inside Intuition: What We Know about Nonverbal Communication** (© 1971). McGraw 1973.

According to Davis, all of us communicate nonverbally, most of the time without being aware of it. This book discusses the cultural, sexual, and geographic similarities and differences in nonverbal communication. Good bibliography included.

Dillard, J. L. **All-American English: A History of the English Language in America.** Random 1975.

A history of American English with many details about language changes as English developed from colonial times.

Dohan, Mary Helen. **Our Own Words.** Knopf 1974.

A new, thorough history of the American language that carries the story of English into the electronic age. Worthwhile for anyone whose curiosity about language extends to phrases like "lightning bug," "hornswoggle," and "yellowjacket." Hundreds of examples.

Fast, Julius. **Body Language** (© 1970). PB 1971.

Fast employs the science of kinesics, the study of the relationship between body motions and communication, to examine territory, space, masks, touch, postures, as well as "winking, blinking, and nods." Good bibliography for the novice.

Funk, Charles Earle. **Heavens to Betsy! and Other Curious Sayings.** Har-Row 1955.

A lively compilation of how more than 400 colorful and familiar expressions in our language originated and developed. A good reference work, this volume also makes fun reading. (See also *Horsefeathers,* Har-Row; *Thereby Hangs a Tale,* Har-Row; and *A Hog on Ice,* Har-Row.)

Gallant, Roy A. **Man Must Speak: The Story of Language.** Random 1969.

Starting with communication in animals, Gallant traces communication through speech and writing into the age of the satellite.

Gardner, Martin. **Codes, Ciphers and Secret Writing.** S&S 1972.

A simple basic introduction to the world of secret writ-

ing; Gardner covers all the standard items of cryptog-
raphy as well as some of the more bizarre methods.

Gelb, I. J. **A Study of Writing** (© 1952). U of Chicago
Pr 1963.

A serious discussion of the general principles governing the use and evolution of writing. Charts, drawings,
and bibliography cover forerunners of writing, word-
syllabic and syllabic systems, as well as the alphabet
and the evolution of writing.

Girsdansky, Michael. **The Adventure of Language** (©
1963). Fawcett World 1967.

A basic handbook for those interested in languages.
For the casual reader, it gives fascinating insights into
the nature of human and cultural psychology.

Hayakawa, S. I., editor. **The Use and Misuse of Language** (© 1962). Fawcett World 1973.

These eighteen essays from *ETC.: A Review of General Semantics* cover the art of communication, semantics, the arts, and human insights.

Hellman, Hal. **Communications in the World of the
Future.** M Evans 1969.

A good survey of the advances in communication, this
book tells of a world of communication satellites, lasers,
and machines that talk to other machines. Drawings,
diagrams, and photographs help tell this story of tomorrow.

Laird, Charlton. **The Miracle of Language** (© 1953).
Fawcett World 1973.

Laird's lively, imaginative work traces language from
its origins through its strange development to the complex means of communication we use today.

Lambert, Eloise, and Mario Pei. **Our Names.** Lothrop
1960.

In addition to the story of peoples' names, this book
examines the names of things like animals, institutions,
flags, and the seasons.

Maddox, Brenda. **Beyond Babel: New Directions in
Communication.** S&S 1972.

An informative survey of the present and a projection

of the near future in communications. The author talks about the changes in communication, their political and social implications, and the frequent resistance to change.

McGough, Elizabeth. **Your Silent Language.** Morrow 1974.

An investigation of kinesics, more commonly referred to as body language. Written from a teenager's point of view, the book covers such areas as handshakes, courting, aggression, and head movements.

Morris, William, and Mary Morris. **Dictionary of Word and Phrase Origins,** 3 vols. Har-Row 1962 (Vol. I), 1969 (Vol. II), and 1971 (Vol. III).

These books give concise, clear answers to hundreds of questions about our language, the latest usage, derivations, and inconsistencies.

Morris, William, and Mary Morris, editors. **Harper Dictionary of Contemporary Usage.** Har-Row 1975.

A panel of 136 well-known people, mostly writers, is used to determine the degree of acceptability of certain words in our language (like *Ms.*) or the difference between words often confused or used as synonyms (like *imply* and *infer*).

Nash, Walter. **Our Experience of Language.** St Martin 1971.

This book examines language not as an object for definition and analysis, but as something we use and respond to every day. There is a good appendix of examples of English from 1014 to the present.

Neal, Harry Edward. **Communication from Stone Age to Space Age** (© 1960). Messner 1974.

An introduction to communication with an emphasis on communication devices such as the pen, pencil, and typewriter. Begins with an explanation of grunts and giggles and concludes with outer space and ESP.

Newman, Edwin. **Strictly Speaking.** Bobbs 1974.

Veteran newsman Newman explores what he considers to be the sorry state of the English language in America. He attacks stereotypes, clichés, errors, and jargon in our language.

Nierenberg, Gerard I., and Henry H. Calero. **How to Read a Person Like a Book** (© 1971). PB 1973.

People do reveal their beliefs and conflicts through nonverbal communication in the ways they sit and gesture and stand. The authors suggest some ideas about learning how to read the subtle nonverbal talk of other people. (See also *Meta-Talk: Guide to Hidden Meanings in Conversation,* PB.)

Pei, Mario. **Double-Speak in America.** Hawthorn 1973.

Beginning with a discussion of new "weasel words" (words coined to obscure or distort meaning), the author writes about the way words are used to hide meaning or purpose and the way people in power use those words.

Pei, Mario. **The Families of Words** (© 1962). St Martin 1974.

This book traces the roots of many of our most common words to their original meanings and shows how some words have changed in meaning through time. (See also *The Story of Language,* NAL.)

Pei, Mario. **The Story of Latin and the Romance Languages.** Har-Row 1976.

History and geography, in addition to linguistics, are brought to bear on the origin and development of Latin and its various transformations that produced the family of Romance languages.

Shipley, Joseph T. **Word Play.** Hawthorn 1972.

This guide defines and explains dozens of word games and gives countless examples of each. Those familiar with riddles, anagrams, and conundrums will find that they've only scratched the surface of possible games.

Smith, Elsdon C. **The Treasury of Name Lore.** Har-Row 1967.

Names are an important part of any language. This book explains how names fit into language, the classification and origin of descriptive surnames, and nicknames. (See also *American Surnames,* Chilton.)

Thum, Gladys, and Marcella Thum. **The Persuaders: Propaganda in War and Peace.** Atheneum 1972.

Is propaganda as American as apple pie? This book

examines the role propaganda has played in the development of this country, from presidential campaigns and advertising to war and Prohibition.

Weekley, Ernest. **The Romance of Words** (© 1911). Dover 1912.

A reissue of an informal, nontechnical exposition of the English language. Weekley provides brief, simple coverage of nearly all the important divisions of etymology. Also included are many unusual word histories.

Wentworth, Harold, and Stuart Berg Flexner, editors. **The Pocket Dictionary of American Slang** (© 1960). PB 1968.

Because language is constantly changing, this book is, by definition, dated. However, it offers a thorough explanation of the slang terms of the past.

Wolfe, James Raymond. **Secret Writing: The Craft of the Cryptographer.** McGraw 1970.

Interspersed with intriguing historical incidents is a solid explanation of secret writing. Transposition, substitution, frequency count, grid, and skytale are some of the areas covered.

MYTH AND FOLKLORE

Baumann, Hans. **The Stolen Fire.** Pantheon 1973.

Legends of heroes and rebels from Eastern Europe, Siberia, Africa, Asia, Australia, and America.

Black Elk (editor Joseph Epes Brown). **The Sacred Pipe: Black Elk's Account of the Seven Rites of the Oglala Sioux** (© 1953). Penguin 1971.

Black Elk, at the age of almost ninety, tells the seven rites of his tribe's religion so that it will be preserved. He describes the ceremonies and tells the importance of the sacred pipe in order that "peace may come to those peoples who can understand. . . ."

Buck, William. **Mahabharata.** U of Cal Pr 1974.

The *Mahabharata* is an epic of India about a feud between two branches of an Indian ruling family that results in a gigantic battle.

Bulfinch, Thomas (editor Edmund Fuller). **Bulfinch's Mythology** (© 1863). Dell 1959.

This standard handbook of mythology is divided into "The Age of Fable" (Prometheus to *Beowulf*), "The Age of Chivalry" *(Launcelot of the Lake* to *Morte d'Arthur)*, and "The Legends of Charlemagne" (the Paladins to the Battle of Roncesvalles).

Campbell, Joseph. **Myths to Live By** (© 1972). Bantam 1973.

Mythology is seen as something alive today, with the author noting the relationship between myth and science, love, religion, and politics. A difficult but rewarding book. Mature.

Carawan, Guy, and Candie Carawan, editors. **Voices from the Mountains.** Knopf 1975.

Appalachian folksongs and recollections of the last forty years touching on labor union struggles, mining disasters, and the battle of a strong and free people to run their own lives and world.

Carter, Dorothy Sharp, editor. **Greedy Mariani and Other Folktales of the Antilles.** Atheneum 1974.

This collection, selected from the folktales of Cuba, Haiti, Jamaica, Puerto Rico, and the Dominican Republic, includes animal tales, tales of magic, and how and why tales of origin.

Davidson, H. R. Ellis. **Gods and Myths of Northern Europe.** Penguin 1964.

Myths, legends, and folklore of the principal Scandinavian and Norse gods like Odin, Thor, and Freyr.

de Angulo, Jaime. **Indian Tales** (© 1953). Ballantine 1974.

The author, who lived among the Pit River Indians of California, began writing these stories about animal-humans for his children. Some are authentic translations of Indian tales; others are purely out of the mind of the author.

Deutsch, Babette. **Heroes of the Kalevala: Finland's Saga.** Messner 1940.

This retelling of the Finnish epic brings excitement and

humor to the feats of singer-magician Vainamoinen and other heroes.

Dorson, Richard M. **American Folklore.** U of Chicago Pr 1959.

This topical history of American folklore by a leading folklorist is an excellent introduction to the field.

Dorson, Richard M. **Buying the Wind: Regional Folklore in the United States.** U of Chicago Pr 1964.

A wealth of oral material collected from Maine Downeasters, Pennsylvania Dutchmen, Southern Mountaineers, Louisiana Cajuns, Illinois Egyptians, Southwest Mexicans, and Utah Mormons.

Emrich, Duncan. **American Folk Poetry: An Anthology.** Little 1974.

This anthology captures the richness of the American oral tradition ranging from children's songs, play-party games, love songs, and child ballads to religious, war, occupational, and westward expansion pieces. An extensive bibliography on the American folksong compiled by Joseph C. Hickerson of the Library of Congress is a valuable addition to the collection.

Emrich, Duncan. **Folklore on the American Land.** Little 1972.

As an introduction to American folklore, this book has wide coverage of tales, songs, superstitions, riddles, folk grammar, photographs, and engaging commentary on folk medicine, weather, birth, marriage, and death.

Evans, Bergen. **Dictionary of Mythology: Mainly Classical** (© 1970). Dell 1972.

Arranged alphabetically and cross-referenced, the items in the *Dictionary* are largely from Greek, Roman, and Norse legends.

Evslin, Bernard. **The Green Hero: Early Adventures of Finn McCool.** Four Winds 1975.

The youthful adventures of Finn McCool, the popular giant of Irish lore, are retold in a highly readable style. The charm and imagination of the Irish people are reflected in each of these legends.

Evslin, Bernard. **Heroes, Gods and Monsters of the Greek Myths** (© 1967). Bantam 1975.

The author retells the stories of ancient Greece—of Zeus and the gods of Olympus, of Prometheus and Orpheus, of Perseus and Theseus, of Midas and Pygmalion. From this panorama of antiquity emerges the ever familiar struggle of Good and Evil, of Light and Darkness.

Feldmann, Susan, editor. **The Storytelling Stone: Myths and Tales of the American Indians** (© 1965). Dell 1971.

This collection of fifty-two representative myths and tales of the American Indians contains stories of creation, the underworld, the flood, the theft of fire, and tales of heroes and supernatural journeys of men, animals, and gods to rival the myths of the ancient Greeks and Romans.

Fowke, Edith, editor. **The Penguin Book of Canadian Folk Songs.** Penguin 1973.

The influence of France and Britain is seen in many of the eighty-two songs of this collection. Songs are grouped under such categories as love, the sea, the land, the woods, and social life.

Goodrich, Norma Lorre. **Ancient Myths.** NAL 1960.

Myths and legends from Egypt, Greece, Crete, Troy, Persia, India, and Rome.

Goodrich, Norma Lorre. **The Medieval Myths.** NAL 1961.

Stories and myths of the Middle Ages—*Beowulf, The Song of Roland,* and *Prince Igor* (a twelfth-century Russian epic), among others.

Graves, Robert. **Greek Gods and Heroes.** Dell 1960.

Graves retells the ancient legends of Greece with wit and humor.

Green, Roger Lancelyn. **The Tale of Troy.** Penguin 1959.

Green retells the story of the Trojan War, from Paris's abduction of the beautiful Helen to the exploits of Achilles in the long seige of Troy to Odysseus's incredible journey home. (See also *Tales of the Greek Heroes,* Penguin.)

Green, Roger Lancelyn, editor. **Tales of Ancient Egypt**
(© 1968). Penguin 1973.

Legends of ancient Egypt, the gods men worshipped,
boy magicians, the land of the dead, and sea serpents.

Grinnell, George Bird. **Pawnee Hero Stories and Folk-
Tales.** U of Nebr Pr 1961.

First published in 1889, this book contains the recorded
legends and tales of the Pawnee Indians as they were
told to Grinnell. In addition, the author shares his
knowledge about Pawnee life, customs, religions, and
history from his visits with the tribe in the 1870s. (See
also *Blackfoot Lodge Tales: The Story of a Prairie
People,* U of Nebr Pr; and *By Cheyenne Campfires,*
U of Nebr Pr.)

Harris, Rosemary. **Sea Magic and Other Stories of En-
chantment.** Macmillan 1974.

Ten stories of the supernatural ranging from the ten-
der "Sankichi's Gift" (Japan) to the weird elements
of "The Graveyard Rose" (Germany).

Helfman, Elizabeth S. **Signs and Symbols of the Sun.**
Seabury 1974.

A generously illustrated exploration of the importance
of the sun as a symbol throughout history—in mythology, religion, science, and art.

Hooke, Samuel H. **Middle Eastern Mythology.** Penguin
1963.

Much of Greek, Roman, and Celtic folklore and myth
has its roots in the mythology of the ancient Near East,
Palestine, Egypt, and Mesopotamia. Here are myths
about creation, hell, floods, and great heroes.

Hull, Denison B., translator. **Aesop's Fables.** U of Chicago Pr 1960.

Hull seeks to recapture the original flavor of Aesop's
fables with a verse translation which allows readers to
provide the moral themselves rather than having it
stated directly.

King, Cynthia. **In the Morning of Time: The Story of
the Norse God Balder.** Four Winds 1970.

The central story is that of Balder, Norse god of innocence and goodness; Odin, Frigga, Thor, Loki, and other characters of Norse mythology are also presented.

Lomax, Alan, editor. **The Penguin Book of American Folk Songs.** Penguin 1965.

Notes by the editor and piano arrangements by Elizabeth Poston enhance this collection of 111 ballads, spirituals, work songs, cowboy songs, and love songs from colonial to modern times.

Marriott, Alice. **Saynday's People: The Kiowa Indians and the Stories They Told** (© 1947). U of Nebr Pr 1963.

The first half of the book contains Kiowa Indian stories of the trickster and hero Uncle Saynday, while the second half describes the lifestyle, government, ceremonies, cooking, crafts, and healing practices of the now vanished life of the Kiowas. Numerous drawings illustrate the making of clothes, tools, etc.

Marriott, Alice, and Carol K. Rachlin. **American Indian Mythology** (© 1968). NAL 1972.

The Indian myths in this collection are gathered from over twenty North American tribes and are representative of the religious philosophies of those tribes. Included are stories of creation, the coming of corn, the dancing feather, and death.

Matson, Emerson N., editor. **Longhouse Legends.** Nelson 1968.

Based on the translations of Martin Sampson, chief of the Swinomish tribe, this book recounts thirteen ancient legends of the Puget Sound Indians of the Pacific Northwest.

Mercatante, Anthony S. **Zoo of the Gods: Animals in Myth, Legend and Fable.** Har-Row 1974.

Man's relationship with more than 100 animals from myths, legends, and fables is the focus here. Attention is given to animals of the mind: unicorns, harpies, dragons, and the like.

Miller, Joseph. **Tales from the Wandering Gypsies.** Miller Bks 1969.

Miller presents a collection of eighteen original fables

filled with humor and warmth; each tale ends with a moral.

Morgan, Fred T. **Ghost Tales of the Uwharries.** Blair 1968.

An assortment of ghost tales from the folklore of the Uwharrie Mountains of central North Carolina.

Narayan, R. K. **The Ramayana.** Viking Pr 1972.

A prose retelling of the great epic of India in which Prince Rama courts his beloved Sita and battles her kidnapper.

Nequatewa, Edmund. **Truth of a Hopi: Stories Relating to the Origin, Myths and Clan Histories of the Hopi** (© 1967). Northland 1973.

Ancient stories of the Hopi Indian past as well as brief histories of various clans of the Hopi, showing how legends and culture intermingle.

Paredes, Americo, editor. **Folktales of Mexico.** U of Chicago Pr 1970.

Traditional legends, animal tales, and jokes of the Mexican people.

Reed, A. W. **Myths and Legends of Australia** (© 1965). Taplinger 1973.

This collection contains fifty-five myths of Australian aborigines that explain the origins of the world, the behavior of the elements, and animal characteristics.

Rugoff, Milton, editor. **A Harvest of World Folk Tales.** Viking Pr 1968.

This broad collection of folktales represents nineteen world areas.

Schwartz, Alvin. **Cross Your Fingers, Spit in Your Hat.** Lippincott 1974.

A collection of superstitions and other folk beliefs on such topics as love and marriage, children, friends and neighbors, school, money, plants, the weather, and death. The illustrations add a touch of humor.

Sedgwick, Paulita. **Mythological Creatures: A Pictorial Dictionary.** HR&W 1974.

Alphabetically arranged and with illustrations based

on classical descriptions, this work identifies creatures of myth and folklore from many countries.

Seki, Keigo, editor (translator Robert J. Adams). **Folktales of Japan.** U of Chicago Pr 1963.

Seki, a leading folklore scholar in Japan, edited this readable collection of tales which reflect the rich traditions of ancient Japanese villagers.

Stanford, Gene, and Barbara Stanford, editors. **Myths and Modern Man.** WSP 1972.

This retelling of mythologies from many races and cultures is organized around five fundamental concerns: Where did we come from? How do men and women differ? What is the perfect individual? Can people live together in peace? Is death the end?

Synge, Ursula. **Weland: Smith of the Gods.** S G Phillips 1973.

Weland, the smith, is the subject of a Norse myth about courage, endurance, and revenge.

Traveller Bird. **The Path to Snowbird Mountain: Cherokee Legends.** FS&G 1972.

Traveller Bird tells sixteen legends of the Cherokee Indians as told to him by his grandfather. Included are creation stories, "Why the Possum's Tail Is Bare," "The Man Who Became a Lizard," and "The Origin of Corn and Beans."

Tyler, Hamilton A. **Pueblo Gods and Myths** (© 1964). U of Okla Pr 1972.

Descriptions and discussions of the deities of the Pueblo Indians including Hopis, Zunis, and Keres. Wherever possible, the author makes comparisons with famous Greek gods and myths. Mature.

Vitaliano, Dorothy B. **Legends of the Earth: Their Geologic Origin.** Ind U Pr 1973.

Geomythology is a new science devoted to discovering possible scientific explanations for the origins of myths and folklore and events they describe. Earthquakes, plagues, and volcanic eruptions may have led to myths like the lost continent of Atlantis and the parting of the Red Sea.

Weslager, C. A. **Magic Medicines of the Indians** (© 1973). NAL 1974.

A detailed and scholarly examination of various medical cures—some of them miraculous—used by American Indians, including several hundred different plants plus various ceremonies of medicine men. Mature.

Whedbee, Charles Harry. **The Flaming Ship of Ocracoke & Other Tales of the Outer Banks.** Blair 1971.

Tales and legends from North Carolina's historic coastal folklore offering a combination of unusual, awesome, and sometimes horrifying events. (See also *Legends of the Outer Banks & Tar Heel Tidewater,* Blair.)

Wigginton, Eliot, editor. **The Foxfire Book.** Anch Pr 1972.

This product of the work of high school students presents the folk culture of the north Georgia mountains and the southern highlands, from mountain recipes and weather signs to detailed instructions for soap-making and chimney building. (See also *Foxfire 2* and *Foxfire 3,* Anch Pr.)

OUR RELIGIONS

Allegro, John. **The Dead Sea Scrolls.** Penguin 1956.

The author discusses the Dead Sea Scrolls, their importance to studies of the New Testament, and the possibility of further discoveries of this kind.

Asimov, Isaac. **Asimov's Guide to the Bible: Old Testament** (© 1968). Avon 1971.

A helpful guide to understanding names of people, towns, and things not otherwise explained in the Old Testament. (See also *Asimov's Guide to the Bible: The New Testament,* Avon.)

Bryant, Anita. **Mine Eyes Have Seen the Glory** (© 1970). Bantam 1972.

The author tells what her faith has meant to her, starting with her early remembrances of childhood and continuing through her life as a well-known entertainer.

Buddha. **The Teachings of the Compassionate Buddha.**
NAL 1955.

Ways of looking at the world and within oneself which
have influenced countless numbers of people, especially in Asia. The *Dhammapada* ("The Way of
Truth") is an important part of Buddhism. Mature.

Cheney, Sheldon. **Men Who Have Walked with God**
(© 1945). Dell 1974.

An outline of religions and mysticism, particularly
Eastern religions. A difficult and mature book.

Cohen, Daniel. **The New Believers.** M Evans 1975.

The author discusses several of the new religious
groups which have become popular in recent years and
which have had a particular appeal to the young. The
beliefs, the practices, and the founders of such groups
and movements as the Children of God, the Jesus
People, the Divine Light Mission, Transcendental
Meditation, witchcraft, and satanism are included.

Cohen, Daniel. **The Spirit of the Land: Revivalism in
America.** Four Winds 1975.

A history of religious revivalism in America from 1801
to the current Jesus Movement and such famous re-
vivalists as Billy Sunday, Dwight L. Moody, and Billy
Graham.

Conze, Edward, editor and translator. **Buddhist Scriptures.** Penguin 1959.

A good survey of the basic writing and teaching of
the Golden Age of Buddhist literature. The collection
emphasizes texts for the layman rather than for the
monk, showing their humanity rather than their pro-
fundity.

Craven, Margaret. **I Heard the Owl Call My Name.**
Doubleday 1973.

With only two years to live, a young minister is sent
to his church's most difficult parish—a remote Indian
village near the rugged seacoast of British Columbia.
There he learns to live with the poverty, strength, and
unfamiliar beliefs of the Kwakiutl Indians. Fiction.

Deloria, Vine, Jr. **God Is Red** (© 1973). Dell 1975.

Deloria offers an alternative to Christianity, which he

feels has failed in its theology and in its application to life today. He suggests that humanity must search for God in terms of our land, seeking a source of religion in beliefs of the American Indians. Mature.

Douglas, Lloyd C. **The Robe** (© 1942). PB 1975.

A young Roman nobleman takes Christ's robe after helping in the Crucifixion. Fiction.

Epstein, Isidore. **Judaism.** Penguin 1959.

A short history of Judaism including discussions of various aspects of the faith and the contributions of individuals who have helped shape the history of Judaism.

Gaer, Joseph. **How the Great Religions Began.** NAL 1954.

Using the life stories of the founders or leaders of the world's great religions, the author explains many religious faiths.

Gaines, Steven S. **Marjoe: The Life of Marjoe Gortner.** Har-Row 1973.

Ordained at the age of four, Marjoe became a nationally famous evangelist. As he entered his teens, Marjoe lost his religious effectiveness, and as he matured he departed more and more from religion and went into the entertainment world.

Garnett, Emmeline. **Tormented Angel: A Life of John Henry Newman.** FS&G 1966.

Newman decided, at age forty-four, to leave the Church of England, in which he had taken Orders, and to enter the Roman Catholic Church. The resulting furor did not prevent him from becoming a highly influential religious leader who died a cardinal of the Church.

Garvin, Philip, and Julia Welch. **Religious America.** McGraw 1974.

The television series of the same name provides the basis for the text and photographs of this book which deals with the religious experiences and beliefs of a number of Americans.

Gleason, Judith. **Orisha: The Gods of Yorubaland.** Atheneum 1971.

Poems and stories about the Orisha, who are not quite

African gods, but who walk the earth and represent truth, creation, and love.

Greene, Graham. **The Power and the Glory** (© 1940). Bantam 1968.

A Mexican Catholic priest living in a society that has virtually outlawed religion tries to find who he is and what he can do for his people. Mature fiction.

Grubb, Davis. **The Night of the Hunter** (© 1953). Avon 1968.

Harry Powell, a mad, self-ordained messianic preacher, is convinced that the Lord has annointed him to kill evil men and women. Learning from a murderer that robbery loot has not been found, Powell marries and kills the robber's widow and then searches for the widow's two children to get the money. Fiction.

Guillaume, Alfred. **Islam** (© 1954). Penguin 1961.

The author traces the historical background of Islam, writes about Muhammad, the founder of Islam, and discusses aspects of Islam from its beginning to the 1950s. Included are some speculations about Islam in the future.

Gurney, A. R., Jr. **The Gospel According to Joe.** Har-Row 1974.

The story of Christ and salvation retold in a modern setting, with political rallies, riots, and troops in the streets replacing the events and characters in the familiar Biblical story. Fiction.

Herrigel, Eugene (translator R. F. C. Hall). **The Method of Zen** (© 1960). VinRandom 1974.

Methods and training in Zen Buddhism are discussed with an attempt to "explain" Zen to the Westerner.

Holmes, Marjorie. **Nobody Else Will Listen: A Girl's Conversations with God** (© 1973). Bantam 1974.

The feelings of a young girl about parents, girl friends, boy friends, school, and other topics are expressed through her conversations with God. (See also *Who Am I, God?*, Bantam.)

Hulme, Kathryn. **The Nun's Story** (© 1956). PB 1974.

A nun struggles to keep her vows but becomes increasingly concerned over whether she made the right choice when she entered the convent. Fiction.

Johnson, Clive, editor. **Vedanta** (© 1971). Bantam 1974.

A collection of Hindu scripture, commentary, and poetry.

Kelen, Betty. **Confucius in Life and Legend.** Nelson 1971.

The life of Confucius, his teachings, his philosophy, his early training, and other pertinent materials related to the man whose name is associated with the wisdom of the East.

King, Marian. **Mary Baker Eddy: Child of Promise.** P-H 1968.

The life story of the founder of Christian Science, emphasizing those periods of her life which were important to her spiritual growth.

Knudson, R. R. **Jesus Song.** Delacorte 1973.

Fifteen-year-old Joy Cheever, disillusioned with the religious teachings around her in Washington, D.C., finds a group of Jesus People in Canada. After difficult times, the group writes a successful religious Indian rock opera and Joy finds the meaning of Jesus. Fiction.

Lao-tzu (translator D. C. Lau). **Lao Tzu.** Penguin 1963.

Considered to be the principal classic in the thought of Taoism, the work is a collection of wise sayings, compiled in about the fourth century B.C. The *Lao Tzu* (also titled *Tao-te Ching,* meaning the "classic of the Way and virtue") encourages a philosophy of meekness as the surest path to survival. (See also *Tao-te Ching,* VinRandom.)

Lewis, C. S. **Out of the Silent Planet** (© 1943). Macmillan 1965.

In this first volume of an allegorical trilogy about religion and humanity, a Cambridge professor accidentally becomes involved in a secret space trip and discovers a plot of a mad scientist aimed at the inhabitants of Malacandra. (See also *Perelandra,* Macmillan; and *That Hideous Strength,* Macmillan.) Fiction.

Marshall, Catherine. **A Man Called Peter.** McGraw 1951.

Peter Marshall was a Scot immigrant who became chaplain of the United States Senate, but he never lost his feeling for people in all walks of life. His wife tells both of his relationship with God and with people.

Mascaro, Juan, translator. **The Bhagavad Gita.** Penguin 1962.

Taking place on a battlefield, the *Gita* is an eighteen-part discussion between Krishna and Arjuna on the nature and meaning of Love, Light, and Life. A classic of Sanskrit literature and the central text of the Hindu religion, it is believed to have been written about 500 B.C. (See also *The Song of God: Bhagavad-Gita,* NAL.)

Mascaro, Juan, translator. **The Dhammapada.** Penguin 1973.

A brief collection of more than 400 aphorisms which illustrate the Buddhist moral system. Pointing out the path to Nirvana, the *Dhammapada* includes such categories as transient pleasures, self-possession, life, and watchfulness.

Maugham, Robin. **The Sign.** McGraw 1974.

In the year A.D. 20, a time of religious and political quarrels before John the Baptist's appearance, a young man appears claiming to be the Messiah. The author portrays both the religious beliefs and the social and political climate of this time. Some readers may be offended by the discussion of homosexuality. Fiction.

Meltzer, Milton. **World of Our Fathers: The Jews of Eastern Europe.** FS&G 1974.

Jewish life in Eastern Europe up to the time of large-scale emigration to the U.S., including such topics as family life and the pogroms or massacres.

Morris, James. **The Preachers.** St Martin 1973.

Morris discusses and dissects the work, influence, and power of nine modern well-known ministers and evangelists, sometimes sympathetically, sometimes not, from A. A. Allen to Billy Graham.

Needleman, Jacob. **The New Religions.** Doubleday 1970.

The author analyzes the appeal of Eastern religions and teachings to modern humanity. Mature.

Nettinga, James Z., editor. **Quotations from the Bible for Modern Man.** PB 1973.

Bible passages arranged according to provocative themes: "Are You Caught in an Identity Net?"; "Do You Want to Swing Free?"; "Star Trek"; "The 'Do You Want to Do It Yourself?' Kit"; and "Profiles of Faith." Most are from the King James Version. Imaginatively illustrated.

Pickthall, Mohammed, translator. **The Meaning of the Glorious Koran** (© 1970). NAL n.d.

The author attempts to present the meaning of the *Koran,* a work which he says cannot be translated and still retain the beauty and power of the original.

Prabhavananda, Swami, and Frederick Manchester, translators. **The Upanishads** (©1948). NAL 1961.

A translation of the oldest of India's most sacred Hindu scriptures treating the nature of man and the universe. Mature.

Rampa, T. Lobsang. **The Third Eye** (© 1956). Ballantine 1972.

Rampa writes of his experiences in a Tibetan lamasery, where he had an "operation" that opened the Third Eye, allowing him to observe the auras of those about him and to determine what they are really thinking.

Rice, Edward. **The Five Great Religions.** Four Winds 1973.

In a text liberally illustrated with photographs, the author discusses Judaism, Christianity, Buddhism, Hinduism, and Islam, attempting to point out beliefs, differences, similarities, and origins of the various faiths.

Rodinson, Maxime (translator Anne Carter). **Mohammed** (© 1971). VinRandom 1974.

The life story of the founder of Islam and the impact Islam has had on Arab society and culture, yesterday and today.

Rogers, Dale Evans. **The Woman at the Well** (© 1970).
Bantam 1972.

The author tells of the influence of her Christian faith
on her life and discusses some of the problems she sees
society facing today.

Seeger, Elizabeth. **Eastern Religions.** T Y Crowell 1973.

Five major religions of the East—Hinduism, Buddhism,
Confucianism, Taoism, and Shinto—are explained in
terms of their legends, teachings, and prominent personalities.

Smith, Charles Merrill. **How to Talk to God When You
Aren't Feeling Religious** (© 1971). Bantam 1973.

The author talks to God about a variety of topics, including the professional clergy, sex, heroes, and bitterness.

Smith, Don Ian. **Wild Rivers and Mountain Trails.** Abingdon 1972.

The mountain wilderness of central Idaho provides the
backdrop for the author's examination of his faith and
his attempt to better understand his God.

Sohl, Robert, and Audrey Carr, editors. **The Gospel
According to Zen.** NAL 1970.

Brief comparisons between the writings of Zen masters
and selections from the Bible with essays about religion and humanity's spiritual plight today.

Stroup, Herbert. **Founders of Living Religions.** Westminster 1974.

The lives and faiths of eight founders of living religions.

Swann, Thomas Burnett. **How Are the Mighty Fallen.**
DAW Bks 1974.

A retelling of the Biblical David and Jonathan story,
with the Cyclops, Sirens, history, and fantasy woven together to give the story a new look which some may
find disturbing. Fiction.

Synge, Ursula. **The People and the Promise.** S G Phillips 1974.

The story of the Exodus from Egypt is told through
the eyes of the people who lived at that time. Fiction.

Taylor, Ellen G. **Song of Abraham.** Pyramid Pubns 1973.

The story of Abraham and his followers and the beginning of Judaism, described sympathetically and with vivid insight. Fiction.

Van Over, Raymond, editor. **Taoist Tales.** NAL 1973.

Stories, parables, poetry, and anecdotes by writers and thinkers fascinated by Taoism, the religion that has influenced Chinese thought and action for better than 1,500 years.

Waley, Arthur, translator. **The Book of Songs** (© 1937). Grove 1960.

The Book of Songs contains one of the most important collections of poetry in world literature and is one of the Five Confucian Classics. The followers of Confucius used the songs both for instruction and as examples.

Wouk, Herman. **This Is My God: The Jewish Way of Life** (© 1959). PB 1973.

The author of *The Caine Mutiny* explains what the Jewish way of life is. Wouk discusses the faith, the history, and the laws of Jews. A helpful glossary of Hebrew terms is included. Mature.

FINE ARTS

Adams, Laurie. **Art Cop.** Dodd 1974.

Detective Robert Volpe of the New York City Police is both an artist and a cop, so what better assignment for him than director of the Art Squad, a unit which puzzles out thefts from museums and galleries as well as art frauds and forgeries.

Ames, Evelyn. **A Wind from the West.** HM 1970.

The New York Philharmonic made its last foreign tour under the direction of Leonard Bernstein in the summer of 1968, and this account of the trip reveals a great deal about both orchestra and conductor.

Apel, Willi, and Ralph T. Daniel, editors. **The Harvard Brief Dictionary of Music** (© 1960). PB 1961.

A dictionary of musical terms, works, trends, and movements.

Battcock, Gregory, editor. **The New Art: A Critical Anthology.** Dutton 1973.

The twenty-two essays in this collection describe recent trends in American art, with discussions of film, conceptual art, happenings and improvisations, as well as painting and sculpture.

Bernstein, Leonard. **The Infinite Variety of Music** (© 1966). NAL 1970.

Bernstein analyzes classical music, jazz, and Muzac in five television scripts and a series of essays.

Bernstein, Leonard. **The Joy of Music** (© 1959). NAL 1967.

The conductor of the New York Philharmonic discusses Beethoven's *Fifth Symphony,* the world of jazz, the art of conducting, musical comedy, modern music, Bach, and opera.

Bing, Rudolf. **5000 Nights at the Opera** (© 1972). Popular Lib 1973.

Bing, for twenty-two years the general manager of New York City's Metropolitan Opera, takes the reader backstage to witness the triumphs and disasters of one of the world's great opera companies.

Casals, Pablo (with Albert E. Kahn). **Joys and Sorrows.** S&S 1970.

Casals lived a long and rich life, playing the cello for Queen Victoria in the 1890s and for President Kennedy in the 1960s, winning admirers for his interpretations of Bach's music, and showing courage in refusing to play in his homeland, Spain, because of its totalitarian regime.

Clark, Kenneth. **Another Part of the Wood.** Har-Row 1975.

A great art scholar tells about his early life and his discovery and growing appreciation for art, the artists and art critics he has known, and what he believes important about art. Mature.

Closson, Ernest. **History of the Piano.** St Martin 1974.

The piano is a latecomer among keyboard instruments, having been preceded by the clavichord, the harpsichord, and the virginal, but once established this instrument became the center of musical life.

Cohen, George M. **A History of American Art.** Dell 1971.

The arts of architecture, painting, sculpture, and graphics are surveyed from the colonial period to the present.

Collier, James Lincoln. **Inside Jazz.** Four Winds 1973.

Jazz, America's contribution to music, is traced from its beginnings among the blacks of New Orleans through its development into blues, Dixieland, and progressive.

Constant, Alberta Wilson. **Paintbox on the Frontier: The Life and Times of George Caleb Bingham.** T Y Crowell 1974.

Bingham, a painter of the early nineteenth century, depicted common people living on the western frontier of his time—fur trappers, Indians, politicians, and people in general. Illustrated with many black and white and color reproductions of his paintings.

de Mille, Agnes. **Speak to Me, Dance with Me.** Little 1973.

The author struggled with the early criticism that she was not "built right" for a dancer to become one of the leading dancer-choreographers in America, reshaping the dance in the musical theater.

Esterow, Milton. **The Art Stealers.** Macmillan 1973.

Stealing art treasures has been the goal of many individuals, from Vincenzo Perugia, who stole the Mona Lisa in 1911, to modern plunderers who ransack archaeological finds.

Flexner, James Thomas. **The Double Adventure of John Singleton Copley.** Little 1969.

Copley, who grew up in colonial Boston without the opportunity to see great paintings, developed a style independent of the academic painters of Europe and emerged as the first major artist of the New World.

Furlong, William Barry. **Season with Solti: A Year in the Life of the Chicago Symphony.** Macmillan 1974.

Georg Solti is one of today's great conductors. The chronicle of one year with the Chicago Symphony portrays the joys and frustrations of working with musicians and creating a deservedly famous orchestra.

Harman, Carter. **A Popular History of Music.** Dell 1969.

A nontechnical history of classical music touching upon major composers and their works. One section is devoted to jazz and modern electronic music.

Harnan, Terry. **African Rhythm-American Dance: A Biography of Katherine Dunham.** Knopf 1974.

Dunham, American dancer and choreographer, sought to bring the mood of African dance into works that she developed for her own dance company, which she assembled only after years of struggle.

Haverstock, Mary Sayre. **Indian Gallery: The Story of George Catlin.** Four Winds 1973.

Catlin spent a large portion of his life painting portraits of American Indians in the unexplored parts of the country in the mid-1800s. Illustrated with his paintings and drawings, this book is the story of Catlin's travels, adventures, insights, and paintings, much of it quoted from his own writings.

Hemming, Roy. **Discovering Music.** Four Winds 1974.

The author gives specific recommendations for the beginner who would like to collect classical records. Performers, composers, and specific musical works are discussed.

Holbrook, Sabra. **Joy in Stone: The Cathedral of Reims.** FS&G 1973.

For over fifteen centuries the cathedral of Reims has adapted to the joys of kings and bishops and to the sorrows of war and revolution. The author thus traces the soul of a nation in one of the landmarks of France.

Horwitz, Sylvia L. **Toulouse-Lautrec: His World.** Har-Row 1973.

Though hampered by a bone disease that left him deformed, Henri Toulouse-Lautrec made his mark as an artist, capturing the world of Paris dance halls and cafés in his own unique style. Photographs of the artist and his work accompany this account of his life.

Jacobson, Robert. **Reverberations: Interviews with the World's Leading Musicians.** Morrow 1974.

Over thirty great names in the world of classical music—composers, conductors, singers, and instrumental-

ists—discuss their careers in this collection of personal
interviews.

Kaiser, Joachim (translators David Woolridge and
George Unwin). **Great Pianists of Our Time** (© 1971).
Herder & Herder 1972.

Brief biographies of twenty of the major concert
pianists of our time, from the pianistic elder statesmen
like Artur Rubenstein and Vladimir Horowitz to
younger men like Glenn Gould and Van Cliburn.

Kallem, Anne E. (with Louisa B. Hellegers and Steven
Morgenstern). **Giant Book of Crafts.** Sterling 1976.

An expensive but inclusive survey of crafts that goes
well beyond the usual craft book by covering many
unusual arts (for example, net making).

Kelen, Emery, editor. **Leonardo da Vinci's Advice to
Artists.** Nelson 1974.

The editor selects comments from da Vinci's notebooks
and his *Treatise on Painting* about his experiences,
his experiments, and his suggestions or recommendations about painting. Many da Vinci illustrations. (See
also Emery Kelen, editor, *Fantastic Tales, Strange
Animals, Riddles, Jests and Prophecies of Leonardo
da Vinci,* Nelson.)

Klein, Mina C., and H. Arthur Klein. **Kathe Kollwitz:
Life in Art.** HR&W 1972.

The first complete biography of this very gifted
German artist who, through her works, relates themes
which are very close to her life—social injustice, oppression, causes related to peace, "the joys and sorrows
of maternity, the fathomless mystery of death."

Macaulay, David. **Cathedral: The Story of Its Construction.** HM 1973.

Macaulay describes and illustrates with detailed drawings the step-by-step process of building a Gothic cathedral in thirteenth-century France.

Marek, George R. **Toscanini.** Atheneum 1975.

Arturo Toscanini was one of the great symphony orchestra conductors of all time. His career in Italy
and the United States, his explosive temper at rehearsals, and the great conductor as a sensitive human
being are portrayed.

Mazo, Joseph H. **Dance Is a Contact Sport.** Sat Rev Pr 1974.

A New York drama and ballet critic spends the spring of 1973 with the New York City Ballet watching rehearsals, observing dancers, and capturing the backstage life of a ballet company.

Mills, John FitzMaurice. **Treasure Keepers.** Doubleday 1974.

One of the major problems facing directors of museums and art galleries is how to protect art works against time and air and vandals. Another problem is how to detect forgeries and fakes.

Myers, Bernard S., and Shirley D. Myers, editors. **Dictionary of Twentieth-Century Art.** McGraw 1974.

A reference work, alphabetically arranged, on contemporary painters, sculptors, graphic artists, and architects, from Alvar Aalto, Finnish architect, to William Zorach, American sculptor.

Newmeyer, Sarah. **Enjoying Modern Art** (© 1955). NAL 1957.

Modern art from Vincent Van Gogh to Jackson Pollock is traced through major movements and painters.

Peyser, Joan. **The New Music: The Sense behind the Sound** (© 1971). Dell 1972.

A history of the development of twentieth-century classical music and its influences. Four musicians and their work are discussed: Arnold Schoenberg, Anton von Webern, Igor Stravinsky, and Edgard Varèse.

Posell, Elsa Z. **American Composers.** HM 1963.

This introduction to American composers of the late nineteenth and twentieth centuries includes brief biographies of twenty-nine representative musicians.

Posell, Elsa Z. **Russian Composers.** HM 1967.

Short biographies of major Russian composers, such as Fëdor Glinka, Modest Moussorgsky, Pëtr Tchaikovsky, Sergei Rachmaninoff, Igor Stravinsky, Sergei Prokofiev, and Dimitri Shostakovich.

Quick, John. **Artists' and Illustrators' Encyclopedia.** McGraw 1969.

An alphabetical list of terms used in fine arts, photography, printing, and graphic arts, from "Abbozzo" to "yardstick compass." Many illustrations.

Samachson, Dorothy, and Joseph Samachson. **The Russian Ballet and Three of Its Masterpieces.** Lothrop 1971.

The two great ballet companies of Russia, the Bolshoi and the Kirov, developed under the patronage of the Russian aristocracy and survived the revolution to remain among the foremost companies of the world, especially as showcases for the grand productions of the romantic period.

Seroff, Victor. **The Real Isadora.** Dial 1971.

The life of Isadora Duncan, founding spirit of the modern dance movement, reads more like a novel than a biography and contains romance, political intrigue, tragedy, and scandal.

Shanet, Howard. **Philharmonic: A History of New York's Orchestra.** Doubleday 1974.

Music, musicians, and conductors associated with the New York Philharmonic from its origin in 1839 to the present.

Von Westerman, Gerhart (editor Harold Rosenthal and translator Anne Ross). **Opera Guide.** Dutton 1968.

This guide is both a history of opera from its birth in sixteenth-century Florence to the present and a collection of plot summaries, important musical motifs, and stage designs of the more important works.

Wechsberg, Joseph. **The Glory of the Violin.** Viking Pr 1973.

All the great violins were made before 1744. Seventeenth-century fiddlers were applauded when they made their instruments bark like dogs. Nicolò Paganini, the great virtuoso, once lost his violin in a gambling bout. These are only three of the colorful details which fill this history of the violin.

Wilson, Ellen. **American Painter in Paris: A Life of Mary Cassatt.** FS&G 1971.

Among the most accomplished of the French Impressionist painters was a woman named Mary Cassatt, an American from Philadelphia, whose father scorned her early dreams of traveling to Europe to study painting.

Zobeley, Fritz (translator Ann O'Brien). **Portrait of Beethoven.** Herder & Herder 1972.

Born into a family of musicians, Ludwig van Beethoven demonstrated his promise with the publication of his first sonatas at age thirteen. Despite disillusionment in love and eventual deafness, he became one of the monumental composers in musical history.

ALL THE WORLD'S A STAGE

Anderson, Maxwell. **Eleven Verse Plays, 1929–1939.** HarBraceJ 1940.

Some of the plays included in this anthology are *Elizabeth the Queen, Mary of Scotland, Winterset,* and *Valley Forge.*

Beckett, Samuel. **Krapp's Last Tape and Other Dramatic Pieces** (© 1957). Grove 1960.

The play in this collection, *Krapp's Last Tape,* is about what happens when a man plays a tape that he had recorded thirty years before on his thirty-ninth birthday. The collection also includes two radio plays and two pantomimes.

Beckett, Samuel. **Waiting for Godot.** Grove 1954.

This play is a good introduction to the theater of the absurd, with a cast of characters who aimlessly fill up their lives with trivia while waiting for "Godot" without really knowing why they are waiting, or who or what "Godot" is. Mature.

Benedict, Stewart H., et al., editors. **Your Own Thing and Twelfth Night** (© 1970). Dell 1973.

A comparison of Shakespeare's *Twelfth Night* and the successful off-Broadway rock musical *Your Own Thing* is provided in this book, which includes both plays.

Bettenbender, John, editor. **Three English Comedies** (© 1966). Dell 1972.

The manners, customs, and follies of the eighteenth century are satirized in three comedies by Oliver Goldsmith and Richard Sheridan.

Clurman, Harold, editor. **Famous American Plays of the 1930s** (© 1959). Dell 1973.

The five plays by Samuel Behrman, Clifford Odets,

William Saroyan, Robert Sherwood, and John Steinbeck represent the despair and hope of the 1930s.

Clurman, Harold, editor. **Seven Plays of the Modern Theater.** Grove 1962.

The frankness and bestiality of many modern plays is seen in this collection which includes *Waiting for Godot, A Taste of Honey, The Balcony, Rhinoceros, The Birthday Party, The Connection,* and *The Quare Fellow.*

Corrigan, Robert W., editor. **Twentieth-Century British Drama.** Dell 1965.

British drama of the twentieth century is represented in this volume by *Heartbreak House, Loyalties, Private Lives, The Chalk Garden, A Man for All Seasons,* and *The Knack.*

Driver, Tom F. **Romantic Quest and Modern Query: History of the Modern Theater** (© 1970). Dell 1971.

The author discusses the accomplishments of many playwrights, describes the theater from which each developed, and argues that romanticism is present in drama's search for reality. Mature nonfiction.

Elder, Lonne, III. **Ceremonies in Dark Old Men** (© 1965). NAL 1974.

Set in the Harlem of the present, this play realistically captures the hopes, the cynicism, the tragedy, and the humor of a group of blacks concerned with love, lust, money, and a means of escaping their way of life in the ghetto.

Freedley, George, editor. **Three Plays about Crime and Criminals.** WSP 1962.

Arsenic and Old Lace, Kind Lady, and *Detective Story* provide entertaining reading about a variety of criminal types and criminal acts.

Gassner, John. **Masters of the Drama.** Dover 1953.

A comprehensive and critical study of drama from its beginnings to the middle of this century, examining drama from almost every nation and discussing theatrical trends. Nonfiction.

Gibson, William. **American Primitive** (© 1971). Bantam 1974.

The diaries and letters of Abigail and John Adams help to make this play a realistic portrayal of Boston and Philadelphia during the colonial period.

Gibson, William. **The Miracle Worker.** (© 1960). Bantam 1964.

Helen Keller's frustrations and fears stem from her life as a deaf mute. But Annie Sullivan brings meaning to Helen's world by slowly making Helen aware of language and communication.

Guthrie, Tyrone. **My Life in the Theatre.** McGraw 1959.

Guthrie takes the reader on a behind-the-scenes tour of the greatest theaters in the world as he tells of his life as a director. Nonfiction.

Hadas, Moses, editor. **Greek Drama** (© 1965). Bantam 1968.

The brilliance and grandeur of Greek tragedy and the satirical nature of Greek comedy can be seen in these nine plays by Aeschylus, Sophocles, Euripides, and Aristophanes.

Hansberry, Lorraine. **A Raisin in the Sun—The Sign in Sidney Brustein's Window.** NAL 1966.

Hansberry creates universal characters as she looks at life frankly and realistically in these two plays set in two very different worlds of New York City.

Harris, Julie (with Barry Tarshis). **Julie Harris Talks to Young Actors.** Lothrop 1971.

Harris gives a personal and practical account of every phase of the acting profession. Nonfiction.

Hellman, Lillian. **The Collected Plays** (© 1971). Little 1972.

This collection of all the author's plays as she has revised them offers slices of life that might offend some readers. Her characters are people whose standards are far from conventional. Mature.

Hewes, Henry, editor. **Famous American Plays of the 1940s** (© 1960). Dell 1973.

This volume of plays by Maxwell Anderson, Carson

McCullers, Arthur Miller, and Thornton Wilder reflects the development of drama during the war and the postwar years.

Houghton, Norris. **The Exploding Stage** (© 1971). Dell 1973.

The author focuses on the history and criticism of twentieth-century theater to encourage readers to attend the theater and increase their knowledge of it. Nonfiction.

Houghton, Norris, editor. **Seeds of Modern Drama,** Vol. III (© 1963). Dell 1974.

The plays of Anton Chekhov, Gerhart Hauptmann, Henrik Ibsen, August Strindberg, and Émile Zola in modern translations represent the beginning of realism in the theater.

Irwin, Vera R., editor. **Four Classical Asian Plays.** Penguin 1972.

This collection offers a wide variety of classical Asian drama.

Jacobs, Jim, and Warren Casey. **Grease.** PB 1972.

The fifties come alive in this rock 'n' roll musical about girls in pedalpushers and bobby sox and guys in ducktails, pegged pants, and black leather jackets.

Jacobs, Susan. **On Stage: The Making of a Broadway Play.** Knopf 1972.

A Broadway play turns into reality as the author shows the reader what is involved in writing and producing a Broadway play. Nonfiction.

Jonson, Marian. **A Troubled Grandeur: The Story of England's Great Actress, Sarah Siddons.** Little 1972.

A love of the theater and a revolutionary spirit that caused her to break with the traditions of the theater of her time and to reject her parents' advice characterized Siddons, a famous eighteenth-century actress. Nonfiction.

Koch, Kenneth. **A Change of Hearts: Plays, Films, and Other Dramatic Works** (© 1953). VinRandom 1973.

The anthology presents the wide scope and versatility of the author as we see him using and parodying vari-

ous types of plays, theatrical experiences, and subjects.
Nonfiction.

Kopit, Arthur. **Indians** (© 1969). Bantam 1971.

A zany but poignant Wild West Show, starring Buffalo
Bill Cody, Sitting Bull, Wild Bill Hickok, Geronimo,
Annie Oakley, Jesse James, Chief Joseph, and numerous others, which (in sometimes strong language)
condemns white exploitation of Indians.

Kuner, M. C. **Thornton Wilder: The Bright and the
Dark.** T Y Crowell 1972.

The life of one of the most popular American playwrights is examined, with an analysis of his style,
the techniques he used, and the themes that are present in his novels and plays. Nonfiction.

Lawrence, Jerome, and Robert E. Lee. **Inherit the Wind**
(© 1955). Bantam 1969.

The authors base their play on the real life trial of
Thomas Scopes. Scopes is accused of teaching evolution contrary to a state law and two famous lawyers
appear, one to defend him and the right to think freely,
one to support the state and the cause of the Bible.

Lawrence, Jerome, and Robert E. Lee. **The Night
Thoreau Spent in Jail** (© 1970). Bantam 1972.

Thoreau's search for personal truth and his plea for
nonviolence is traced in this work which focuses on the
night he spent in jail for not paying his poll tax.

Little, Stuart W. **Off Broadway: The Prophetic Theater** (© 1972). Dell 1974.

The importance of the off-Broadway theater is shown
in this work tracing its influence on the Broadway
theater from 1952 to the present. Nonfiction.

MacInnes, Helen. **Home Is the Hunter.** HarBraceJ
1964.

In a two-act comedy we find out what really happens
to Ulysses when he finally returns home to Ithaca from
his many journeys.

Meredith, Scott. **George S. Kaufman and his Friends.**
Doubleday 1974.

This biography shows Kaufman's many sides as author

and director of such hits as *You Can't Take It with You, The Man Who Came to Dinner,* and *The Front Page.* Nonfiction.

Mersand, Joseph, editor. **Three Dramas of American Realism.** WSP 1961.

Idiot's Delight by Robert Sherwood, *Street Scene* by Elmer Rice, and *The Time of Your Life* by William Saroyan demonstrate the influence of realism on the American theater.

Mersand, Joseph, editor. **Three Plays about Business in America.** WSP 1964.

The corrupting influence of business on the human spirit is reflected in *The Adding Machine, Beggar on Horseback,* and *All My Sons.*

Miller, Arthur. **The Crucible** (© 1953). Bantam 1966.

Based on the witchcraft trials in Salem, Massachusetts, in 1692, this play emphasizes the irresponsible emotional acts that led to imprisonment and death for many innocent victims.

Miller, Arthur. **The Price** (©1969). Bantam 1972.

The death of their father brings together two brothers, one a policeman and the other a surgeon, causing them to reflect on the significance of their lives.

Momeyer, Arline Bryand, and Walter M. Bach. **All the World's a Stage.** Chris Mass 1969.

Shakespeare comes to life as a real person in this play skillfully written in Elizabethan blank verse. He is shown in the many and varied roles that he played in his own life, including those of actor, playwright, and producer.

Olfson, Lewy, editor. **50 Great Scenes for Student Actors** (© 1970). Bantam 1972.

This collection, arranged by scenes for a woman and man, for two men, and for two women, provides a wide variety of acting experiences for students.

O'Neill, Eugene. **Six Short Plays of Eugene O'Neill** (© 1919). VinRandom 1965.

O'Neill writes about the tragic aspects of life because

he believes that it is through tragedy that one discovers the true meaning of life.

Osborne, John. **Inadmissible Evidence.** Grove 1965.

Bill Maitland, the protagonist of this play, is a middle-
aged lawyer who subjects himself to a very thorough
and ultimately very disastrous self-analysis.

Osborne, John. **Look Back in Anger** (© 1956). Bantam
1967.

Jimmy Porter, the original "angry young man" in his
attack on the Establishment, represents the frustrations of people who hate middle-class complacency.

Piro, Richard. **Black Fiddler.** Morrow 1971.

Piro, a music-drama teacher in a junior high school,
works with his black and Puerto Rican students to put
on *Fiddler on the Roof*. In the process, the anti-
Semitism of some students emerges, and the story
becomes one of music, human relations, and human
understanding. Nonfiction.

Popkin, Henry, editor. **Modern British Drama.** Grove
1964.

Plays that reflect the concerns of modern British
writers, essays by playwrights and directors, and an
introduction that is historical and analytical make up
this collection of six of the best plays of the modern
theater. Mature.

Quintero, José. **If You Don't Dance They Beat You.**
Little 1974.

The American theater comes alive in this self-portrait
of one of the most highly regarded directors of the
American stage. One of the highlights occurs when
Quintero tells of his productions of *The Iceman Com-
eth* and *Long Day's Journey into Night*. Nonfiction.

Radice, Betty, and Robert Baldick, editors (translator
Joshua Cooper). **Four Russian Plays.** Penguin 1972.

These four plays represent the greatest achievements
of Russian playwrights before Chekhov (late nineteenth century). The plays are *The Infant, Chatsky,
The Inspector,* and *Thunder*.

Radice, Betty, and Robert Baldick, editors (translator

Liu Jung-en). **Six Yüan Plays.** Penguin 1972.

These plays from the Yüan dynasty (1280–1369) represent the earliest type of Chinese drama.

Richards, Stanley, editor. **Ten Great Musicals of the American Theatre.** Chilton 1973.

This volume contains the texts and lyrics of some of the best musicals in the history of the American theater including *Porgy and Bess, West Side Story, Fiddler on the Roof, 1776,* and *Company.*

Richardson, Jack. **Gallows Humor.** Dutton 1961.

These two interrelated one-act plays examine order and chaos in the modern world. The first play takes place in the cell of a lawyer who has murdered his wife; the second in the kitchen of the murderer's hangman.

Sackler, Howard. **The Great White Hope** (© 1968). Bantam 1972.

Based on the career of Jack Johnson, the first black heavyweight boxing champion, the rise and fall of a heavyweight titleholder is chronicled as he runs from country to country.

Shaw, George Bernard. **Pygmalion** (© 1913). Penguin 1961.

The Greek myth about Pygmalion creating a statue and falling in love with it was the inspiration for Shaw's story of a flower girl. Shaw's opinions on middle-class morality, marriage, and other social issues are a part of the play and the epilogue to the play.

Smith, Michael, editor. **The Best of Off Off-Broadway.** Dutton 1969.

Seven of the plays that appeared off-Broadway in the last years of the 1960s show the excitement and scope of the movement which gave new playwrights the opportunity to display their talents.

Speaight, Robert. **Shakespeare on the Stage: An Illustrated History of Shakespearian Performance.** Little 1973.

In this beautifully illustrated history, the author begins with Shakespeare's Globe Theatre and traces the popularity of Shakespeare through the ages, showing how the plays were adapted and sometimes altered and how the proscenium arch affected the acting and staging of the plays. Mature nonfiction.

Strasberg, Lee, editor. **Famous American Plays of the 1950s** (© 1962). Dell 1974.

Plays by Edward Albee, Maxwell Anderson, Lillian Hellman, and Tennessee Williams show the depth and sensitivity of many playwrights of the 1950s.

Sweetkind, Morris, editor. **Ten Great One Act Plays.** Bantam 1968.

The author has included plays representing a wide range of writers in time, subject matter, and technique to give the reader the best that the genre has to offer.

Turner, Darwin T., editor. **Black Drama in America: An Anthology** (© 1971). Fawcett World 1973.

The editor has selected plays about the black experience in America. Along with the plays *(Take a Giant Step, Purlie Victorious, The Toilet, We Righteous Brothers),* the editor has included an essay on black drama and its place in American culture. Mature.

Vonnegut, Kurt, Jr. **Between Time and Timbuktu; or, Prometheus-5, a Space Fantasy** (© 1972). Dell 1974.

This space fantasy, an experimental television play about a young poet who wins a jingle contest and is sent off into the time-space warp as his prize, combines excerpts from other stories and novels of the author.

Vonnegut, Kurt, Jr. **Happy Birthday, Wanda June** (© 1971). Dell 1974.

Vonnegut retells the homecoming of ancient Ulysses, who returns after a long absence to discover that his wife has two suitors.

Walcott, Derek. **Dream on Monkey Mountain and Other Plays.** FS&G 1970.

These four plays written by the director of the Trinidad Theatre Workshop demonstrate the vitality and scope of theater that is currently being performed in the West Indies.

Wasserman, Dale, and Joe Darion. **Man of La Mancha** (© 1966). Dell 1969.

The dreams of Don Quixote are portrayed in this musical adaptation of Cervantes's novel.

Weiss, M. Jerry, editor. **Ten Short Plays** (© 1963). Dell 1973.

This edition captures a wide variety of themes and shows the power of the one-act play in works by Sherwood Anderson, Maxwell Anderson, William Saroyan, Tennessee Williams, and others.

Wesker, Arnold. **The Wesker Trilogy** (© 1959). Penguin 1964.

In *Chicken Soup with Barley, Roots,* and *I'm Talking about Jerusalem,* two Jewish families trying to protect and practice their socialist beliefs exemplify problems facing working class people in the twentieth century.

Woodyard, George, editor. **The Modern Stage in Latin America: Six Plays.** Dutton 1971.

These six plays represent trends in current Latin American drama.

Zindel, Paul. **The Effect of Gamma Rays on Man-in-the-Moon Marigolds** (© 1970). Bantam 1973.

A mother, embittered because her childhood dreams have not been fulfilled, takes out her frustrations on her two daughters.

POETRY

Adoff, Arnold, editor. **I Am the Darker Brother: An Anthology of Modern Poems by Black Americans** (© 1968). Collier Macmillan 1970.

Poetry voicing hope, despair, and pride by many black poets.

Aldan, Daisy, editor. **Poems from India.** T Y Crowell 1969.

This volume is a sampling of poems written in most of India's fourteen language groups. From the majesty of ancient hymns to the vivid imagery of modern poems, the reader experiences the moods and ages of India.

Allen, Donald M., editor. **The New American Poetry.**
Grove 1960.

An exploration of the major trends in American poetry
during the years 1945–60 and selections from the work
of important poets of that period.

Allen, Samuel, editor. **Poems from Africa.** T Y Crowell
1973.

An assembly of poems by Africans, beginning with
poems from the oral tradition, reflecting the "multi-
cultural, multilingual complexity of the continent."

Allen, Terry D., editor. **The Whispering Wind: Poetry
by Young American Indians.** Doubleday 1972.

Poems by young Indian writers working at the Institute of American Indian Arts reflecting the dreams,
loves, fears, and lore of the writers.

Angelou, Maya. **Just Give Me a Cool Drink of Water
'for i Diiie** (© 1971). Bantam 1973.

Brief poems that are direct, approachable, and lyric
by a popular black poet. (See also her 1975 collection,
Oh Pray My Wings Are Gonna Fit Me Well, Random.)

Atwood, Margaret. **Power Politics.** (© 1971). Har-Row
1973.

Poems about modern mythologies and the victors and
villains of modern life.

Baron, Virginia Olsen, editor (translator Chung Seuk
Park). **Sunset in a Spider Web.** HR&W 1974.

This is a slim, delicately illustrated book of *sijo* (literally, "melody of the times"), one of the oldest and
most popular poetry forms in Korean literature. The
poetry is highly reminiscent of haiku with its brief,
concentrated form which often depicts the beauty of
nature and the passing of time.

Bernikow, Louise, editor. **The World Split Open: Four
Centuries of Women Poets in England and America.**
VinRandom 1974.

As the subtitle indicates, this collection covers four
centuries of women poets in England and America
from 1552 to 1950.

Berrigan, Daniel. **Prison Poems.** Unicorn Pr 1973.

Berrigan wrote these poems during his term at Danbury Federal Penitentiary. He was convicted of taking part in the destruction of draft board records, and his poems reflect his concern with problems of our lives today.

Bierhorst, John, editor. **In the Trail of the Wind: American Indian Poems and Ritual Orations** (© 1971). Dell 1975.

This anthology of 126 traditional poems and chants from over forty different Indian tribes of both North and South America is arranged by theme (for instance, on beginnings, home, war, death, and dreams) so that readers can compare poems from different tribes.

Bradbury, Ray. **When Elephants Last in the Dooryard Bloomed** (© 1973). Knopf 1974.

More than fifty poems touch on Bradbury's boyhood, everyday occurrences, and his thoughts about home, life, and space travel.

Brandon, William, editor. **The Magic World: American Indian Songs and Poems** (© 1971). Morrow 1972.

Songs and poems from such Indian tribes as the Modoc, Maya, Nahuatl, Pima, Hopi, Tewa, Iroquois, and Tlingit. Some selections contain sexually explicit language.

Breman, Paul, editor. **You Better Believe It: Black Verse in English.** Penguin 1973.

Some were born in the eighteenth century, some in the twentieth; they come from Ghana and Jamaica, Malawi and the United States. But all of these poets have three things in common: they write in English, they are black, and they celebrate being black.

Carruth, Hayden, editor. **The Voice That Is Great within Us: American Poetry of the Twentieth Century.** Bantam 1970.

A mammoth anthology of modern American poetry, from the work of Robert Frost and Carl Sandburg to the poetry of Jim Harrison and Diane Wakoski.

Chipman, Bruce L., editor. **Hardening Rock.** Little 1972.

Lyrics of the golden oldies from the gilded age of rock—from Chuck Berry to Pat Boone, from "Splish Splash" to "Little Deuce Coupe"—with photographs that catch the mood of the era.

Cole, William, editor. **A Book of Animal Poems.** Viking
Pr 1973.

Poems about dogs, cats, horses, and just about any
creature found in the barnyard or in the wilds.

Cronyn, George W., editor. **American Indian Poetry:
An Anthology of Songs and Chants** (© 1918). Liveright 1970.

This anthology of songs and chants about war, love,
birth, work, death, and nature was a pioneering work
originally published as *The Path on the Rainbow*. Most
of the translations are by non-Indians, and some of
the songs are only interpretations of the originals.

Day, A. Grove, editor. **The Sky Clears: Poetry of the
American Indians** (© 1951). U of Nebr Pr 1964.

Day discusses Indian poetry and presents over 200
poems, translated more in the spirit than in the exact
words of the originals, from about forty different tribes,
including the Mayas and Aztecs.

Evans, Mari. **I Am a Black Woman.** Morrow 1970.

A black woman poet writes about her past and present
life.

Frost, Robert. **A Pocket Book of Robert Frost's Poems.**
WSP 1962.

Perhaps more than any other twentieth-century poet,
Frost has captured the imagination of Americans with
his evocations of rural life and, more generally, with
his probing of ideals as they succeed or fail in life,
rather than simply in the mind.

Giovanni, Nikki. **Black Feeling, Black Talk-Black Judge-
ment.** Morrow 1970.

A young black poet seeks her own identity. Some
poems clearly and articulately express the anger felt
by some blacks towards whites, but Giovanni is too
skillful a poet to be discounted as merely a militant.

Giovanni, Nikki. **My House.** Morrow 1972.

Giovanni has been called the "Princess of Black
Poetry," and a look through these pages should tell
you why. She writes with compassion about her grandmother wanting to teach her to bake rolls, on the one

hand, and with outrage about children maimed by na-
palm on the other, with a variety of moods in between.

Gunderson, Keith. **A Continual Interest in the Sun and
Sea.** Abelard 1971.

Poems about the author's family but even more about
the world of the ocean.

Henderson, Harold G., editor. **An Introduction to Haiku:
An Anthology of Poems and Poets from Basho to
Shiki.** Anchor Pr 1958.

A history of the development of haiku, a brief, lyric
form of Japanese poetry with images almost always
drawn from nature, along with many examples of this
very popular form of poetry.

Hopkins, Lee Bennett, and Sunna Rasch, editors. **I
Really Want to Feel Good about Myself.** Nelson 1974.

Fourteen drug addicts in a poetry class write poems
about their problems and their attempts at rehabilitat-
ing themselves.

Howard, Vanessa. **A Screaming Whisper.** HR&W 1972.

Bittersweet poems about the condition of being a black
in a nation that has frequently done evil to nonwhites.

Hughes, Langston. **Selected Poems of Langston Hughes**
(© 1959). VinRandom 1974.

Recognized as one of America's foremost poets, the author brings together those poems which he wanted "to
preserve from his six previously published volumes,
from the privately printed, limited edition, *Dear Lovely
Death,* and from his previously unpublished works."

Iverson, Lucille, and Kathryn Ruby, editors. **We Become New: Poems by Contemporary American Women.** Bantam 1975.

Poems about the condition of women today by American women poets as different as June Jordan, Erica
Jong, Elizabeth Sargent, Robin Morgan, Carolyn Ki-
zer, and Anne Sexton.

Keithley, George. **The Donner Party.** Braziller 1972.

The tragic story of the Donner Party's wagon train to
California is told in verse form. The good times along
the way and the awful ending of the journey are vividly portrayed.

Kherdian, David, editor. **Settling America: The Ethnic Expression of Fourteen Contemporary Poets.** Macmillan 1974.

Fourteen poets of different ethnic backgrounds explore and describe their beliefs and their way of looking at our country.

Klonsky, Milton, editor. **Shake the Kaleidoscope.** PB 1973.

A collection of the poems of more than one hundred modern British and American poets, including Ted Hughes, Kenneth Koch, Gregory Corso, Denise Levertov, and Erica Jong.

Kramer, Aaron, editor. **On Freedom's Side: An Anthology of American Poems of Protest.** Macmillan 1972.

Poems of protest by white, Indian, and black poets.

Kumin, Maxine. **House, Bridge, Fountain, Gate.** Viking Pr 1975.

Richly textured, affirmative poems written since the publication of her collection, *Up Country*, which was awarded the Pulitzer Prize in 1973. The subjects of the poems range from growing up in the 1930s and early 1940s to being Jewish in Danville, Kentucky, to being both a home gardener and lover.

Larrick, Nancy, editor. **On City Streets** (© 1968). Bantam 1969.

Over a hundred city kids helped the editor select the poems for this book; what they have chosen shows the variety of city life and city people, the sad as well as the ridiculous.

Larrick, Nancy, editor. **Room for Me and a Mountain Lion.** M Evans 1974.

Whether in the mountains, in the woods, or on the prairie, poets, like all people, have relished the special feeling of open space around them. The poems in this anthology celebrate getting outside to keep in touch with what is going on inside.

Lester, Julius, and David Gahr, editors. **Who I Am.** Dial 1974.

The themes of self-awareness, childhood, city life, the surroundings of the country, and love are vividly conveyed through photographs and the well-selected poems which accompany them.

Lewis, Richard, editor. **I Breathe a New Song: Poems of the Eskimo.** S&S 1971.

Ninety Eskimo poems and a few myths are included here, with illustrations.

Lomax, Alan, and Raoul Abdul, editors. **Three Thousand Years of Black Poetry.** Dodd 1970.

Thirty centuries of many kinds of poetry from many nations make up this anthology.

Lucie-Smith, Edward, editor. **British Poetry since 1945.** Penguin 1970.

The major British poets to emerge since World War II are represented in this comprehensive collection, which includes both brief essays describing the various "groups" of poets and short biographical introductions to each of the writers.

Lucie-Smith, Edward, editor. **Holding Your Eight Hands: An Anthology of Science Fiction Verse.** Doubleday 1969.

Science fiction poetry is not necessarily futuristic or written exclusively by science fiction writers. Includes poems by Brian Aldiss, John Brunner, Robert Conquest, and C. S. Lewis.

Lueders, Edward, and Primus St. John, editors. **Zero Makes Me Hungry.** Lothrop 1976.

A collection of contemporary poems which evoke new and unexpected images of modern life and glimpses of unimagined possibilities. Nicely illustrated.

Mao Tse-tung (translators Willis Barstone and Ko Ching Po). **The Poems of Chairman Mao.** Har-Row 1972.

Although obviously political in nature, Mao's poems often contain the gentle beauty that is found in Oriental poetry. The poems are expressions of the decades of struggle, the hope for a new China, and the final victory over the Nationalist forces.

Masters, Edgar Lee. **Spoon River Anthology** (© 1915). Macmillan 1962.

More than 200 residents of Spoon River speak from

their graves in this collection of brief monologue-poems. They speak frankly of hypocrisy, injustice, hatred, poverty—even their town's secret sex life.

Merriam, Eve. **The Double Bed.** M Evans 1972.

Poems about women and their place in marriage and the role of marriage in American life.

Mezey, Robert, editor. **Poems from the Hebrew.** T Y Crowell 1973.

The 2,000 years of Hebrew poetry in this collection include selections from the sages of the Old Testament, the medieval writers of Moorish Spain, and the poets of modern Israel. In other volumes of the Crowell Poems of the World Series are selections from Africa, France, Germany, India, Ireland, Italy, and Latin America.

Molloy, Paul, editor. **Beach Glass and Other Poems.** Four Winds 1970.

A large selection of American poems emphasizing the embodiment of experience rather than the expression of ideas.

Murphy, Beatrice M., editor. **Today's Negro Voices.** Messner 1970.

A collection of "right-on" poems from black youths who poignantly cry out in today's langauge.

Niatum, Duane, editor. **Carriers of the Dream Wheel: Contemporary Native American Poetry.** Har-Row 1975.

An attractively illustrated collection of contemporary poems dealing with personal, cultural, and universal experiences by sixteen outstanding Native American poets, among them N. Scott Momaday, James Welch, Duane Niatum, Roberta Hill, Anita Endrezze Probst, Simon J. Ortiz, Wendy Rose, and other less well known young writers.

Parker, Elinor, editor. **Four Seasons, Five Senses.** Scribner 1974.

The ninety poems in this collection—some old, some recent—are divided into four sections exploring the moods of each of the seasons.

Peck, Richard, editor. **Sounds and Silences.** Dell 1970.

    The more than 100 poems in this inexpensive collection are divided into a dozen thematic sections dealing with love, identity, pain, war, and the like. The poems are recent and varied, including rock and folk song lyrics.

Phillips, Robert, editor. **Moonstruck: An Anthology of Lunar Poetry.** Vanguard 1974.

    Historically, the moon has been regarded as a goddess, a source of lunacy, and a fit object to aim a rocket at. This anthology explores our lunar fascination, from ancient times through the Apollo missions.

Pichaske, David R., editor. **Beowulf to Beatles.** Free Pr 1972.

    Poetry from many ages and places with some short discussions of the poems. The poets include E. E. Cummings, Joni Mitchell, Pete Seeger, Bob Dylan, William Butler Yeats, and the Beatles.

Randall, Dudley, editor. **The Black Poets.** Bantam 1971.

    Black poets like Claude McKay, Jean Toomer, Countee Cullen, Gwendolyn Brooks, Imamu Amiri Baraka, June Jordan, Don L. Lee, Ishmael Reed, and Nikki Giovanni write about their hopes, dreams, and fears and about their black brothers and sisters.

Reddy, T. J. **Less than a Score, But a Point: Poems.** VinRandom 1974.

    The author, a black, was sentenced to twenty years in prison in North Carolina because of his civil rights and antiwar activities. The poems are angry and sensitive cries about the injustices suffered by blacks today.

Rich, Adrienne. **Diving into the Wreck.** Norton 1973.

    Rich unflinchingly discloses her vision of women, love, and sex tyrannized by a masculine world, admonishing the victims not to be "ignorant of the fact this way of grief/ is shared, unnecessary/ and political." Cowinner of the National Book Award for poetry in 1974. Mature.

Sexton, Anne. **The Awful Rowing Toward God.** HM 1975.

    Published after the poet took her own life, many of

these thirty-nine poems are meditations on God and death articulating the fear and fascination each held for Sexton. Mature.

Snyder, Gary. **Turtle Island.** New Directions 1974.

Awarded the Pulitzer Prize for poetry in 1975, this collection of nearly sixty poems combines Snyder's background in Zen philosophy with his passion to rediscover the past of the North American continent ("Turtle Island") and the roots of contemporary America.

Tedlock, Dennis, translator. **Finding the Center: Narrative Poetry of the Zuni Indians.** Dial 1972.

These nine stories are quite unlike other translated Indian tales. Tedlock has translated them in such a way that the original rhythm, pitch, and especially the pauses and silences used by the Zuni storytellers are preserved. The stories can therefore be chanted as they were meant to be.

Updike, John. **Verse** (© 1963). Fawcett World 1971.

Poems, both serious and humorous, by the distinguished American novelist and short story writer.

Wakoski, Diane. **The Motorcycle Betrayal Poems.** S&S 1971.

Wakoski's chief subject is herself: betrayed by her lovers, by her art, and even by her face, she writes with both wit and anger about the problems of being a woman and a poet. Mature.

Williams, Mason. **The Mason Williams Reading Matter.** Doubleday 1969.

Poems serious and funny by the popular musician and lyricist.

Williams, Oscar, editor. **Immortal Poems of the English Language.** PB 1952.

This collection remains a bargain excursion through seven centuries of some of the most significant and treasured poetry written in English.

Yevtushenko, Yevgeny (editor Robin Milner-Gulland). **Yevtushenko, Selected Poems.** Penguin 1962.

The modern Russian poet speaks about justice and injustice, prejudice and lies.

SHORT STORIES

Aiken, Joan, et al., editors. **Authors' Choice.** T Y Crowell 1974.

Eighteen authors select their favorite stories, which range from the forthright humor of Damon Runyon to Vera and Bill Cleaver's story of Dr. Sickles, Flora Katherine, and Jesse who search the woods for "wild, green gold."

Allen, Donald M., and Robert Creeley, editors. **New American Story.** Grove 1965.

Stories by ten contemporary writers (LeRoi Jones, Edward Dorn, and Jack Kerouac, for example), many dealing with the world of the dispossessed poor. Mature.

Angus, Douglas, and Sylvia Angus, editors. **Contemporary American Short Stories** (© 1967). Fawcett World 1973.

Stories by social critics such as James Purdy and Tillie Olsen are among those included in this anthology.

Angus, Douglas, and Sylvia Angus, editors. **Great Modern European Short Stories** (© 1967). Fawcett World 1973.

Albert Camus, D. H. Lawrence, and Heinrich Böll are but a few of the European authors included in this large collection.

Babel, Isaac (editor Walter Morison). **Isaac Babel: The Collected Stories.** NAL 1955.

A collection of the author's short fiction demonstrating his rich irony and lyricism.

Bellow, Saul, editor. **Great Jewish Short Stories.** Dell 1963.

The stories range from the ancient to the modern and capture the essence of the Jewish experience.

Breé, Germaine, editor. **Great French Short Stories** (© 1960). Dell 1974.

Breé has brought together some of the outstanding French writers of the short story. Included here are such writers as Honoré de Balzac, Albert Camus, and Félix Fénéon, who wrote the following short story: "Abandoned by Delorce, Cecilia Ward refused to take him back except in marriage. The situation seemed indecent to him so he stabbed her."

Capote, Truman. **The Grass Harp and a Tree of Night and Other Short Stories** (© 1951). NAL 1961.

Capote, author of the novel *In Cold Blood,* includes "Jug of Silver" and "Shut a Final Door" in this collection of ten stories.

Cebulash, Mel, editor. **The Fallen Angel and Other Stories.** Schol Bk Serv 1970.

"Hearts and Hands" by O. Henry, "Two Men Named Collins" by Damon Runyon, "That Strange Mr. Lake" by Marilyn Pergerson, and "The Test" by Phil Aponte are but a few of the stories in this collection.

Chekhov, Anton (editor David Greene). **Great Stories By Chekhov.** Dell 1959.

These stories display Chekhov's mastery of realism and irony and his deep sympathy for the frustrations and difficulties of the people of nineteenth-century Russia.

Clark, Eleanor. **Dr. Heart—A Novella and Other Stories.** Pantheon 1974.

Clark explores the odd ways by which human beings reveal themselves in a collection spanning her entire career from 1937 to the present. Female characters are the major focus of attention in many of her stories. Mature.

Coover, Robert. **Pricksongs and Descants** (© 1969). NAL 1970.

This third book by Coover includes stories that challenge the assumptions of our age. Mature.

Crane, Milton, editor. **50 Great American Short Stories.** Bantam 1965.

James Agee's "A Mother's Tale," a shattering parable of life, death, and the inexorable vise of fate, is one among many contemporary and classic stories by American writers in this collection.

Crane, Milton, editor. **50 Great Short Stories.** Bantam 1968.

Selections from many of the world's finest short story

writers: Guy de Maupassant, James Joyce, Katherine Mansfield, and others.

Crane, Stephen (editor Austin M. Fox). **Maggie and Other Stories by Stephen Crane** (© 1960). WSP 1974.

Crane's short stories, like his novel *The Red Badge of Courage,* carefully and convincingly describe characters and settings; some of the selections here are "The Pace of Youth," "The Second Generation," and "The Monster."

Dinesen, Isak. **Shadows on the Grass** (© 1961). Vin-Random 1974.

Dinesen gives a fictional account of the years she spent managing a coffee plantation in Africa. This volume contains four sketches about life in Kenya, including its people, land, and customs.

Elkin, Stanley. **Criers and Kibitzers, Kibitzers and Criers** (© 1965). NAL 1973.

Selections in this volume are sometimes hilarious, sometimes tragic.

Flores, Angel, editor. **Great Spanish Short Stories.** Dell 1974.

Flores has chosen stories representative of the last 400 years of the Spanish literary tradition.

Flower, Dean, editor. **Counterparts: Classic and Contemporary American Short Stories.** Fawcett World 1971.

John Updike's "The Christian Roommates" and Ralph Ellison's "Did You Ever Dream Lucky?" are examples of the contemporary American short stories in this volume.

Foley, Martha, editor. **The Best American Short Stories, 1974.** HM 1974.

A cross section of outstanding American short fiction pieces published in 1974. Readers will find works by authors such as William Saroyan, John Updike, and Maxine Kumin. (See also *The Best American Short Stories, 1973,* HM.)

Goldstone, Herbert, et al., editors. **Points of Departure— A Collection of Short Fiction.** P-H 1971.

Stories written by American authors within the last

twenty-five years dominate this collection that speaks of love, innocence, marriage, identity, and war.

Good, Merle, editor. **People Pieces.** Herald Pr 1974.
A collection of Mennonite and Amish stories.

Goodman, Roger B., editor. **75 Short Masterpieces: Stories from the World's Literature.** Bantam 1961.
Selections in this collection represent an international array of writers.

Goodman, Roger B., editor. **The World's Best Short Short Stories.** Bantam 1967.
Sholom Aleichem tells a fascinating tale about "A Wedding Without Musicians" and Richardo Palma tells "How the Devil Lost His Poncho" in this collection.

Greene, Graham. **Collected Stories.** Viking Pr 1973.
The author includes in this collection of forty stories "May We Borrow Your Husband?," "A Sense of Reality," "The Blessing," and "Church Militant." In his introduction, Greene says that "the short story for the novelist is often a form of escape—escape from having to live with another character for years on end. . . ." Mature.

Haslam, Gerald. **Okies: Selected Stories.** New West Pubns 1973.
The author's experiences as a farm worker and his acquaintance with migrant workers give authenticity to his stories, collected here for the first time. Mature.

Hemingway, Ernest. **The Nick Adams Stories** (© 1972). Bantam 1973.
Nick Adams, Hemingway's great fictional hero, sheds light on Hemingway the man in this collection, which includes "The Killers," "The Light of the World," and "Fathers and Sons."

Henry, O. (editors Richard Corbin and Ned E. Hoopes). **Surprises: 20 Stories By O. Henry.** Dell 1966.
Perhaps the best known and most popular American short story writer, O. Henry has an unusual ability to put special meaning and excitement into his tales of

people whose lives are seemingly dull and drab. Almost all of his stories have a surprise ending.

Houghton, Norris, editor. **Great Russian Short Stories.** Dell 1958.

Great Russian writers such as Leo Tolstoy, Fyodor Dostoevsky, Ivan Turgenev, and Anton Chekhov share in common a concern for human nature and love and pity for all human beings.

Huxley, Aldous. **Collected Short Stories.** Bantam 1973.

Huxley, best known for his novel *Brave New World*, presents a subtle study of suspected murder in "The Gioconda Smile," one of twenty-one stories collected here.

Isherwood, Christopher, editor. **Great English Short Stories.** Dell 1957.

All the ingredients of great short stories, such as love, loneliness, adventure, crime, humor, and ghosts, appear in this collection of works by British writers W. Somerset Maugham, Joseph Conrad, Rudyard Kipling, George Moore, and others.

Jones, James. **The Ice Cream Headache and Other Stories.** Delacorte 1968.

Jones, best known for his war novel *From Here to Eternity*, focuses upon war and loneliness, courtship and marriage. Mature.

Klinkowitz, Jerome, and John Somer, editors. **Innovative Fiction, Stories for the Seventies.** Dell 1972.

"The Cleveland Wrecking Yard," "Sea," "Sea Rider," and "The Babysitter" are only a few of the stories found in this volume by new writers taking different approaches to life and fiction.

Lass, Abraham, and Leonard Kriegel, editors. **Masters of the Short Story.** NAL 1971.

Twenty-seven stories from such countries as Mexico, England, Ireland, and Russia; the volume contains a biographical sketch of each author and a discussion of each story.

Lucas, Alec, editor. **Great Canadian Short Stories.** Dell 1971.

Selections from the works of Canadian short story

writers like Thomas Haliburton and Ray Smith, ranging from the early nineteenth century to the present.

Mann, Thomas (translator H. T. Lowe-Porter). **Death in Venice and Seven Other Stories** (© 1930). VinRandom 1966.

Mann's stories are complex and notable for their detail and irony. In the title story, Gustave Aschenbach, a brilliant and admired writer, seeks perfect beauty but finds its opposite in the splendor and decay of Venice. The strange magician Cipolla captivates and, at the same time, humiliates his audience in "Mario and the Magician" until the docile Mario suddenly turns on him. Mature.

Mansfield, Katherine. **Stories.** VinRandom 1956.

Readers will enjoy stories like "The Man without a Temperament," "The Stranger," "The Voyage," and "Prelude." Mature.

Maugham, W. Somerset. **The Complete Short Stories of W. Somerset Maugham** (© 1952). WSP 1970.

Some of Maugham's well-known stories such as "Princess September," "Mr. Know All," "The Pool," and "The Happy Man."

McCullers, Carson. **The Ballad of the Sad Cafe and Other Stories.** Bantam 1967.

Stories about people who are "lost" and who are often desperately seeking to escape their isolation through love.

Mercier, Vivian, editor. **Great Irish Short Stories.** Dell 1964.

Mercier believes that a great short story must "echo in the reader's mind" after he or she has closed the book. The author shows how and why the Irish genius for storytelling developed. Included in this collection are works by Samuel Beckett, James Joyce, and William Butler Yeats.

Miller, Arthur. **I Don't Need You Anymore.** Viking Pr 1967.

Miller's title story is about a few late summer days in the life of a five-year-old boy.

O'Connor, Flannery. **The Complete Stories.** FS&G 1972.

O'Connor's stories, such as "A Good Man Is Hard to Find," "Everything That Rises Must Converge," and "Revelation," deal with characters in the country and small towns of the South who are forced by usually violent means to realize the connections between human life and the mysteries of the divine.

O'Flaherty, Liam. **The Wounded Cormorant and Other Stories.** Norton 1973.

The author writes short stories in Gaelic, a Celtic language of Ireland and Scotland, and in English. The pervasive theme in this collection is the relationship between people and nature. Mature.

Pasinetti, P. M., editor. **Great Italian Short Stories.** Dell 1959.

The writers in this collection represent over 600 years of Italian civilization in stories which reveal "the extremes of spirituality and ribaldry" of a people.

Poe, Edgar Allan (editor Richard Wilbur). **18 Best Stories by Edgar Allan Poe** (© 1965). Dell 1974.

Poe's weirdness and dramatic power are clear in the short stories found in this collection.

Porter, Katherine Anne. **Flowering Judas and Other Stories** (© 1965). NAL 1970.

Porter includes in this volume many of her well-known stories ranging in time and place from revolutionary Mexico to pre-Nazi Berlin, from rural Texas to bohemian New York.

Prescott, Orville, editor. **Mid-Century: An Anthology of Distinguished Contemporary American Short Stories** (© 1971). WSP 1973.

The twenty short stories in this collection were written around the end of World War II.

Rosen, Kenneth, editor. **The Man to Send Rain Clouds: Contemporary Stories by American Indians.** Viking Pr 1974.

Unlike most Indian stories which are folktales taken from ancient oral traditions, these nineteen short stories are contemporary and largely written by young, well-educated Indians whose writing often bears the scars of bitterness, repression, and the struggle for self-determination, although many of the writers retain some of the old traditions and beliefs.

Saki (editors Richard Corbin and Ned E. Hoopes). **Incredible Tales: Saki Short Stories.** Dell 1966.

Saki, the pseudonym of H. H. Munro, displays his wit, his love of practical jokes, his interest in the supernatural, and his ability to satirize human frailty.

Schaefer, Jack. **The Collected Stories of Jack Schaefer.** HM 1966.

Each of the thirty-two stories in this volume concerns itself with some aspect of the West. The characters are brave, likeable, and comic at times.

Schaefer, Jack. **The Short Novels of Jack Schaefer.** HM 1967.

Several of Schaefer's more popular short novels, such as *Shane, First Blood,* and *The Canyon.* Schaefer is a storyteller who not only uses sentiment and tragedy, but also wry humor in almost every story.

Simon, John, editor. **Fourteen for Now: A Collection of Contemporary Stories** (© 1969). Har-Row 1972.

A collection of short stories written after World War II.

Singer, Isaac Bashevis. **A Crown of Feathers.** FS&G 1973.

Singer's stories touch many themes, including "Grandfather and Grandson," which deals with the "generation gap."

Sohn, David A., editor. **Ten Modern American Short Stories.** Bantam 1965.

A collection of stories ranging from the turmoil of school campuses to the discipline of a Chinese commune.

Spender, Stephen, editor. **Great German Short Stories.** Dell 1960.

A universal theme pervading most of these stories and, in fact, much of German writing is the struggle between the spiritually healthy and unhealthy way of life.

Stafford, Jean. **The Collected Stories.** FS&G 1969.

The author includes stories under the following subtitles as a way of demonstrating the broadness of her experiences in various sections of this country: "The Innocents Abroad," "The Bostonians and Other Manifestations," and "Cowboys and Indians, and Magic Mountains."

Stansbury, Donald L., editor. **Impact: Short Stories for Pleasure.** P-H 1971.

Contemporary stories such as Ralph Ellison's "Game," Hernando Tellez's "Just Lather, That's All," and Charles Einstein's "The New Deal." Mature.

Stegner, Wallace, and Mary Stegner, editors. **Great American Short Stories.** Dell 1957.

A variety of writers comment on the humor and pathos of the human condition in America. Among the better known authors included are Edgar Allan Poe, James Thurber, Ambrose Bierce, John Steinbeck, and Hortense Calisher.

Steinbeck, John. **The Long Valley** (© 1956). Bantam 1970.

Thirteen of John Steinbeck's great stories are brought together in one volume of such classics as "The Red Pony," "The Leader of the People," and "The Vigilante."

Stuart, Jesse. **A Jesse Stuart Harvest** (© 1965). Ballantine 1974.

Stuart celebrates the South with eighteen of his best short stories depicting his native Kentucky.

Taylor, Peter. **The Collected Stories of Peter Taylor.** FS&G 1971.

This volume includes "Dean of Men," "The Other Times," "The Fancy Woman," and other stories selected by the author.

Traven, B. **The Night Visitor and Other Stories** (© 1966). Hill & Wang 1973.

A hacienda deep in the Mexican bush where a lonely American recreates in his imagination an eerie world of Indian folk legend sets the tone for this volume of Traven stories.

Warren, Robert Penn, and Albert Erskine, editors.
Short Story Masterpieces. Dell 1954.

Thirty-six short stories of enduring quality, offering
reading from the humor of James Thurber to the irony
of Ernest Hemingway.

POPULAR CULTURE

Arnold, Eddy. **It's a Long Way from Chesters County**
(© 1969). Pyramid Pubns 1970.

The story of the great country music singer, from his
Tennessee childhood to his adult life as a popular
entertainer.

Berle, Milton (with Haskel Frankel). **Milton Berle:
An Autobiography.** Delacorte 1974.

The performer who dominated the early days of television tells the frank story of his life and loves along
with stories about the first years of television.

Berton, Ralph. **Remembering Bix.** Har-Row 1974.

Bix Beiderbecke was one of the great cornetists of the
jazz age. A prodigy at seven, an admired musician at
twenty-one, and dead at twenty-eight, he was both a
romantic figure and a very lonely human being.

Cohn, Nik. **Rock from the Beginning** (© 1969). PB
1970.

Comments on songs and musicians, from the beginning
of rock music until the late 60s.

Cole, Maria (with Louie Robinson). **Nat King Cole.**
Morrow 1971.

A great popular singer, Cole was the first black star
to have a national radio and television show, but he
could find no national sponsor for his television show
and was driven off the air.

Dance, Stanley. **The World of Swing.** Scribner 1974.

The 1930s, the swing era of jazz, are recounted through
the careers of forty of the greatest artists of that period, bandleaders like Claude Hopkins, instrumental-
ists like Cozy Cole, and singers like Billie Holiday.

Davis, Clive (with James Willwerth). **Clive: Inside the**

Record Business. Morrow 1975.

From the time he joined Columbia Records in 1965 until he left in 1973, Davis may have been the single most important figure in the changing world of the rock and roll recording business.

Davis, Sammy, Jr., Jane Boyar, and Burt Boyar. **Yes I Can: The Story of Sammy Davis, Jr.** (© 1965). PB 1972.

The story of the popular black singer and entertainer, including his problems growing up among show business people, his friends, and his personal life. He is occasionally bitter but mostly optimistic about America and its racial problems.

Deford, Frank. **Five Strides on the Banked Track: The Life and Times of the Roller Derby.** Little 1971.

Roller derby is one of the most popular entertainments in America. The fans, the players, the teams, and the travel are touched on by the author.

Denisoff, R. Serge. **Great Day Coming: Folk Music and the American Left** (© 1971). Penguin 1973.

An examination and criticism of folk music since the 1930s and its connection with political movements. Some artists discussed are Pete Seeger, Woody Guthrie, Burl Ives, Bob Dylan, Joan Baez, and the Weavers.

Easton, Carol. **Straight Ahead: The Story of Stan Kenton.** Morrow 1973.

Stan Kenton was and is one of the most influential men in modern music; this biography covers both his life and the changes he caused in music, particularly with his progressive jazz.

Edmonds, I. G. **The Magic Man: The Life of Robert-Houdin.** Nelson 1972.

Robert-Houdin was the father of modern magic. His life and his tricks (one even stopped a war) influenced other magicians, especially an even more famous performer, Harry Houdini.

Edmondson, Madeleine, and David Rounds. **The Soaps: Daytime Serials of Radio and TV.** Stein & Day 1973.

History, anecdotes, and details about radio and TV soap operas, from "The Goldbergs" to "Another World."

Ellington, Edward Kennedy. **Music Is My Mistress.** Doubleday 1973.

Duke Ellington was one of the innovators of modern music. In this book, he talks about jazz musicians he has known, his feelings about music generally, and places he has been during his long career.

Friedman, Myra. **Buried Alive: The Biography of Janis Joplin** (© 1973). Bantam 1974.

Joplin died of a heroin overdose at twenty-seven. She had been one of the great singers of the rock music scene, but she was also a young woman with serious personal problems and little self-respect.

Gillett, Charlie. **The Sound of the City: The Rise of Rock 'n' Roll** (© 1970). Dell 1972.

A history of rock 'n roll music from 1954 to 1969. Musicians, trends, styles, and the writing of music and lyrics are covered.

Goldstein, Richard, editor. **The Poetry of Rock.** Bantam 1969.

Lyrics of rock songs by writers Chuck Berry, John Lennon and Paul McCartney, the Doors, Bob Dylan, John Phillips, Janis Ian, Paul Simon, and others.

Goreau, Laurraine. **Just Mahalia, Baby.** Word Bks 1974.

Mahalia Jackson, the great gospel singer, and those close to her talk to the author about her life, gospel music, black life, religion, and civil rights.

Greene, Bob. **Billion Dollar Baby.** Atheneum 1974.

A newspaper columnist joins the touring Alice Cooper band in the winter of 1973 to learn what makes the group work as hard as they do.

Guralnick, Peter. **Feel Like Going Home.** Dutton 1971.

Portraits of the major figures in blues and rock 'n' roll, from the music of the Delta to today, Muddy Waters to Charlie Rich.

Hamilton, Charles, and Diane Hamilton. **Big Name Hunting: A Beginner's Guide to Autograph Collecting.** S&S 1973.

Autograph collecting is a popular hobby, and the authors tell the beginner how to get started, how to purchase autographs, some problems that await the uninformed collector, and some stories about autographs and autograph collecting.

Harris, Christie, and Moira Johnston. **Figleafing Through History: The Dynamics of Dress.** Atheneum 1971.

The history of clothing and the uses of clothing to conceal or reveal. Fads, fancies, styles, trends, and whims are discussed. Many illustrations.

Jares, Joe. **Whatever Happened to Gorgeous George?** P-H 1974.

Professional wrestling was once both a popular and a colorful spectacle. Gorgeous George and other outlandish but fascinating wrestlers are described.

Jones, Hettie. **Big Star Fallin' Mama: Five Women in Black Music.** Viking Pr 1974.

Illustrated biographies of Ma Rainey, Bessie Smith, Mahalia Jackson, Billie Holiday, and Aretha Franklin, with some suggested books and records.

Jones, LeRoi. **Blues People: Negro Music in White America.** Morrow 1963.

Both a history of black people and the music they have written and played. Jones covers the period from slavery to modern times, with many comments about jazz, blues, and swing groups.

Knight, Curtis. **Jimi: An Intimate History of Jimi Hendrix.** Praeger 1974.

Hendrix was a superstar of British rock 'n' roll who also became a major success in the United States. His death and the myths that grew out of his life are described.

LaGuardia, Robert. **The Wonderful World of TV Soap Operas.** Ballantine 1974.

A brief history of soap operas leads into a detailed discussion of TV soap operas today with stories about writers, actors, and famous bloopers.

Lee, Stan. **Origins of Marvel Comics.** S&S 1974.

Lee introduces the major heroes of Marvel comic

books: the Phantastic Four, Spider-Man, Thor, the
Hulk, and Dr. Strange. Many color illustrations.

Lupoff, Dick, and Don Thompson, editors. **All in Color
for a Dime** (© 1970). Ace Bks 1971.

A collection of articles about comic books—the major
heroes, series, and publishers—and their impact on
readers and American society. Well illustrated.

McCabe, Peter, and Robert D. Schonfeld. **Apple to the
Core: The Unmaking of the Beatles.** PB 1972.

The Beatles story from the beginning to the end, with
comments about records they made and the influence
they had on modern music. The Beatles sometimes
do not emerge as heroes in this frank study.

McGregor, Craig, editor. **Bob Dylan: A Retrospective.**
Morrow 1972.

A collection of articles about Bob Dylan, his music,
his writing, his concerts, and his thoughts.

Mellers, Wilfrid. **Twilight of the Gods: The Beatles in
Retrospect** (© 1973). Viking Pr 1974.

Comments on the Beatles' music—the early songs, the
Sgt. Pepper album, and all the other records and concerts that changed the course of American popular
music. A good glossary of musical terms will help the
beginner in reading this book.

Morse, David, editor. **Grandfather Rock** (©1972). Dell
1973.

A collection of classic poetry paired by theme with
modern rock lyrics. For example, Homer's "The Si-
rens' Song" is paired with Eric Clapton and Martin
Sharp's "Tales of Brave Ulysses," and William Butler
Yeats's "The Dawn" is paired with John Lennon and
Paul McCartney's "The Fool on the Hill."

Nassour, Ellis, and Richard Broderick. **Rock Opera.**
Hawthorn 1973.

The history of the rock opera *Jesus Christ Superstar,*
from the record album to the Broadway hit to the
motion picture. Many photographs.

Nicholas, A. X., editor. **The Poetry of Soul.** Bantam
1971.

A collection of the lyrics of soul music as recorded or

written by Otis Redding, Aretha Franklin, Sonny Charles, and others.

Nicholas, A. X., editor. **Woke Up This Mornin': Poetry of the Blues.** Bantam 1973.

Lyrics of blues songs by writers Leadbelly, Blind Lemon Jefferson, Bessie Smith, Big Bill Broonzy, Muddy Waters, B. B. King, and others.

Nite, Norm N., editor. **Rock On: The Illustrated Encyclopedia of Rock n' Roll.** T Y Crowell 1974.

Brief biographical and historical sketches of more than 1,000 popular artists of rock 'n' roll during the 1950s and early 1960s, with lists of the most popular records of each artist.

Nye, Russel. **The Unembarrassed Muse: The Popular Arts in America.** Dial 1970.

A long and fascinating book covering many facets of popular culture: minstrel shows, dime novels, early boys' books, bluegrass, radio, television, films, bestsellers, and much more.

Pettit, Florence H. **How to Make Whirligigs and Whimmy Diddles and Other American Folkcraft Objects.** T Y Crowell 1972.

Instructions and patterns for making American folkcraft objects, including a carved cherrywood goose, a pinecone cardinal, and corn-shuck dolls. Elaborately illustrated and directed at the beginner. Bibliography.

Pleasants, Henry. **Serious Music—And All That Jazz!** (© 1969). S&S 1971.

A music critic who is devoted to classical music but believes it may have reached a dead end argues that rock may prove to be the important music of our time.

Propes, Steve. **Golden Oldies: A Guide to 60s Record Collecting.** Chilton 1974.

A brief history of record collecting and trends of popular music in the 1960s is followed by a long section on the prominent groups and individuals of the period and their individual records.

Purdy, Claire Lee. **Gilbert and Sullivan: Masters of Mirth and Melody.** Messner 1946.

When writer William S. Gilbert and composer Arthur

S. Sullivan joined forces, they produced a series of unparalleled comic opera successes, for instance, *H.M.S. Pinafore, Pirates of Penzance,* and *The Mikado.*

Robinson, Jerry. **The Comics: An Illustrated History of Seventy-five Years of Comic Strip Art.** Putnam 1974.

A history of comic strips, beginning in the year 1896. Many illustrations of both black and white and color strips.

Robinson, Richard. **Electric Rock.** Pyramid Pubns 1971.

A thorough presentation of information about rock music equipment, brands, prices, recording information, and tips for beginners and experienced musicians.

Robinson, Richard. **Pop, Rock and Soul.** Pyramid Pubns 1972.

John Denver, the Beatles, the Rolling Stones, Cat Stevens, and many other popular musicians are interviewed and discussed.

Rolling Stone Magazine Editors. **Knockin' On Dylan's Door: On the Road in '74.** PB 1974.

Several writers contribute brief accounts of Bob Dylan's musical tour of the United States in 1974, his first since 1966. A good picture of the rock and roll scene, its music, its fans, its fanatics. For *Rolling Stone* magazine's lengthy 1976 history of rock, see also *The Rolling Stone Illustrated History of Rock & Roll,* distributed by Random.

Rooney, James. **Bossmen: Bill Monroe and Muddy Waters.** Dial 1971.

Rooney compares and contrasts the careers and music of two important men in popular music, Bill Monroe, a star in bluegrass and country music, and Muddy Waters, the great man of Chicago blues.

Rowsome, Frank, Jr. **The Verse by the Side of the Road.** Dutton 1965.

In early 1927 the Burma-Shave Company began putting signs advertising its product along America's highways. As time passed, the signs grew funnier and became a part of almost every American motorist's life until 1963 when the signs began disappearing from the roadways. The entire list of Burma-Shave signs from 1927 to 1963 is included.

Russell, Ross. **Jazz Style in Kansas City and the Southwest.** U of Cal Pr 1971.

A fascinating discussion of blues, ragtime, and jazz during the 1920s and 1930s, with many stories about jazz musicians. Some excellent photographs and a lengthy list of books and records.

Sarlin, Bob. **Turn It Up! (I Can't Hear the Words)** (© 1973). S&S 1974.

Sarlin writes about many contemporary songwriters and performers in rock 'n' roll music. Joni Mitchell, Bob Dylan, and Randy Newman are only three of many covered.

Schicke, C. A. **Revolution in Sound.** Little 1974.

When Thomas Edison invented the phonograph in 1877, he called it "my baby." After many innovations, from cylinder to disc, from 78 rpm to 33 rpm, from monophonic to stereophonic, his baby now brings music to millions.

Shaw, Arnold. **The Rockin' Fifties.** Hawthorn 1974.

A history of the popular music scene during the 1950s.

Shestack, Melvin, editor. **The Country Music Encyclopedia.** T Y Crowell 1974.

Biographies of the leading figures in country music, from Roy Acuff through Faron Young. Lists of country music records, country music radio stations, and a sample of country songs conclude the book.

Somma, Robert, editor. **No One Waved Good-Bye.** Dutton 1971.

A collection of essays covering the effect of the deaths of rock 'n' roll stars—such as Janis Joplin, Jimi Hendrix, and Brian Epstein—on other musicians.

Stambler, Irwin, and Grelun Landon. **Golden Guitars.** Four Winds 1971.

The origin and development of country and western

music, its trends, styles, music, and musicians. Johnny Cash, Glen Campbell, and Bobbie Gentry, among others, are profiled.

Stedman, Raymond William. **The Serials: Suspense and Drama by Installment.** U of Okla Pr 1971.

The serial is apparently an American dramatic invention, and the author gives the history and details of movie, radio, and television serials. Many illustrations.

Stewart, John. **The Circus Is Coming.** Westminster 1973.

A history of the circus and many of its animal acts and daredevil performers.

Thomas, J. C. **Chasin' the Trane.** Doubleday 1975.

Although he died when he was only forty years old, John Coltrane created a legend through the use of black and Indian music and his great skill with the saxophone.

Welk, Lawrence (with Bernice McGeehan). **Ah-One, Ah-Two: Life with My Musical Family.** P-H 1974.

One of the most popular bandleaders in America had his television show cut out from under him and set out to develop a network of TV stations to show his syndicated musical programs.

Whitcomb, Ian. **After the Ball: Pop Music from Rag to Rock** (© 1972). Penguin 1974.

A history of the beginnings of popular music—ragtime, jazz, swing, and rock 'n' roll—treating trends, styles, and musicians.

Williams, Martin. **The Jazz Tradition** (© 1970). NAL 1971.

The development and trends in jazz, from the work of Jelly Roll Morton to Duke Ellington and on through the work of John Coltrane.

Wolfe, Tom. **The Pump House Gang** (© 1968). Bantam 1969.

Articles and ideas about many facets of popular culture by the leading writer in the field in America. (See also *The Kandy-Kolored Tangerine-Flake Streamline Baby,* PB.)

HUMOR AND SATIRE

Adamson, Joe. **Groucho, Harpo, Chico and Sometimes Zeppo** (© 1973). S&S 1975.

Subtitled "A history of the Marx Brothers and a satire on the rest of the world," this account of the famous comedy team covers their career from the early days of vaudeville and the movies and continues with Groucho to the present. Dialogue excerpts from their routines and many photographs. Nonfiction.

Allen, Woody. **Getting Even.** Random 1971.

A collection of hilarious essays written by one of the funniest men around. Best known as a television and movie comedian, Allen demonstrates in this book not only his original comic perspective but also his genuine writing talent.

Allen, Woody. **Without Feathers.** Random 1975.

A collection of many of Allen's articles about love and death and humanity living in our absurd world.

Amis, Kingsley. **Lucky Jim** (© 1953). Viking Pr 1958.

A satire of campus life in a British university where young faculty members struggle in a system dedicated to turning out "the white-collar proletariat." Fiction.

Armour, Richard. **Out of My Mind.** McGraw 1972.

These short pieces cover a range of subjects, from selecting Christmas trees to the reading habits of the young, with a variety of intentions from sprightly nonsense to sharp satire. Nonfiction.

Armour, Richard. **Twisted Tales from Shakespeare.** McGraw 1957.

A critic and humorist offers funny summaries of six plays by Shakespeare, some satiric study questions, and many puns. (See also *The Classics Reclassified,* McGraw.) Nonfiction.

Asimov, Isaac. **Isaac Asimov's Treasury of Humor.** HM 1971.

A lifetime's collection of favorite jokes, anecdotes, and limericks with copious notes on how to tell them and why. The material is divided according to comic device (anticlimax, paradox, tables turned, etc.) and subject matter (ethnic, marriage, bawdy, etc.). Nonfiction.

Berger, Arthur Asa. **The Comic-Stripped American.** (© 1973). Penguin 1974.

The author believes that we can get both amusement and understanding about America and the American Dream from reading popular comic strips. Beginning with comics no longer printed, such as "The Yellow Kid" and "Krazy Kat," Berger moves on to currently published comics such as "Little Orphan Annie," "Dick Tracy," and "Peanuts." Nonfiction.

Berger, Phil. **The Last Laugh: The World of the Stand-Up Comics.** Morrow 1975.

Interviews with and comments on the humor of comedians Jonathan Winters, Richard Pryor, Milton Berle, Cheech and Chong, Rodney Dangerfield, Woody Allen, and others. Nonfiction.

Bernstein, Burton. **Thurber: A Biography.** Dodd 1975.

The life of James Thurber, one of America's most delightful humorists—his admiration for strong people, his bullying of others less strong, and his love of writing. Nonfiction.

Block, Herbert. **Herblock Special Report.** Norton 1974.

A biased record of Nixon's career told through the cartoons and commentary of Pulitzer Prize winner Herbert Block of the *Washington Post*. Demonstrating the devastating effectiveness of a sustained satiric campaign running many years, over 450 cartoons testify to Block's prophetic vision and artistry.

Blume, Judy. **Are You There, God? It's Me, Margaret** (© 1970). Dell 1972.

Besides having to worry about adjusting to a new school in a new environment, twelve-year-old Margaret Simon has to cope with a Christian mother, a Jewish father, and a late-to-blossom figure. Fiction.

Brautigan, Richard. **The Hawkline Monster: A Gothic Western** (© 1967). S&S 1974.

Armed with a trunkful of weapons, two gunmen set off to kill the monster living in the ice caves under Miss Hawkline's house. The language is often ribald and candid in this modern fantasy. Mature fiction.

Brautigan, Richard. **Trout Fishing in America** (© 1969). Dell 1971.

Brautigan mirrors the spiritual environment of his

time with a unique style, marked by flashes of comic perception. Funny but seldom satiric, Brautigan's casual chattiness has helped make him one of the "in" writers of the 1970s. Fiction.

Broun, Heywood. **The Fifty-first Dragon** (© 1921). P-H 1968.

A brief tongue-in-cheek tale of a timid knight who is conned into heroic deeds. Readers of medieval romances will enjoy the comic contrasts provided by this story of Gawaine le Coeur-Hardy, dragon-killer. Fiction.

Brown, Joe David. **Paper Moon** (© 1971). NAL 1972.

In the tall-tale tradition of *Huckleberry Finn,* eleven-year-old Addie Pray, a born con artist, exploits the gullible as she and Long Boy journey through the South during the Great Depression. Fiction.

Buchwald, Art. **I Never Danced at the White House** (© 1973). Fawcett World 1975.

A collection of newspaper columns written by a funny journalist on the post-Watergate scene. Buchwald can see the humor in such universals as TV watching, generational sparring, and observing the American political scene. Nonfiction.

Cerf, Bennett, editor. **Stories to Make You Feel Better.** Random 1972.

After a lifetime of reading and people-watching, Cerf presents his favorite anecdotes and jokes to counteract depression and provide a laugh for the day. Nonfiction.

Cervantes, Miguel de. **Don Quixote.** Penguin 1950.

Written in 1605, this is the story of impoverished and emaciated Alonzo Quizano, who believes so completely in romance and chivalry that he changes his name to Don Quixote de la Mancha, dons armor, acquires a squire, and sets out to rescue heroines and fight villains in seventeenth-century Spain. Mature fiction.

Chase, Chris. **How to Be a Movie Star, or a Terrible Beauty Is Born** (© 1968). Har-Row 1974.

A humorous glimpse behind the scenes of show business through the eyes of a would-be actress. Chase, a delightful personality who was nearly discovered many times, is able to describe the hazards of the acting profession and still entertain the reader with a light-hearted account of what makes actresses persevere against overwhelming odds. Nonfiction.

Cole, William. **Oh, What Nonsense!** Viking Pr 1966.

Although this collection has the format of a children's book, its 821 nonsense verses appeal to all ages. An unusual anthology since some obvious masters of nonsense are omitted and fresh examples are presented instead.

Crews, Harry. **Car** (© 1972). PB 1973.

Herman Mack's boast that he will eat a car, half a pound a day in half-ounce cubes, becomes a public relations spectacle in this satire on America's love of cars. Some readers may object to some of the language. Fiction.

Davis, Douglas M., editor. **The World of Black Humor.** Dutton 1967.

Fifteen of America's finest contemporary novelists are presented in this anthology of excerpts, selected as illustrations of "black humor." These writers respond to the absurdity of humanity's condition by lashing out in satiric bursts of anger and mirth. Represented are such authors as William Burroughs, Walker Percy, Peter De Vries, John Barth, and James Purdy. Mature fiction.

De Vries, Peter. **Into Your Tent I'll Creep.** Little 1971.

A young man marries his former high school teacher and agrees to do the housekeeping while she continues her career, but it doesn't work out that way. Fiction.

Dickens, Charles. **Hard Times** (© 1854). Penguin 1969.

Dickens satirizes the evils of industrialism by contrasting such characters as the ideal worker, Stephen Blackpool, and the ruggedly individualistic manufacturer, Mr. Bounderby. Utilitarianism and the educational abuses it fostered are ironically depicted in Coketown's Mr. Gradgrind, whose school stifles imagination in its pursuit of the facts. Fiction.

Elliott, Bob, and Ray Goulding. **Write If You Get Work: The Best of Bob and Ray.** Random 1975.

Bob and Ray were two extremely funny writers and

performers on radio. They now appear on TV and the stage and make some very funny commercials. This is a collection of some of their best material, satires on radio announcers, soap operas, mystery shows, and children's shows.

Emrich, Duncan, editor. **The Nonsense Book.** Four Winds 1970.

An award-winning collection for any reader with a taste for the nonsensical. Includes riddles, rhymes, tongue-twisters, puzzles, and jokes from American folklore.

Feiffer, Jules, compiler. **The Great Comic Book Heroes.** Dial 1965.

Samples from the best-loved comic strips of the 1930s and 1940s—"Superman," "Captain Marvel," "Batman," and "Wonder Woman"—with commentary by satiric cartoonist Jules Feiffer. Nonfiction.

Fox, William Price. **Moonshine Light, Moonshine Bright** (© 1967). Bantam n.d.

Earl Edge and his buddy Coley Simms, fifteen year olds living in Columbia, South Carolina, in the late 1940s, have many comic adventures during the summer when their heart's desire is getting a car. Fiction.

Fox, William Price. **Southern Fried Plus Six** (© 1968). Ballantine 1974.

This collection of highly entertaining stories owes much of its effectiveness to the author's use of the motifs and tone of native American humor. Many of the best stories are set in the rural South of the 1920s and 1930s with moonshiners, short-order cooks, and loose women springing to life. Fiction.

Friedman, Bruce Jay. **A Mother's Kisses** (© 1964). PB 1970.

Joseph, a seventeen-year-old Jewish boy from New York City trying to get into college, is assisted at every turn by his flamboyant mother who is so colorfully portrayed that she becomes almost a caricature of the overprotective mother. Fiction.

Gardner, Herb. **The Goodbye People.** FS&G 1974.

The author of *A Thousand Clowns* again focuses on the appeal of a nonconformist lifestyle. Hope for a second chance comes to a disillusioned wife with a new nosejob, an aging Coney Island businessman dreaming of a comeback, and a job-dominated middle-aged designer who breaks out of the rut. Fiction.

Gay, John. **The Beggar's Opera.** Dover 1973.

A classic social and political satire written in 1729, Gay's musical play is still stageworthy. Although composed as a parody filled with topical references, a modern reader need not recognize the allusions to get pleasure from the action-filled plot about eighteenth-century pickpockets, hussies, and highwaymen.

George, Peter. **Dr. Strangelove, or How I Learned to Stop Worrying and Love the Bomb** (© 1964). Bantam 1972.

A novelization of Stanley Kubrick's film of the same name, this is black comedy about nuclear war between the United States and Russia triggered by a mad American general who has a paranoid fear that Communism and other forces are trying to take over America. Fiction.

Gill, Brendan. **Here at "The New Yorker."** Random 1975.

Harold Ross began the *New Yorker,* America's leading magazine of sophisticated humor, in 1925. This history by one of the magazine's writers covers the fifty years of its existence with observations and anecdotes about writers James Thurber, Robert Frost, John O'Hara, and many others. Mature nonfiction.

Glashan, John. **Speak Up You Tiny Fool!** Dial 1966.

Readers of *Holiday* magazine may be acquainted with Glashan's pen and ink work, but most of the cartoon sequences originally appeared in England. The tiny, bearded, and bespectacled cartoon character finds himself in situations familiar to all.

Gogol, Nikolai Vasilievich. **Dead Souls.** NAL 1961.

An 1842 novel set in Russia when serfs were registered and counted as "souls" and those who died between registrations were called "dead souls." The rogue Chichikov, wishing to marry an heiress, acquires legal ownership of some dead souls so that he can fraudulently set himself up as a man of means. Mature fiction.

Gould, John. **The Parables of Peter Partout.** Little 1965.

Peter Partout, woodbox philosopher of Peppermint

Corner, Maine, writes letters to the editor that are tall tales at their best. Nonfiction.

Guareschi, Giovanni. **The Little World of Don Camillo** (© 1951). WSP 1973.

Stories about life in the small Italian village which comprises the little world of its priest, Don Camillo. There is warmth and humor in his continual opposition to left-wingers, especially his rival, Mayor Peppone, and in his personal relationship with God. Fiction.

Guthman, Les, editor. **The King and Us: Editorial Cartoons by Conrad.** Clymer 1974.

The editor uses work by Pulitzer Prize winner Paul Conrad, cartoonist for the *Los Angeles Times,* and selections from former President Nixon's statements on Watergate to make satirical and pointed statements about America today. Nonfiction.

Hasek, Jaroslav. **The Good Soldier Schweik** (© 1923). NAL 1930.

Schweik is an open and simple-minded man forced into the armed forces of his country. His leaders all tell him how wonderful it is to die for a country, but Schweik cannot understand. Fiction.

Hein, Piet. **Grooks** (© 1966). Doubleday 1969.

A "grook" is a short poem with a point accompanied by a simple drawing. These poems are funny and sometimes sad, revealing some truths about all of us. (See also *Grooks 2, Grooks 3,* and *Grooks 4,* Doubleday.)

Heller, Joseph. **Catch-22** (© 1961). Dell 1973.

An American bombardier in World War II seeks a way to avoid the combat missions that his glory-mad commander constantly orders, while black market fortunes are made, lives are lost, and the war is somehow won. A bitterly funny war novel which, through a purposely vague theme and structure and antiheroic main character, satirizes a world Heller sees as absurd. Fiction.

Hersey, John. **My Petition for More Space.** Knopf 1974.

Set in the near future when overpopulation forces strict control of living space, the main character stands in a line waiting his turn at the petition window to demand more space than the normal seven by eleven feet. Fiction.

Holbrook, Hal. **Mark Twain Tonight!** Pyramid Pubns 1959.

Holbrook has traveled around the country portraying Mark Twain, performing selections from Twain's works. This collection offers brief excerpts of these selections as Holbrook uses them.

Hooker, Richard. ***M*A*S*H Goes to Maine** (© 1972). PB 1973.

Combining their medical clinic with a fish outlet ("The Finestkind Clinic and Fishmarket"), Hawkeye, Trapper John, and two colleagues continue their madcap adventures in Spruce Harbor, Maine. Fiction.

Hughes, Langston. **The Best of Simple.** Hill & Wang 1961.

This collection of the best stories about Jesse B. Simple, the black "Everyman," presents rare vignettes of life in Harlem. Fiction.

Ionesco, Eugene (translator Donald M. Allen). **The Bald Soprano** (in **Four Plays**). Grove 1958.

The play, which centers on a simple social act—one married couple visiting the home of another—satirizes, through its comic dialogue, the inability to communicate.

Kelly, Walt. **Pogo Revisited.** S&S 1974.

This book contains three Pogo classics, *Instant Pogo, The Jack Acid Society Book,* and *The Pogo Poop Book,* featuring adventures of the inhabitants of Okefenokee Swamp—Pogo the possum, Churchy the turtle, and Albert the alligator.

Kidner, John. **The Kidner Report.** Acropolis 1972.

A satirical guide for anyone who wants to succeed as a Washington bureaucrat. Excellent material for analysis of bureaucratic jargon—its protective vocabulary, formula phrasing, and catchwords for adding weight when substance is light. Nonfiction.

Koch, Eric. **The Leisure Riots.** Tundra Bks 1973.

A comic, futuristic novel about the zany campaigns of a Washington think tank, a group of intellectuals working under a Nazi-like leader who are assigned to combat an underground movement trying to disrupt leisure time activities in an America freed from the drudgeries of work. Fiction.

Koestler, Arthur. **The Call Girls** (© 1973). Dell 1974.

Intellectuals representing different branches of the arts and sciences meet at an international symposium to present their views on the world predicament and to offer approaches for working out plans for survival. Satiric and grimly humorous. Mature fiction.

Kosinski, Jerzy. **Being There** (© 1971). Bantam 1972.

A simple, satiric tale about a mentally retarded young man raised in utter isolation with only a garden and a TV set to occupy his attention. What happens to him when he is forced into the outside world provides a sharp contrastive picture of innocence and experience. Mature fiction.

Levenson, Sam. **In One Era and Out the Other** (© 1973). PB 1974.

Autobiographical reminiscences of a popular comedian from some of his folksy comic routines on television that contrast the present with the good old days. Non-fiction.

Lewinstein, Stephen R. **Computer Coach.** Westminster 1971.

Hubert Rollins is no athlete, but he is a mathematical wizard. When the coach of the Randolph Institute of Technology baseball team is fired after losing fifty-six straight games, computer expert Rollins applies for the coaching job with some mathematical angles to turn a losing squad into a winner. (See also *Double Play,* Westminster.) Fiction.

Livingston, Myra Cohn, editor. **What A Wonderful Bird the Frog Are.** HarBraceJ 1973.

Poems about people and things that writers as different as Thomas Hardy, E. B. White, Jonathan Swift, and Ogden Nash have thought funny.

McHale, Tom. **Farragan's Retreat** (© 1971). Bantam 1972.

In this satiric whodunit, a wealthy Philadelphian is assigned by his conservative family to murder his own son, a militant intellectual dodging the draft in Canada. Language may offend some readers. Fiction.

Milligan, Spike. **Adolph Hitler: My Part in His Downfall** (© 1971). Harper Mag Pr 1974.

Gunner Milligan's humorous account of barracks life in the British Army in the early days of World War II. Some language may offend some readers. Fiction.

Milligan, Spike. **The Goon Show Scripts.** St Martin 1973.

"The Goon Show" was for years one of the most popular and wacky radio comedy shows in England. The three stars were Spike Milligan, Harry Secombe, and Peter Sellers. Contains nine scripts. Nonfiction.

Murdoch, Iris. **Under the Net.** Viking Pr 1964.

Centering on a group of offbeat but attractive Londoners, the fast-moving plot abounds in humorous episodes in which tangled relationships result in unforeseen complications. Fiction.

Nash, Ogden. **The Old Dog Barks Backwards.** Little 1972.

A posthumous collection of seventy-seven short pieces which have never appeared before in book form. Although lacking in a basic theme, these comic verses reflect the contemporary scene.

Nichols, John. **The Milagro Beanfield War.** HR&W 1974.

Joe Moudragón taps an irrigation canal to irrigate his meager and parched land. Joe becomes a symbol to other downtrodden farmers in their battle with Anglo water barons. Some language may offend some readers. Mature fiction.

Orwell, George. **Animal Farm** (© 1945). NAL 1974.

A revolt of farmyard animals leads to the fall of the human owners. This satirical fable, written as an allegory of the Russian Revolution, is really about the nature of power. Fiction.

Parker, Dorothy. **The Portable Dorothy Parker** (© 1944). Viking Pr 1973.

Parker was at the center of the New York City literary scene during the 1920s and 1930s. Her sharp wit and pointedly feminine viewpoint make this collection of stories, articles, poems, and book reviews captivating reading.

Peple, Edward. **A Night Out** (© 1909). Blair 1960.

Omar Ben Sufi, an aristocratic Persian cat of the purest breed, is lured from his "little $80,000 cottage" by a tramp cat. This is the amusing, tongue-in-cheek tale of the night's adventures and Omar's brief taste of the dangers and joys he has missed during his sheltered life. Fiction.

Percy, Walker. **Love in the Ruins, or the Adventures of a Bad Catholic at a Time Near the End of the World** (© 1971). FS&G 1973.

A psychiatrist with a world-saving invention, a bevy of women in love with him, and a burning ambition for the Nobel Prize struggles through Bantu riots and hospital shenanigans set in the near future. Fiction.

Perelman, S. J. **Vinegar Puss.** S&S 1975.

A collection of twenty-two pieces of humor by one of the great contemporary masters of satire and sophisticated wit.

Rogers, W. G. **Mightier than the Sword.** HarBraceJ 1969.

A comprehensive history of writers who have used cartoon and caricature to express "outrage against injustice and tyranny, contempt for stupidity, or grief over tragedy." Mature nonfiction.

Roth, Philip. **Our Gang.** Bantam 1972.

A political satire whose targets are unmistakable, with such main characters as President Trick E. Dixon, Vice President What's-his-Name, Attorney General Malicious, Ex-President Lyin' B. Johnson, and Jacqueline Charisma Colossus. Mature fiction.

Schultz, Charles M. **The Snoopy Festival.** HR&W 1974.

A collection of 700 Snoopy cartoon strips with Snoopy playing his many roles—World-Famous Author, Flying Ace, and Joe Cool being just a few.

Schwartz, Alvin, editor. **Witcracks: Jokes and Jests from American Folklore.** Lippincott 1973.

Humorous examples of outlandish lies, riddles, conundrums, puns, numbskull tales, "hate" and "sick" jokes, and shaggy dog stories. This illustrated collection includes favorites about Little Audrey, Little Willie, and the Little Moron as well as elephant, knock-knock, and Confucius-say jokes. Nonfiction.

Spach, John Thom. **Time Out from Texas.** Blair 1969.

Two hicks go to New York City to play pro basketball. Not used to city-slicker ways, the brothers cause continuous havoc. Fiction.

Swift, Jonathan. **Gulliver's Travels.** Dell n.d.

A brilliant satire of European society and culture written in 1726. Lemuel Gulliver, seaman, recounts his experiences with the tiny Lilliputians, the giant Brobdingnagians, the Laputan scientists, and the Houyhnhnms. Fiction.

Thurber, James. **The Thurber Carnival** (© 1931). Dell 1964.

The best from the work of one of America's greatest humorists. Includes short stories, fables, and cartoons.

Thurber, James. **The Years with Ross** (© 1959). Ballantine 1975.

Humorist James Thurber describes the wild and sometimes wacky world of the *New Yorker* magazine. Harold Ross was the eccentric but brilliant founder and editor of the magazine. Nonfiction.

Trudeau, G. B. **The President Is a Lot Smarter than You Think** (© 1971). HR&W 1973.

A series of "Doonesbury" cartoon collections that reflect the contemporary world through the adventures of its college-age comic characters, including Michael Doonesbury, a Sunday liberal; Mark Slackmeyer, a militant always at odds with his father; B. D., a football player with Vietnam experience; and Phred, his Vietcong friend. Satiric views of Washington politics, war, women's liberation, and other current issues.

Twain, Mark. **The Adventures of Huckleberry Finn** (© 1884). WSP 1973.

Huck Finn, a teenage nonconformist, escapes with a runaway slave down the Mississippi River from a civilized life he cannot adjust to. By letting the reader see America and a cross section of its people through Huck's eyes, Twain creates a masterpiece of comic satire. Fiction.

Twain, Mark. **The Mysterious Stranger and Other Stories** (©1916). NAL 1962.

A collection of some of Twain's humor, from the light-heartedness of "The Celebrated Jumping Frog of Calaveras County" to the bitterness of "The Man That Corrupted Hadleyburg" and "The Mysterious Stranger." Fiction.

Twain, Mark (editor Frederick Anderson). **A Pen Warmed-Up in Hell.** Har-Row 1972.

Subtitled "Mark Twain in Protest," this collection of little-known miscellaneous pieces reveals the master of humor as a pessimistic critic of society appalled by the same evils that abound today—militarism, racism, and greed. Nonfiction.

Twain, Mark. **Pudd'nhead Wilson** (© 1894). Bantam 1959.

On the same day in 1830, two boys are born, one the son of a prosperous landowner, the other the son of his mulatto slave girl. To help advance her child, the slave arranges to substitute her child for the other boy. Then the trouble starts. Fiction.

Untermeyer, Louis, editor. **Great Humor.** McGraw 1972.

A collection of humorous materials—wit, whimsy, and satire—gathered from a survey of 2,000 years of writings in half a dozen languages.

Voltaire, Francoise Marie de. **Candide, Zadig & Stories.** NAL 1961.

Written in 1759 as a satire of the philosophy of optimism, *Candide* is the tale of an innocent's adventures through what his tutor calls "the best of possible worlds." Fiction.

Vonnegut, Kurt, Jr. **Breakfast of Champions** (© 1973). Dell 1974.

A self-satirizing novel about "two lonesome, skinny, fairly old white men on a planet which [is] dying fast," according to the narrator, Kilgore Trout, a science fiction writer and Pontiac dealer who is going insane. Fiction.

Vonnegut, Kurt, Jr. **God Bless You, Mr. Rosewater** (© 1965). Dell 1974.

Eliot Rosewater, super-rich, super-sensitive lover of all

humankind, is considered insane because of his offbeat views, humble lifestyle, and servile dedication to the world's derelicts. But Rosewater finds solace in alcohol and his hobby of fire-fighting. (See also *Cat's Cradle*, Dell.) Fiction.

Vonnegut, Kurt, Jr. **Welcome to the Monkey House** (© 1950). Dell 1974.

A collection of some of Vonnegut's shorter works. The writer presents the logic of black comedy in twenty-five tales. Fiction.

Waugh, Evelyn. **The Loved One** (© 1948). Dell 1962.

A macabre novel satirizing California upper middle-class society, especially its burial customs. Dennis Barlow, employed in a Hollywood pet cemetery, falls in love with Aimee Thanatogenos, a mortuary cosmetician, but gets competition from Mr. Joyboy, an embalmer at the deluxe funereal compound. Fiction.

Weiss, M. Jerry, editor. **Tales Out of School.** Dell 1967.

A selection of stories and sketches about school by America's best-known writers of humor. Such authors as Bel Kaufman, Max Shulman, and Robert Benchley are represented. Fiction.

Wells, H. G. **Tono-Bungay** (© 1909). NAL 1961.

The discovery of Tono-Bungay, a patent medicine, brings fortune and adventures in London to the scientist who discovered it. Fiction.

West, Nathanael. **A Cool Million** (© 1936). Avon 1973.

To help his widowed mother forestall a mortgage foreclosure, young Lem Pitkin sets out for New York to seek his fortune. Before his whirlwind adventures are over, he has unselfishly given of himself—a piece at a time. Fiction.

West, Nathanael. **The Day of the Locust** (© 1950). Bantam 1962.

A satirical novel about Hollywood in the 1930s. Artist Todd Hackett sees his hopes dashed, like those of his grotesque acquaintances—a would-be actress, a dying vaudevillian, a down-and-out cowboy, a dwarf, and a good-hearted bookkeeper. Fiction.

Wibberley, Leonard. **The Mouse That Roared** (© 1955). Bantam 1971.

A satirical farce about a small country whose declaration of war against the United States is not taken seriously until, through a series of ludicrous accidents, it achieves a position of global bargaining power. Fiction.

Wilbur, Richard. **Opposites.** HarBraceJ 1973.

Drawings and poems about the opposites to all kinds of words; for instance, a poem about the opposite of *fox* or of *prince* or of *July*.

Wilson, Tom. **Life Is Just a Bunch of Ziggys.** Sheed 1973.

Straight-to-the-mark cartoon humor. Funny one-pagers about Ziggy, an antihero we can all identify with.

Wodehouse, P. G., and Scott Meredith, editors. **A Carnival of Modern Humor.** Delacorte 1967.

Two writers specializing in humor have selected what they consider to be thirty of the best pieces of humor by writers of the twentieth century. Included are gems from James Thurber, Clarence Day, Jean Kerr, Stephen Leacock, Robert Benchley, and others. Nonfiction.

Youngman, Henny. **Henny Youngman's Greatest One-Liners** (© 1970). PB n.d.

Popular comic Henny Youngman presents the best of his short, short jokes. Nonfiction.

MASS MEDIA

A. Seeing Films: Genres and Topics

Barsam, Richard Meran. **Nonfiction Film: A Critical History.** Dutton 1973.

A comprehensive critical history of nonfiction films with an emphasis on those produced in Great Britain and the United States.

Bogle, Donald. **Toms, Coons, Mulattoes, Mammies, & Bucks: An Interpretive History of Blacks in American Films** (© 1973). Bantam 1974.

Bogle establishes various stereotypes of blacks found

in the movies, tracing them from the early days through
the 1970s. Individual films are treated in depth to show
the roles blacks performed and how the stereotypes
changed historically.

Fenin, George N., and William K. Everson. **The Western from Silents to the Seventies.** Grossman 1973.

The western film began in 1903 with *The Great Train Robbery*. The authors discuss the history, styles, actors, and changes in western films with many still photographs.

Fordin, Hugh. **The World of Entertainment: Hollywood's Greatest Musicals.** Doubleday 1975.

This book is devoted to the musicals produced by Arthur Freed during his thirty years at Mero-Goldwyn-Mayer.

French, Philip. **Westerns: Aspects of a Movie Genre** (© 1973). Viking Pr 1974.

French's analysis includes topics such as politics and the western, heroes and villains, Indians and blacks, violence, and the "post-westerns."

Gabree, John. **The Gangster in Films.** Pyramid Pubns 1973.

Among the topics treated in this book are biographical gangster films, detective films, and films from the 1930s to the 1970s. Recent films like *Bonnie and Clyde* and *The Godfather* are compared with earlier films.

Gifford, Denis. **Science Fiction Film.** Dutton 1971.

Major films in the genre, dating from the 1900s to the late 1960s, are emphasized in the discussions; minor films are also mentioned and related to the central topics. A useful index lists directors, production companies, and alternate titles for over 500 films.

Haskell, Molly. **From Reverence to Rape: The Treatment of Women in the Movies.** HR&W 1974.

Haskell maintains that movies have reinforced the idea of women's inferiority, and she shows the forms that sexual stereotypes have taken. Discussing movies chronologically and topically, the author shows how women have been reduced from one type of sexism, that is, as objects of veneration, to a more recent one where they are presented as objects of humiliation and subjugation.

Kagan, Norman. **War Films.** Pyramid Pubns 1974.

A readable and concise history that treats war films chronologically. Surveys films from *The Birth of a Nation* to *Dr. Strangelove* and **M*A*S*H.*

Kaminsky, Stuart M. **American Film Genres: Approaches to a Critical Theory of Popular Film.** Pflaum-Standard 1974.

Among the genres discussed are gangster films, westerns, caper films, horror and science fiction, musicals, and comedies. Two chapters are devoted to genre directors Don Siegel and John Ford.

Kitses, Jim. **Horizons West: Studies in Authorship in the Western Film** (© 1969). Ind U Pr 1970.

Kitses begins with a discussion of the dominant themes and images of the American West. The emphasis of the book is on three major directors in the genre: Anthony Mann, Budd Boetticher, and Sam Peckinpah.

Lahue, Kalton C. **Continued Next Week: A History of the Moving Picture Serial** (© 1964). U of Okla Pr 1969.

A history of the silent serials, which were a popular offering of the American film industry from 1914 to 1930. Lahue discusses the major stars, films, changes in types of films, and audience response to the serials.

Lahue, Kalton C., and Terry Brewer. **Kops and Custards: The Legend of Keystone Films.** U of Okla Pr 1968.

A detailed history of Mack Sennett's Keystone comedies. The authors discuss specific films and the stars of these famous comedies. (See also Lahue's *World of Laughter: The Motion Picture Comedy Short, 1910–1930,* U of Okla Pr.)

Lucas, George, Gloria Katz, and Willard Huyck. **American Graffiti.** Ballantine 1973.

This book contains the scenario of the film, a listing of the cast and music, and seventy illustrations. The text evokes the film's depiction of being a teenager in the early 1960s.

Maddux, Rachel, Stirling Silliphant, and Neil D. Isaacs. **Fiction into Film** (© 1970). Dell 1972.

In this work the reader follows the step-by-step process of what is involved when an original story, "A Walk in the Spring Rain," is made into a screenplay and then into a motion picture.

Manchel, Frank. **Cameras West.** P-H 1971.

An informal history of the western from *The Great Train Robbery* (1903) to *Butch Cassidy and the Sundance Kid* (1969). The book includes a discussion of major stars; classic westerns such as *The Virginian, Stagecoach,* and *High Noon;* and the impact of technical developments.

Manchel, Frank. **Terrors of the Screen.** P-H 1970.

This book begins with a discussion of the origin of horror films in France and their development in Germany by Wegener, Weine, and others. The rest of the book provides a chronological overview of horror films, concluding with *Rosemary's Baby* and *The Planet of the Apes* (1968).

Manchel, Frank. **When Movies Began to Speak.** P-H 1969.

This brief history of the sound era in films describes the development of sound and the contributions of major sound pioneers such as Case, Lubitsch, and Disney.

Manchel, Frank. **When Pictures Began to Move.** P-H 1969.

Drawings are used to illustrate how "pictures began to move." Movie stills from early films are included.

Maynard, Richard A., editor. **Africa on Film: Myth and Reality.** Hayden 1974.

Analysis and criticism of the representation of Africa in films and examples of the myth of Africa in popular literature and films.

Maynard, Richard A., editor. **The American West on Film: Myth and Reality.** Hayden 1974.

A collection of essays which explore the West as depicted in literature and in films. The last section deals with the trends in westerns since 1960 and the cowboy antihero.

Maynard, Richard A., editor. **The Black Man on Film: Racial Stereotyping.** Hayden 1974.

Topics include a discussion of responses to *Birth of a Nation;* the stereotyping of blacks in films from 1929–1955; a "new" image as represented by the first black movie star, Sidney Poitier; and a consideration of trends for the future, as seen in such films as *Shaft* and *Super Fly.*

Moss, Robert F. **Karloff and Company: The Horror Film.** Pyramid Pubns 1974.

Beginning with silent films, Moss surveys developments in horror movies.

O'Leary, Liam. **The Silent Cinema.** Dutton 1965.

Besides a brief section on the invention of the cinema, chapters are devoted to one-reelers, feature films, silents of the war years, and a lengthy discussion of the cinema between 1919–1929.

Rosenthal, Alan. **The New Documentary in Action: A Casebook in Film Making** (© 1971). U of Cal Pr 1972.

Topics include direct cinema, television journalism, reenactments, specials, and sponsored films. Among those interviewed are Allan King, Frederick Wiseman, Allen Funt, and Norman McLaren.

Sennett, Ted. **Lunatics and Lovers.** Arlington Hse 1973.

An entertaining look at the "screwball comedies" of the 1930s and 1940s. Sennett's analysis of the types of stories and characters which typified these films includes the "Cinderella syndrome," "poor little rich girls (and boys)," and "boss-ladies and other liberated types."

B. Seeing Films: Focus on Directors

Fleming, Alice. **The Moviemakers: A History of American Movies through the Lives of Ten Great Directors.** St Martin 1973.

Each of the eleven essays surveys the contributions and style of a particular director. Beginning with the career of Edwin S. Porter, the book summarizes the work of Griffith, Sennett, DeMille, Flaherty, Lubitsch, Capra, Ford, Disney, Hitchcock, and Kubrick.

Glatzer, Richard, and John Raeburn, editors. **Frank Capra: The Man and His Films** (© 1974). U of Mich Pr 1975.

This anthology examines the man who directed such films as *It Happened One Night, Lost Horizon,* and *Mr. Smith Goes to Washington.*

Harcourt, Peter. **Six European Directors: Essays on the Meaning of Film Style.** Penguin 1974.

Beginning with an introduction to film criticism, Harcourt closely examines the work of Eisenstein, Renoir, Buñuel, Bergman, Fellini, and Godard.

Higham, Charles, and Joel Greenberg. **The Celluloid Muse: Hollywood Directors Speak** (© 1969). NAL 1972.

The authors interviewed fifteen Hollywood directors, covering the Hollywood scene from the beginning of talking pictures until modern times.

Kagan, Norman. **The Cinema of Stanley Kubrick.** HR&W 1972.

An intensive analysis of the work of the man who directed *Dr. Strangelove, 2001: A Space Odyssey,* and *A Clockwork Orange.*

Minnelli, Vincente (with Hector Arce). **I Remember It Well.** Doubleday 1974.

The father of Liza Minnelli, former husband of Judy Garland, and one of the most important directors at MGM, Minnelli shares his life and his experiences with actors and producers from 1940 to the present.

Perry, George. **The Films of Alfred Hitchcock.** Dutton 1965.

This succinct, chronological treatment of Hitchcock's work covers the silent films through *Topaz.*

Richie, Donald. **The Films of Akira Kurosawa.** U of Cal Pr 1965.

Kurosawa is a Japanese film director who has made an international reputation for himself with the films *Rashomon, Ikiru, The Seven Samurai,* and others.

Samuels, Charles Thomas. **Encountering Directors** (© 1972). Cap Putnam 1973.

Samuels interviews eleven major directors, including Truffaut, Fellini, Bergman, Renoir, and Hitchcock.

Sarris, Andrew. **The American Cinema: Directors and Directions, 1929–1968** (© 1968). Dutton 1969.

Sarris groups 200 American directors into eleven categories and briefly discusses the work of each director. (See also *Interviews with Film Directors,* Avon.)

Walsh, Raoul. **Each Man in His Time: The Life Story of a Director.** FS&G 1974.

Walsh has been a Hollywood director from the time of the talkies, working with actors as different as John Wayne, Mae West, Clark Gable, and Jimmy Cagney.

C. Seeing Films: History and Criticism

Agel, Jerome, editor. **The Making of Kubrick's "2001"** (© 1970). NAL 1972.

The book includes "The Sentinel" by Arthur C. Clarke, the short story which was the basis for the film; articles from various magazines on the making of *2001*; portions of the script which were eliminated; a number of interviews with Kubrick; audience response to the film; and reviews.

Armes, Roy. **Film and Reality: An Historical Survey.** Penguin 1974.

This difficult, informative book surveys how realism has been presented in movies in the last eighty years. Three major traditions are discussed: directors who saw films as a direct link with reality, those who saw films as imitating life, and those concerned with "inner reality"—the world of dreams and illusions.

Benchley, Nathaniel. **Bogart.** Little 1975.

A biography of film star Humphrey Bogart that pictures him as both human and admirable.

Bogdanovich, Peter. **Pieces of Time: Peter Bogdanovich on the Movies** (© 1973). Dell 1974.

Collected film essays by the director of *Paper Moon, The Last Picture Show,* and *Daisy Miller.* Includes

Bogdanovich's impressions of actors, directors, movies, and Hollywood.

Cawkwell, Tim, and John M. Smith, editors: **The World Encyclopedia of the Film.** T Y Crowell 1972.

Alphabetized entries of many actors, directors, and producers listing their work and an alphabetized list of films with information about dates and stars and production people. A basic reference tool for film enthusiasts.

Corliss, Richard. **Talking Pictures: Screenwriters in the American Cinema, 1927–1973.** Overlook Pr 1974.

Corliss examines 100 Hollywood movies in terms of screenwriters' contributions. The work of thirty-six writers is discussed.

Crist, Judith. **TV Guide to the Movies.** Popular Lib 1974.

This book contains reviews of over 1,500 films shown on television.

Crowther, Bosley. **The Great Films: Fifty Golden Years of Motion Pictures.** Putnam 1967.

This well-illustrated film history provides an introduction to and commentary on major developments in the movies.

Durgant, Raymond. **The Crazy Mirror: Hollywood Comedy and the American Image.** Dell 1972.

Nostalgia, social history, and film criticism are included in this study of comic movie trends, from slapstick to recent comedy.

Edwards, Anne. **Judy Garland.** S&S 1974.

Garland was both a film star from her youth and a very troubled woman who died long after she had become a legend.

Frank, Gerold. **Judy.** Har-Row 1975.

Judy Garland's life story taken from her personal papers and letters and interviews with those closest to the popular and tragic Hollywood star.

Gish, Lillian (with Ann Pinchot). **Lillian Gish: The Movies, Mr. Griffith, and Me.** P-H 1969.

Gish was one of America's first movie stars. She

worked with the great film director D. W. Griffith and knew almost all the major figures in the early days of American filmmaking.

Kael, Pauline. **Deeper into Movies** (© 1973). Bantam 1974.

This is a collection of 150 movie reviews by one of America's most well known film critics. The reviews, written for the *New Yorker* between 1969 and 1972, provide the opportunity to see, in Kael's words, "the interaction of movies and our national life during a frantic time." (See also *Going Steady*, Bantam; *Kiss Kiss Bang Bang*, Bantam; *I Lost It at the Movies*, Bantam; and *Reeling*, Little.

Kardish, Laurence. **Reel Plastic Magic: A History of Films and Filmmaking in America.** Little 1972.

In seven chapters, Kardish provides a compact yet detailed history of the movies, ranging from the early Kinetoscope to today's experimental films.

Kauffmann, Stanley. **A World on Film.** Dell 1967.

This collection of film criticism and articles on films written between 1958 and 1965 is arranged in sections showing how external pressures of culture, acting techniques, and attitudes of various countries influence movie productions.

Knight, Arthur. **The Liveliest Art: A Panoramic History of the Movies** (© 1957). NAL 1971.

This history of the movies traces the cinema's growth from 1895. Includes the author's annotated list of the hundred best books on films.

Latham, Aaron. **Crazy Sunday: F. Scott Fitzgerald in Hollywood** (© 1971). PB 1972.

The last years of author F. Scott Fitzgerald's life, which he spent trying to earn a living writing for the movies, are the focus of this book. Latham discusses Fitzgerald's screenplays and portrays a writer in despair. For a 1976 treatment of Fitzgerald's years in Hollywood—and those of four other distinguished writers—see Tom Dardis, *Some Time in the Sun*, Scribner.

Maltin, Leonard. **Movie Comedy Teams.** NAL 1974.

Individual chapters are devoted to major comedians such as Laurel and Hardy, Wheeler and Woolsey, the

Marx Brothers, the Three Stooges, and Abbott and Costello. Each chapter includes a brief biography of the performers, critiques of their films, and plot summaries.

Manvell, Roger. **Chaplin.** Little 1974.

Throughout the book, Manvell is concerned with relating Chaplin's life and work to broader social and political issues.

Nobile, Philip, editor. **Favorite Movies: Critics' Choice.** Macmillan 1973.

A collection of film critics' essays on their favorite movies. Among the critics included are Dwight Macdonald, Peter Bogdanovich, Jay Cocks, John Simon, Judith Crist, Molly Haskell, and Richard Schickel.

Quigly, Isabel. **Charlie Chaplin: Early Comedies.** Dutton 1968.

Brief analyses and many photographs comprise this book that focuses on Chaplin's films made between 1914 and 1918.

Robinson, David. **Buster Keaton.** Ind U Pr 1969.

A study of the comedies of Buster Keaton. Films are described, analyzed, and related to the circumstances in which they were made.

Sennett, Ted, editor. **The Movie Buff's Book.** Pyramid Pubns 1973.

Part of a series of brief screen biographies of major Hollywood performers. Each volume is devoted to a star and includes a filmography of the performer's work.

Shales, Tom. **The American Film Heritage: Impressions from the American Film Institute Archives.** Acropolis 1972.

This anthology of "impressions," written and visual, is a good resource book. Not intended as a film history, the discussions and photographs dramatically convey the development of the movies.

Simon, John. **Movies into Film: Film Criticism 1967–1970** (© 1971). Dell 1972.

A collection of essays by one of America's most caustic and controversial film critics.

Swindell, Larry. **Body and Soul: The Story of John Garfield.** Morrow 1975.

Garfield, a Hollywood film star of the 1940s, was born on New York City's lower East Side. A tough kid living in a tough city slum, Garfield became interested in acting and succeeded as one of the first movie antiheroes.

Tuska, John. **The Filming of the West.** Doubleday 1976.

Organized into seven periods, one hundred representative westerns made between 1903–1972 are discussed in terms of cast, production work, and financing.

Windeler, Robert. **Sweetheart: The Story of Mary Pickford.** Praeger 1974.

Pickford's career began in 1909 and ended in 1932 when she retired. This book provides many stories about stars, directors, and the movie business.

Wood, Michael. **America in the Movies.** Basic 1975.

The author believes that the movies of the 1940s and 1950s reveal what America believed in and what it may believe in yet. He discusses such films as *Singin' in the Rain, Best Years of Our Lives, Citizen Kane, Gone with the Wind,* and *The Ten Commandments.*

Zolotow, Maurice. **Shooting Star: A Biography of John Wayne.** S&S 1974.

The life of John Wayne: his football days at the University of Southern California, his early cowboy movies, his first starring role in a major film, *Stagecoach,* and his many western films since then. The book covers Wayne's politics, marriages, and his relations with and feelings about Hollywood directors and friends.

D. Seeing Films: Film Study

Bluestone, George. **Novels into Film.** U of Cal Pr 1957.

The introductory essay, "The Limits of the Novel and the Limits of the Film," presents a thorough discussion of the differences and similarities between the two forms. The remainder of the book analyzes six films based on novels: *The Informer, Wuthering*

Heights, Pride and Prejudice, The Grapes of Wrath, The Ox-Bow Incident, and *Madame Bovary.*

Gottesman, Ronald, and Harry Geduld, editors. **Guidebook to Film.** HR&W 1972.

This book contains annotations of books and periodicals and a list of theses and dissertations about films; guides to museums, archives, and film schools; sources for equipment and supplies; distributors of films; film organizations, festivals, and contests; types of movie awards; and a glossary of film terminology.

Jacobs, Lewis, editor. **Introduction to the Art of the Movies.** FS&G 1960.

The chronological format of the essays enables the reader to see how attitudes toward film have changed and how critics at different stages of film development reacted to the medium.

Jacobs, Lewis, editor. **The Movies As Medium.** FS&G 1970.

Thirty-six directors present brief statements on filmmaking. Other sections deal with "The Plastic Elements" (image, movement, time and space, color, and sound) and "The Plastic Structure" (composition and form).

Jinks, William. **The Celluloid Literature: Film in the Humanities.** Glencoe 1974.

An introduction to film that focuses on the relationship between narrative film and literature. Topics such as language, point of view, structure, and sound are discussed.

Kuhns, William. **Movies in America.** Pflaum-Standard 1972.

Kuhns focuses on two aspects of films in America: "the sophistication and broadening of the movies as an art form, and the complex interrelationships between a period and the movies of that period."

Kuhns, William, and Robert Stanley. **Exploring the Film.** Pflaum-Standard 1968.

A range of topics, including visual language, filmic drama, the documentary, and film criticism, among others, makes up this introduction to film.

Perkins, V. F. **Film as Film.** Penguin 1972.

Individual chapters are devoted to early films and criticism; the relationship between technology and filmmaking; the concepts of form, imagery, empathy; and the ways in which films are a "collective enterprise."

Sadoul, Georges (editor and translator Peter Morris). **Dictionary of Film Makers.** U of Cal Pr 1972.

Biographical information and critical evaluations are given for over 1,000 filmmakers from sixty countries.

Sadoul, Georges (editor and translator Peter Morris). **Dictionary of Films.** U of Cal Pr 1972.

Approximately 1,300 films from fifty countries, including America, are discussed.

Stephenson, Ralph, and J. R. Debrix. **The Cinema as Art.** Penguin 1965.

Presents the relationship between film aesthetics and such topics as space, time, sound, and "reality."

E. Making Films

Andersen, Yvonne. **Make Your Own Antimated Movies.** Little 1970.

This brief volume provides an introduction to making animated films. Technical points are clearly explained, and each step in producing the animation is illustrated.

Brosnan, John. **Movie Magic.** St Martin 1974.

After a brief definition of special effects, Brosnan provides topical and chronological discussions of how "mechanical effects," such as car crashes or explosions, and "photographic effects," such as rear projection or optical printers, are used to create illusions in the movies.

Herman, Lewis. **A Practical Manual of Screen Playwriting for Theater and Television Films.** NAL 1963.

The book's three sections concern plot and characters; camera shots and special effects; and elements that enhance a script, such as tempo, props, sound, music, and format.

Horvath, Joan. **Filmmaking for Beginners.** Nelson 1974.

Among the topics included are the camera, the script, and the techniques of shooting. Editing, sound, and animation are also discussed.

Kael, Pauline, Herman J. Mankiewicz, and Orson Welles. **The Citizen Kane Book.** Little 1971.

Kael discusses Welles's movie *Citizen Kane* as well as the complete shooting script, including major frames from the film. There is also a section on the "cutting continuity"—the record of how the movie was edited.

Kuhns, William, and Thomas F. Giardino. **Behind the Camera.** Pflaum-Standard 1970.

A comprehensive guide to filmmaking that discusses cameras, lenses, composition, lighting, sound, shooting scripts, editing, and special effects, among other things. Photographs and drawings are used to provide examples of the equipment and topics discussed.

Lambert, Gavin. **The Making of "Gone with the Wind."** Little 1973.

This book ranges from the career of the film's producer, David O. Selznick, to how the original novel was written; and from the casting of the stars to technical details and production costs. Particularly interesting is the description of how the burning of Atlanta was achieved on the screen.

Livingston, Don. **Film and the Director** (© 1953). Putnam 1970.

Every aspect of filmmaking, ranging from basic screen techniques to the commercial aspects, is included here.

Manoogian, Haig P. **The Film-Makers Art.** Basic 1966.

Discussions of the filmmaker's perspective, film structure and craft, planning, production, and editing.

Morrow, James, and Murray Suid. **Moviemaking Illustrated: The Comicbook Filmbook.** Hayden 1973.

The authors use the comic book panel format to illustrate the topics discussed.

Pincus, Edward. **Guide to Filmmaking** (© 1969). NAL 1972.

Major sections focus on types of films, cameras, exposures, filming procedures, lighting, processing, and editing.

Platt, Joan, editor. **Young Animators and Their Discoveries: A Report from Young Filmakers Foundation.** Praeger 1973.

In a collection of twelve interviews, amateur filmmakers tell how they create animated films and special effects.

Trojanski, John, and Louis Rockwood. **Making It Move.** Pflaum-Standard 1973.

This comprehensive handbook contains step-by-step directions for making animation without film, handmade films, puppet-doll animation, object animation, cut-out animation, kinestasis, pixillation, and motion distortion.

F. Television and Radio

Anderson, Chuck. **The Electric Journalist: An Introduction to Video.** Praeger 1973.

The book treats such topics as how videotape systems work, the basic techniques of editing and production, and problems of street shooting and interviewing.

Cavett, Dick, and Christopher Porterfield. **Cavett.** HarBraceJ 1974.

The life story of the television personality and talkshow host, his growing up in Nebraska, his beginnings in show business, his show and his guests, and many comments on television and its values and problems.

Epstein, Edward Jay. **News from Nowhere: Television and the News.** VinRandom 1973.

Epstein examines economic, political, and organizational factors that shape television news. Besides looking at how news is gathered, organized, and presented, Epstein suggest ways television could improve its handling of news reporting.

Friendly, Fred W. **Due to Circumstances beyond Our Control. . . .** VinRandom 1967.

A former president of the Columbia Broadcasting System combines personal memoirs with a critique of the television industry.

Galanoy, Terry. **Tonight!** Warner Bks 1972.

The most popular talk-show in television history is the "Tonight Show." The author gives an anecdote-filled history of the show and its four hosts: Jerry Lester, Steve Allen, Jack Paar, and Johnny Carson.

Gerrold, David. **The Trouble with Tribbles.** Ballantine 1973.

Gerrold describes how he wrote and sold an episode for "Star Trek." He traces the episode's development through a rough outline to final revised draft.

Gerrold, David. **The World of "Star Trek."** Ballantine 1973.

The development of the TV show, its writers, stars, and technicians, and the fans' reactions. The book includes a listing of each episode's writers and actors.

Herron, Edward A. **Miracle of the Air Waves: A History of Radio.** Messner 1969.

From the discovery of the wireless by the Italian scientist Guglielmo Marconi, radio has undergone many changes, from a toy and a scientific curiosity to a means of world communication for news, entertainment, and culture.

Hilliard, Robert L., editor. **Understanding Television: An Introduction to Broadcasting.** Hastings 1964.

The growth, organization, and impact of television studio and control equipment, producing, writing, directing, and staging.

Hoyt, Olga G., and Edwin P. Hoyt. **Freedom of the News Media.** Seabury 1973.

The authors examine specific threats to media in the 1970s. Topics include problems of censorship, media bias, and professional ethics in both print and electronic media. Case histories and legal decisions provide concise, clear examples of major issues.

Johnson, Nicholas. **How to Talk Back to Your Television Set.** Bantam 1970.

A former member of the Federal Communications Commission discusses the impact of television and how reforms can be made. The first chapters deal with television's influence, the problems of corporate control and censorship, and the growth of communications technology such as cable television. After discussing the problems and implications, Johnson turns to how Congress and the FCC might create changes.

Koch, Howard. **The Panic Broadcast: Portrait of an Event.** Little 1970.

Koch recounts the famous radio show of October 30, 1938, when Orson Welles's Mercury Theatre performed *Invasion from Mars*. Many listeners did not realize the "invasion" was a radio drama.

Lackmann, Ron. **Remember Radio.** Putnam 1970.

A nostalgic look at radio from the late 1930s to the early 1950s, this book contains photos of the original stars, excerpts from scripts, cast listing, and advertisements.

Lackmann, Ron. **Remember Television.** Putnam 1971.

Television's early years are the subject of this pictorial essay. Lackmann briefly discusses major shows produced between 1947 and 1958.

Mayer, Martin. **About Television.** Har-Row 1972.

An examination of modern television, its development, quality, news programs, comedies, advertising.

Murrow, Edward R. (editor Edward Bliss, Jr.). **In Search of Light: The Broadcasts of Edward R. Murrow, 1938–1961** (© 1967). Avon 1974.

Murrow was a distinguished American radio and TV news reporter assigned to London during World War II. This collection of his broadcasts covers virtually all the big stories he reported on in his career. Mature.

Newcomb, Horace. **TV: The Most Popular Art.** Doubleday 1974.

Television is, the author argues, our most popular art form, and he comments on westerns, mysteries, soap operas, sports shows, adventure shows, and situation comedies.

Rhymer, Paul (editor Mary Frances Rhymer). **The Small House Half-Way Up in the Next Block.** McGraw 1972.

One of the most popular daytime comedies on radio

during the 1940s was "Vic and Sade." Ray Bradbury suggests in his foreword why the show was so popular with so many people, including young people. The remainder of the book consists of thirty scripts.

Shulman, Arthur, and Roger Youman. **The Television Years.** Popular Lib 1973.

A pictorial survey from 1947 to 1972, this book provides brief essays on changing styles, programs, and fads in television.

Skornia, Harry J. **Television and the News: A Critical Appraisal.** Pacific Bks 1968.

Skornia explores problems of handling news, including censorship and legal problems. Three case histories examine news problems in depth.

Stasheff, Edward, and Rudy Bretz. **The Television Program: Its Direction and Production.** Hill & Wang 1951.

A comprehensive, often technical, discussion of how television shows are created. Among the topics are program formats, camera concepts, pictorial composition, direction, and production.

Trapnell, Coles. **Teleplay: An Introduction to Television Writing.** Hawthorn 1974.

Practical advice from a television writer and producer on how to write a television play and outline, working with actors, and selling the script.

Whitfield, Stephen E., and Gene Roddenberry. **The Making of "Star Trek."** Ballantine 1968.

This history will appeal to fans of "Star Trek" as well as to those interested in how a television show is conceived and produced. Written with the cooperation of Gene Roddenberry, the program's producer, the text includes memos, letters, production notes, and excerpts from scripts.

G. Other Mass Media

Cantor, Muriel G. **The Hollywood TV Producer.** Basic 1971.

TV producers—their relationship with writers, directors, and actors; their role in terms of the network and of the viewing audience; their concerns in selecting shows; and how their values shape the program's contents.

Cirino, Robert. **Don't Blame the People.** VinRandom 1971.

Cirino explores the implications for society when the communications system can be used by special interest groups. He discusses how media have manipulated issues such as hunger in America, auto safety, effects of smoking, pollution, and overpopulation, among others.

Cirino, Robert. **Power to Persuade: Mass Media and the News.** Bantam 1974.

Through 150 case studies of decision making in media, Cirino presents issues such as objectivity in media, censorship, and the influence of advertisers.

Gordon, John. **Stuff, Etc.** Lippincott 1970.

A collage with text describing how we dehumanize ourselves and destroy our language through advertising and mass media.

McLuhan, Marshall. **Understanding Media: The Extensions of Man.** NAL 1964.

McLuhan believes that the medium is the message: we need to study both what people send as a message and the means or media used. He comments on films, comics, ads, games, phonograph records, TV, and many other media. An influential and sometimes difficult book by an often provocative thinker. (See also *War and Peace in the Global Village,* Bantam.) Mature.

McLuhan, Marshall, and Quentin Fiore. **The Medium Is the Massage: An Inventory of Effects.** Bantam 1967.

A mixed-media presentation of how electronic technology is changing people's lives. A good introduction to McLuhan's theories.

Stein, M. L. **Shaping the News.** WSP 1974.

A journalist describes how news is gathered, written, and edited; how internal censorship and external pressures often control the news; and how the media may influence voting, life styles, and social change. Mature.

Stein, Robert. **Media Power: Who Is Shaping Your Picture of the World?** HM 1972.

Stein explores the implications of how the media increasingly shape people's view of reality. He discusses how media power is affecting various aspects of American journalism, such as the underground press, New Journalism, large newspapers, and magazines.

Stevens, Paul. **I Can Sell You Anything.** Ballantine 1972.

An advertising man describes how ads are made, why they work, and how one can avoid being misled by advertisements.

Tebbel, John. **The American Magazine: A Compact History.** Hawthorn 1969.

Tebbel traces the developments in American magazines from 1741 to the late 1960s.

Tebbel, John. **The Compact History of the American Newspaper.** Hawthorn 1969.

An overview of the role of newspapers in American society from colonial times to the present. Among the topics discussed are censorship, propaganda, tabloids, development of journalism as a business, changes in newspaper style and design, and the role of news services and syndicates. For the history of a single major newspaper, the *New York Times,* see Gay Talese, *The Kingdom and the Power,* Bantam.

Valdes, Joan, and Jeanne Crow, editors. **The Media Reader.** Pflaum-Standard 1975.

The book is divided into three main sections: "The Workings" provides an introduction to the processes of media; "The Mass Message" focuses on the effects of media; and "The Personal Message" examines communication through media such as film, photography, and popular music.

Valdes, Joan, and Jeanne Crow. **The Media Works.** Pflaum-Standard 1973.

An overview of newspapers, radio, television, magazines, comics, popular songs, and "underground" media. Topics range from brief histories of the various media to analyses of specific advertising techniques.

SPORTS

Acton, Jay. The Forgettables (© 1973). Bantam 1974.

Acton describes the games and players of the Potts-town (Pennsylvania) Firebirds in their final season of minor league football. Though the season culminates in a championship, the book is not about success or glory but about people who dream of the big time and who will never get there. Nonfiction.

Angell, Roger. The Summer Game (© 1972). Popular Lib 1973.

A sportswriter covers ten years of baseball and the stars of that decade like Willie Mays, Whitey Ford, Maury Wills, Hoyt Wilhelm, Don Larson, and Curt Flood. Nonfiction.

Ashe, Arthur (with Frank Deford). **Arthur Ashe, Portrait in Motion.** HM 1975.

Ashe, the 1975 Wimbledon champion, covers one year of his life and tennis playing. He explains the world of professional tennis, the players, matches, and travel, his experiences in South Africa, and what it means to be a black man playing a predominantly white professional sport. For the 1976 biography of Bill Tilden, an earlier tennis great, see Frank Deford, *Big Bill Tilden: The Triumphs and the Tragedy,* S&S. Nonfiction.

Baldwin, Stan, Jerry Jenkins, and Hank Aaron. Bad Henry. Chilton 1974.

The biography of Henry Aaron, baseball superstar who broke Babe Ruth's lifetime home run record. Nonfiction.

Barkow, Al. Golf's Golden Grind. HarBraceJ 1974.

Greatness in golfing does not come from winning one tournament but from winning consistently on the tour. The author covers major events and golfers from the 1890s, when golf was a sport of the upper class, to the present, with golf now being played by millions. Nonfiction.

The Baseball Encyclopedia. Macmillan 1976.

The complete baseball reference book—records of individual players and teams, the baseball Hall of Fame, batting and pitching leaders, world champion teams, and all-star games. (See also *A Baseball Century: The First 100 Years of the National League,* Macmillan.) Nonfiction.

Beddoes, Richard, Stan Fischler, and Ira Gitler. **Hockey! The Story of the World's Fastest Sport.** Macmillan 1973.

A history of hockey in the United States and Canada with details and stories about the players, teams, and controversies. Nonfiction.

Bell, Marty. **The Legend of Dr. J.** Coward 1975.

Julius Erving, Dr. J to those who know pro basketball, has been called the greatest basketball player of our time. His decision to enter the American Basketball Association when it was considered second-rate by the sports establishment is only part of his story. Nonfiction.

Berry, Barbara. **The Thoroughbreds.** Bobbs 1974.

The author traces the history of thoroughbreds and thoroughbred horse racing from the time when it was the sport of royalty to the present day. Included are stories about such famous horses as Man o' War, Citation, and Secretariat. Nonfiction.

Blount, Roy, Jr. **About Three Bricks Shy of a Load.** Little 1974.

Blount spent the 1973 football season observing the Pittsburgh Steelers, a team apparently destined for the Super Bowl but for that year denied the achievement. The accounts of games and players are often frank and rowdy. Nonfiction.

Bradley, Bill. **Life on the Run.** Quadrangle 1976.

Bradley, a forward for the New York Knicks, presents a succinct but informative look inside pro basketball. A skilled and intelligent writer, he gives more than a player's view of the game in addressing its issues and problems.

Brondfield, Jerry. **Woody Hayes and the 100-Yard War.** Random 1974.

Hayes is the head football coach at Ohio State University, where he has been both successful and highly controversial. Episodes involving his charm and success—and toughness and nastiness—illustrate his complexity. (See also Robert Vare, *Buckeye,* Harper Mag Pr.) Nonfiction.

Bryant, Paul W., and John Underwood. **Bear.** Little 1974.

Paul "Bear" Bryant has been a most successful coach of football at the University of Alabama for twenty-eight years. Maybe more important than his winning record has been his reputation as a genuinely decent human being who doesn't subordinate character to football skills. Nonfiction.

Chadwick, Bill, and Hal Bock. **The Big Whistle.** Hawthorn 1974.

Chadwick lost the sight in his right eye in a hockey game, but he came back to play again and later became a referee in the National Hockey League. Nonfiction.

Chavoor, Sherman, and Bill Davidson. **The 50-Meter Jungle.** Coward 1973.

Chavoor, who coached Mark Spitz to seven Olympic gold medals, tells how great swimmers are trained and the problems and prejudices that many swimmers encounter. Nonfiction.

Cope, Myron. **The Game That Was.** T Y Crowell 1974.

Through interviews with players of the early days of pro football, the author creates a history of the conditions, plays, and games that changed the sport from a nearly ignored game to the most popular spectator sport in America today. Nonfiction.

Cox, William R. **The Running Back.** Bantam 1974.

Touch Conover is kicked off his college football team for fighting and feels lucky to get a spot on the Titans, a semiprofessional minor league team. He finds that getting from the Titans to a real pro team is a long, tough road. (See also *Playoff,* Bantam.) Fiction.

Creamer, Robert W. **Babe: The Legend Comes to Life.** S&S 1974.

A delinquent sent to St. Mary's Industrial School for Boys in Baltimore when he was very young, Babe Ruth grew up to become the greatest baseball player of his time and a national hero. He was also the subject of many heroic stories, many of them untrue.

The author tries to separate the truth about Babe Ruth from the myths. Nonfiction.

Davis, Mac. **Sports Shorts** (© 1959). Bantam 1969.

Short pieces, some of them no more than a paragraph or two, about strange or exciting moments in sports. (See also *Baseball's Unforgettables,* Bantam.) Nonfiction.

DeLillo, Don. **End Zone** (© 1972). PB 1973.

The football team at small Logos College badly needs a fast backfield man. Taft Robinson seems to be the answer until he becomes fascinated by mysticism. The narrator, Gary Harkness, is even a less typical jock. Mature fiction.

Diagram Group. **Rules of the Game.** Paddington-Two Continents 1974.

Sports and games from many nations, with rules and regulations. Sports common to the United States—football, baseball, and track and field—are listed, but so are less well known sports like jai alai, Gaelic football, cricket, and korfball. Nonfiction.

Dickey, Glenn. **The Jock Empire: Its Rise and Deserved Fall.** Chilton 1974.

A sportswriter for the *San Francisco Chronicle,* the author writes about the villains and bums and nice guys of professional sports in biting and frank language. Nonfiction.

Dryden, Ken (with Mark Mulvoy). **Face-Off at the Summit.** Little 1973.

The authors recount the tension, excitement, politics, and controversies surrounding the 1972 hockey series between the Canadian all-stars and a team from the Soviet Union. Nonfiction.

Durant, John. **Highlights of the Olympics, from Ancient Times to the Present.** Hastings 1973.

The individual stars, the records, and the color of the Olympic games, especially since 1896. Nonfiction.

Eskenazi, Gerald. **The Derek Sanderson Nobody Knows.** Follet 1973.

Twenty-six-year-old hockey star Derek Sanderson wound up with one of the largest contracts in sports history—$2.6 million. Sanderson is a flashy hockey player admired by many other players. Nonfiction.

Fleming, Alice, editor. **Hosannah the Home Run! Poems about Sports.** Little 1972.

Poems about baseball, golf, football, boxing, tennis, track and field, basketball, skating, and hockey.

Flood, Curt (with Richard Carter). **The Way It Is.** PB 1972.

A former star outfielder of the St. Louis Cardinals tells about his life and his decision to challenge the "reserve clause" which allowed baseball team owners to determine what team a player must play for. Nonfiction.

Fox, Larry. **The O. J. Simpson Story: Born to Run.** Dodd 1974.

From a ghetto in San Francisco to the Buffalo Bills, O. J. Simpson has always been a runner. This biography includes the football records O. J. set at the University of Southern California and later with the Buffalo Bills. Nonfiction.

Frazier, Walt, and Ira Berkow. **Rockin' Steady: A Guide to Basketball and Cool.** P-H 1974.

The great New York Knicks guard tells about his philosophy and style of basketball playing and living. Nonfiction.

Gilman, Kay Iselin. **Inside the Pressure Cooker: A Season in the Life of the New York Jets.** Berkley Pub 1974.

A sportswriter talks about the New York Jets, the players and their problems, the coaching staff, the game, and the controversies surrounding a once winning team now on a losing streak. Nonfiction.

Glanville, Brian. **History of the Soccer World Cup.** (1973). Collier Macmillan 1974.

Many photographs of stars and games accompany this history of World Cup soccer competition from 1930 through 1970. Nonfiction.

Golesworthy, Maurice, editor. **The Encyclopaedia of Cricket.** St Martin 1974.

Although cricket has never been popular in the United

States, the sport is extremely popular in England and in many of its former colonies. Anyone curious about this game will find rules, players, and details alphabetically arranged here. Nonfiction.

Hall, Donald, Gerard F. McCauley, Charles Morgan, John A. Parrish, and James T. Wooten. **Playing Around: The Million Dollar Infield Goes to Florida.** Little 1974.

During spring 1973, several nonplayers joined the Pittsburgh Pirates baseball team for one week of spring training. Poet Hall, literary agent McCauley, physician Parrish, journalist Wooten, and American Civil Liberties Union Director Morgan write about the fun, mishaps, and frustrations of living the dream of playing major league baseball. Nonfiction.

Harris, Mark. **Bang the Drum Slowly** (© 1956). Dell 1973.

Henry Wiggen, star pitcher of the New York Mammoths, writes about Bruce Pearson, third-string catcher, who is slowly dying of Hodgkins disease. Because of Wiggen's interest in him personally and professionally, Pearson becomes both a better player and a more sensitive human being. Fiction.

Heller, Peter, editor. **In This Corner . . . !** S&S 1973.

Forty world boxing champions tell their own stories, including championship fights and their problems as boxers. Nonfiction.

Heward, Bill (with Dimitri V. Gat). **Some Are Called Clowns.** T Y Crowell 1974.

Once, almost all small towns were visited by barnstorming baseball teams trying to entertain the crowd and pick up a buck or two. This is the story of one of the last of the barnstorming teams, the Indianapolis Clowns, in their forty-fourth year of busing from town to town and living lonely lives on the road. Nonfiction.

Hollander, Zander, editor. **The Modern Encyclopedia of Basketball.** Four Winds 1972.

Beginning with a history of basketball, the book includes a year-by-year account of college basketball from 1937 to 1972 and professional basketball from 1946 to 1972. Records, stars, rules, teams—almost anything anyone would want to know about basketball. Nonfiction.

Hollander, Zander, and Hal Bock, editors. **The Complete Encyclopedia of Ice Hockey.** P-H 1974.

Teams, players, records, rules, and history are covered in this mammoth account of a popular sport. Nonfiction.

Holoway, John. **Voices from the Great Black Baseball Leagues.** Dodd 1975.

From 1886 to 1947, when Jackie Robinson was signed by the Dodgers, some of the best baseball played in America was between black teams. The author traveled across the country interviewing veterans of black baseball and getting stories about legendary stars like Josh Gibson, Newt Allen, Buck Leonard, Hilton Smith, Cool Papa Bell, and Satchel Paige. Nonfiction.

Jackson, C. Paul. **Rose Bowl Pro.** Hastings 1970.

Bo Greyam, star left halfback for Michigan State, wants to play pro football so badly that he allows his feelings to influence his play for his college team. (See also *Second Time Around Rookie,* Hastings.) Fiction.

Jennison, Keith E., editor. **The Concise Encyclopedia of Sports.** Watts 1970.

Rules, some history, and many illustrations of more than fifty sports and games. Nonfiction.

Jordan, Pat. **A False Spring.** Dodd 1975.

As a high school baseball pitcher, Jordan was a certainty to make the major leagues in no time at all. But pitching in the minors was no snap and instead of becoming the star everyone knew he'd be, he slowly recognized that he'd never get anyplace in baseball. Honest about sports and sex and graphic in language and situations. Nonfiction.

Jordan, Pat. **The Suitors of Spring.** Dodd 1973.

Profiles of baseball pitchers, well-known ones like Tom Seaver, retired ones like Bo Belinsky and Johnny Sain, and comparative unknowns like Art DeFilippis and Steve Dalkowski. Nonfiction.

Kahn, Roger. **The Boys of Summer.** NAL 1973.

The Brooklyn Dodgers of the 1950s were one of baseball's all-time great teams. The author thoughtfully describes the players then and where and what they are now. Nonfiction.

Karst, Gene, and Martin J. Jones, Jr. **Who's Who in Professional Baseball.** Arlington Hse 1973.

Alphabetically arranged biographies of over 1,500 professional baseball players from 1846 to the present. Nonfiction.

Kaye, Ivan N. **Good Clean Violence: A History of College Football.** Lippincott 1973.

A history of college football from its beginning. The author writes about the coaches, many of the major players and games, and the changes that have taken place in the rules and the action in the last 103 years. Nonfiction.

Killy, Jean-Claude (with Al Greenberg). **Comeback.** Macmillan 1974.

At thirty, Killy was regarded as a has-been. Then after five years with no skiing competition, the World Cup and Olympic champion started on his comeback trail which eventually led to his winning the Grand Prix. Nonfiction.

Knudson, R. R. **Fox Running.** Har-Row 1975.

Fox Running runs for many reasons, but when she is asked to run for a university by a former Olympic runner, she is not sure that she can run on someone else's terms. Fiction.

Knudson, R. R., and P. K. Ebert, editors. **Sports Poems.** Dell 1971.

Football, basketball, baseball, and a variety of minor sports, from surfing to bronco busting, figure in these poems, including the popular standard "Casey at the Bat" and some of those prefight harangues by Muhammad Ali. For a 1975 collection of short stories combining sports and science fiction, see Martin Harry Greenberg, et al., editors, *Run to Starlight: Sports through Science Fiction,* Delacorte.

Koppett, Leonard, editor. **The New York Times at the Super Bowl.** Quadrangle 1974.

By reprinting columns from the sports section of the *New York Times,* the author gives a day-by-day pic-

ture of Super Bowl games from the first one in 1967
to Super Bowl VIII in 1974. Nonfiction.

Libby, Bill. **Classic Contests of Sports.** Hawthorn 1974.
Brief accounts of memorable sports events in baseball,
basketball, golf, football, hockey, boxing, auto racing,
horse racing, tennis, and track and field covering the
last fifty years. Nonfiction.

Lipsyte, Robert. **Sportsworld: An American Dream-
land.** Quadrangle 1975.
A well-executed examination of contemporary professional sports by a sportswriter who isn't often taken
in by the flamboyance of his subject or promotional
views of it. Nonfiction.

Lorimer, Lawrence T., editor. **Breaking In.** Random
1974.
Spencer Haywood, Mickey Mantle, Althea Gibson, and
Don Schollander are among nine outstanding athletes
who tell about their early careers. Nonfiction.

Lyttle, Richard B. **A Year in the Minors.** Doubleday
1975.
The San Jose Bees are a typical modern minor league
baseball club made up mostly of college-educated
young players who have one or two years to find out
if they have any hope of making the majors. Many
details and stories about training young players and
promoting minor league teams. Nonfiction.

McCallum, John. **The World Heavyweight Boxing
Championship: A History.** Chilton 1974.
This is the story of twenty-four heavyweight cham-
pions from John L. Sullivan to George Foreman.
Nonfiction.

McCallum, John, and Charles H. Pearson. **College
Football U.S.A. 1869 . . . 1972.** McGraw 1972.
A history of football, the early days, the All-Ameri-
cans, some exciting games, Knute Rockne, records of
schools, the evolution of the rules of football, football
awards, and the bowl games. Nonfiction.

McKay, John (with Jim Perry). **McKay: A Coach's
Story** (© 1974). Atheneum 1975.
Many coaches regard McKay as one of the great foot-

ball thinkers and coaches of all time. His University of Southern California teams won many Rose Bowl games and several national championships. Nonfiction.

McWhirter, Norris, and Ross McWhirter. **Guinness Sports Record Book.** Bantam 1974.

The third edition offers records in all sports. Nonfiction.

Miller, Peter. **The 30,000-Mile Ski Race.** Dial 1972.

The most demanding international ski competition is the World Cup, a fifteen-race grand tour in the three Alpine events of downhill, slalom, and giant slalom. Miller recreates the races and the work of the skiers preparing for the World Cup. Nonfiction.

Morris, Jeannie. **Brian Piccolo: A Short Season** (© 1971). Dell 1972.

Piccolo's life, his short career as a Chicago Bear football player, his friendship with star running back Gale Sayers, and his fight against cancer. Nonfiction.

Morrison, Lillian, editor. **Sprints and Distances: Sports in Poetry and the Poetry in Sports.** T Y Crowell 1965.

An anthology of poetry about golf, baseball, hiking, boxing, boating, running, football, and other sports.

Mosedale, John. **The Greatest of All: The 1927 New York Yankees.** Dial 1974.

Most baseball fans would agree that the 1927 New York Yankees were probably the greatest hitting team in history. With Babe Ruth hitting 60 home runs and first baseman Lou Gehrig hitting 47 home runs and driving in a record 175 runs, the Yankees had an incredibly great year, even for a fine team used to good years. Nonfiction.

Musick, Phil. **Who Was Roberto? A Biography of Roberto Clemente.** Doubleday 1974.

Clemente won four batting titles, made over 3,000 hits, and was an extraordinary rightfielder. This is his story, from his boyhood days in Puerto Rico until his death in a plane crash on New Year's Eve, 1972. Nonfiction.

Newcombe, Jack. **Six Days to Saturday: Joe Paterno and Penn State.** FS&G 1974.

Beginning with the football game just concluded, the

author covers the next six days as coaches and football team prepare for the next game. Nonfiction.

Orr, Jack. **The Black Athlete: His Story in American History** (© 1969). Pyramid Pubns 1970.

Black athletes are an integral part of amateur and professional athletics today, but the author uncovers a history of black athletes that will surprise many readers. Nonfiction.

Pepe, Phil. **Great Comebacks in Sport.** Hawthorn 1975.

Short accounts of great teams and great players that have come back from failure—the New York Jets, Sandy Koufax, Joe Louis, the old Boston Braves, the New York Knicks, Muhammad Ali. Nonfiction.

Pepe, Phil. **The Wit and Wisdom of Yogi Berra.** Hawthorn 1974.

Berra may not have a beautiful face, but he has had an interesting life and has had some funny things happen to him. Nonfiction.

Peterson, Robert. **Only the Ball Was White.** P-H 1970.

Until 1947, black players were barred from playing in organized baseball, except in the Negro leagues. Great players like Jackie Robinson, Roy Campanella, and Satchel Paige played in poorly designed baseball parks under bad conditions for teams like the Birmingham Black Barons, the Indianapolis Clowns, and the Kansas City Monarchs. Nonfiction.

Plimpton, George. **One for the Record: The Inside Story of Hank Aaron's Chase for the Home-Run Record.** Har-Row 1974.

Probably the most exciting event of the 1974 sports year was Aaron's breaking the home run record of Babe Ruth. Plimpton follows Aaron's quest for the new record from the last weeks of the 1973 season until April 8, 1974, when Aaron hit his 715th home run. Nonfiction.

Ralbovsky, Martin. **Destiny's Darlings: A Little League Team Twenty Years Later.** Hawthorn 1974.

In 1954, a team from Schenectady, New York, won the world championship of Little League baseball. Twenty years later, the author interviewed the players on the team, now in their thirties, none of them having lived up to their early athletic promise and some of them bitter because of fame that had come too early in their lives.   Nonfiction.

Rappoport, Ken. **The Trojans: A Story of Southern California Football.** Strode 1974.

Since 1888, the University of Southern California has played football, and during modern times, USC has won five national championships, played in many Rose Bowl games, and placed many players on All-American teams. (See also Will Perry, *The Wolverines: A Story of Michigan Football;* Clyde Bolton, *The Crimson Tide: A Story of Alabama Football;* Denne H. Freeman, *Hook 'Em Horns: A Story of Texas Football;* Jim Weeks, *The Sooners: A Story of Oklahoma Football;* and Wilbur Snypp, *The Buckeyes: A Story of Ohio State Football,* all published by Strode.) Nonfiction.

Reichler, Joseph. **Baseball's Great Moments.** Crown 1974.

Descriptions of highlights in baseball beginning with the hitting of Ted Williams in the 1946 All-Star game. Nonfiction.

Rentzel, Lance. **When All the Laughter Died in Sorrow** (© 1972). Bantam 1973.

A star receiver with the Dallas Cowboys football team and married to a film star, Rentzel became more and more aware that winning was not just necessary—it was an obsession. When he lost, he could not accept defeat; finally, a psychological problem forced him into acts that nearly ruined his life and his career. Mature nonfiction.

Robinson, Sugar Ray (with Dave Anderson). **Sugar Ray.** Viking Pr 1970.

For his weight, Robinson is often said to have been the greatest prizefighter ever to enter the ring. He grew up in Detroit and New York City ghettos, began his rise in the Golden Gloves amateur competition, and finally became a champion. Unfortunately, he found that financial and professional success did not necessarily lead to personal success.   Nonfiction.

Russell, Bill (as told to William McSweeny). **Go Up for Glory** (© 1966). Noble 1968.

Russell was a great college basketball center at the

University of San Francisco and became one of the pro's greatest centers with the Boston Celtics. Tom Heinsohn was a famous Celtic teammate of Russell's and now coaches that team. For his autobiography, published in 1976, see Tommy Heinsohn (with Leonard Lewin), *Heinsohn, Don't You Ever Smile?*, Doubleday. Nonfiction.

Ryan, Bob. **Wait till I Make the Show: Baseball in the Minor Leagues.** Little 1974.

Ryan takes the reader into the world of small towns and the baseball minor leagues, the bus rides, the adoring fans, the veterans on the way down, and the future heroes on the way up. Nonfiction.

Sabin, Lou. **Record-Breakers of the Major Leagues.** Random 1974.

Brief stories about several major league baseball players who broke records: Lou Brock stealing bases, Henry Aaron hitting home runs, Tom Seaver pitching, Mickey Mantle hitting homers and striking out. Nonfiction.

Sayers, Gale (with Al Silverman). **I Am Third** (© 1970). Bantam 1972.

Sayers, black and shy, and Brian Piccolo, white and uninhibited, were close friends and teammates on the Chicago Bears professional football team. Sayers became one of the greatest running backs in pro football history while Piccolo died at an early age from cancer. (See also William Blinn, *Brian's Song,* Bantam.) Nonfiction.

Schaap, Dick. **Massacre at Winged Foot: The U.S. Open Minute by Minute.** Random 1974.

The U.S. Open is the single most important golf tournament in the world. The author covers the 1974 Open at Winged Foot Golf Club in Mamaroneck, New York, where Hale Irwin defeated far better known golfers like Jack Nicklaus and Gary Player. Nonfiction.

Schoor, Gene. **Football's Greatest Coach: Vince Lombardi.** Doubleday 1974.

Lombardi was a great college football player, but he did not become the coach of a professional team until late in life. Then he built a football empire and his own legend at Green Bay. Nonfiction.

Schoor, Gene. **The Jim Thorpe Story: America's Greatest Athlete**. Messner 1951.

Thorpe, an American Indian, was a magnificent football player. He excelled in track and field, but his victories in the 1912 Olympics and the gold medals he was awarded were taken from him because he played professional ball and had not lied about it, as many athletes of his time did. Nonfiction.

Schuyler, Pamela R. **Through the Hoop: A Season with the Celtics.** HM 1974.

Photographer Schuyler interviewed Tom "Satch" Sanders, former Celtic star and presently Harvard basketball coach, about the work, training, and games of the Boston Celtics professional basketball team. Many photographs of the Celtic players. Nonfiction.

Shaw, Gary. **Meat on the Hoof** (© 1972). Dell 1973.

When he attended the University of Texas, Shaw soon discovered that playing football meant total dedication and pain. He began to question whether football was that important, especially when players were hurt in practice and their injuries ignored. Nonfiction.

Smith, Red. **Strawberries in the Wintertime.** Quadrangle 1974.

Smith has been a reporter and sportswriter ever since he graduated from Notre Dame, and for most of his life he has written about sports for either the *New York Herald Tribune* or the *New York Times*. This is a collection of his columns about the many aspects of sports that have intrigued him. (See also Jerome Holtzman, *No Cheering in the Press Box,* HR&W.) Nonfiction.

Smith, Robert. **Baseball.** S&S 1970.

Beginning with 1845, when Alexander Cartwright conceived the game of baseball, Smith writes about players, teams, records, and World Series games that make up the history of the sport. Nonfiction.

Sobol, Ken. **Babe Ruth and the American Dream.** Random 1974.

Ruth was more than a great baseball hitter. He was such a national hero his drinking sprees and his foul mouth were ignored or forgiven. Sobol attempts to determine the truth about this complex and little-understood man. Nonfiction.

Steinmark, Freddie. **I Play to Win.** Little 1971.
University of Texas football player Freddie Steinmark learned he had cancer only six days after his team had been voted number one in the nation. Though his left leg was amputated, Freddie never gave up fighting for his life. Nonfiction.

Treat, Roger, editor. **The Encyclopedia of Football.** A S Barnes 1974.
Despite its title, the book covers only professional football, but its coverage of players, teams, history, scores, league standings, and other facts about pro football is extensive. Nonfiction.

Tutko, Thomas, and Umberto Tosi. **Sports Psyching: Playing Your Best Game All of the Time.** J P Tarcher 1976.
Athletes in every sport know the problem of "choking" at a crucial moment. This book offers techniques for avoiding such problems and for generally improving one's competitive attitude and performance.

Twombly, Wells. **Blanda: Alive and Kicking** (© 1972). Avon 1973.
George Blanda had a remarkable career in pro football: first, a star quarterback for many years in the National Football League and the Old American Football League, then a field goal kicker for the Oakland Raiders and the oldest active player in the pro ranks. Nonfiction.

Wagenheim, Kal. **Clemente!** (© 1973). WSP 1974.
The life of Roberto Clemente, from his early life in Puerto Rico to his greatness as an outfielder for the Pittsburgh Pirates until his death in an airplane crash in 1972. Nonfiction.

Wolf, David. **Foul! The Connie Hawkins Story.** Paperback Lib 1972.
A savage picture of college and professional sports, particularly basketball, through the life story of ghetto-born Connie Hawkins, who fought his way out of New York City. Gifted in sports but not in school,

Hawkins lasted only a short time in college and was involved in a point-shaving gambling episode. Years later, he was finally exonerated. Nonfiction.

Wooden, John (with Jack Tobin). **They Call Me Coach** (© 1972). Bantam 1973.

The life story and philosophy of the one-time high school coach and English teacher who became the basketball coach at UCLA and, over the years, one of the most successful basketball coaches in history. (See also Dwight Chapin and Jeff Prugh, *The Wizard of Westwood: Coach John Wooden and His UCLA Bruins,* HM.) Nonfiction.

Woodley, Richard. **Team: A High School Odyssey.** HR&W 1973.

Although the author uses fictitious names for both people and towns, this is about a real high school football team, from its practice sessions through wins and losses. The close relationship between the players and their coach is stressed. Nonfiction.

Zimmerman, Paul. **The Last Season of Weeb Ewbank.** FS&G 1974.

Ewbank had coached the Baltimore Colts to two world championships and the New York Jets to one world championship. At sixty and in his last year as coach of the Jets, he wanted to go out a winner. Instead, the year for both the Jets and Ewbank was very close to a total disaster. Nonfiction.

ON THE MOVE

Bledsoe, Jerry. **The World's Number One, Flat-Out, All-Time Great, Stock Car Racing Book.** Doubleday 1975.

Race car drivers, promoters, and racing fans are the subjects of this often frank study of the auto racing circuit, from the small race tracks to Daytona. Nonfiction.

Burman, Ben Lucien. **Blow for a Landing** (© 1938). Ballantine 1974.

The Mississippi River comes to life in this entertaining story about Willow Joe and his many quests. Fiction.

Butterworth, W. E. **Wheels and Pistons: The Story of the Automobile.** Four Winds 1971.

A well-illustrated history of the automobile. Nonfiction.

Cottrell, Leonard. **Up in a Balloon.** S G Phillips 1970.

An account of the 200-year history of gas-filled balloons in which heroic individuals—both men and women—entertained crowds, furthered atmospheric research, helped fight wars, and were the forerunners of today's astronauts. Nonfiction.

Cuthbertson, Tom. **Bike Tripping.** Ten Speed Pr 1972.

Practical information about bicycles, equipment, safety, repairs, trips, road racing, and just about anything else a bike rider would like to know. (See also *Anybody's Bike Book: An Original Manual of Bicycle Repairs,* Ten Speed Pr.) Nonfiction.

Edmonds, I. G. **Minibikes and Minicycles** (© 1973). Archway 1975.

Information about bikes and cycles—safety, repair, troubleshooting, and planning trips. Nonfiction.

Engel, Lyle Kenyon. **The Complete Book of Autoracing.** Bantam 1970.

Brief sections on the history of auto racing: great races, stock car competition, drag racing, and rally competition. Nonfiction.

Engel, Lyle Kenyon. **The Complete Motorcycle Book.** Four Winds 1974.

The art and sport of motorcycling, including discussions of different kinds of motorcycles, rules for safe driving, motorcycle maintenance, and racing. Nonfiction.

Engel, Lyle Kenyon, and *Auto Racing* Magazine Editors. **The Indianapolis "500"** (© 1970). Four Winds 1972.

Drivers, cars, records, and accidents are all discussed in this illustrated history of America's most famous automobile race; covers the years 1911–1969. Nonfiction.

Fenner, Phyllis R., editor. **Where Speed Is King: Stories of Racing Adventure.** Morrow 1972.

Short stories of adventure, mystery, thrills, and speed centering on racing and race drivers. (See also *Behind the Wheel: Stories of Cars on Road and Track,* Morrow.) Fiction.

Fletcher, Colin. **The Man Who Walked Through Time** (© 1967). VinRandom 1972.

An account of a man's hike through the entire length of the Grand Canyon, a feat never before accomplished. Fletcher's two-month struggle against the elements in the beautiful but inhospitable canyon gave him a sense of nature's vastness. Nonfiction.

Fletcher, Colin. **The New Complete Walker.** Knopf 1974.

An expert hiker describes the joy of hiking and the equipment needed to make it safe and fun, from shoes to food, backpacks to tents, first aid to maps. Appendices include information on retailers of equipment and on hiking groups. Nonfiction.

Gordon, John Steele. **Overlanding: How to Explore the World on Four Wheels.** Har-Row 1975.

The author, an experienced traveler, gives helpful, specific information on driving anywhere in the world. Facts about costs, how to handle insurance and customs, mechanics, and road damage. Nonfiction.

Halacy, D. S., Jr. **On the Move: Man and Transportation.** Macrae 1974.

A history of people's constant movement around the earth: some of the reasons they have wanted to move, some of the ways they have used in the past, and ways they will likely use in the future. Nonfiction.

Krueger, Robert. **Gypsy on Eighteen Wheels: A Trucker's Tale.** Praeger 1975.

Truck drivers and the lives they lead with hitchhikers, waitresses, the highway patrol, and deadlines. Many excellent photographs. Nonfiction.

Langer, Richard W. **The Joy of Camping.** Sat Rev Pr 1973.

A guide celebrating the joy and freedom of camping in any season with suggestions for making any hiking or backpacking trip more enjoyable. Nonfiction.

Leek, Stephen, and Sybil Leek. **The Bicycle—That Curious Invention** (© 1973). Nelson 1974.

German Baron von Drais invented the bicycle in 1816,

but even he could not have predicted the changes his invention and its place in society would undergo during the next 100 years. Many illustrations. Nonfiction.

Leete, Harley M., editor. **The Best of Bicycling!** (© 1970). PB 1972.

Information about bicycling around the world for sport, for traveling, for health, or for adventure. Information about bike clubs and techniques of biking and many other things. Nonfiction.

Libby, Bill. **Foyt.** Hawthorn 1974.

A. J. Foyt has won more national championship races and more national driving titles than any other auto racer. Nonfiction.

Lyttle, Richard B. **The Complete Beginner's Guide to Backpacking.** Doubleday 1975.

A well-illustrated guide to backpacking, covering wearing apparel, safety, bedding, shelter, cooking equipment, the backpack itself, and trip planning. Nonfiction.

Manning, Harvey. **Backpacking One Step at a Time.** VinRandom 1973.

An illustrated guide with specific tips on equipment, procedures, and dangers. Nonfiction.

McCready, Albert L., and Lawrence W. Sagle. **Railroads in the Days of Steam.** Am Heritage 1960.

The early history of the American railroad industry told through paintings and photographs. Nonfiction.

McKay, Don, editor. **On Two Wheels.** Dell 1971.

An anthology of stories, poems, songs, and essays about the art and joy of riding motorcycles.

Merrill, Bill. **The Hikers & Backpackers Handbook** (© 1972). Arc Bks 1974.

A practical and fact-filled guide for planning and completing short and overnight hikes, including advice on almost all related concerns, from planning menus to selecting shoes. Nonfiction.

Morris, Taylor. **The Walk of the Conscious Ants.** Knopf 1972.

A college professor and seventeen students hiked for

forty days through New Hampshire, Maine, and Canada. Along the way, they met suspicious policemen and natives, but they learned about themselves and what they could endure. Nonfiction.

Olney, Ross R. **Great Moments in Speed.** P-H 1970.

Great car races and great racers from 1903 until today are the subjects of this book about the spills and thrills of speed racing. Nonfiction.

Publications International Ltd. **Complete Buying Guide: Camping Equipment and Recreational Vehicles.** PB 1973.

Evaluations of camping equipment, such as tents, lanterns, backpacks, stoves, and sleeping bags, and recreational vehicles, such as four-wheel drives, tent trailers, motorhomes, and pickups. Nonfiction.

Revson, Peter, and Leon Mandel. **Speed with Style: The Autobiography of Peter Revson.** Doubleday 1974.

Revson was handsome and wealthy; he was also one of the greatest and most famous car racers in the world, winning several Grand Prix races and living a colorful life until his death in a car wreck in 1973. Nonfiction.

Riviere, Bill. **Pole, Paddle, and Portage: A Complete Guide to Canoeing** (© 1969). Little 1974.

Details, with many photographs, of almost anything one would want to know about canoeing—its excitement, the equipment, portaging, and planning a canoeing trip. Nonfiction.

Russell, Terry, and Renny Russell. **On the Loose** (© 1969). Ballantine 1971.

Color photographs of the scenic beauty of the American West are on pages opposite prose and poetry by naturalists and others who write about life, nature, and humanity. Nonfiction.

Ryback, Eric. **The High Adventures of Eric Ryback** (© 1971). Bantam 1973.

Ryback dreamed of walking alone from the Canadian border to the Mexican border. This is his record of the dangers and adventures of the 132 days it took him to walk the 2,500 miles. Nonfiction.

Scalzo, Joe. **Stand on the Gas.** P-H 1974.

Sprint car racing is described along with its famous races and drivers like Bobby Unser and Mario Andretti. Nonfiction.

Shoumatoff, Alex. **Florida Ramble.** Har-Row 1974.

Shoumatoff set off in his old car to ramble around Florida finding out about the state's people, natural wonders, flophouses, orange groves, retirement communities, and anything else that attracted his attention. Nonfiction.

Smith, Robert. **A Social History of the Bicycle.** McGraw 1972.

Beginning with the early development of the bicycle and the allegations that the contraption was dangerous and a tool of the devil, the author chronicles the development and use of the bicycle and its impact upon American life and habits. Nonfiction.

Stout, James, and Ann Stout. **Backpacking with Small Children.** T Y Crowell 1975.

Both authors are experienced backpackers and their advice on equipment, clothing, and other matters is both sensible and lively. Nonfiction.

Thomas, Bill. **Tripping in America off the Beaten Track.** Chilton 1974.

An alphabetized, state-by-state list of interesting but little-known places worth exploring. Nonfiction.

Wallach, Theresa. **Easy Motorcycle Riding** (© 1970). Bantam 1971.

Brief chapters about driving motorcycles intelligently and safely, buying a first motorcycle, and the enjoyment and adventure anyone can have riding a motorcycle. Nonfiction.

SCIENCE, TODAY AND TOMORROW

Angrist, Stanley W. **Other Worlds, Other Beings.** T Y Crowell 1973.

If life exists on other planets in our solar system or elsewhere in the galaxy, the conditions there will have to match a series of criteria which would exclude most planets.

Armstrong, Neil, Michael Collins, and Edwin E. Aldrin, Jr. **First on the Moon: The Astronauts' Own Story.** Little 1970.

The men of *Apollo 11,* the first manned spacecraft to land on the moon, describe in detail the events leading up to and following that moment in July 1969 when Armstrong stepped onto the lunar dust.

Barnett, Lincoln. **The Universe and Dr. Einstein** (© 1957). Bantam 1974.

Einstein's theories of relativity revolutionized twentieth-century science. This account of his discoveries makes all the intricacies of $e = mc^2$ relatively intelligible.

Bova, Ben. **Starflight and Other Improbabilities.** Westminster 1973.

How can we expect to explore even the star nearest to our sun when the trip would take 80,000 years? This and other problems of travel to the outer reaches of the solar system and beyond are discussed in this volume.

Bova, Ben. **The Weather Changes Man.** A-W 1974.

Prehistoric people not only survived the last Ice Age, they also underwent physical and cultural adaptations that permitted them to live in the various climates of the globe.

Branley, Franklyn M. **The End of the World.** T Y Crowell 1974.

Someday life on earth and then earth itself must end. The author describes the steps by which earth will be claimed by the sun billions of years from now.

Branley, Franklyn M. **Pieces of Another World.** T Y Crowell 1972.

Before the first moon rocks were analyzed, scientists speculated about what they might reveal, and while the experts were largely correct, there were still some surprises.

Calder, Nigel. **The Life Game.** Viking Pr 1974.

The explosion of scientific investigation in the years since Darwin proposed his theories has yielded new information about evolution from a number of disciplines. Recent advances in molecular biology, geology, and anthropology contribute to this updated account of the rules governing the "life game." Mature.

Clarke, Arthur C. **Report on Planet Three and Other Speculations.** Har-Row 1972.

A collection of tongue-in-cheek essays by scientist and science fiction writer Clarke which demonstrates not only his keen insight into the workings of our planet but also his sense of humor. Mature.

Clarke, Arthur C., and Chesley Bonestell. **Beyond Jupiter** (© 1972). Little 1973.

The author of *2001: A Space Odyssey* describes a remarkable event in outer space that will take place in the late 1970s, the orbital alignment of the five outermost planets in the solar system. This occasion will provide scientists a unique opportunity to investigate these planets with a single space probe.

Cross, Wilbur, and Susan Graves. **The New Age of Medical Discovery.** Hawthorn 1972.

Robot guinea pigs, telemedicine, deep-freeze techniques, computers endowed with memory banks—these may be common elements of medical practice in A.D. 2000.

Dineley, David. **Earth's Voyage through Time** (© 1973). Knopf 1974.

A detailed survey of the planet on which we live, beginning with its birth 4.5 million years ago. This book considers many questions that have long puzzled scientists about the origin of earth and the changes it is constantly undergoing.

Drummond, A. H., Jr. **The Population Puzzle.** A-W 1973.

Studies of animals both in the laboratory and in the wild suggest that overcrowding causes strange changes in behavior and that there may be strict limits to the level of crowding that humans will be able to tolerate.

Engdahl, Sylvia Louise. **The Planet-Girded Suns.** Atheneum 1974.

The idea that there may be inhabited planets circling stars in other solar systems has not always been popular. This book traces the history of the idea and presents a summary of current opinion on the age-old question, "Are we alone in the universe?"

Evans, Howard Ensign. **Life on a Little Known Planet**
(© 1968). Dell 1972.

The little-known planet is earth, but the life is the
world of insects and their marvelous mechanisms for
adaptation and survival.

Ferguson, Marilyn. **The Brain Revolution: The Frontiers of Mind Research** (© 1973). Bantam 1975.

Research into the functions and abilities of the human
brain, including material on biofeedback and the effects
of psychedelic drugs, dreams, and meditation.

Halacy, D. S., Jr. **The Energy Trap.** Four Winds 1975.

Even though diminishing supplies of organic fuels
have forced scientists to explore other energy sources,
nuclear fusion and solar power are still in their
planning stages as solutions to the energy crisis.

Halacy, D. S., Jr. **The Weather Changers.** Har-Row
1968.

Everybody talks about the weather, but this book
shows what some people have been doing about it.
Halacy describes efforts to induce rain, suppress hail
and lightning, disperse fog, and modify hurricanes,
as well as changes caused by air pollution.

Hawkins, Gerald S. **Splendor in the Sky.** Har-Row
1969.

A history of astronomy: how the Egyptians, Greeks,
and Romans viewed the heavens; what discoveries of
Copernicus, Kepler, and Newton brought to our understanding of stars and planets; and what currently is
of major interest to astronomers.

Heintze, Carl. **Genetic Engineering.** Nelson 1974.

The discovery of the structure of the molecules responsible for heredity may eventually give us the power to
manipulate the future of humanity.

Hellman, Hal. **Transportation in the World of the Future.** M Evans 1974.

Transportation, especially in urban areas, is already
a problem, but the future promises even greater con-
centrations of people in sprawling cities. The author
explores the possibilities for innovation in travel systems of all sorts.

Hey, Nigel. **How Will We Feed the Hungry Billions?** Messner 1971.

Famine and exploding populations in poorer areas of the world are in the headlines today. Developing new strains of crops, irrigating now arid lands, and farming the seas are some of the solutions for averting hunger in the future.

Jacker, Corinne. **The Biological Revolution.** Parents 1971.

The author reviews the work in biology, surgery, bionics, and cybernetics during the last twenty-five years and details some work that is currently underway in these fields, particularly that dealing with the question, "Is there intelligent life in outer space?"

Jastrow, Robert. **Red Giants and White Dwarfs** (© 1969). NAL 1971.

The director of the Goddard Institute for Space Studies describes the nature of the universe, from the smallest subatomic particles to the grandest of galactic structures, pointing out along the way earth's place in this scheme.

Klass, Philip J. **Secret Sentries in Space.** Random 1971.

In this account of the development of satellite reconnaissance, the author describes both how spy-in-the-sky systems operate and what they have done to change the techniques of intelligence gathering.

Langone, John. **Goodbye to Bedlam: Understanding Mental Illness and Retardation.** Little 1974.

People suffering mental illness were once treated worse than prisoners or traitors. The author discusses modern approaches to mental illness and some of the therapies open to doctors.

Lewis, Richard S. **The Voyages of Apollo: The Exploration of the Moon.** Quadrangle 1974.

The voyages of the Apollo missions (1969–1972) have given scientists much information about the moon. Details about its surface and other findings are analyzed.

Lewis, Richard S., and Jane Wilson. **Alamogordo Plus Twenty-five Years.** Viking Pr 1971.

The 1945 nuclear explosion near Alamogordo, New Mexico, ushered in the atomic era. The implications of that event as they have unfolded in the years since are discussed here in a series of essays which describe the scientific, political, and moral aftermath of that fateful July day.

McPhee, John. **The Curve of Binding Energy.** FS&G 1974.

Theodore Taylor, a theoretical physicist, was instrumental in the design of the first atomic weapons and later designed an atomic-powered space rocket that was never built. He presently works on systems for safeguarding nuclear materials from potential do-it-yourselfers.

Metzger, Norman. **Men and Molecules.** Crown 1972.

These eleven essays were adapted from a series of radio broadcasts sponsored by the American Chemical Society. The subjects range from the chemistry of aging to the prevention of polluted oceans. Mature.

Morgenthau, Hans. **Science: Servant or Master?** NAL 1972.

Not everyone is pleased with the direction that contemporary science has taken in this country. The author investigates what he feels to be vital problems concerning the relationship of science to politics, technology, and morality. Mature.

Pallas, Norvin. **Calculator Puzzles, Tricks and Games.** Sterling 1976.

All manner of games and other entertainments for those who know arithmetic and have access to a pocket calculator. (See also Edwin Schlossberg and John Brockman, *The Pocket Calculator Game Book,* Morrow.)

Raphael, Bertram. **The Thinking Computer: Mind inside Matter.** W H Freeman 1976.

A comprehensive survey and explanation of artificial intelligence, including robots and the latest generation of computers.

Rapport, Samuel, and Helen Wright, editors. **Science: Method and Meaning.** WSP 1964.

This collection of scientific essays spans the last 100 years and includes topics from a variety of disciplines, yet each essayist grapples with the same fundamental question: how does a scientist approach his or her work?

Richardson, Robert S. **The Stars and Serendipity.** Pantheon 1971.

Some great astronomical discoveries have been made when the discoverers were in fact looking for something else; these finds include the planet Uranus, the sunspot cycle, and radio waves from outer space.

Rocks, Laurence, and Richard Runyon. **The Energy Crisis.** Crown 1972.

Several possible solutions to the mounting crisis in securing and controlling the use of our energy resources are outlined in this sometimes hopeful, sometimes pessimistic account of what may be possible and what may not be.

Rusch, Richard B. **Computers: Their History and How They Work.** S&S 1969.

An introduction to mechanical brains, how they function, and their place in the world today and tomorrow.

Russell, Helen Ross. **Earth, the Great Recycler.** Nelson 1973.

Spaceship Earth is composed of a series of delicately balanced systems: water, energy, food, and the earth itself, which together comprise the ecosphere, the narrow band on the planet that supports life.

Sagan, Carl, and Thornton Page, editors. **UFO's—A Scientific Debate** (© 1972). Norton 1974.

This collection of essays about the probability that unidentified flying objects might be extraterrestrial space probes neither assumes that UFOs are myth nor that they are the craft of "little green men." Mature.

Shapley, Harlow. **The View from a Distant Star: Man's Future in the Universe** (© 1963). Dell 1967.

This book addresses itself to truly "universal" questions: Can humanity survive the contamination of this world? What place and value do we have in the universe? Do life forms similar to us exist on other planets?

Silverstein, Alvin, and Virginia Silverstein. **The Code of Life.** Atheneum 1972.

Genetics, the scientific study of heredity, made rapid

advances with the discovery of the structure of DNA, a complex molecule that serves as the master code for the structure and characteristics of all living things.

Smith, Norman F. **Uphill to Mars, Downhill to Venus.** Little 1970.

An engineer for the National Aeronautics and Space Administration explains the problems of getting a rocket into space, maintaining it during its flight, and getting it safely back to earth.

Stehling, Kurt R. **Computers and You** (© 1972). NAL 1973.

The promise of the computer age is great, with the application of computer technology to such problems as diagnosing disease, forecasting the weather, and streamlining government bureaucracy.

Sullivan, Walter. **We Are Not Alone.** McGraw 1966.

The science editor of the *New York Times* describes the evidence that suggests man may not be the only intelligent being in the universe and the dilemmas, political, moral, and religious, that we might face upon encountering other intelligent beings.

Taylor, Gordon Rattray. **The Biological Time Bomb** (© 1968). NAL 1969.

Recent breakthroughs in biology present a range of possible changes for the future, including artificial organs and prolonged life expectancy, and such controversial issues as test-tube babies and personality modification.

Taylor, John W. R. **Rockets and Missiles** (© 1970). Bantam 1972.

This fully illustrated introduction to the world of rockets traces their history from tenth-century China and speculates about their future possiblities for both space travel and scientific investigation.

Vergara, William C. **Science in the World around Us** (© 1973). WSP 1974.

This book contains answers to a whole series of questions that at one time or another might puzzle us, from "How does an aerosol can work?" to "What makes a Mexican jumping bean jump?"

Von Ditfurth, Hoimar. **Children of the Universe.** Atheneum 1974.

Human beings may be just inhabitants of a smallish planet in a modest solar system, but nevertheless this German scientist sees all phenomena in the universe as participating in an interrelated cosmic event. Mature.

Ward, Ritchie. **The Living Clocks** (© 1971). NAL 1972.

Biochronometry, a branch of biology which investigates rhythms that regulate the life processes, explains such diverse phenomena as the migration of birds, the nectar gathering of bees, and the stress patterns of human beings. Mature.

Watson, James D. **The Double Helix** (© 1968). NAL 1969.

The inside story of one of the greatest discoveries in biochemistry, the structure of DNA, the heredity molecule, has become a modern classic. Told by one of the men who participated in the discovery, the account bristles with the personal intrigues of life inside and outside the laboratories.

Weiss, Malcolm. **The World within the Brain.** Messner 1974.

The least understood of all human organs, the brain coordinates all functions of the body and all aspects of our behavior. New discoveries about the workings of the brain present possibilities for the treatment of brain-related disorders but also problems for the discoverers. For example, to what degree should this new knowledge be used to control human behavior?

Whitney, Charles A. **The Discovery of Our Galaxy.** Knopf 1971.

Present day understanding of the nature of the universe has developed from a series of discoveries and speculations that have won some individuals fame and others a trip to the stake.

DIGGING INTO OUR PAST

Alsop, Joseph. **From the Silent Earth** (© 1962). Har-Row 1964.

Alsop writes of the Greek Bronze Age civilization

(c. 3500 B.C.), its abrupt end, and its discovery many years later. Over 100 photos, maps, a foldout chronological table, and bibliography.

Ardrey, Robert. **The Territorial Imperative** (© 1966). Dell 1971.

The author examines the territorial drive of animals and birds to control and defend land or airspace and argues that territorial needs are also felt by humans. (See also *African Genesis,* Dell; and *The Social Contract,* Dell.) Mature.

Baldwin, Gordon C. **Inventors and Inventions of the Ancient World.** Four Winds 1973.

Many photographs illustrate the story of how many of our most basic discoveries—fire, the calendar, housing, and the domestication of plants and animals—were made and how many were made more than once. Bibliography.

Baldwin, Gordon C. **Race Against Time: The Story of Salvage Archaeology.** Putnam 1966.

When dams or roads or houses are being constructed and archaeological finds are made, salvage archaeologists are brought in to work under definite time-limits.

Bascom, Willard. **Deep Water, Ancient Ships: The Treasure Vault of the Mediterranean.** Doubleday 1976.

Bascom attempts to pinpoint the location of ancient undersea wrecks in the Mediterranean. Includes charts, tables, drawings, and photographs.

Bass, George F. **Archaeology under Water** (© 1966). Penguin 1972.

An introduction to the whys and wherefores of underwater archaeology, its problems, its successes, its scientific history and future.

Berlitz, Charles. **Mysteries from Forgotten Worlds** (© 1972). Dell 1973.

Berlitz believes that an advanced civilization existed in the Americas thousands of years before Columbus and that this civilization was enriched by visitors from Europe and the Far East. He also explores the legend of the lost continent of Atlantis. Bibliography.

Bibby, Geoffrey. **The Testimony of the Spade.** Knopf 1956.

Written as a companion to C. W. Ceram's *Gods, Graves, and Scholars* (also annotated in this section), this book traces the culture of our early ancestors north from the Alps to Scandinavia and west from Russia to Ireland. Annotated bibliography.

Bray, Warwick, and David Trump. **The Penguin Dictionary of Archaeology** (© 1970). Penguin 1972.

From "Abbevillian" to "Ziwiyeh," this reference book concisely describes, in more than 1,600 entries, the sites, cultures, periods, techniques, terms, and personalities of archaeology.

Brennan, Louis A. **Beginner's Guide to Archaeology.** Stackpole 1973.

The relationships between survey, test, digging, recording, study-analysis, and reporting are described, with details of professional know-how given for each step. Concludes with guides to sites, museums, resources, and periodicals.

Brennan, Louis A. **The Buried Treasure of Archaeology.** Random 1964.

Two topics of archaeology are of primary interest here: first, the effects of shifting weather patterns on ancient people; second, the archaeological importance of areas outside of the Middle East.

Bronowski, Jacob. **The Ascent of Man** (© 1973). Little 1974.

Begun as a series of TV scripts, this inquiry into humanity and its growth covers great inventions, discoveries, and advancements throughout history.

Brunhouse, Robert L. **In Search of the Maya** (© 1973). Ballantine 1974.

The reader experiences the excitement of the discovery of the Mayan civilization and the adventures of the eight amateur archaeologists involved in the search.

Buck, Peter H. **Vikings of the Pacific** (© 1959). U of Chicago Pr 1972.

The romantic story of the settlement of Polynesia by a Stone Age people.

Bushnell, G. H. S. **The First Americans.** McGraw 1968.

The civilizations and cultures of peoples in Mexico, Central America, Peru, and Ecuador before the ninth century. Many illustrations.

Calder, Nigel. **The Restless Earth: A Report on the New Geology.** Viking Pr 1972.

Based on a 1972 British television special, this book explains the work of the "new geologists" who believe earthquakes, volcanoes, and mountain ranges are all caused by a single process: the movement of huge plates that make up the earth's outer shell.

Carter, Howard. **The Tomb of Tutankhamen.** Dutton 1972.

The 1922 discovery of Tutankhamen's tomb was the most important archaeological find in Egypt's Valley of the Kings, because the tomb had not yet been found and looted by grave robbers.

Ceram, C. W. **The First American: A Story of North American Archaeology** (© 1971). NAL 1972.

The history of early dwellers in America told through archaeological findings. One section is devoted to answering the question "What is archaeology?"; the remainder of the book is about burial mounds, Mesa Verde, Bandelier, and other Indian ruins and artifacts. Many illustrations, some in color.

Ceram, C. W. **Gods, Graves, and Scholars** (© 1967). Bantam 1972.

The adventures, accidents, and men that contributed to the development of the science of archaeology; explorations at Troy and in Egypt, Babylonia, and Mexico are described.

Ceram, C. W. **The March of Archaeology** (© 1958). Knopf 1970.

A pictorial history of archaeology with accounts of findings in Pompeii, Crete, Egypt, Babylon, and Mexico.

Collier, James Lincoln. **The Making of Man.** Four Winds 1974.

Collier traces the evolution of prehistoric peoples in terms of how they hunted, made tools, built homes, cared for their children, and dealt with their peers.

Cottrell, Leonard. **Reading the Past: The Story of Deciphering Ancient Languages.** CCPr Macmillan 1971.

A brief history of humanity's desire to understand ancient written languages and how that knowledge has helped us understand civilizations like those of Egypt, Crete, and Babylonia.

Coy, Harold. **Man Comes to America.** Little 1973.

The story of prehistoric peoples in America before the time of the Aztecs. When did they first arrive, how did they exist, and what remains to establish their early existence in America?

Day, Michael H. **Fossil Man** (© 1970). Bantam 1971.

The most concrete evidence for the evolution of our species consists of the fossil bones of human-like creatures who preceded the appearance of modern man. This lavishly illustrated book traces our development from primates, with an emphasis on the evidence of fossil remains, and includes a list of books to read and places to visit.

De Camp, L. Sprague. **Great Cities of the Ancient World.** Doubleday 1972.

A study of the major cities of antiquity: Thebes, Nineveh, Tyre, Babylon, Athens, Carthage, and others. Fine photos, drawings, diagrams, and bibliography.

Fairservis, Walter A., Jr. **The Ancient Kingdoms of the Nile.** NAL 1962.

The political and cultural history of Nubia, Egypt, and the Sudan are surveyed. Fairservis recreates the past using geology, geography, paleontology, and archaeology.

Fay, Gordon S. **The Rockhound's Manual.** Har-Row 1972.

This manual covers rock collecting, identification, and storage and also deals with field work—map reading, use of survey tools, making field and lab tests, and staking a claim. Includes color photos, tables, and a list of selected books and magazines.

Ford-Johnston, J. **History from the Earth.** NYGS 1974.
Archaeological investigations in the Near East, Africa,
India, China, America, and Europe.

Franzen, Greta. **The Great Ship "Vasa."** Hastings 1971.
In 1628 the warship *Vasa* sank to a depth of 100 feet.
This is the story of how the ship was found and raised
300 years later and preserved as a monument to marine archaeology.

Gardner, Martin. **Fads and Fallacies in the Name of
Science.** Dover 1957.
A study of human gullibility and the grotesque dealing with several absurd theories of modern "pseudo-
scientists" and the strange, frequently tragic cults
spawned by these theories. Included are the flat earth
societies, the hollow earth cults, and the sensation
created by Bridey Murphy.

Hamblin, Dora Jane. **Buried Cities and Ancient Trea-
sures.** S&S 1973.
Hamblin explores Turkey, the land of Troy, and the
Euphrates River. Good photos and short bibliography.

Hapgood, Charles H. **Maps of the Ancient Sea Kings.**
Chilton 1966.
The author offers evidence that advanced civilizations
inhabited our world before the end of the Ice Age,
thousands of years before the great Egyptian and
Greek civilizations.

Hawkes, Jacquetta, and Bernard V. Bothmer. **Pharaohs
of Egypt.** Am Heritage 1965.
A behind-the-scenes look at the life of the pharaohs,
especially during the period known as the New Kingdom. Plenty of photos and a brief bibliography.

Heyerdahl, Thor. **Aku-Aku** (© 1958). PB 1960.
The stone statues of a lost civilization on Easter Island are a major mystery to scientists. The author
excavated there and offers some ideas about the builders of the statues.

Ivanoff, Pierre (translator Elaine P. Halperin). **Mayan
Enigma: The Search for a Lost Civilization.** Dela-
corte 1971.
Seeking answers to certain mysteries about the Mayan

civilization, the author spent two years with the descendants of the Mayans, whose civilization is more primitive than that of their ancestors.

Johnstone, Paul. **The Archaeology of Ships.** Walck 1974.

Many ancient ships sank because of battles and storms. Modern archaeologists have learned much about ancient civilization by investigating remains of these ships.

Larue, Gerald A. **Your Future in Archaeology.** Rosen Pr 1970.

Larue examines the qualities and education necessary to pursue a career in archaeology. Besides explaining the field itself, the book discusses such things as colleges and universities offering archaeology programs, employment opportunities, and writing resumes.

Lauber, Patricia. **Who Discovered America?** Random 1970.

Who discovered America before Columbus did? Anthropologists investigate unusual clues as they seek answers: Peruvian mummies with silky red hair, the use of blowguns with poison darts, and a lump of Rhode Island coal found in Greenland. Many photographs and maps. Bibliography.

Leakey, L. S. B. **By the Evidence: Memoirs, 1932–1951.** HarBraceJ 1974.

Leakey covers the years when he made important anthropological finds at his diggings in the Olduvai Gorge in Africa that startled the scientific world and established that humans first appeared on earth much earlier than scientists had believed.

Matthews, William H., III. **Fossils: An Introduction to Prehistoric Life.** B&N 1962.

Primarily an amateur collector's handbook that offers many good suggestions to those interested in fossil collecting and also gives a general introduction to earth history and the many types of prehistoric plants and animals. Includes bibliography, sources of geological information in each state, and a list of museums displaying fossils.

McKern, Sharon S. **Exploring the Unknown: Mysteries in American Archaeology.** Praeger 1972.

Before the coming of whites to America, several vast and well-developed civilizations—the Mayan, the Aztec, the Inca—had arisen. The author gives a record of those civilizations from their relics, ruins, and burial grounds.

Millar, Ronald. **The Piltdown Men.** Ballantine 1974.

Hailed as the "missing link" in the evolution of human beings, the Piltdown Man was discovered in 1912 and dismissed fifty years later as a hoax.

Moore, Ruth. **The Earth We Live On.** Knopf 1971.

A comprehensive study of geological discovery. Although many theories are explained, the strong point of this classic is its emphasis on the adventures of prominent geologists.

Nance, John. **The Gentle Tasaday: A Stone Age People in the Philippine Rain Forest.** HarBraceJ 1975.

In 1960 a tribe of cave-dwelling Indians, the Tasaday, was discovered in a Philippine rain forest. Unaware of the outside world, the tribe welcomed Manuel Elizalde, a young Philippine millionaire and amateur scientist, as if he were a god.

Noble, Iris. **Treasure of the Caves: The Story of the Dead Sea Scrolls.** Macmillan 1971.

In 1947 a young goatherd in the Dead Sea area stumbled upon one of the great archaeological discoveries of our time: scrolls inscribed with ancient Hebrew biblical texts. The author reviews discoveries of more scrolls, their translations, and their meaning.

Pace, Mildred Mastin. **Wrapped for Eternity.** McGraw 1974.

The archaeological findings, including burial customs, tombs, and the activities of grave robbers, derived from the study of Egyptian burial sites. Many illustrations.

Pearl, Richard M. **How to Know the Minerals and Rocks** (© 1955). NAL 1957.

Written for students, collectors, and hobbyists, this is a basic field guide to more than 125 of the most important minerals and rocks, including gems, ores, and metals. Each description is accompanied by a well-labeled drawing illustrating the characteristic features of the rock or mineral.

Pfeiffer, John E., and Carleton S. Coon. **The Search for Early Man.** Am Heritage 1963.

Probes the question of whether humans have inherited any peaceable characteristics from their hunter-warrior ancestors. Particular emphasis is placed on two digs near the famous Lascaux caves.

Robbins, Maurice. **The Amateur Archaeologist's Handbook** (© 1965). T Y Crowell 1973.

The how, why, when, and where for the amateur beginning the hobby of archaeology. Plenty of charts, drawings, and photos. Thorough appendices of sites, museums, courses of study, as well as an outstanding annotated bibliography.

Saggs, H. W. F. **The Greatness That Was Babylon** (© 1962). NAL 1968.

A detailed study of day-to-day life in Mesopotamia describing Babylonian gods, heroes, language, laws, medicine, arts, and sciences.

Scott, Joseph, and Lenore Scott. **Egyptian Hieroglyphs for Everyone.** Funk & W 1968.

The fundamentals of the ancient form of Egyptian writing, illustrated by inscriptions on existing remains with explanations of each in words and clear drawings.

Silverberg, Robert. **Clocks for the Ages.** Macmillan 1971.

Silverberg describes the history and methods of the archaeological dating of ancient peoples and their artifacts.

Silverberg, Robert. **The Mound Builders** (© 1970). Ballantine 1974.

The earth mounds in Ohio, Illinois, Indiana, and Missouri have fascinated scientists for years. Who made them? Have the makers disappeared or were they Indian tribes? What were the mounds used for? (See also *Lost Cities and Vanished Civilizations,* Bantam.)

Stern, Philip Van Doren. **The Beginnings of Art.** Four Winds 1973.

Art did not begin with the Greeks; rather, it began

with ancient cave dwellers and their drawings, scattered over a large part of Europe. Well illustrated with both line drawings and photographs.

Sutton, Ann, and Myron Sutton. **Among the Maya Ruins: The Adventures of John Lloyd Stephens and Frederick Catherwood.** Rand 1967.

In 1839 Stephens and Catherwood went into the jungles of Central America on a secret mission for President Van Buren. They soon forgot their mission as they discovered long-lost Mayan cities.

Von Hagen, Victor W. **The World of the Maya.** NAL 1960.

Von Hagen uses the everyday life of the Maya, which was dominated by complex rituals, to explain the Mayan astronomical calculations, analyze their writing and pictures, and describe the high quality of their sculptural arts. Bibliography and photos included. (See also *The Realm of the Incas,* NAL; and *The Aztec: Man and Tribe,* NAL.)

Wellard, James. **The Search for the Etruscans.** Sat Rev Pr 1973.

Wellard shows how serious archaeologists competed with individuals interested in obtaining artifacts for private sale during the rediscovery of the Etruscan civilization in Italy.

White, Peter. **The Past Is Human.** Taplinger 1976.

A British archaeologist counters the currently popular claims that aliens from outer space visited earth in the distant past by showing that the "evidence" of these visits can be explained by the technological capabilities of ancient civilizations.

NATURE

Abbey, Edward. **Desert Solitaire: A Search in the Wilderness** (© 1968). Ballantine 1971.

For two summers, Abbey worked as a seasonal park ranger at Arches National Monument in Utah. He had no great love for tourists, but he has an abiding love for the desert and its inhabitants.

Amory, Cleveland. **Man Kind? Our Incredible War on Wildlife.** Har-Row 1974.

Amory, president of the Fund for Animals, details the indiscriminate and cruel slaughter of animals. He contends that we have too often killed for bloodlust or because of an animal's undeserved reputation as a killer (wolves and coyotes, for example).

Batten, Mary. **The Tropical Forest.** T Y Crowell 1973.

The mysteries of the tropical forest are revealed in this well-illustrated book, which includes discussions of plants, animals, and insects.

Behme, Robert L. **Shasta and Rogue: A Coyote Story.** S&S 1974.

The author and his family rescued and raised two abandoned coyote pups. Shasta and Rogue soon became loyal and loving members of the family who proved many of the unfavorable stories about coyotes to be completely wrong.

Brooks, Paul. **The Pursuit of Wilderness.** HM 1971.

A conservationist describes recent battles to save wilderness and wildlife from industry, mining interests, the Atomic Energy Commission, housing developers, and army engineers.

Brower, Kenneth, editor, and Eliot Porter. **Galapagos,** 2 vols. Ballantine 1970.

A collection of prose passages by Herman Melville, Charles Darwin, and others and color photographs by Porter portray the history of these famous islands.

Bruemmer, Fred. **Encounters with Arctic Animals.** McGraw 1972.

For seven years the author lived with Eskimos, observing their world and its animal life: polar bears, seals, caribou, walruses, and musk oxen. Many beautiful color and black and white photographs of endangered species.

Buchenholz, Bruce. **Doctor in the Zoo.** Viking Pr 1974.

Prose and photographs document the activities of a chief veterinarian at a zoo during a week which included the delivery of a monkey by Caesarian section, the treatment of a gorilla for rheumatic fever, and the arrival of four baby elephants.

Burton, Maurice. **Animals of Europe: The Ecology of the Wildlife.** HR&W 1973.

Color photographs of the animals of Europe and a history of animal life on the continent.

Callahan, Philip S. **Insect Behavior.** Four Winds 1970.

The life of insects: the ways they eat, reproduce, communicate, and protect themselves. Includes a section of projects for observing, collecting, and photographing insects.

Caras, Roger A. **Monarch of Deadman Bay** (© 1969). Bantam 1972.

A realistic and detailed novel about the Kodiac bear, tracing the story of one bear from conception to death. Fiction.

Carrighar, Sally. **Home to the Wilderness.** HM 1973.

Carrighar found joy and a way out of the concrete jungle of civilization by observing and writing about the lives, rituals, and habits of animals.

Carrighar, Sally. **One Day on Beetle Rock** (© 1944). Ballantine 1973.

Ten stories by a skilled writer and naturalist about animals living in the High Sierra.

Collett, Rosemary. **My Orphans of the Wild.** Lippincott 1974.

For a decade, the Collett family has been rescuing and caring for injured wild animals, and this book is the story of those years and a guide for helping wild animals.

Corbett, James E. **Man-Eaters of Kumaon** (© 1945). Bantam 1962.

Professional hunter Corbett writes about tigers who have turned man-eater and his hunting and killing of those tigers.

Diolé, Philippe (translator J. F. Bernard). **The Errant Ark: Man's Relationship with Animals.** Putnam 1974.

Diolé argues that animals are essential to humanity and that our attempts to stave off the extinction of many animal species today are doomed to failure unless we rethink our present approaches. Mature.

Douglas-Hamilton, Iain, and Oria Douglas-Hamilton. **Among the Elephants.** Viking Pr 1975.

A Scottish zoologist and a photographer went to an East African game preserve, their job being to chart the migration of elephants and to determine whether they are near extinction. They learned to recognize all 450 individual elephants in their preserve, and they describe the elephants' lives and society.

Dowden, Anne Ophelia. **Wild Green Things in the City.** T Y Crowell 1972.

This fully illustrated book examines the weeds and wildflowers that survive and grow despite the brick and asphalt of the city.

Durrell, Gerald. **A Bevy of Beasts.** S&S 1973.

To his family's dismay, Durrell became zookeeper at England's Whipsnode, one of the first zoos to devise natural habitations for its animals. Durrell tells about his humorous encounters with wolves, lions, wombats, polar bears, and many other animals.

Emboden, William A. **Bizarre Plants: Magical, Monstrous, Mythical.** Macmillan 1974.

Emboden's illustrated book explores the real and imaginary plants which have amazed and intrigued people and the strange and sometimes bawdy folktales that grew up around the plants.

Evans, Edna H. **Famous Horses and Their People.** Greene 1975.

Real life stories of famous people and the horses they rode.

Fletcher, Colin. **The Winds of Mara** (© 1972). Knopf 1973.

In the late 1960s, the author returned to Mara, Kenya's great animal sanctuary, to study African wildlife and to determine the impact civilization has had on the animals and birds.

- Gilbert, Bil. **Chulo.** Knopf 1973.

Gilbert and three other young naturalists study the coatimundi, a nearsighted and lanky member of the raccoon family that lives in tribes and has an incredibly effective system of communication.

Greenway, James C., Jr. **Extinct and Vanishing Birds of the World.** Dover 1967.

This work is a revised publication of a 1958 study prepared by the American Committee for International Wild Life Protection and provides encyclopedic accounts of extinct and vanishing forms of birds.

Grzimek, Bernhard, and Michael Grzimek (translators El and D. Rewald). **Serengeti Shall Not Die** (© 1960). Ballantine 1973.

A father and son team of naturalists write about the Serengeti National Park in Tanzania: the animals, the natural predators, and the human predators who threaten to destroy whole species for money.

Halliday, William R. **Depths of the Earth: Caves and Cavers of the United States** (© 1966). Har-Row 1975.

Descriptions of caves and the people who explore and investigate them, with accounts of their natural and scientific discoveries.

Halmi, Robert. **In the Wilds of North America.** Four Winds 1971.

Halmi presents both basic and little-known information about the game animals of North America: the grizzly, the elk, the mountain goat, the wild boar, and other animals.

Hannum, Alberta Pierson. **Look Back with Love: A Recollection of the Blue Ridge.** Vanguard 1969.

The culture and life of the Southern highlanders is preserved in this personal recollection of the author's mountain friends.

Hoopes, Ned E., editor. **The Wonderful World of Horses, Fifteen Superb Stories.** Dell 1966.

Mustangs, wild horses, broncos, and playful colts are the central characters of these stories written by Nathaniel Hawthorne, William Saroyan, John Steinbeck, and others. Fiction.

Hulme, Kathryn. **Look a Lion in the Eye: On Safari through Africa.** Little 1974.

In 1971, three women and their guide spent a month traveling in a Land Rover visiting the wild game reserves in Kenya and northern Tanzania.

Hyde, Dayton O. **Yamsi** (© 1971). Ballantine 1974.

The owner of an Oregon ranch writes about his love for his work, his animals, and his soil. Many photographs in this account of one year on the ranch.

Jenkins, Alan C. **Wild Life in Danger.** St Martin 1973.

Many animals are in imminent danger of extinction, often because people want land or furs or souvenirs. But other individuals are concerned and are finding ways to protect endangered species.

Kains, M. G. **Five Acres and Independence: A Handbook for Small Farm Management** (© 1935). Dover 1973.

This work provides a number of proven, basic agricultural practices in working a small farm and discusses a variety of activities, including setting seeds, raising bees, and raising and preserving fruits and vegetables.

Keith, Sam, editor. **One Man's Wilderness: An Alaskan Odyssey.** Alaska Northwest 1973.

Keith has edited the journal of Richard Proenneke, who spent eighteen months alone in the Alaskan wilderness.

Kirk, Ruth. **Desert: The American Southwest.** HM 1973.

The starkness and the beauty of the deserts of California, Nevada, Utah, and Arizona, with many photographs by the author and her husband.

Krutch, Joseph Wood. **The Best Nature Writing of Joseph Wood Krutch** (© 1970). PB n.d.

All of his life Krutch was a sensitive observer of nature. Here he writes of animals, dunes, flowers, and the Grand Canyon, and of our ability to despoil nature. Mature.

Krutch, Joseph Wood. **Grand Canyon** (© 1958). Anch Pr 1962.

Krutch, a professor at Columbia University, moved west when he retired. His love and awe of the wonders of the Grand Canyon are evident in this account of its geological past and its picturesque present. (See also *The Great Chain of Life,* Pyramid Pubns; and *The Desert Year,* Viking Pr.)

Laycock, George. **Wild Animals, Safe Places.** Four Winds 1973.

Humanity encroaches more and more each year upon the wilderness of animals, but some animal sanctuaries have been set aside. The four described here are Yellowstone National Park, Mt. McKinley National Park, the Hawaiian Islands National Wildlife Refuge, and Everglades National Park. (See also *Wild Travelers,* Four Winds.)

Lineweaver, Thomas H., III, and Richard H. Backus. **Natural History of Sharks** (© 1970). Anch Pr 1973.

A fact-filled and fascinating summary of what is known about sharks: evolution, reproduction, anatomy, and physiology.

Lorenz, Konrad Z. **King Solomon's Ring** (© 1952). NAL 1972.

Lorenz shares his knowledge and theories about animals in discussing the dogs, birds, and fish he has raised.

MacKinnon, John. **In Search of the Red Ape.** HR&W 1974.

A first-person account of the author's years of studying the orangutan, the most mysterious of the world's great apes, in the jungles of Borneo and Sumatra.

Matthiessen, Peter. **The Cloud Forest** (© 1961). Pyramid Pubns n.d.

The people, animals, birds, and beauty of the jungle environment are vividly described as Matthiessen shares his adventure-packed journey through South America.

Matthiessen, Peter. **Oomingmak: The Expedition to the Musk Ox Island in the Bering Sea.** Hastings 1967.

Matthiessen describes a 1964 expedition to capture musk ox calves. The expedition's purpose was to see if the calves could be raised domestically for their wool, thus aiding the Eskimo economy.

Maxwell, Gavin. **Ring of Bright Water** (© 1960). Ballantine 1974.

Although this popular book details Maxwell's life and adventures in the wilderness and his life with his otter pets, the real hero and heroine in this book are the otters, Mijbil and Edal.

McCoy, J. J. **Our Captive Animals** (© 1971). Seabury 1972.

An examination of "captive wild animal environments," such as zoos, game farms, and menageries; the care of captive animals; and the role of zoos in the preservation of endangered species.

McHugh, Tom. **The Time of the Buffalo.** Knopf 1972.

A close-up view of the buffalo's habits and life cycle tracing the history of the great American bison in the ecology of the grass plains and in the life of the American Indian and settler.

McPhee, John. **Encounters with the Archdruid.** FS&G 1971.

David Brower, an ardent and militant conservationist, takes on three opponents—a mineral engineer, a resort developer, and a dam builder—in a battle to save nature for future generations.

McPhee, John. **The Survival of the Bark Canoe.** FS&G 1975.

Henri Vaillancourt makes birch-bark canoes in the same way Indians made them. McPhee describes the building of these canoes and a 150-mile canoe trip he took with Vaillancourt in the Maine woods and streams.

Merne, Oscar J. **Ducks, Geese and Swans.** St Martin 1974.

An introduction to the *Anatidae* family of birds; includes maps and full-color illustrations of each of the 140 species described.

Mowat, Farley. **A Whale for the Killing** (© 1972). Penguin 1973.

In addition to the stories about whaling and the descriptions of life on the southwest coast of Newfoundland, Mowat describes the unfortunate fate of a female fin whale who was stranded in a cove where local people tormented and shot the gentle creature for "sport" while Mowat tried to save her life.

Murphy, Robert. **The Peregrine Falcon.** HM 1964.

This novel is about the first year in the life of a female peregrine falcon as she learns to survive in the Canadian wilderness and then begins her long autumn migration to the Florida Keys. Fiction.

Napier, Prue. **Monkeys and Apes** (© 1972). Bantam 1973.

Part of Bantam's Knowledge through Color series, this is a beautifully illustrated introduction to the world of primates and includes a detailed but restrained discussion of the reproduction cycle.

Olson, Sigurd F. **Open Horizons.** Knopf 1969.

Olson has been a naturalist ever since his boyhood on a Wisconsin farm. He writes about the spiritual, psychological, and physical values of living in the wilderness.

Prince, J. H. **The Universal Urge.** Nelson 1972.

Courtship and mating are universal urges in all animals, though the rituals associated with them may vary widely.

Richards, John. **The Hidden Country.** S G Phillips 1973.

The "hidden country" flourishes in the city but is frequently overlooked: the world of insects and plants.

Rood, Ronald. **Animals Nobody Loves** (© 1971). Bantam 1972.

This book contains the inside story about creatures that nobody likes: fleas, bats, pigs, vultures, rats, spiders, and other unpopular creatures.

Roots, Clive. **Animals of the Dark.** Praeger 1974.

Roots, a collector of rare animals for zoos, discusses the reptiles, birds, and mammals of the night and how they survive.

Russell, Franklin. **Corvus the Crow.** Four Winds 1972.

This sensitive but realistic story gives an account of a crow's life through a full cycle of seasonal change and emphasizes how animals must adapt to the continually changing conditions of life. Fiction.

Russell, Helen Ross. **Winter Search Party.** Nelson 1971.

This book investigates the curious question of where

insects go during the winter and explains how to find, recognize, and collect insects and other invertebrates during the winter.

Ryden, Hope. **God's Dog.** Coward 1975.

The author's two years of close observation of coyotes convinced her that these much-maligned and hunted animals deserve our respect and affection. Many photographs.

Ryden, Hope. **Mustangs: A Return to the Wild.** Viking Pr 1972.

Ryden studies American wild horses as they struggle to survive in the arid bush country.

Schaller, George B. **Golden Shadows, Flying Hooves** (© 1973). Dell 1975.

Schaller tells of the three adventurous years he and his family spent on the plains of Tanzania while he made his famous study of lion behavior and of other African predators. (See also *The Year of the Gorilla,* U of Chicago Pr.)

Short, Lester L. **Birds of the World.** Bantam 1976.

A very inexpensive introduction to the vast world of birds with brief descriptions of 140 selected species, each accompanied by a color photograph.

Storer, John H. **Man in the Web of Life** (© 1968). NAL 1972.

The interaction and interdependence between people, society, and the natural world—an attempt to understand the complex forces that make human nature what it is.

Sullivan, Walter. **Continents in Motion.** McGraw 1974.

Sullivan, science editor for the *New York Times,* explains how the revolutionary theory of "continental drift"—the theory that the landmasses of our planet are constantly moving—came into being and how the drift has influenced and affected the natural world.

Sutton, Ann, and Myron Sutton. **Guarding the Treasured Lands: The Story of the National Park Service.** Lippincott 1965.

The beginning of the National Park Service and the work of rangers, naturalists, archaeologists, and historians employed by the Service.

Sutton, Ann, and Myron Sutton. **The Wilderness World of the Grand Canyon: Leave It as It Is.** Lippincott 1971.

A husband and wife team of naturalists describes the plants and animals in the Grand Canyon, the geological history of the canyon, and the damage done to it by people.

Teal, John, and Mildred Teal. **Life and Death of the Salt Water Marsh** (© 1969). Ballantine n.d.

The marshes of the East Coast of the U.S., life forms found there, and the destruction of marshes so important to the environment.

Teal, Mildred, and John Teal. **Pigeons and People.** Little 1972.

Information about the many kinds of pigeons, including the dodo, the passenger pigeon, the rock dove, and the "city pigeon." The history of these birds stands as an ecological warning.

Teale, Edwin Way. **A Naturalist Buys an Old Farm.** Dodd 1974.

Teale writes about life on a small Connecticut farm, detailing his search for such a home and the natural wonders and beauty he discovered on his few acres.

Tompkins, Peter, and Christopher Bird. **The Secret Life of Plants** (© 1973). Avon 1974.

This study explores the fascinating possibility that plants are capable of feeling and expressing emotion, reading minds, serving as lie detectors, and other activities which were believed to be beyond the potential of plants.

Van Lawick, Hugo. **Solo: The Story of an African Wild Dog** (© 1974). Bantam 1975.

This true story of an abandoned wild puppy's struggle to survive was the basis for the award-winning TV documentary, "The Wild Dogs of Africa." (See also *Innocent Killers,* Ballantine.)

Van Lawick-Goodall, Jane. **In the Shadow of Man** (© 1971). Dell 1972.

For ten years the author observed a herd of wild chimpanzees in Tanzania. Study of their families, their relationships, and the treatment of their young convinced her that these supposedly wild animals have developed a tribal civilization akin to humans.

Von Frisch, Karl, and Otto Von Frisch. **Animal Architecture.** HarBraceJ 1974.

How animals ingeniously use stone, wood, clay, and other natural materials to construct homes with hinged doors, wells 120 feet deep, air conditioning systems, and other such features.

Wenkam, Robert. **Kauai and the Park Country of Hawaii** (© 1967). Ballantine 1969.

A testimony in prose, poetry, and pictures to the beauty of these Pacific islands and a plea to protect their beauty from commercial exploitation.

Wilkes, Paul. **Fitzgo: The Wild Dog of Central Park.** Lippincott 1973.

Paul and Joy Wilkes noticed a brown and white dog living in Central Park in New York City. The dog clearly took good care of himself, but he was independent and unwilling to be friends with humans. Then one old man tried hard to win the dog's affection.

Wolf, Marguerite Hurrey. **I'll Take the Back Road.** Greene 1975.

In 1948, the author and her family left the city to move to rural Vermont. Her love of the farm and the back roads, animals, and people of Vermont is obvious.

Young, Stanley P., and Edward A. Goldman. **The Puma: Mysterious American Cat.** Dover 1946.

A report about the history, life habits, economic status, and control of the puma, from its place in Inca and Aztec cultures to modern field studies of this giant American cat.

Young, Stanley P., and Edward A. Goldman. **The Wolves of North America,** 2 vols. Dover 1944.

Volume I is a detailed discussion of the history of wolves as well as a report of twenty-five years of field studies. Volume II is a data-filled, scientific classification of the species found on this continent.

ECOLOGY

Abbey, Edward. **The Monkey Wrench Gang.** Lippincott 1975.

Three men and a woman who hate our industrialized and mechanized society decide to blow up the Glen Canyon dam. Fiction.

Baron, Robert Alex. **The Tyranny of Noise.** St Martin 1970.

An authority on noise abatement and the dangers of noise to human beings establishes the case for noise controls and legislation.

Barry, James P. **The Fate of the Lakes: A Portrait of the Great Lakes.** Baker Bk 1972.

A pictorial and narrative account of the current and future roles of the Great Lakes as economic and recreational resources and of the many types of pollutants which threaten the survival of the lakes.

Brooks, Paul. **The Pursuit of the Wilderness** (© 1962). HM 1971.

In words and pictures, this book describes six battles won by those who want to preserve our wilderness heritage.

Carson, Rachel. **Silent Spring** (© 1962). Fawcett World 1973.

Carson was one of the first ecologists to see the potential dangers of pesticides for plants, animals, and human beings. Her warnings were often ignored but have since become the watchwords of many ecologists and conservationists.

Commoner, Barry. **The Closing Circle: Nature, Man, and Technology.** Knopf 1971.

Commoner defines ecology, gives case histories of ecological disasters (smog in Los Angeles and water pollution in Lake Erie), demonstrates that our technological proficiency has led and will lead to more ecological nightmares, and shows how we can change to give ourselves a chance for survival.

Douglas, William O. **The Three Hundred Year War: A Chronicle of Ecological Disaster.** Random 1972.

The Supreme Court justice recounts what humankind has done to befoul the air, the water, the animals, and itself and suggests ways we may yet win the battle to save the world. Mature.

East, Ben. **The Last Eagle.** Crown 1974.

A fictional account of the life cycle of the eagle that speaks strongly about humanity's senseless destruction of the environment. Fiction.

Eastlake, William. **Dancers in the Scalp House.** Viking Pr 1975.

A group of Indians decides to explode an atomic bomb on a dam under construction since the dam will flood their land. Fiction.

Ehrlich, Paul. **The Population Bomb** (© 1968). Ballantine 1971.

Ehrlich's highly controversial book explores the possible effects of the worldwide population explosion on our air, food, and water supplies and possible effects on our moral codes. (See also Paul Ehrlich and Richard L. Harriman, *How to Be a Survivor,* Ballantine.) Mature.

Falk, Richard A. **This Endangered Planet: Prospects and Proposals for Human Survival** (© 1971). Vin-Random 1972.

An overview of the world environmental crisis, its causes, and some badly needed worldwide strategies for the future. Mature.

Fallows, James M. **The Water Lords.** Bantam 1971.

A writer for one of Ralph Nader's task forces on American pollution reports on the environmental crisis in Savannah, Georgia, where the Savannah River is being contaminated by sewage and industrial wastes.

Fisher, Tadd. **Our Overcrowded World.** Parents 1969.

The facts about the population crisis, an examination of the special problems faced by developing nations, and an objective examination of moral issues involved.

Godfrey, Arthur, editor. **The Arthur Godfrey Environmental Reader.** Ballantine 1970.

An excellent introduction to environmental studies with excerpts from such major works in the field as Rachel Carson's *Silent Spring,* Wesley Marx's *The Frail Ocean,* and William Wise's *Killer Smog.*

Graham, Frank, Jr. **Where the Place Called Morning Lies.** Viking Pr 1973.

Twelve years ago, Graham and his wife moved to the Maine seacoast to be free from air and water pollution. They gradually discovered that decisions made by marine engineers, oil companies, and others affect the whole world of nature, from Japan to Texas to Maine.

Grayson, Melvin J., and Thomas R. Shepard, Jr. **The Disaster Lobby: Prophets of Ecological Doom and Other Absurdities.** Follett 1973.

An examination of alleged negative effects the ecology, consumer, and feminist movements have had upon the American economy and lifestyle. The books takes to task everyone from Rachel Carson to Gloria Steinem. A conservative view of contemporary issues.

Halacy, D. S., Jr. **Now or Never: The Fight Against Pollution.** Four Winds 1971.

The types of pollution confronting modern humanity—air, water, noise, and others—and what is being done and what the reader can do to change the situation.

Hickel, Walter J. **Who Owns America?** (© 1971). Warner Bks 1972.

The former secretary of the interior records his hopes for conservation by the Nixon administration and his final disillusionment. He suggests that we all own America and that we must all work to keep it safe from those who would destroy it instead of preserve it.

Jones, Holway R. **John Muir and the Sierra Club: The Battle for Yosemite.** Sierra 1965.

The history of the Sierra Club and the battle to save Yosemite from commercialization is also a history of the changing social attitude toward the wilderness—an attitude which holds that wilderness areas are necessary for ecological balance as well as natural beauty.

Little, Charles E., and John G. Mitchell. **Space for Survival: Blocking the Bulldozer in Urban America.** PB 1971.

This Sierra Club handbook is aimed at anyone who would like to keep some open space in the city and who would like to keep housing tracts from swallowing up space that could be used for parks and recreation areas.

Maddox, John. **The Doomsday Syndrome: An Attack on Pessimism** (© 1972). McGraw 1973.

Maddox takes issue with popular concern over population growth, pollution, and the depletion of natural resources and disagrees with those who doubt humanity's ability to solve such problems.

Marine, Gene. **America the Raped** (© 1969). Avon 1972.

The author believes that the ecology of our continent is in danger and that the crisis is due to the "engineering mentality" which has raped the land and wildlife. Mature.

Marzani, Carl. **The Wounded Earth.** A-W 1972.

A detailed but readable examination of the earth's ecosystems, of people as polluters, and of our need to solve some major pollution problems. The book is optimistic, suggesting how technology can be used to correct humanitys' past ecological blunders.

McCoy, J. J. **Shadows over the Land.** Seabury 1970.

The author is convinced that life on earth may end soon if humanity does not do something about pesticides and polluted air and water. A list of books, films, and organizations concludes this warning.

Millard, Reed. **Natural Resources—Will We Have Enough for Tomorrow's World?** Messner 1972.

Our supply of natural resources is dwindling, and the author explores some problems in finding new resources and suggests how we will have to face the problem.

Moser, Don. **A Heart to the Hawks.** Atheneum 1975.

Mike Harrington thinks about girls sometimes, but most of the time he is absorbed in his study of nature and natural history. Then a land developer plans to build on the woodland that Mike studies, and Mike sets out to fight the intruder. Fiction.

Packard, Vance. **The Waste Makers** (© 1960). PB 1963.

Packard argues that most Americans bear the responsibility for our conspicuous consumption and even more

conspicuous waste since we are in some way involved
in the businesses guilty of wasting materials and creating the resource, power, and ecological dilemmas we
face today.

Papanek, Victor. **Design for the Real World.** Pantheon
1971.

Papanek, dean of the School of Design at the California Institute of the Arts, discusses designing products
and tools to benefit people, not manufacturers and
profitmakers. He and his students have devised a tin-
can radio costing nine cents and an educational TV
costing eight dollars to manufacture. Mature.

Pawley, Martin. **The Private Future: Causes and Consequences of Community Collapse in the West.** Random 1974.

Worried about the collapse of Western civilization, the
author analyzes what madness and drives of humanity have led to our present predicament. He contends
that we have lost our sense of community, our ability
to identify with others. Mature.

Perry, Richard. **The Polar Worlds.** Taplinger 1973.

A comparative study of the Arctic and Antarctic focusing on native species' ability to adapt to ecological
imbalances. Perry concludes that Antarctica's wildlife
is relatively safe but that the Arctic's ecology is pre-
carious.

Pringle, Laurence. **Pests and People.** Macmillan 1972.

The case against the use of stronger and stronger pesticides which might be more appropriately called "bio-
cides" and a plea for the use of alternative methods
for dealing with insect pests.

Sand, George X. **The Everglades Today: Endangered
Wilderness.** Four Winds 1971.

This book speaks lyrically of the history, beauty, and
wonder of the Everglades and lashes out at those who
have and would destroy this tropical wilderness. Photographs.

Schroeder, Henry A. **The Poisons around Us.** Ind U Pr
1974.

A factual and detailed examination of metals and
other elements as pollutants and as substances bene-

ficial to human life, including the relationship of pollutants to human health.

Sears, Paul B. **Where There Is Life: An Introduction
to Ecology.** Dell 1970.

This work, which avoids technical jargon, is a good
starting point in the study of the safeguarding of our
resources and life support systems.

Smith, Grahame J. C., Henry J. Steck, and Gerald
Surette. **Our Ecological Crisis.** Macmillan 1974.

Three essays explore the ecological dilemma from the
biological, economical, and political points of view.
Mature.

Smith, W. Eugene, and Aileen M. Smith. **Minamata.**
HR&W 1975.

A horrifying report of the damage done to human
beings when toxic wastes were dumped into Minamata
Bay in southern Japan. The authors detail the effects
of the mercury poison on those who did not die immediately and the legal battles between the people and
the company dumping the poisonous materials.

Snyder, Ernest E. **Please Stop Killing Me!** NAL 1971.

Snyder notes the many ways humanity and technology
have increased the likelihood of death in the twentieth
century through radiation, smog-induced cancer, and
toxic poisoning in foods or water. He concludes by
suggesting ways humanity can stave off some of its
self-induced ills.

Stadler, John, editor. **Eco-Fiction.** WSP 1971.

This collection has stories by such authors as Ray
Bradbury, Edgar Allan Poe, E. B. White, and others,
all concerned with ecology. Fiction.

Sterling, Philip. **Sea and Earth: The Life of Rachel
Carson** (© 1970). Dell 1974.

The life of the woman whose book *Silent Spring*
warned the world about the dangers of pesticides. While
she was attacked by many groups for her comments,
she became a heroine to many people who wanted to
save humanity from itself.

Stoutenburg, Adrien. **Out There** (© 1971). Dell 1972.

In the twenty-first century, five teenagers and Aunt

Zeb leave the protective dome of "New City" to explore the world of nature which was ravaged and destroyed by twentieth-century humanity's disregard for its natural environment. Fiction.

Udall, Stewart L. **The Quiet Crisis** (© 1963). Avon 1964.

The former secretary of the interior warns the nation about the destruction of our natural resources and animals and the great American wildernesses through the fouling of the air, water, and land and recommends ways to save our land and ourselves.

Wise, William. **Killer Smog.** Ballantine 1970.

In December 1952, 4,000 London residents died when the city was overwhelmed by smog. The author describes what led to the smog, what we should learn from the catastrophe, and what we can do to lessen the chances of a repetition.

Zwick, David (with Marcy Benstock). **Water Wasteland** (© 1971). Bantam 1972.

A study of water pollution by one of Ralph Nader's groups working on American pollution. Who and what is causing water pollution and what can be done to stop it.

SKIES AND MOUNTAINS

Aldrin, Edwin E., Jr. (with Wayne Warga). **Return to Earth** (© 1973). Bantam 1974.

"Buzz" Aldrin, second man to walk on the moon, tells of his challenging exploits as an astronaut and of the devastating depression that overcame him when the journey was over, an illness which required hospitalization and psychiatric counseling before he regained his health.

Bonington, Chris. **Annapurna: South Face.** McGraw 1971.

This first-person account of the historic climb up the treacherous south face of Annapurna—one of the most formidable mountains in the world—presents a detailed picture of the planning, the challenge, and the tragedy which were elements of the climb.

Bova, Ben. **In Quest of Quasars** (© 1969). CCPr Macmillan 1970.

Quasars, bluish star-like bodies that emit unusual amounts of radio energy from the most distant reaches of the universe, receive a thoughtful examination. Included with the numerous photographs and illustrations are discussions of novae, pulsars, and other galaxies.

Bradbury, Ray, et al. **Mars and the Mind of Man.** Har-Row 1973.

Two astronomers, two science fiction writers, and a science editor met the day before *Mariner 9* arrived at Mars in 1971 and discussed their ideas about the famous planet. And, a year later, they reacted to their original statements in the light of the *Mariner 9* discoveries.

Brown, Peter. **Astronomy in Color.** Macmillan 1972.

This encyclopedic publication offers concise explanations of our present knowledge about the solar system and other galaxies, including pulsars, quasars, and black holes. Eighty pages are devoted to full-color photographs and drawings from American, British, and Australian sources. Mature.

Clarke, Arthur C. **The Promise of Space.** Har-Row 1968.

Describes the accomplishments of space technology during the 1950s and 1960s and discusses various possibilities for the future, including the building of cities on other planets and traveling to distant stars. Mature.

Clarke, Arthur C., and Robert Silverberg. **Into Space: A Young Person's Guide to Space.** Har-Row 1971.

This revision of Clarke's 1954 history of rocketry, *Going Into Space,* reviews the amazing amount of new information that has been generated by space accomplishments in the 1960s.

Cleare, John. **Mountains.** Crown 1975.

Mountains have always been important in our mythologies, our religions, our history, and our love of nature. The author examines the geology of mountains and the adventures of people who have tried to scale them.

Collins, Michael. **Carrying the Fire.** FS&G 1974.

Collins, the Apollo astronaut who guided the command module while Armstrong and Aldrin landed on the moon, recounts his years with the space program.

Douglas, William O. **My Wilderness: The Pacific West** (© 1960). Pyramid Pubns 1968.

The author, a Supreme Court justice and an ardent conservationist, writes of his experiences along the Pacific Ocean but especially his hikes and horseback rides into the Olympic Mountains and the High Sierra.

Dwiggins, Don. **Into the Unknown: The Story of Space Shuttles and Space Stations.** Childrens 1971.

A history of the development of space stations and shuttles with discussion of future prospects for 100-person space stations and interplanetary probes.

Fenner, Phyllis R., editor. **Perilous Ascent: Stories of Mountain Climbing.** Morrow 1970.

Ten stories about mountain climbing, from a young mountaineer in Germany to the search for the Abominable Snowman. Fiction.

Gann, Ernest K. **Ernest K. Gann's Flying Circus.** Macmillan 1974.

Flying and fliers in America, from the planes they love—be it an Armstrong-Whitworth Argosy or a Boeing 377 Stratocruiser—to the glories of flight itself.

Gentry, Curt. **The Killer Mountains** (© 1968). Ballantine n.d.

Many legendary lost mines, especially the Lost Dutchman Mine, are reputed to be in the Superstition Mountains of Arizona. Men have died or been killed searching for the Lost Dutchman.

Grissom, Betty, and Henry Still. **Starfall.** T Y Crowell 1974.

Grissom may have been a shy, small-town girl, but the man she married thrust her into the public spotlight with him. He was Gus Grissom, an astronaut and one of three men to die in the 1967 flash fire in the Apollo command module.

Halacy, D. S., Jr. **The Coming Age of Solar Energy.** Har-Row 1973.

A history of solar energy, with discussions of the promising prospects of orbiting solar power plants, thermal energy from the sea, and the proposal for a 5,000-square mile, pollution-free solar power plant in the desert of the Southwest that could supply energy for the entire United States.

Haston, Dougal. **In High Places** (© 1972). Macmillan 1973.

Haston has been a mountain climber most of his life. This story covers his climbs, from a railway bridge in Scotland to the Alps and Mt. Everest.

Heiman, Grover. **Aerial Photography: The Story of Aerial Mapping and Reconnaissance.** Macmillan 1972.

Emphasizing military more than civilian applications, this is the history of photography as a means of reconnaissance and mapping. Heiman also describes the development of aircraft which have been especially useful for aerial photography.

Herzog, Maurice. **Annapurna** (© 1952). Dutton 1953.

Herzog led a French expedition to the Himalayan Mountains to be the first group to climb 26,493-foot Annapurna.

Hillary, Sir Edmund. **Nothing Venture, Nothing Win.** Coward 1975.

Hillary was the first white person to stand on the summit of 29,028-foot Mount Everest. He also led an expedition in search of the Abominable Snowman.

King, Clarence. **Mountaineering in the Sierra Nevada** (© 1872). U of Nebr Pr 1970.

King was a geologist, mining engineer, and mountain climber who loved the California Sierra Nevada. His description is especially fresh and fascinating because his climbing came when the whole range was virtually unknown wilderness to the rest of the country.

Klass, Philip J. **UFOs Identified.** Random 1968.

A new scientific theory is presented by the author to account for the appearances of UFOs, some likely reported by cranks but some identified by scientists and aviators.

Lavender, David. **The Rockies** (© 1968). Har-Row 1975.

The history of the Rockies, beginning in 1859, is traced

in this book, which includes people, places, events, and philosophies which shaped this region of America.

Maclean, Alistair. **Breakheart Pass.** Doubleday 1974.

During the 1870s, a trainload of passengers is caught by a blizzard in the Rocky Mountains. Fiction.

Macvey, John W. **Whispers from Space.** Macmillan 1973.

Because intelligent life almost certainly exists elsewhere in the universe, earth's humans have attempted to contact distant galaxies. Macvey examines the theories of extraterrestrial life, archaeological mysteries, advances of radio astronomy, mathematical language for interstellar communications, and methods of long-distance space travel. Mature.

Mooney, Michael M. **The "Hindenburg."** Dodd 1972.

The dirigibles built by the Zeppelin Company of Germany had a record of more than a million air-miles of accident-free travel. Zeppelin's *Hindenburg* was to be the greatest of these flying machines, but on its eleventh flight the passengers did not know what the officers knew—that a bomb had been planted to blow up the dirigible.

Moore, Patrick, and David A. Hardy. **Challenge of the Stars: A Forecast of the Future Exploration of the Universe.** Rand 1972.

Beyond our moon lie the planets, their moons, and distant stars. Through text and dramatic paintings, Moore and Hardy take the reader on a tour of what might someday be seen and experienced by earth's explorers.

Moore, Patrick, and Iain Nicolson. **Black Holes in Space.** Norton 1976.

Two astronomers lay out the evidence for black holes, superheavy masses in space from which neither matter nor light can escape.

Muir, John. **The Mountains of California** (© 1894). Anch Pr 1961.

One of the great naturalists, explorers, and conservationists of his time, Muir relates his experiences in the California Sierras, the animals, the winds, the majesty. (See also *The Yosemite,* Anch Pr.)

Muirden, James. **The Amateur Astronomer's Handbook: A Guide to Exploring the Heavens** (© 1968). T Y Crowell 1974.

Muirden's guide to viewing stars, planets, and other celestial bodies through a telescope includes equipment selection, mirror making, and advice on building your own telescope. Mature.

Neely, Henry M. **A Primer for Star-Gazers.** Har-Row 1970.

A thorough and simplified introduction to the basics of locating stars and enjoying star-gazing. Neely's original ideas and step-by-step directions are accompanied by nearly 100 "sky pictures" and charts.

Peltier, Leslie C. **Guideposts to the Stars: Exploring the Skies throughout the Year.** Macmillan 1972.

Peltier explains how, without costly telescopes or elaborate charts, an unfamiliar observer can learn to recognize fifteen of the brightest stars which then lead to neighboring stars and constellations. Also contains brief chapters on planets, comets, meteors, variable stars, novae, and zodiacal light.

Polgreen, John, and Cathleen Polgreen. **The Stars Tonight.** Har-Row 1967.

Helps beginning star-gazers locate key stars, constellations, and various nebulae with the naked eye.

Read, Piers Paul. **Alive: The Story of the Andes Survivors.** Lippincott 1974.

An airplane carrying Uruguayan rugby players to a game in Chile crashed in the Andes in October 1972. The survivors endured cold and hunger, and two of them finally left to find help.

Roberts, David. **Deborah: A Wilderness Narrative.** Vanguard 1970.

Roberts and his best friend attempted to scale Mt. Deborah in Alaska. Their failure was due to bad luck, bad weather, and a breakdown of their friendship.

Roberts, David. **The Mountain of My Fear.** Vanguard 1968.

Four Harvard students tried to climb Alaska's Mt.

Huntington in 1965. Roberts conveys the fear and thrills of climbing and the horror of watching a companion fall to his death.

Ronan, Colin A. **Discovering the Universe: A History of Astronomy.** Basic 1971.

From the ancient efforts to comprehend the order of the universe to the present use of radio telescopes and interplanetary spaceprobes, Ronan describes the fascinating history of astronomy. In a later book (*Astronomy,* B&N), Ronan explores the struggles, both successful and unsuccessful, in the 2,000-year study of astronomy. Mature.

Rose, Eugene A. **High Odyssey.** Howell-North 1974.

Orland Bartholomew explored the California Sierra Nevada and during six months in 1928–1929 made the first solo climb of Mt. Whitney. Rose reconstructed the story from Bartholomew's diary.

Scott, Sheila. **Barefoot in the Sky** (© 1973). Macmillan 1974.

Scott was the first solo pilot to fly directly over the North Pole in a light aircraft. She broke over 100 world air records and has been in many air races.

Sharpe, Mitchell R. **"It Is I, Sea Gull": Valentina Tereshkova, First Woman in Space.** T Y Crowell 1975.

On June 16, 1963, a Russian spaceship blasted off and went into orbit. The cosmonaut was Tereshkova, the first woman to be directly involved in a spaceshot. Her biography also gives a history of the development of Soviet science and space knowledge.

Silverberg, Robert. **Ghost Towns of the American West** (© 1968). Ballantine n.d.

After the gold and silver rushes were over, ghost towns remained behind. Silverberg tells about the past glories and present conditions of ghost towns throughout the West.

Smith, Norman F. **Wings of Feathers, Wings of Flame: The Science and Technology of Aviation.** Little 1972.

After a few chapters on the history of aviation, the author discusses how planes fly, how to learn to fly, and many scientific facts about aviation.

Snyder, Howard H. **The Hall of the Mountain King.**
Scribner 1973.

Snyder and two friends joined a 1967 expedition to
climb 20,320-foot Mt. McKinley in Alaska. Of the
twelve men who began the climb, only five survived,
in part because of inexperience, in part because of bad
luck and bad weather.

Thomas, Lowell. **Lowell Thomas' Book of the High
Mountains.** Messner 1964.

Thomas touches on the geological formation of mountains; their beauty and magnificence; mountains in
Europe, Asia, Africa, and North and South America;
and mountain climbing. Many photographs.

Underhill, Miriam. **Give Me the Hills** (© 1971). Ballantine 1973.

Underhill has climbed mountains in Europe and North
America and led the first all-women climbing team to
conquer the Matterhorn in Switzerland. She conveys
her love of and awe for mountains.

Wolters, Richard A. **Once upon a Thermal.** Crown
1974.

The author describes why and how he took up the
sport of gliding and his experiences in learning how
to glide and competing with other gliders.

OCEANS

Alsar, Vital (with Enrique Hank Lopez). **La Balsa:
The Longest Raft Voyage in History.** Readers Digest
Pr 1973.

On May 29, 1970, four men set sail on a balsa raft.
Their destination—Australia, 8,000 miles from their
Ecuadorian homes. Their purpose—to establish the
validity of the scientific hypothesis that ancient South
American Indians had sailed far from their homeland.

Arnov, Boris, Jr. **Homes beneath the Sea: An Introduction to Ocean Ecology.** Little 1969.

Glimpses into tide pools, coral reefs, and the sea bottom from the point of view of ocean ecology showing
the vital importance of the most minute of sea creatures
to the entire life of the ocean community.

Bailey, Maurice, and Maralyn Bailey. **Staying Alive!**
(© 1974). Ballantine 1975.

A contemporary survival story of a couple adrift in
two rubber rafts in the Pacific. Catching fish with
safety pins and turtles and birds by hand, talking for
endless days about food and the new boat they would
build, they withstood frequent storms and isolation
for an incredible 117 days.

Bardach, John. **Harvest of the Sea.** Har-Row 1968.

Bardach first surveys and evaluates our present knowledge of the oceans and methods of investigating them.
Then he describes some of the possible uses of the
oceans' resources, such as farming fish. Mature.

Beach, Edward L. **Dust on the Sea.** HR&W 1972.

The author, a former commander on submarines, tells
the story of patrol submarines in the last days of
World War II in the Pacific. (See also *Run Silent,
Run Deep,* PB.) Fiction.

Behrman, Daniel. **The New World of the Oceans: Men
and Oceanography.** Little 1969.

Behrman describes advances and problems with marine
science from the point of view of various oceanographers as well as from his own personal experiences.

Bell, R. C., editor. **Diaries from the Days of Sail.** HR&W
1974.

Paintings and drawings enliven this collection of three
diaries of nineteenth-century sailing experiences. One
diary is by a young man on tour sailing from London
to North America; the second is by an emigrant on
his way to Australia; the third by a seventeen year old
on his first voyage as a professional sailor.

Benchley, Peter. **Jaws** (© 1974). Bantam 1975.

Somewhat contrived (especially some of the sex-ori-
ented passages), the novel is nevertheless a tension-
filled story about what happens to a small Long Island
resort town when a twenty-foot-long great white
shark—the most vicious creature in the sea—begins to
devour unsuspecting swimmers. Mature fiction.

Bentley, John. **The "Thresher" Disaster** (© 1974) Doubleday 1975.

The story of the nuclear-powered submarine *Thresher,*

which sank in April 1963 with 129 men aboard and the naval inquiry that followed the disaster.

Borgese, Elisabeth Mann. **The Drama of the Oceans.** Abrams 1976.

Text and pictures explore the shores and oceans of the world. Physical and biological aspects are covered, as are the human uses of the ocean environment, past, present, and future.

Caras, Roger A. **Sockeye: The Life of the Pacific Salmon.** Dial 1975.

A well-written narrative of the life of an individual salmon featuring its arduous journey from the ocean back to its breeding place.

Chichester, Sir Francis. **"Gipsy Moth" Circles the World** (© 1968). PB 1969.

Chichester kept a diary of his 226-day voyage around the world in his yacht, *Gipsy Moth*. What made his trip remarkable was that he sailed alone.

Clark, Eugenie. **The Lady and the Sharks.** Har-Row 1969.

Exciting adventures with sharks, sea turtles, and giant manta rays fill this story of Clark's ten years as researcher and director of the Cape Haze Marine Laboratory in Florida. (See also *Lady with a Spear,* Har-Row.)

Coombs, Charles. **Deep-Sea World: The Story of Oceanography.** Morrow 1966.

The formation of the world's oceans and the ways humanity can use the ocean resources intelligently are covered in this study of the science of oceanography.

Cousteau, Jacques-Yves, and Philippe Diolé. **Diving Companions.** Doubleday 1974.

Colorful adventures with sea lions, elephant seals, and walruses as experienced by Cousteau and his internationally famous team of scientist-explorers aboard the research ship *Calypso*. (Earlier publications of Cousteau are *World Without Sun,* Har-Row; *The Silent World,* Ballantine; and *The Living Sea,* PB.)

Critchlow, Keith. **Into the Hidden Environment: The Oceans** (© 1972). Viking Pr 1973.

The purpose of this book is "to project into the submarine world, to whet the appetites of future explorers, and to present the issues involved in our oceanic destiny."

Daugherty, Charles Michael. **Searchers of the Sea: Pioneers in Oceanography.** Viking Pr 1961.

Stories of famous ocean explorers who charted the currents, mapped the shorelines, measured the depths, and studied marine life from the South Seas to the Arctic.

Diolé, Philippe (translator Alan Ross). **The Undersea Adventure.** Messner 1953.

Diolé describes the poetry and beauty of the undersea world and the death and violence, too. One section is about undersea archaeology.

Gaskell, Thomas F. **The Gulf Stream** (© 1972). NAL 1974.

The Gulf Stream: geography, hydrography, climate, explorations, ecology, and stories from throughout history of famous voyages, exploratory adventures, military exploits, and sea monsters.

Graham, Robin Lee (with Derek Gill). **Dove** (© 1972). Bantam 1974.

The youngest sailor to sail around the world alone, Graham describes the fierceness of the storms, the beauty of living a free life with an attractive girl in the South Pacific, and the incredible loneliness of the five-year journey he began at age sixteen.

Hass, Hans (translator Ewald Osers). **Challenging the Deep: Thirty Years of Undersea Adventure.** Morrow 1972.

The autobiography of Hass, a pioneer of ocean exploration and a popularizer of skin diving and underwater photography.

Heyerdahl, Thor. **The "RA" Expeditions.** NAL 1972.

Heyerdahl struck out across the Atlantic in a reed boat to prove his theory about ancient people's colonization of the Western Hemisphere.

Hickling, C. F., and Peter Brown. **The Seas and Oceans in Color** (© 1973). Macmillan 1974.

A compact analysis of the nature of the seas and oceans and a description of the food and mineral resources available for future development.

Horsfield, Brenda, and Peter Bennet Stone. **The Great Ocean Business** (© 1972). NAL 1974.

A study of the ocean floor, particularly the effects and significance of continental drift, and the ecological and political factors in oceanography. Mature.

Limburg, Peter R., and James B. Sweeney. **Vessels for Underwater Exploration.** Crown 1973.

With pictures and text, the authors present the fascinating history—both accomplishments and failures—of undersea craft, from the first diving bells and fanciful submarines to the most sophisticated modern research submersibles and underwater habitats.

Lipscomb, James. **Cutting Loose.** Little 1974.

Five young men, accompanied by a three-member film crew, sailed a sixty-foot schooner from California to Singapore, battling storms and reefs, encountering fascinating people and sights in the South Seas, and struggling throughout the year-long journey with their personal values, goals, and relationships with each other. Mature.

MacInnis, Joe. **Underwater Man** (© 1974). Dodd 1975.

MacInnis gives a firsthand account of his life underwater, his treasure hunting, his search for a missing plane off Venezuela, the rescue of a diver in Lake Michigan.

Marx, Robert F. **The Lure of Sunken Treasure.** McKay 1973.

An experienced diver describes underwater explorations for the remains of Spanish treasure ships, the Swedish man-of-war *Vasa,* and a sunken city.

Marx, Wesley. **The Frail Ocean** (© 1967). Ballantine 1969.

The beauty and wealth of the sea and an urgent warning about the need to protect it from future damage. Mature.

Matthiessen, Peter. **Blue Meridian** (© 1971). NAL 1973.

The story of the filming of the movie *Blue Water, White Death* in which a courageous crew of underwater photographers searched for months to film close-up action shots of the most feared creature of the sea, the great white shark.

Matthiessen, Peter. **Far Tortuga.** Random 1975.

Modern life and tourism have almost destroyed the turtle fisheries, but in the Caribbean Sea, Raib Avers and his men on the schooner *Lillias Eden* set out to catch green turtles. Mature fiction.

McCoy, J. J. **A Sea of Troubles.** Seabury 1975.

The oceans offer great promise if we learn to take care of their resources. The author comments on what we are doing right and wrong with sewage and industrial wastes.

Mostert, Nöel. **Supership.** Knopf 1974.

Mostert takes the reader on a long but absorbing journey through the quarter-mile-long oil tanker, *Ardshiel,* describing the ship and its operations, which threaten the lives of the crew, the security of coastal towns, and the very life and balance of the world's oceans. Mature.

Norris, Kenneth S. **The Porpoise Watcher.** Norton 1974.

Porpoises—especially those named Kathy, Alice, Keiki, and Pono—and whales—pilots, grays, and sperms—are the subjects of Norris's account of his personal and scientific experiences. Most informative are his descriptions of capturing and training pilot whales and various kinds of porpoises.

O'Brien, Esse Forrester. **Dolphins—Sea People.** Naylor 1964.

Although much information on dolphin behavior and language has been gathered since this book was written, O'Brien offers many insights into the life and behavior of these intelligent and entertaining mammals. Famous dolphin personalities—such as Mitzi (Flipper), Smily, and Carolina Snowball—are featured.

Pennington, Howard. **The New Ocean Explorers: Into the Sea in the Space Age.** Little 1972.

Three ocean disasters of the 1960s were the sinking of the U.S. nuclear submarine *Thresher,* the dropping of a hydrogen bomb into the sea when an American bomber exploded off the coast of Spain, and the oil spillage from the tanker *Torrey Canyon* off England. In all these, oceanographers were involved in trying to keep the oceans free from pollution.

Robertson, Dougal. **Survive the Savage Sea** (© 1973). Bantam 1974.

After killer whales rammed and sank their schooner in 1972, a family of six struggled to survive in a nine-foot dingy against sun, sharks, storms, and starvation. The father vividly describes the ingenious ways that kept them alive in the Pacific for thirty-seven days.

Scheffer, Victor B. **The Year of the Whale.** Scribner 1969.

Based on facts, this story describes the first year in the life of a sperm whale. Fiction.

Scott, Frances, and Walter Scott. **Exploring Ocean Frontiers: A Background Book on Who Owns the Seas.** Parents 1970.

The authors here describe some of the developments of ocean technology that will hopefully lead to better international laws of the sea.

Thompson, Thomas. **Lost!** Atheneum 1975.

Two men and a woman struggled to survive after their thirty-one-foot trimaran flipped over in a freak Pacific storm. More than a record of the physical struggle for survival, this true account describes the conflict between one man's belief in himself and the other man's fundamentalist and all-consuming belief in God's will.

Throckmorton, Peter. **Shipwrecks and Archeology: The Unharvested Seas** (© 1969). Little 1970.

Decrying the lack of care with which many amateur divers search shipwrecks for treasures, the author describes the growth of techniques in marine archaeology, many of them based on his personal experiences.

With text and photographs, Throckmorton takes the reader into the wrecks of the *Heraclea,* the *Artemis,* the *Nautilus,* and many ancient ships. Mature.

Tomalin, Nicholas, and Ron Hall. **The Strange Last Voyage of Donald Crowhurst.** PB 1970.

Crowhurst sailed from England as one of many in a contest to sail solo around the world. He doctored records and instruments to make them appear that he had won the race (though he never left the Atlantic Ocean), but decided he could not lie to others and took drastic action to save face.

Trumbull, Robert. **The Raft** (© 1942). Pyramid Pubns n.d.

This is the true story of the heroic endurance of three navy flyers who survived the Pacific in a tiny rubber raft for thirty-four days.

Walton, Bryce. **Harpoon Gunner.** T Y Crowell 1968.

The story of a sixteen year old's experiences on a modern whaling ship hunting the nearly extinct blue whale. Eric had always dreamed of becoming a king gunner like his father, but he has second thoughts about his intentions as he learns to respect the giant mammals he is hunting. Fiction.

Ward, Ritchie. **Into the Ocean World: The Biology of the Sea.** Knopf 1974.

More than a collection of facts about marine biology, this book presents the biographies of some of the people who have made significant advances into the earth's least explored frontier. Mature.

Wertenbaker, William. **The Floor of the Sea: Maurice Ewing and the Search to Understand the Earth.** Little 1974.

The dramatic discovery of continental drift was the result of years of work by Ewing, founder of the world's leading marine geophysical research center. Mature.

DIRECTORY OF PUBLISHERS

A & W Visual Library A & W Visual Library, 95 Madison Avenue, New York, NY 10016

A S Barnes A.S. Barnes & Co., Inc., P.O. Box 421, Cranbury, NJ 08512

A-W Addison-Wesley Publishing Co., Inc., Jacob Way, Reading, MA 01867

Abelard Abelard-Schuman Ltd., 666 Fifth Avenue, New York, NY 10019

Abingdon Abingdon Press, 201 Eighth Avenue, South, Nashville, TN 37202

Abrams Harry N. Abrams, Inc., 110 East 59th Street, New York, NY 10022

Ace Bks Ace Books, 1120 Avenue of the Americas, New York, NY 10036

Acropolis Acropolis Books, 2400 17th Street, N.W., Washington, DC 20009

Aladdin Aladdin Books. Orders to: Book Warehouse, Inc., Vreeland Avenue, Boro of Totowa, Paterson, NJ 07512

Alaska Northwest Alaska Northwest Publishing Co. Orders to: 130 Second Avenue, South, Edmonds, WA 98020

Am Heritage American Heritage Publishing Co., 1221 Avenue of the Americas, New York, NY 10036

Am West American West Publishing Co. Orders to: Charles Scribner's Sons, Shipping & Service Center, Vreeland Avenue, Totowa, NJ 07512

Anch Pr Anchor Press. Orders to: Doubleday & Co., Inc., 501 Franklin Avenue, Garden City, NY 11530

Ann Forfreedom Ann Forfreedom, 1947 Bell, No. 26, Sacramento, CA 95825

Arbor Hse Arbor House Publishing Co., 641 Lexington Avenue, New York, NY 10021

Arc Bks Arc Books. Orders to: Arco Publishing Co., Inc., 219 Park Avenue, South, New York, NY 10003

Archway Archway Paperbacks, 630 Fifth Avenue, New York, NY 10020

Arco   Arco Publishing Co., Inc., 219 Park Avenue, South, New York, NY 10003

Ariel   Ariel, Box 9183, Berkeley, CA 94709

Arlington Hse   Arlington House Publishers, 165 Huguenot Street, New Rochelle, NY 10801

Assn Pr   Association Press, 291 Broadway, New York, NY 10007

Atheneum   Atheneum Publishers. Orders to: Book Warehouse, Inc., Vreeland Avenue, Boro of Totowa, Paterson, NJ 07512

Avon   Avon Books, 959 Eighth Avenue, New York, NY 10019

Award Hse   Award House. Orders to: Award Books, 350 Kennedy Drive, Hauppauge, NY 11788

Baker Bk   Baker Book House, 1019 Wealthy Street, S.E., Grand Rapids, MI 49506

Ballantine   Ballantine Books, Inc. Orders to: Random House, Inc., 457 Hahn Road, Westminster, MD 21157

B&N   Barnes & Noble, Inc. Orders to: Harper & Row, Publishers, Inc., Keystone Industrial Park, Scranton, PA 18512

Bantam   Bantam Books, Inc. Orders to: 414 East Golf Road, Des Plaines, IL 60016

Basic   Basic Books, Inc., 10 East 53rd Street, New York, NY 10022

Beacon Pr   Beacon Press, Inc., 25 Beacon Street, Boston, MA 02108

Berkley Pub   Berkley Publishing Corp. Orders to: G. P. Putnam's Sons, 200 Madison Avenue, New York, NY 10016

Blair   John F. Blair, Publisher, 1406 Plaza Drive, S.W., Winston-Salem, NC 27103

Bobbs   Bobbs-Merrill Co., 4300 West 62nd Street, Indianapolis, IN 46268

Bradbury Pr   Bradbury Press, 2 Overhill Road, Scarsdale, NY 10583

Braziller   George Braziller, Inc., 1 Park Avenue, New York, NY 10016

Brigham   Brigham Young University Press, 205 University Press Building, Provo, UT 84602

Canfield Pr Canfield Press. Orders to: Harper & Row, Publishers, Keystone Industrial Park, Scranton, PA 18512

Cap Putnam Capricorn Books. Orders to: G. P. Putnam's Sons, 200 Madison Avenue, New York, NY 10016

Caxton Caxton Printers, Ltd., P.O. Box 700, Caldwell, ID 83605

CCPr Macmillan Crowell-Collier Press. Orders to: Macmillan Publishing Co., Inc., Front & Brown Street, Delran Township, Riverside, NJ 08075

Charterhouse Charterhouse Books, Inc. Orders to: David McKay, Inc., 750 Third Avenue, New York, NY 10017

Chelsea Hse Chelsea House Publishers, 70 West 40th Street, New York, NY 10018

Childrens Childrens Press, Inc., 1224 West Van Buren Street, Chicago, IL 60607

Chilton Chilton Book Co. Orders to: Sales Service Department, 201 King of Prussia Road, Radnor, PA 19089

Chr Lit Christian Literature Crusade, Inc., Pennsylvania Avenue, Fort Washington, PA 19034

Chris Mass Christopher Publishing House (Mass), 53 Billings Road, North Quincy, MA 02171

Citation Citation Press. Orders to: Scholastic Book Services, 906 Sylvan Avenue, Englewood Cliffs, NJ 07632

Clymer Clymer Publications, 222 North Virgil Avenue, Los Angeles, CA 90004

Collier Macmillan P.F. Collier, Inc. Orders to: Macmillan Publishing Co., Inc., Front & Brown Street, Delran Township, Riverside, NJ 08075

Columbia U Pr Columbia University Press. Orders to: 136 South Broadway, Irvington-on-Hudson, NY 10533

Cornell U Pr Cornell University Press, 124 Roberts Place, Ithaca, NY 14850

Coward Coward, McCann & Geoghegan, Inc., 200 Madison Avenue, New York, NY 10016

Crown Crown Publishers, Inc., Englehard Avenue, Avenel, NJ 07001

Daughters Daughters, Inc., Plainfield, VT 05667

DAW Bks DAW Books. Orders to: New American Library, 1301 Avenue of the Americas, New York, NY 10019

Delacorte Delacorte Press. Orders to: Dial Press, 1 Dag Hammarskjold Plaza, 245 East 47th Street, New York, NY 10017

Dell Dell Publishing Co., Inc., 1 Dag Hammarskjold Plaza, 245 East 47th Street, New York, NY 10017

Dial Dial Press, 1 Dag Hammarskjold Plaza, 245 East 47th Street, New York, NY 10017

Dillon Dillon Press, Inc., 500 South Third Street, Minneapolis, MN 55415

Dodd Dodd, Mead & Co., 79 Madison Avenue, New York, NY 10016

Doubleday Doubleday & Co., Inc., 501 Franklin Avenue, Garden City, NY 11530

Dover Dover Publications, Inc., 180 Varick Street, New York, NY 10014

Drake Pubs Drake Publishers, Inc., 381 Park Avenue, South, New York, NY 10016

Dutton E. P. Dutton & Co., Inc., 201 Park Avenue, South, New York, NY 10003

Eakins Eakins Press, 155 East 42nd Street, New York, NY 10017

Fairchild Fairchild Publications, Inc., 7 East 12th Street, New York, NY 10003

Fawcett World Fawcett World Library, 1515 Broadway, New York, NY 10036

Feminist Pr Feminist Press, SUNY/College at Old Westbury, Box 334, Old Westbury, NY 11568

Fleet Fleet Press Corp., 160 Fifth Avenue, New York, NY 10010

Follett Follett Publishing Co., 1010 West Washington Boulevard, Chicago, IL 60607

Four Winds Four Winds Press. Orders to: Scholastic Book Services, 906 Sylvan Avenue, Englewood Cliffs, NJ 07632

Free Pr Free Press. Orders to: Macmillan Publishing Co., Inc., Front & Brown Street, Delran Township, Riverside, NJ 08075

Friend Pr Friendship Press, 475 Riverside Drive, New York, NY 10027

FS&G Farrar, Straus & Giroux, Inc., 19 Union Square, West, New York, NY 10003

Funk & W Funk & Wagnalls Co. Orders to: Thomas Y. Crowell Co., 666 Fifth Avenue, New York, NY 10019

Glencoe Glencoe Press. Orders to: Macmillan Publishing Co., Inc., Front & Brown Street, Delran Township, Riverside, NJ 08075

Globe Globe Book Co., Inc., 175 Fifth Avenue, New York, NY 10010

Greene Stephen Greene Press, P.O. Box 1000, Battleboro, VT 05301

Greenwood Greenwood Press, Inc., 51 Riverside Avenue, Westport, CT 06880

Grossman Grossman Publishers, Inc. Orders to: Vikeship Co., 299 Murray Hill Parkway, East Rutherford, NJ 07073

Grove Grove Press, Inc., 53 East 11th Street, New York, NY 10003

H M Gousha H. M. Gousha, 2001 the Alameda, P.O. Box 6227, San Jose, CA 95150

Har-Row Harper & Row, Publishers, Inc. Orders to: Keystone Industrial Park, Scranton, PA 18512

HarBraceJ Harcourt Brace Jovanovich, Inc., 757 Third Avenue, New York, NY 10017

Harper Mag Pr Harper Magazine Press, 2 Park Avenue, New York, NY 10016

Harvard U Pr Harvard University Press, 79 Garden Street, Cambridge, MA 02138

Hastings Hastings House, Publishers, Inc., 10 East 40th Street, New York, NY 10016

Hawthorn Hawthorn Books, Inc., 260 Madison Avenue, New York, NY 10016

Hayden Hayden Book Co., Inc., 50 Essex Street, Rochelle Park, NJ 07662

Herald Pr   Herald Press, 616 Walnut Avenue, Scottdale, PA 15683

Herder & Herder   Herder and Herder, 1221 Avenue of the Americas, New York, NY 10036

Hill & Wang   Hill & Wang, Inc. Orders to: Farrar, Straus, Giroux, Inc., 19 Union Square, New York, NY 10003

HM   Houghton Mifflin Co., 2 Park Street, Boston, MA 02107

Holiday   Holiday House, Inc., 18 East 53rd Street, New York, NY 10022

Howell-North   Howell-North Books, 1050 Parker Street, Berkeley, CA 94710

HR&W   Holt, Rinehart & Winston, Inc., 383 Madison Avenue, New York, NY 10017

Ind U Pr   Indiana University Press, Tenth & Morton Streets, Bloomington IN 47401

Iowa St U Pr   Iowa State University Press, South State Avenue, Ames, IA 50010

J P Tarcher   J. P. Tarcher, Inc. Orders to: Hawthorn Books, Inc., 260 Madison Avenue, New York, NY 10016

Japan Pubns   Japan Publications Trading Co., Inc., 200 Clearbrook Road, Elmsford, NY 10523

John Day   John Day Co., Inc., 666 Fifth Avenue, New York, NY 10019

John Knox   John Knox Press, 341 Ponce De Leon Avenue, N.E., Atlanta, GA 30308

John Muir   John Muir Publications. Orders to: Book People, 2940 Seventh Street, Berkeley, CA 94710

Jonathan David   Jonathan David, Publishers, Inc., 68-22 Eliot Avenue, Middle Village, NY 11379

Knopf   Alfred A. Knopf, Inc. Orders to: Random House, Inc., 400 Hahn Road, Westminster, MD 21157

Kodansha   Kodansha International, Ltd. Orders to: Harper & Row, Publishers, Inc., Keystone Industrial Park, Scranton, PA 18512

Lathrop   Norman Lathrop Enterprises, 2342 Star Drive, Wooster, OH 44691

Lawrence Hill Lawrence Hill & Co., Inc., 150 Fifth Avenue, New York, NY 10011

Lerner Pubns Lerner Publications Co., 241 First Avenue, North, Minneapolis, MN 55401

Lippincott J. B. Lippincott, Co., East Washington Square, Philadelphia, PA 19105

Little Little, Brown & Co. Orders to: 200 West Street, Waltham, MA 02154

Liveright Liveright Publishing Corp. Orders to: W. W. Norton Co., Inc., 500 Fifth Avenue, New York, NY 10036

Lothrop Lothrop, Lee & Shepard Co. Orders to: William Morrow & Co., Inc., 6 Henderson Drive, West Caldwell, NJ 07006

Lowell Pr Lowell Press, 115 East 31st Street, Box 1877, Kansas City, MO 64141

M Evans M. Evans & Co., Inc. Orders to: J. B. Lippincott Co., East Washington Square, Philadelphia, PA 19105

Macmillan Macmillan Publishing Co., Inc. Orders to: Front & Brown Street, Delran Township, Riverside, NJ 08075

Macrae Macrae Smith Co., 225 South 15th Street, Philadelphia, PA 19102

McGraw McGraw-Hill Book Co., 1221 Avenue of the Americas, New York, NY 10036

McKay David McKay Co., Inc., 750 Third Avenue, New York, NY 10017

Messner Julian Messner, Inc. Orders to: Simon & Schuster, Inc., 1 West 39th Street, New York, NY 10018

Miller Bks Miller Books, 409 San Pasqual Drive, Alhambra, CA 91801

Moody Moody Press, 820 North LaSalle Street, Chicago, IL 60610

Morrow William Morrow & Co., Inc. Orders to: 6 Henderson Drive, West Caldwell, NJ 07006

NAL New American Library, 1301 Avenue of the Americas, New York, NY 10019

Nash Pub Nash Publishing Corp. Orders to: E. P. Dutton & Co., Inc., 201 Park Avenue, South, New York, NY 10003

Naylor Naylor Co. Orders to: P.O. Box 1838, San Antonio, TX 78206

NCTE National Council of Teachers of English, Order Department, 1111 Kenyon Road, Urbana, IL 61801

Nelson Thomas Nelson, Inc. Orders to: 407 Seventh Avenue, South, Nashville, TN 37203

New Community New Community Projects, 32 Rutland Street, Boston, MA 02118

New Directions New Directions Publishing Corp. Orders to: J. B. Lippincott Co., East Washington Square, Philadelphia, PA 19105

New West Pubns New West Publications, Civic Center, Box 4037, San Rafael, CA 94903

Noble Noble & Noble Publishers, Inc., 1 Dag Hammarskjold Plaza, 245 East 47th Street, New York, NY 10017

Northland Northland Press, P.O. Box N, Flagstaff, AZ 86001

Norton W. W. Norton & Co., Inc., 500 Fifth Avenue, New York, NY 10036

NYGS New York Graphic Society, Ltd. Orders to: Little, Brown & Co., 200 West Street, Waltham, MA 02154

Overlook Pr Overlook Press. Orders to: Vikeship Co., 299 Murray Hill Parkway, East Rutherford, NJ 07073

P-H Prentice-Hall, Inc., Englewood Cliffs, NJ 07632

Pacific Bks Pacific Books, Publishers, P.O. Box 558, Palo Alto, CA 94302

Paddington Paddington Press Ltd. Orders to: Two Continents Publishing Group, 5 South Union Street, Lawrence, MA 01843

Pantheon Pantheon Books. Orders to: Random House, Inc., 457 Hahn Road, Westminster, MD 21157

Panther Hse Panther House, Ltd., P.O. Box 3552, New York, NY 10017

Paperback Lib Warner Paperback Library, 75 Rockefeller Plaza, New York, NY 10019

Parents Parents Magazine Press, 52 Vanderbilt Avenue, New York, NY 10017

PB Pocket Books, Inc. Orders to: Simon & Schuster, Inc., 630 Fifth Avenue, New York, NY 10020

Penguin Penguin Books, Inc. Orders to: 7110 Ambassador Road, Baltimore, MD 21207

Pflaum-Standard Pflaum/Standard. Orders to: 8121 Hamilton Avenue, Cincinnati, OH 45231

Popular Lib Popular Library, Inc., 600 Third Avenue, New York, NY 10011

Praeger Praeger Publishers, 111 Fourth Avenue, New York, NY 10003

Putnam G. P. Putnam's Sons, 200 Madison Avenue, New York, NY 10016

Pyramid Pubns Pyramid Publications, Inc., 919 Third Avenue, New York, NY 10022

Quadrangle Quadrangle/The New York Times Co. Orders to: Harper & Row, Publishers, Keystone Industrial Park, Scranton, PA 18512

Quinto Sol Pubns Quinto Sol Publications, Inc., P.O. Box 9275, Berkeley, CA 94709

Rand Rand McNally & Co., P.O. Box 7600, Chicago, IL 60680

Random Random House, Inc. Orders to: 457 Hahn Road, Westminster, MD 21157

Readers Digest Pr Reader's Digest Press. Orders to: E. P. Dutton & Co., Inc., 201 Park Avenue, South, New York, NY 10003

Ritchie Ward Ritchie Press, 474 South Arroyo Parkway, Pasadena, CA 91105

Rosen Pr Richards Rosen Press, Inc., 29 East 21st Street, New York, NY 10010

S G Phillips S. G. Phillips, Inc., 305 West 86th Street, New York, NY 10024

S&S Simon & Schuster, Inc., 630 Fifth Avenue, New York, NY 10020

Sat Rev Pr Saturday Review Press. Orders to: E. P. Dutton & Co., 201 Park Avenue, South, New York, NY 10003

Scarecrow Scarecrow Press, Inc., 52 Liberty Street, Box 656, Metuchen, NJ 08840

Schol Bk Serv Scholastic Book Services. Orders to: 906 Sylvan Avenue, Englewood Cliffs, NJ 07632

Scribner Charles Scribner's Sons. Orders to: Shipping & Service Center, Vreeland Avenue, Totowa, NJ 07512

Seabury Seabury Press, Inc., 815 Second Avenue, New York, NY 10017

Shameless Hussy Pr Shameless Hussy Press, Box 424, San Lorenzo, CA 94580

Sheed Sheed & Ward, Inc., 6700 Squibb Road, Mission, KS 66202

Sierra Sierra Club Books. Orders to: Charles Scribner's Sons, Shipping & Service Center, Vreeland Avenue, Totowa, NJ 07512

St Martin St. Martin's Press, Inc., 175 Fifth Avenue, New York, NY 10010

Stackpole Stackpole Books, Cameron & Keller Streets, Harrisburg, PA 17105

Stein & Day Stein & Day, 7 East 48th Street, New York, NY 10017

Sterling Sterling Publishing Co., Inc., 419 Park Avenue, South, New York, NY 10016

Strode Strode Publishers, 6802 Jones Valley Drive, S.E., Huntsville, AL 35802

Swallow Swallow Press, 1139 South Wabash Avenue, Chicago, IL 60605

T Y Crowell Thomas Y. Crowell Co., 666 Fifth Avenue, New York, NY 10003

Taplinger Taplinger Publishing Co., Inc., 200 Park Avenue, South, New York, NY 10003

Tempo G&D Tempo Books. Orders to: Grosset & Dunlap, Inc., 51 Madison Avenue, New York, NY 10010

Ten Speed Pr Ten Speed Press, Box 4310, Berkeley, CA 94704

Tundra Bks Tundra Books of Northern New York, 18 Cornelia Street, Box 1030, Plattsburgh, NY 12901

Twin Circle Twin Circle Publishing Co., Inc., 86 Riverside Drive, New York, NY 10024

Two Continents Two Continents Publishing Group, Ltd. Orders to: 5 South Union Street, Lawrence, MA 01843

U of Ariz Pr University of Arizona Press, P.O. Box 3398, Tucson, AZ 85722

U of Cal Pr University of California Press, 2223 Fulton Street, Berkeley, CA 94720

U of Chicago Pr University of Chicago Press. Orders to: 11030 South Langley Avenue, Chicago, IL 60628

U of NM Pr University of New Mexico Press, Albuquerque, NM 87131

U of Okla Pr University of Oklahoma Press, 1005 Asp Avenue, Norman, OK 73069

Unicorn Pr Unicorn Press, P.O. Box 3307, Greensboro, NC 27402

U of Minn Pr University of Minnesota Press, 2037 University Avenue, S.E., Minneapolis, MN 55455

U of Nebr Pr University of Nebraska Press, 901 North 17th Street, Lincoln, NB 68508

Vanguard Vanguard Press, Inc., 424 Madison Avenue, New York, NY 10017

Van Nos Reinhold Van Nostrand Reinhold Co. Orders to: 300 Pike Street, Cincinnati, OH 45202

Viking Pr Viking Press, Inc. Orders to: Vikeship Co., 299 Murray Hill Parkway, East Rutherford, NJ 07073

VinRandom Vintage Books. Orders to: Random House, Inc., 457 Hahn Road, Westminster, MD 21157

Walck Henry Z. Walck, Inc. Orders to: David McKay Co., Inc., 750 Third Avenue, New York, NY 10017

Walker & Co Walker & Co., 720 Fifth Avenue, New York, NY 10019

Warner Bks Warner Books, Inc., 75 Rockefeller Plaza, New York, NY 10019

Watts Franklin Watts, Inc. Orders to: Grolier, Inc., 845 Third Avenue, New York, NY 10022

Westminster   Westminster Press, Room 905, Witherspoon Building, Philadelphia, PA 19107

W H Freeman   W. H. Freeman and Co. Publishers, 660 Market Street, San Francisco, CA 94104

Wollstonecraft   Wollstonecraft, Inc., 6399 Wilshire Boulevard, Los Angeles, CA 90048

Word Bks   Word, Inc., P.O. Box 1790, Waco, TX 76703

WSP   Washington Square Press, Inc. Orders to: Simon & Schuster, Inc., 630 Fifth Avenue, New York, NY 10020

AUTHOR INDEX

TITLE INDEX

459